IMPLEMENTING TOWN PLANNING: THE ROLE OF TOWN PLANNING IN THE DEVELOPMENT PROCESS

Series: Exploring Town Planning

Series Editor   Clara Greed

IMPLEMENTING TOWN PLANNING: THE ROLE OF TOWN PLANNING IN THE DEVELOPMENT PROCESS

Edited by Clara Greed

Contributing Authors: John Allinson, Janet Askew, Jim Claydon, Linda Davies, Clara Greed, Jennifer Tempest, and Robin Tetlow

LONGMAN

Longman Group Limited,
Longman House, Burnt Mill, Harlow,
Essex CM20 2JE, England
and Associated Companies throughout the world.

© Longman Group UK Limited 1996

First published 1996

British Library Cataloguing-in-Publication Data

A catalogue record for this book is available from the British Library

ISBN 0-582-23423-9

Set by 8 in 10/12 pt New Baskerville
Produced through Longman Malaysia, PP

CONTENTS

LISTS OF TABLES AND FIGURES

SERIES EDITOR PREFACE

Implementing Town Planning is a sequel to *Introducing Town Planning*. That book is written for newcomers, especially first-year students on built environment courses, but also the general public. It covers the historical, social, legal and organisational aspects of town planning. This book is aimed at second-year students and above, undertaking more detailed project work, and seeking to relate their studies to the real world of planning and development. Several of its chapters are based on case studies and are written by planning practitioners drawing on their up-to-date knowledge of development issues. They illustrate some of the conflicts and differences of opinion over plan making and implementation and, where appropriate, they provide a more discursive treatment. Overall, the emphasis is upon practical planning issues rather than academic planning theory.

A third volume is intended; *Investigating Town Planning* will incorporate a diverse range of topical issues, reflecting the varied and fragmented nature of modern town planning policy and practice. For although there is only one planning system, the statutory local government system, it may be argued that nowadays there is no longer one version of town planning, but many 'plannings' as manifested in trends both in academia and professional practice. Each type has its own adherents and policy priorities, often it would seem operating in splendid isolation, if not outright disagreement, with other representatives of the world of town planning. The third volume will seek to capture this diversity, drawing on a team of contributors who are specialists in different areas of town planning. It will combine economic and market-led perceptions of town planning alongside environmental or 'green' planning perspectives, but will also include material which considers the relationship of town planning with housing policy.

All three volumes are seeking to challenge readers with the eternal question, What exactly is town planning? And they take many perspectives, including social, economic, physical, visual, environmental and governmental. Much of the work of the planner might also be undertaken by the surveyor, housing manager or architect, indeed nowadays the professional boundaries themselves are increasingly in a state of flux, with new professional groupings emerging, and old allegiances weakening. Therefore it is hoped that readers, in using this book, will not only find useful substantive material, but also be challenged to reflect upon the scope, purpose and nature of town planning.

During the 1990s there has been a resurgence of interest in urban design, and I intend to make this the subject of two further volumes 4a and 4b, in joint editorship with Marion Roberts of the University of Westminster; 4a on the agenda of urban design, and 4b on 'how to do it'. Under this heading one can identify a cluster of related policy areas, including estate layout, townscape, urban conservation, planning for the disabled, crime and design, traffic calming, public art, and to some extent the more detailed aspect of women and planning. The volume on urban design will cover the more traditional townscape dimensions – what an area looks like – but will also comprise material on more recent interpretations of its purpose, interpretations which focus on how people use an area. Further volumes are also proposed.

ACKNOWLEDGMENTS

Thanks to Richard Larcombe, development director of CISC for permission to use extracts in Chapter 2 and Appendix 2.

The Pipeline Diagram, *The Land Market and Development Process* is reproduced by Jim Claydon in Chapter 3, courtesy of Sue Barrett, the School of Advanced Urban Studies, Bristol.

Thanks are due to Michael Parkes, community planner, King's Cross Railway Lands Group, for help in providing material used by Janet Askew.

Thanks to Women's Design Service and the London Women and Planning Forum of the London Boroughs, and especially to Sue Cavanagh and Ruth Cadbury.

Thanks to Chris Wade and Paul Dyke at the University of the West of England, the graphics unit of the Faculty of the Built Environment for preparing the diagrams in Chapter 10 and to all those who worked on the other illustrations.

Thanks to Bellway Homes plc and in particular to their group planner, Nick Cook MRTPI, Paul Bullivant, director of the Bristol Churches Housing Association, and Kendall Kingscott, architect, for their cooperation and to Oldfield King Group for the illustrations in relation to the York Gate site.

THE CONTRIBUTORS

John Allinson BA (Hons), MPhil, MRTPI is a senior lecturer in town planning at the Faculty of the Built Environment, University of the West of England, Bristol. His specialist subjects include the property development process, information technology and research methods. He is national course manager for the RTPI Joint Distance Learning Diploma. Prior to taking his present post in 1990 he worked in three different planning offices over the last ten years, his specialist area being planning research and statistical analysis within the context of structure plan production and economic development. He has also spent three years in consultancy working on corporate computer systems for local authorities, becoming team leader. He is a contributor to a range of planning journals, including *Town and Country Planning, Planning Practice and Research* and *The Planner*. Currently he is undertaking research on the development process in relation to 'difficult sites'.

Janet Askew BSc, Dip TP, MRTPI is an associate lecturer at the University of the West of England and also has her own planning consultancy. After graduating from the University of Wales at Cardiff she worked in forward planning and development control in the public and private sectors in England, Wales and Scotland. She was a planner in the Shetland Islands during the boom in the 1970s and she was involved in the planning for the development of the oil terminal. In the course of her work in the private sector she has been involved in a number of major projects, including work on urban regeneration of inner city sites in London and Bristol. She has specialised in analysis of potential future uses of redundant land in both urban and rural settings. She has also worked on tourism plans for major waterways, and on retail, commercial and residential schemes. Her current research interest is concerned with the link between planning and the resources for implementing development.

Jim Claydon MSc, MRTPI is director of studies of the School of Town and Country Planning at the University of the West of England. He has been a lecturer there over thirteen years, and for nine years before that he was a local authority planner in Devon and Leicestershire. His practice experience ranges across strategic planning, development control and consultancy, in which he is still active. For fifteen years he has been heavily involved in professional training for councillors and planners. His research interests include economic development and negotiations in planning. He gained his first degree in geography at London University followed by a postgraduate diploma at Kingston Polytechnic (now Kingston University). In 1983 he was awarded an MSc in public policies studies at Bristol University and has been a member of the Royal Town Planning Institute since 1974.

Linda Davies is a chartered town planner who combines her practice and teaching experience in the hope that each continues to benefit the other. For some five years she has been a senior associate lecturer in the School of Town and Country Planning at the University of the West of England, specialising in local planning, development control and local government studies. Her academic publications include *Regional Planning Guidance* and *Aspects of Equality*. In her spare time she is an executive committee member and ethnic minority liaison officer for the south-west branch of the Royal Town Planning Institute, and also an external tutor at the College of Estate Management, Reading. Having spent some fifteen years in local government, mostly for Scottish inner urban areas but also for rural Wiltshire, she brings to this book a wide range of experience.

Clara Greed BSc (Hons), MRTPI, FASI, FRGS, PhD is a senior lecturer in town planning in the Faculty of the Built Environment, University of the West of England, previously working in the Department of Surveying, and now part of the Planning School. She is the author of the first volume in this series, *Introducing Town Planning*, and has published widely on built environment matters, including *Women and Planning* (1994) and *Surveying Sisters* (1991) on women chartered surveyors. She is a chartered town planner, fellow of the Architects and Surveyors Institute and a member of several committees related to the built environment professions. As a member of the Planning and Strategy Group of the Construction Industry Standing Conference (CISC), she helped to produce Part A (Planning) of the CISC map for the assessment of professional competence at NVQ levels 4 and 5. She is interested in equal opportunities issues and is chair of the Faculty Access Initiative.

Jennifer Tempest BA (Hons), MA, Dip CP, MRTPI, having obtained her professional qualifications at Oxford Polytechnic, worked for over ten years in district council planning departments in Oxfordshire, Wiltshire and Somerset. All these posts involved working in development control at increasingly senior levels. From 1985 to 1988 she was a principal planning officer with North Wiltshire District Council, responsible for development control in the northern half of the district. Following maternity leave, she moved out of local government to work as a freelance planning consultant and teacher at the school of planning. She joined The Planning Practice on a full-time basis in 1989. Her work includes extensive involvement with the regional and district health authorities, and now with the privatised NHS trusts. The Planning Practice has a broad client base in both the public and private sectors, undertaking work on all aspects of the planning process.

Robin Tetlow, MSc, Dip Surv, FRTPI, FRICS, FCIOH is a director of the Oldfield King Group, a multidisciplinary consultancy which offers a range of planning, development, design and engineering services. He heads the specialist planning and housing divisions of the group, and since establishing the Bristol office in 1985 has acted for a wide variety of public and private sector clients. He studied estate management at De Montfort University, Leicester, and town planning at Heriot-Watt University, where his dissertation 'City Centre Office Development' was given a special commendation. Before joining Oldfield King he spent eight years working for housing associations based in London, Norwich, Cardiff and Southampton. He was principal author of *Development: A Guide for Housing Associations* (National Federation of Housing Associations 1986) and has written many articles on planning and housing issues. He is a visiting lecturer on planning and housing in the Faculty of the Built Environment at the University of the West of England.

PART I

THE DEVELOPMENTAL AND PROFESSIONAL CONTEXT

Chapter 1

IMPLEMENTATION: PERSPECTIVES AND PERCEPTIONS

Clara Greed

Introduction

This book investigates the implementation process that produces development, with particular attention to the role of town planning as seen within the property development and construction context. Town planners are but one of the groups of urban professionals involved. They work alongside surveyors, architects, valuers, property investment specialists, civil engineers, construction managers and others. Many of these other professional groups are likely to see their professional role as that of advisors to the client, namely the developer, on how to get the best financial return from the site. Property is a commodity like any other, so the aim of the private sector property professional is to get through the different stages of the development process, and thus to achieve construction as rapidly as possible. The sooner they achieve construction, the sooner they can get a return on the investment involved (Rydin 1993). To such groups, implementation means achieving new development with the emphasis on the end product. A major hurdle to achieving development is gaining of planning permission from the local authority in the first place. Indeed those working in the private sector may see planners as the enemy and view the statutory planning process negatively.

In contrast, town planners bring to their work another agenda, and therefore a somewhat different definition of implementation. To planners, implementation might mean a process resulting in the successful carrying out of planning policies, and of specific plans, thus achieving certain long-term policy objectives. These are different objectives from those of the private sector developer. They are likely to relate to social provision of amenities, good design, environmentally sensitive development and a concern with wider issues related to overall urban form and transportation policies; they are unlikely to be concerned exclusively with the development of a specific site. The 'occasion of the development' is their window of opportunity to implement this wider agenda. Therefore, for planners, implementation (of planning strategies or land use plans), might be measured in what has *not* been built, and in what has been conserved, protected, altered or improved. As illustrated in Volume I of this series (Greed 1993: 5) one elderly planner measured his lifetime achievement in the fact that through operating a successful development control system, in his local planning authority area, he had prevented the green belt being built upon, thus preventing two adjacent conurbations from joining up and destroying another stretch of countryside. The scope and objectives of modern town planning are discussed in Volume I of this series *Introducing Town Planning* and it is strongly recommended that those readers unfamiliar with the rudiments of town planning in Britain consult Volume I, or a similar introductory text, before proceeding further.

Overall, the town planner's perspective as to the time-scale of implementation is likely to be longer than that of the private sector property professional. Many planning documents and development plans are drawn up to cover long periods of time, typically from five years up to thirty years or more. Indeed, planning is essentially an activity concerned with the future. Planning is concerned with deciding what course of action to take in respect of a particular urban issue before it happens, for example, predicting growth in traffic volumes and developing transportation planning strategies accordingly. Admittedly many of the grandiose schemes of the postwar heyday of town planning have been discredited, because planning for the future so often proved to be unrealistic. Future policies have often proved to be based on inaccurate forecasts of population growth, the economy and development demands. Much modern town planning is therefore more incremental, cautious and short-term in approach. But the planner's time-scale is still likely to be longer than that of the private sector developer, who having developed a site, is free to move on to another site, or indeed to another town or city altogether. In contrast it may take many years for a particular planning policy to be achieved, and to bear fruit. This example also highlights another of the important distinctions in perspective: planners are essentially implementing policies rather than development *per se*.

The question of what sort of policies planners are seeking to implement, and whose interests are represented in the process are extremely important. As already indicated, they are of a broader environmental and social nature than the objectives of the developers. But in the first part of the book, they are taken as given; this is to avoid introducing too many issues all at once. The way the planner approaches the implementation process, and the negotiating strategies involved, are inevitably informed by the local planning authority's policy priorities. The chapters gradually shift their emphasis from the process of implementation to the kinds of policies, and whether they reflect the needs of the general public, as against the developer or the planner. In other words, the book moves from covering planning processes and procedures to considering policies and people's needs. This is important because the implementation process can come across as somewhat 'peopleless', and as a two-cornered fight between the developer and the planner, even when planning is ostensibly promoted as being for the benefit of urban society.

Plans and policy implementation

Planners working in local authority planning offices, the main implementary level of planning in Britain, are responsible for making plans and operating the development control system. Their client is not a single developer, but society itself, and their site is not just one building plot, but they may be responsible for producing development plans for a whole local area, city or county. As indicated above, planners are likely to include in their planning policy agenda, topics related to social, economic, political and environmental considerations as well as the purely physical, design and layout constraints of development on the site in question. The broader agenda of the planners is encapsulated in a careers booklet of the Royal Town Planning Institute (RTPI).

> Land is a limited resource. . . . For the general benefit of society, it has been necessary to find ways to balance the demand for different uses of land, to locate land uses so that they are sensibly related to each other, and to ensure that land is not developed in such a way that it spoils the environment. Land use planning has developed to meet the social and economic needs of people.
>
> (RTPI 1990a)

According to this agenda, town planning is essential to the well-being of urban society; the market economy alone cannot provide a satisfactory environment. Without some measure of state intervention through the town planning system, it is assumed that chaos would ensue. Other definitions of the functions of planning centre on the planner's role in bringing forth land for development, reconciling conflicting demands, providing for non-profit-making issues, acting as an urban economist and allocating scarce resources, especially land (Rydin 1993). In all these definitions the planner is not only presented as a policy maker, but as a mediator between conflicting groups, as an urban manager and inevitably as a negotiator seeking to ensure plan implementation is successful by means of the planning process (Greed 1994: 33). Those unfamiliar with the role of the planner might like to read Chapter 2 of Greed (1994), which investigates the different types of planner, and their varying roles as policy makers and urban managers, but also as technicians and administrators 'operating' the municipal planning process. The introductory chapters to Hall (1992) also provide useful background.

In the above definition, which centres on the physical functions of town planning, emphasis is put upon seeking to arrange the land uses in such a way that they work efficiently together. For example, a major concern of modern town planning is the problem of traffic, including the problems of congestion, car parking, accessibility, public transport provision, sustainability and environmental pollution. It has been found over the years that planning more highways, building more roads and increasing car parking spaces, does not necessarily solve the traffic problem. It may simply encourage more of the same problems. However, the relocation of certain high-level traffic-generating land uses, such as office development, to decentralised locations might decrease, or at least spread more evenly, existing traffic flows and thus reduce urban congestion. Indeed the Department of the Environment in early 1994 updated planning policy guidance note PPG 13 *Transport*, in which it officially recognises the need to take into account the interrelationship between land use patterns and likely traffic generation and flow patterns at a city-wide level.[1]

It may be seen from this example, that the town planner's deliberation about a certain development on a particular site are informed, not just by questions of its suitability, or indeed profitability, but by city-wide considerations of the likely impact on land use, transportation patterns, car parking requirements and also wider social needs. Indeed this one little development might be 'the straw which breaks the camel's back', the additional traffic flows generated by it finally bringing the traffic to a halt! (See p. 204 of Volume I.) Looking at issues such as traffic also reveals the fact that there is no one right answer that will please everyone. For the centre of Bristol, some groups simply want a place to park while they go to work; some look upon parking space as a wasteful encouragement of the car at the expense of public transport and valuable developments; and some look to more sustainable ways of organising cities (Blowers 1993). The final choice of policy over a particular issue, or in relation to a particular site, is inevitably a reflection of the influence of various powerful groups in society. Planning policy, it is argued, can never be concerned purely with physical land use issues, as some groups are always likely to benefit more than others (see Volume I, Part IV); the making of plans must also allow for social policy dimensions.

Themes

The chapters in this book are written by a range of planners: members of the Faculty of the Built Environment at the University of the West of England (UWE) and practitioners in Bristol, County of Avon, in the south-west. Some of the examples are from Bristol, but by no means all. In any case, the principles and content are of national relevance, and with some modification, national applicability. Indeed it may be argued that the Bristol planning situation and the city itself are a microcosm of the national situation. For further information on the authors, see the list of contributors. The book comprises a collection of chapters which should ideally be read in sequence, but which may be drawn upon separately in studying different aspects of the implementation process. The book is more than a collection of essays; its chapters are organised into sections that explore different aspects of implementation and which develop different themes.

In summary, sections which investigate the developmental/professional context and the legislative/procedural framework are followed by sections which comprise a series of case studies demonstrating the implementation process and related themes in relation to real site developments. It is not a primary purpose of this book to look at implementation of high-level policy goals from the town planner's perspective, but it does offer examples where the development process provided opportunities for policy attainment. The specific role of central and local government in implementing current planning policies, and details of financial, economic and spatial planning programmes – for example, the role of Enterprise Zones, City Challenge, single regeneration budget and EU incentives and controls – will be explored in the following volume in this series, within the context of investigating the effectiveness of policy making from the town planner's perspective. But many such issues will be touched upon within the story of development as presented in this volume.

One key issue pursued throughout the book is that of the roles and relationships between the different actors in the development process, not least the likelihood of differing perspectives and approaches to conflict resolution. In particular, this volume illustrates the fragmented nature of the development process itself and of the power to implement. Planners have limited powers to carry through their planning objectives alongside all the other private and public actors involved in the development process. A related theme identifies the helps and hurdles which facilitate or frustrate the implementation of planning objectives within the existing governmental and developmental context, so characterised by division of powers.

The second key theme relates more to the social aspects of planning, as in any development process, in spite of complex mechanisms to extract at least limited planning gain, there are likely to be both gainers and losers within the urban community. Therefore, as the book progresses, greater emphasis is put upon who is benefitting, in addition to the property developers themselves. In later chapters attention is given to inner city communities, and the needs of minorities, thus bringing in a social dimension to what may at first sight seem a rather peopleless implementary process. Consideration is also given to what is being implemented, what should be planned in an ideal work and how alternative approaches to implementation might achieve these goals. A particular problem is the definition of the scope and nature of town planning itself, not least from a social perspective. Many of the policies which groups in the community want may be defined as *ultra vires*, that is, not a land use matter. Indeed, an inescapable theme is the tension between the traditional physical land use agenda of planners (and the development fraternity) and the wider social, economic and community based agenda of those on the receiving end of planning policy, who actually live and work in the areas under consideration.

Planning gain

A key theme, running right through the chapters of this book, is the discussion of the issue of planning gain, which nowadays seems to be seen by many as a normal, expected spin-off from the development process. This section introduces the term, but more detailed treatment will be found in subsequent chapters. Within the above RTPI definition of town planning is the implicit theme, 'planning is for people' (Broady 1968). It has long been argued (Hall 1992, Ch. 1) that the property market may be good at providing for economically profitable land uses, buildings and facilities, but that there is again a need for state intervention to ensure that essential, but unfortunately non-profit-making uses are provided as well. These might range from the provision of basic physical infrastructure, such as sewers, drains and roads, to more social facilities, such as schools, community centres, public conveniences, parks and buses. It must be admitted that there has been much criticism by the general public both of the policies implemented and the nature of the implementation process (which is often perceived as somewhat corrupt) although planning gain is for the benefit of society not the profit of individual planners. In the past, many such social amenities were traditionally provided out of rates and taxes, a consensus accepted to varying degrees by all political parties, as part of essential local government expenditure in civilised, advanced societies. However, in recent years there have been major cut-backs in public expenditure, and a trend towards privatisation of erstwhile public goods and services. Attempts have been made to introduce market economy principles into social areas as diverse as education, housing, health and recreation.

Nowadays it may be argued that town planners, and the local government system itself, are considerably weaker than in the past. Back in the postwar reconstruction period, significantly during Labour government, planning, including town planning, was prioritised as a means of organising the economy and built environment. Although their purpose was to create a more productive system, in which the perceived inefficiencies and conflicts of a market economy would be replaced by logical, rational planning, in reality such experiments were readily criticised because the planning policies were unsatisfactory; they did not always deliver the goods. In contrast, the entrepreneurial expansion under the enterprise culture of the 1980s, introduced by the Conservatives under Mrs. Thatcher, caused a major change of direction. It was held that market forces, not state intervention and government funding, worked best in improving the economy and 'solving' society's problems. Private sector solutions for public policy issues were favoured. For example, in the 1980s, the traditional development plan-led approach to urban development, firmly under the control of the planners, was undermined by a series of pro-developer appeal decisions by the secretary of state for the environment. The onus was upon giving rather than refusing permission. This approach resulted in the weakening of green belt policy, significant because 12% of England alone is covered by green belt policy in fourteen different locations. A proliferation of urban fringe development took place, including residential development, and a veritable Store Wars ensued among the retailing giants as they vied for out-of-town superstore

7

locations. Thankfully, at last, there was a volte-face (especially under Secretary of State John Gummer) and the 1990s have seen a return to a greater emphasis upon the primacy of the development plan. Gummer also advised against allowing planning permission for out-of-town developments, presumably because of the transportation and sustainability implications of such developments (PPG 13).[1]

Within this changing political setting, town planners found they had less power to intervene in what had become a market-led situation and to implement their controlling planning policies. Also the local government structure itself had been weakened financially and administratively in the 1980s and 1990s; funding was no longer available for all the social, environmental and infrastructural elements that were normally required to accompany development. Therefore planners needed to adopt other tactics in seeking to carry out effective planning. They looked for alternative means of fulfilling the original intentions of their plans, which inevitably comprise social and environmental as well as physical components. In particular, planners have sought to extract from developers what is known as planning gain, and arguably in the process, they have acquired new forms of informal non-statutory power as negotiators. Thus the issue of planning gain is a key theme in this book, as an integral part of the implementation process.

Over and above the basic statutory procedures, negotiation continues to play a major role in achieving a satisfactory development solution – an implementation acceptable to developers and to planners. But compared with ten years ago, developers are arguably less willing to play ball regarding planning gain. However, negotiation continues to be part of the planner's tool-kit, as will be pursued in later chapters. Regardless of the state of the economy, the way in which the implementation game is played largely depends on the way in which the planners see their role, and upon their degree of power relative to other actors in the development process. A planner's personality can also have an effect. Some planning officers may be strong leaders and take on the role of city manager; they may appear to have everything under control, inspiring within developers a feeling of safety.

Friends or enemies?

From the discussion so far, some readers might imagine the planner and the developer on opposing sides. Nowadays, this is not necessarily so. Later chapters illustrate the increasing emphasis placed upon partnership schemes, in which local authorities and developers pool their expertise and resources to achieve implementation. For example, planners are keen to unlock the developers' financial resources to fund their urban development schemes. On the other hand, local authorities still have powers of compulsory purchase, needed by the developer to facilitate land assembly. Authorities possess in-house local knowledge and a vast range of professional ability, which is relatively cheap compared with private sector expertise. However, some consider that the public/private sector divide has already blurred for reasons beyond town planning. For example, the government's drive to make the public sector more efficient, and to introduce a market situation into public services is likely to lead to major changes in the nature of local government. Some public sector bodies and former nationalised industries are being privatised. For example, the National Health Service has been restructured around a series of localised, private trusts.

More broadly, the whole nature of local government is changing as a more market based structure is emerging. In particular, Compulsory Competitive Tendering (CCT) is gradually being introduced. At first, CCT in local government was limited mainly to manual and semi-skilled occupations in which outside private firms were invited to tender for public sector work contracts. Now CCT is moving into the white-collar and professional levels of local government, the functions of departments such as town planning, surveying, highways, valuation and estates, will probably be opened up for competitive tender. It is likely, therefore, that more town planning work will be undertaken by private planning consultancies. Ironically some of the planners in these consultancies may well be ex-local government planners, who either got out of their own accord at the time of the property boom in the 1980s, or who have gone into the private sector in the 1990s following local government cut-backs and redundancy. There is much debate about the likely effects of these changes, in particular many would argue that town planning cannot be broken up into bits and farmed out to consultants. Long-term, city-wide development plans, in particular, require in-house staff, who can see the whole picture, and ensure continuity of implementation. Many of the issues raised in the above discussion will be highlighted in individual chapters, especially the emphasis on negotiation in the planning process and the role of working with the private sector in achieving implementation.

Contents

In more detail the chapters are as follows. Before tackling the subject of implementation, it is important that the reader is familiar with the nature of the professional groups, development processes and areas referred to in individual chapters. Therefore Chapter 2 provides some basic background, of particular value to those readers starting at Volume II, although they are strongly recommended to consult Volume I *Introducing Town Planning* for the fuller picture. But, as well as background, Chapter 2 also contains new material. Firstly, the planners and the planning system are explained briefly, but more advanced detail will be provided by the other contributors to Volume II in the main body of the text. Secondly, there is a brief summary of the development process; later chapters offer a deeper analysis, taking it as their central theme. The development process was also covered in the second chapter of Volume I. Lastly, there is a consideration of the way in which planners fit into the wider world of the property professions and construction industry. (It should be noted for those who have already read Volume I that this final section, which starts two-thirds of the way through the chapter, covers material not contained in Volume I.) The topic will be investigated with reference to material from the CISC (Construction Industry Standing Conference) 'mapping' exercise, which has sought to delineate and structure the main functions of the various professional groups involved (CISC 1993). A more detailed critique of the CISC mapping exercise *vis-à-vis* town planning is given in Appendix 2 to demonstrate to readers the fluidity and complexity of that part of the professional cake which we call town planning. If one includes the professional, managerial technical, trades and manual levels, there are more than two million people working in the construction industry at the various levels and in the different specialisms. All of them work together to produce the end-product of 'development', that is they are all involved in the implementation process in different ways.

Chapter 2 concludes Part I, 'The Developmental and Professional Context'. Part II, 'The Legislative and Procedural Framework', comprises four chapters and presents the means of achieving implementation. Some inexperienced students seem to imagine that simply identifying what is wrong is all that is needed; they take it for granted that their ideas will be accepted and that the government should do something. In reality, the process of implementation is far more complex, involving a range of governmental and private sector bodies. It is one thing to have good ideas or to draw up planning guidelines and policy statements, but to put them into effect – to achieve implementation – requires a range of tools, including negotiation, management techniques, legal measures, political lobbying, possibly working in cooperation with the private sector and the application of professional expertise and experience. Case studies illustrate aspects of the process in a range of developmental and organisational settings.

Part II provides the framework and will introduce the reader to the context, procedural and legal setting of the development process, as seen from the local authority planner's perspective. Chapter 3, written jointly by Jim Claydon and John Allinson, looks at the development process; the discussion related to a conceptual model called the Pipeline Diagram. Chapter 3 also explains the relevant legislation which governs the operation of the planning system; this provides an explanation of the context of the implementation process, written from the local authority planner's perspective. Although the initiative for development is likely, nowadays, to come chiefly from the private sector, virtually all types of development still require planning permission before development can take place. So the local government planner may be seen, in a sense, as having a relatively powerful controlling and orchestrating role in respect of the progression of the process of development. In particular, Chapter 3 identifies the tools available to the planner to carry out the planning processes effectively. It also identifies the hurdles the developer must overcome.

Not all the tools used by local authorities to shape and control the built environment are within the hands of the planning department. In Chapter 4 John Allinson sets out the other legislative controls and policy areas which affect implementation, including the Building Regulations and the Fire Regulations. Another theme running through the book is that controls which lie outside the direct influence of the planners can act as hurdles to the implementation of effective planning policy. Incidentally, they may also be a hindrance to the private developer. Chapter 4 provides a valuable grounding in order to appreciate this theme. To reiterate, the emphasis in these chapters is upon the wider construction and property development 'site' context of town planning, rather than upon discussion of strategic or economic planning policy issues. The uneasy relationship between planners and other regulators or controllers of the built environment is revisited and further explored in the final plenary chapters of the book; and it crops up frequently in the case studies. Part II is completed by Chapters 5 and 6, written by John Allinson and Janet Askew. They consider ways in which planners might implement their broader social and environmental policy agenda by means of such strategies as planning gain, working in partnership with the private sector within the context of the development process, negotiating satisfactory planning briefs in respect of site development and monitoring ongoing compliance with planning conditions. Planning gain, and the other strategies identified, are all concerned with getting some sort of wider spin-off benefits to the community from the development process, and thus are aimed at implementing at least a small part of the planners' wider policy agenda. The contributors place planning gain within the wider historical context of the betterment debate, that is the question of the extent to which the developer should be expected to plough back his profits for the benefit of the community in contributions to social, amenity and infrastructural provision or through direct taxation, for example. This is another theme which runs all through the book, and for that matter, all through twentieth century planning history; betterment is frequently seen as a spin-off from the successful implementation process.

Part III is entitled 'Resolving Conflict' because it presents different approaches, both statutory and informal, to dealing with the differences of opinion that are bound to emerge between planners and developers. There is a gradual progression in the contents of the book from procedures and processes towards people and policies. Therefore, Part III adopts a somewhat more questioning perspective towards the implementation process and towards the resolution or prevention of conflicts which arise over site development. The chapters also provide a background to Part V, which contains another set of case studies to focus upon the differences of opinion over site development. Chapter 7, written by John Allinson, describes planning inquiries, appeals structures and procedures. In Chapter 8, he describes other forms of statutory hearing as ways of resolving conflict without recourse to the expensive, time-consuming and increasingly litigious appeals system. In Chapter 9, Jim Claydon looks at the potential of negotiation to resolve conflict in the implementation process, arguing that negotiating skills are essential components of the planner's tool-kit.

Part IV, 'The Process in Practice', comprises case studies located in or around the Bristol region. Chapter 10 provides a short background to the planning situation in Bristol and also raises some of the more controversial issues. Chapters 11 and 12 are written from the 'other side', by a private sector planning consultant, Robin Tetlow of Oldfield King Planning. He describes the process involved in seeking to develop a difficult site on the edge of the centre of Bristol. The site was within a somewhat run-down area, viewed as being worthwhile developing in the 1980s in spite of the high costs involved. A planning gain agreement was negotiated to provide a mixed use development combining new-build social housing, and the refurbishment of some very run-down listed buildings and office developments. By the 1990s, the scheme currently being developed is somewhat scaled down in view of the property recession, but the site still has potential for the future when the next economic upturn takes place. This fascinating account of what implementation really involves also provides a vehicle to describe the roles of other members of the built environment professions and construction industry in the development process. Insights are drawn from the author's experience of using the site as a basis for several student professional role-play projects in the last few years, within the Faculty of the Built Environment, University of the West of England, and from doing implementation in the real world in trying to getting the site developed.

Chapter 13 also takes a non-local authority planning perspective. It is written by Jennifer Tempest of The Planning Practice, Bath, a planning consultant who has been working on behalf of a local NHS trust on the management, disposal and development of former NHS sites and buildings which have become available because of current hospital closure programmes. A health trust is a good example of a quasi-public body which has recently emerged as a result of policies seeking to rationalise and introduce a form of privatisation to the National Health Service. This move reflects current central government opinion that entrepreneurial organisational structures are likely to be more efficient and accountable to the public they serve, than traditional bureaucratic public sector organisations. Admittedly some see the disposal of such public sites, especially green belt, as selling the family silver, but their sale, with planning permission on them, can greatly increase health trust revenue. By means of case studies the planning policy issues are illustrated and also the details of procedural and legal aspects are presented in situations where, effectively, one government department is dealing with another, with the health trust taking on the persona of an entrepreneurial developer. In Chapter 14 Janet Askew, planning consultant and planning lecturer, presents a case study of Canon's Marsh in Bristol one of the few remaining vacant sites in the central docklands.

In discussing implementation, one must reflect upon the question, for whom is the planning policy and the ultimate development intended? Part V, 'People, Policies and Power', pursues the theme of using what is essentially a physical, land use based planning system to achieve wider social and economic policies for the community . In Chapter 15 Janet Askew presents a study of the King's Cross railway redevelopment site in London, and makes comparisons with the Canon's Marsh site discussed in Chapter 14. In particular, there has been a much stronger political involvement by local groups, including conservation and community groups, in the King's Cross development process, and generally the planning authority has taken a more proactive and socially motivated approach towards the planning of the site. The community is often the 'third party' in the planning process but often does not have a strong legal right to be represented in the proceedings. Planning gain matters are prominent in the discussions of what can be achieved on the sites. The case study of King's Cross brings out the role of planning briefs and negotiations, as identified in Part IV, in moving towards a satisfactory scheme. Janet Askew also introduces the concept of interim uses; these are uses to which a site can be put for the benefit of the community while the tedious discussion grinds on. Chapters 14 and 15 provide examples of alternative and novel approaches to implementation.

In Chapters 16 and 17 Linda Davies returns to the topical question of planning for women and minorities. Planning is for people, but people are not a unitary group, and in recent years a key issue has been equal opportunities; in particular, which groups derive benefit from current planning policy. Chapters 16 and 17, unlike earlier chapters, are not based around studies of implementation in relation to a particular scheme on a specific site. Instead, they are broader and attempt to incorporate equal opportunities planning policies into the Unitary Development Plan (UDP) policy statements currently being produced by the London boroughs and larger metropolitan authorities. These policy statements affect whole administrative areas. Linda Davies draws on many examples from her research to demonstrate the difficulty of implementing policies which do not quite fit into designated categories within development documents.

There appear to be two main problems in terms of how to package such policies in order to make them effective. Firstly, there is the question of whether such policies should be put in a separate section just on ethnic minorities, for example, or whether they should be integrated and mainstreamed into existing topic sections on transport, etc. Secondly, there is the question of whether the desired policies should be written as general policy statements, such as 'Shopper crèche provision should be included as an integral part of out-of-town retail development,' or written as prescriptive detailed standards, such as specifying so many child care spaces per thousand square metres of floor space. The Department of the Environment, following receipt of many such new-style UDP plans over the last few years, has stipulated that it prefers such issues to be integrated within the mainstream discussion under relevant topic headings, for example, including transport needs of the disabled under the mainstream transportation section, rather than putting them in separate chapters (Department of the Environment 1992a). Also, it would appear that some planning inspectors dislike floor space quotas and detailed standards seeing them as inappropriate at development plan level. Part V does not deal in detail with the actual content of the policies presented, instead it discusses their chances of implementation within the planning system. More fundamentally, such socially oriented policies may be seen as *ultra vires*, outside the remit of physical land use planning. Indeed the tension between a land use based approach to planning, as against a broader social policy oriented approach is a theme developed in these chapters.

In Part VI, 'Alternative Perspectives', the editor returns to the key themes and certain unresolved issues to develop them further. Firstly, in Chapter 18, the question of policy is addressed, that is, what proposals planners should be implementing in an ideal world. There is a progressive shift throughout the book from considering the more prescriptive issues of development procedures and processes towards the conceptual issue of what is being implemented and who it is for. In many of the chapters it has been taken as given that certain good policies inform the objectives of the implementation process, but these have not necessarily been overtly stated. Chapter 18 presents a range of possible policies to the reader. Alternative approaches to achieving implementation of such visionary proposals are considered.

Chapter 19 returns to the question of power, planners' ability (or lack of ability) to make the process happen and to implement policy. With reference to the provision of just one small aspect of amenity provision at the local planning level, it seeks to illustrate the problems planners confront in implementing policy, not least because they do not possess total control over the built environment, but because they share it with a range of other regulatory and policy making bodies, whose activities may either reinforce or undermine the planners' attempts to implement good policy (a theme originally introduced back in Part II). There may be no participation, limited consultation and no comeback on the decisions of such bodies as the British Standards Institution, whose standards can shape key aspects of the built environment. The conclusion draws together the different levels and dimensions of the implementation spectrum, ranging from the city-wide strategic policy level, through the local plan level and down to the nitty-gritty level of street layout and building design, all of which, it is argued, are town planning matters as they affect the way people use cities. In order to understand the problems of implementing effective urban policy, the reader should bear in mind the following cognate questions when reading this book. What counts as a legitimate policy concern of town planning? What is included in, or out, and why?

In Chapter 20 the definition of implementation is revisited, in the light of material presented in the book. It is argued that it may be impossible to give a definition which satisfies everyone, but a range of factors are identified by which the success or failure of the process can be judged. It also re-examines the question of people in the implementation process, that is, the place of the general public and the consumers of planning policy. Members of the public, and more specifically active pressure groups, often find themselves at odds with the planners over environmental matters, inner city issues and basic policy assumptions about the question of how they want to live (Department of the Environment 1972a). They may find, in challenging planning applications, that they have to count as third parties, with limited legal right to contest planning decisions which directly affect them. Also, the role of public participation, politics and pressure group involvement is considered in relation to plan preparation. In the last section, a set of proposals is listed which would enable more effective implementation of modern planning policy.

Overall, this book incorporates three main components. The first component is relatively descriptive; it provides the background information on the legal and procedural framework, and the conceptual context of the process. The second component consists of the case studies, ordered to help the reader obtain a clear progression from looking at largely commercial developments on relatively small sites; through a broader perspective on much larger sites; to implementing social objectives for a whole city or nation. A gradual progression is to be found in the book from looking at the procedural and property development aspects of planning implementation, towards looking far more at the question of what policies were actually being implemented throughout this process. There is progressive emphasis upon the concept that planning is for people, thus upon the means and opportunities the development process offers for the implementation of social policy. The third component consists of the more discursive sections which look beyond the implementary process itself and comment on the nature of the planning policy being implemented. Certain passages in the book are intended to be more unsettling and give an airing to controversial underlying issues; these issues are bound to be bubbling beneath the surface in any discussion of the nature of planning policy and the planning implementation process. This third component is particularly present in chapters written by the editor, but is also present in the more critical and reflective components in all chapters.

[1] Volume II is intended to be more practical than Volume I. Many chapters are written by practitioners, so the reader will find fewer book references and a shorter bibliography. A separate section lists most of the main acts of Parliament, planning policy guidance notes (PPGs), circulars, regulations and order referred to in the text. Check this section for items not found, under Department of the Environment in the reference list. Appendix 1 contains some suggestions for project work which might be of help to lecturers or might be of use to students in self-evaluation or self-directed learning.

Chapter 2

PROCESSES, PARTICIPANTS AND FUNCTIONS

Clara Greed

Definitions

The purpose of this chapter is to provide background material to give an explanatory context for the book as a whole. This is particularly important for those starting at Volume II, but should also be of interest to those who have already covered Volume I. This chapter seeks to describe the main actors in the development process referred to in the following chapters, with particular reference, firstly, to the question of who the planners are, and secondly to development, developers and the development process. Thirdly, the reader is introduced to the broader context of the process of implementation within reference to the construction industry (beyond the boundaries of town planning) using material from CISC (Construction Industry Standing Conference) (CISC 1993). CISC has sought to 'map' the different levels and specialisms involved in the construction process. This is interesting because it has sought to break down all the functions and processes undertaken, and to identify all the participants who are involved in the activities of the construction industries and property professions, including town planners. The reader will also require some basic background on the City of Bristol and the County of Avon, in order to appreciate the nuances of some of the case studies, although the principles are representative of the situation nationally. This will be provided in due course at the start of Part IV.

The planners

Town planning is a relatively small profession. The main professional body to which planners belong is the Royal Town Planning Institute (RTPI) whose membership consists of under 18,000 (Tables 2.1 and 2.2, and see Greed 1993, Ch. 2 for background explanatory material). 80% of planners work in the public sector, chiefly within local government planning departments; the remaining 20% are employed in the private sector, many practising within planning consultancies (although this situation is changing because of increasing privatisation and the introduction of CCT, that is the compulsory

Table 2.1   Membership of the professional bodies as at January 1995

Body	Full members		Student members		Total Members	
RTPI	14534	(20.0%)	3192	(42.0%)	17726	(23.0%)
RICS	70918	(6.1%)	21267	(15.8%)	92185	(8.3%)
ICE	52000	(1.2%)	9285	(11.0%)	80250	(3.5%)
ISE	17131	(1.7%)	6489	(11.9%)	23620	(4.5%)
CIOB	25118	(0.7%)	9439	(4.3%)	33557	(1.7%)
CIOH	8000	(43.0%)	4116	(56.0%)	12300	(44.0%)
ASI	4820	(1.2%)	485	(10.2%)	5305	(1.9%)
ISVA	5774	(6.7%)	1381	(16.5%)	7155	(8.6%)
RIBA	27708	(7.2%)	4102	(28.2%)	31810	(10.0%)
CIBSE	12939	(1.2%)	2225	(4.9%)	15164	(1.8%)
LI	2284	(40.5%)	3653	(42.4%)	3777	(40.0%)
IRRV	2361	N/A	1570	N/A	5751	(24.0%)
NAEA	(non examining body)				9657	(21.1%)

Source: The professional bodies as at January 1995. In some cases there are other intermediate or honorary categories which make up the remainder of the total, who are not
strictly speaking either fully qualified members or students, such as probationers, technicians, international members, graduate associates.

Key: (Female percentages in brackets.)
RTPI = Royal Town Planning Institute; RICS = Royal Institution of Chartered Surveyors;
ICE = Institution of Civil Engineers; ISE = Institution of Structural Engineers; CIOB =
Chartered Institute of Building; CIOH = Chartered Institute of Housing; ASI = Architects
and Surveyors Institute; ISVA = Incorporated Society of Valuers and Auctioneers; RIBA =
Royal Institute of British Architects; CIBSE = Chartered Institution of Building Services
Engineers; NAEA = National Association of Estate Agents; LI = Landscape Institute; IRRV =
Institute of Revenue, Rating & Valuation.

competitive tendering). Planners are but one professional group among
many within the world of the construction and property professions who play
a part in making development happen. However, as part of the municipal
machinery of local government, they are to be found in every county and district across the country. They still have a fair amount of power in that
virtually all development must seek planning permission. Although a small
profession, it comprises a variety of expertise and knowledge areas.

Other property professionals are motivated by a wide range of objectives,
such as the profit motive or the requirement to control the cost factor, or
they may simply see implementation as a technologically challenging civil
engineering project; agendas which might clash with the more altruistic
motives of the planners. Chartered surveyors concerned with the more
commercial and market-led aspects of development, and about the same
number of civil engineers involved in the nitty-gritty of design and construction (Table 2.1). In addition, within local government, other departments
have authority over aspects of land use and development which may, or may
not, be exercised in a manner that brings praise from the planners. The role
of highways, building regulations, environmental health, housing and other
such built environment-related local government departments will be

17

Table 2.2 Membership of the Royal Town Planning Institute

Category	Total	Female	Non-White*	Disabled*
Fellows	613	20	15	5
Members	12688	2553	364	35
Students	3094	1309	180	4
Legal	144	8		
Honorary	63	6		
International	26	8	4	
Retired	807	28	8	28
All	17435	3932	571	72

* Non-white and disabled not divided into m/f, nor ethnic grouping. Source of table, and thus categorisations, RTPI.

Summary: 22% Female, 3.3% 'non-white', 0.4% disabled.

N.B. 80% of town planners are employed in government bodies, mainly local government, but 80% of surveyors (and generally other built environment professions) are to be found in the private sector.

illustrated, where appropriate, within the various chapters. For example, highways departments might have very different objectives from planning authorities, in dealing with traffic management. Likewise, building control and public health regulations which require buildings to conform to modern standards might be in conflict with the sensitive conservation of historic buildings. A recurrent theme is the question of the level of power of the planners to implement change in the built environment. Planners would appear to be relatively weak because of their small numbers, but they have considerable power as part of the wider local government regulatory system.

The planning system

The organisation of the planning system was previously explained in Volume I (Greed 1993, 21). Figure 2.1 illustrates the levels of town and country planning; some contributors have included similar diagrams to reflect their own viewpoints. Before the detailed description of Chapter 3, here is a brief explanation for newcomers. Planning is a function of government at three levels, central government, county local government and district local government. Although the Department of the Environment has a policy-directing role to play at central government level, town planning is primarily a function of local government. In summary, within areas still operating the two-tier system of local government set up under the reorganisation which occurred following the 1972 Local Government Act, the shire county planning authorities produce overall strategic development plans, known as structure plans, setting out macro level policies for the county and city level

Central Government
Department of the Environment

Secretary of State (politician, MP)   Advised by planning professionals (civil servants)
Approves development plans
Gives overall policy guidance
Deals with appeals (assisted by the planning inspectorate)

Also range of other central government departments liaise with DoE on planning issues, e.g. MoD, Home Office, MAFF, Industry, Transport.
Note European EC 'level' environmental impact analysis (EIA)

Regional level

Note no significant regional level at present but vestiges of Regional Economic Planning Boards, committees, plans, e.g. SERPLAN. Growing emphasis on regional liaison by development plan authorities.

Local government

Decisions are made by the politicans (elected councillors on council planning committee) as advised by the professionals (planners who are employed as local government officers). Following recent changes, two types of development plan system are running:

Two-tier system	Unitary system
Counties (47) Structure Plans Overall policy strategy Minerals and waste disposal	*Metropolitan districts (36)* *London boroughs (32)* Unitary Development Plans (combine contents of structure and local plans) Policy implementation Development control
Districts (333) Local plans Implementation of planning Development control (outline and detailed applications)	The planning role of the 6 metropolitan counties passed to metropolitan district councils, and the GLC's role passed to the 32 London boroughs in 1986.

Also range of *ad hoc* bodies and plans including:

Outside the local government system. New Town Development Corporations (few left nowadays), urban development corporations, National Park boards, committees (Countryside Commission, a DoE quango, has overview of rural policies).

Inside the local government system. Additional special types of planning areas, administered by existing districts, e.g. Enterprise Zones and Simplified Planning Zones. Conservation areas administered by local planning authorities, but listing an overall historic buildings policy under English Heritage, a DoE quango.

Fig. 2.1   The levels of town and country planning

as a whole. The districts into which each county is divided (on average four or five per county) operate the more detailed micro implementary level, while being cognisant of the overall policy directives set by the counties. The districts have two main functions, firstly to produce local plans which translate high-level policy into its implications for a particular area, district or village; and secondly they operate the development control system, granting or refusing planning permission. In this they are guided both by the higher-level policies set out in the structure and local plans relevant to the area, and secondly by a complex national system of planning law. For the purposes of planning law, development includes both new building and also change of use on existing premises or land, for example from residential to commercial use. The planning law system is vast and complex; interpretations of the law and of precedent play a large part in the enforcement and negotiation processes. The district level is key to the implementation process. Currently in 1995 a return to a unitary system is gradually being introduced (check professional press for details), as in Avon.

As can be seen from the above brief description there are many levels and areas of expertise within the planning system. Although town planning is a small profession, it contains a wide range of specialist expertise. For example, if one considers the areas that planners need to survey and research in order to produce a development plan, as originally set out in the *Development Plan Manual* (Department of the Environment 1972b) and updated in the *Development Plans: Good Practice Guide Note* (Department of the Environment 1992a) they have to know about the following areas: housing, population and employment; retail development; leisure and recreation; the countryside; minerals; waste disposal sites; and transportation. Nowadays one might add to this list other specialist areas, such as the social aspects of planning, including so-called minority issues such as race, gender and disability; green issues, including ecological issues and planning for sustainability (Blowers 1993); and urban design.

While some planners might specialise in policy making at the level of the development plan and the strategic issues, others, who are equally important, deal with local planning and development control. It is these latter areas which are the implementary levels, where planners deal with the developers, and arguably have the most direct power in shaping the built environment, for example, by negotiating over planning gain; by making planning permissions conditional to certain wider environmental and social requirements; and by overseeing operating design and layout control on site development (for more details about the types of planners read Volume I, and also Hall 1992). Indeed, colleagues are of the opinion that there is no longer one planning profession, but many plannings, often existing in splendid isolation with quite different agendas, for example, green planners, women and planning, urban designers, regional economic planners, European Union planners, environmental assessment specialists, transportation planners and plain old-fashioned land use zoning planners. This policy theme will be the basis of the next volume. However, within the development process, particularly within the case studies of Parts IV and V, one can see how these different agendas interact within the context of the development process.

In the large conurbations there now operates a somewhat different one-tier system, with the planning authority combining the county district functions. In London, since the abolition of the Greater London Council in 1986, the thirty-two London boroughs are the main planning authorities. In the areas previously covered by the metropolitan counties, the planning role has now passed to the metropolitan district councils into which they were divided. The London boroughs and the metropolitan districts are required to produce unitary development plans (UDPs), which combine the functions of structure plans and local plans in one format. Further revisions of the levels and functions of local government, as well as boundary revisions, are currently being produced by the Local Government Commission. It is envisaged that the new authorities will come into operation in either April 1996 or April 1997; the enabling legislation is already in force, namely, the 1992 Local Government Act. As will be illustrated, representatives of the present different levels of the planning system do not necessarily see eye to eye, and there is no guarantee the new system will necessarily be an improvement. There is often considerable ill-feeling between both the county and the district levels, and among different districts if they do not feel the county planners are treating all areas equally fairly in designating development opportunities to their part of the county. Furthermore, there is also likely to be considerable opposition and suspicion of the planning system from the general public, the whole dimension of public participation being a key factor in the implementation process.

Politicians, planners and people

Planners **do not decide** ultimate questions of policy. Planners **give advice** to elected councillors then the councillors make the decisions. The councillors sit on the local council planning committee. It cannot be overstated that town planning is a political process in that it concerns property and land, and deals with people's wants and needs. At a recent workshop of CISC (1993) which consisted mainly of public sector planners, it was concluded that planners are not really policy makers at all; rather they are advisors, researchers, managers – a controversial point for further discussion! In Volume I there was considerable reference to the Great Planner as the visionary thinker, the theoretician, the great man, such as Le Corbusier and Ebenezer Howard; nowadays one might see the local authority planner in quite a different light, as essentially a manager, an administrator, even a technician (Greed 1994: Ch. 2). Indeed, planners might be seen as implementors in the sense that they are carrying out others' commands, rather than operating on the basis of their own initiative and autonomy.

The truth probably lies somewhere between the two. Whatever the official version might be, according to the enabling legislation, those who operate a system (as against those who give the directions) often possess a fair amount of unofficial power simply because they are the ones who are doing the job and know what it is all about. Even the most humble planner as operator or technician of the planning system is not necessarily just following rules, but is likely to use personal judgement and professional discretion in carrying out the most mundane tasks, and therefore possess considerable potential power (Greed 1994, 31). This discussion is part of a wider discussion about the role of individuals within bureaucracies, of which local government is a classic example (see Greed 1994, Ch. 2, in which Weber's concept of the bureaucratic subtype of the technician operator is discussed from a more sociological perspective).

As to the role of the people, for whom planning is meant to be, there is considerable debate as to whether they get much of a chance in such a complex and inevitably bureaucratised system. Public participation has always been a component of the plan making process ever since the days of the 1971 Town and Country Planning Act, which made it a mandatory requirement. However, as will be seen in later chapters, current attempts to speed up the planning system and powers for local authorities to validate their own plans (as explained in Part II) mean there is less attention given to formal public inquiries (and the examination in public of the development plan) and arguably a reduction in the requirements for full public involvement in local planning. Also the various ad hoc bodies set up to deal with town planning issues, such as urban development corporations, may be subject to no statutory requirement that public participation should take place, this being a bone of contention both over the London Docklands Development Corporation and the Bristol Development Corporation (BDC). For an explanation of the role of ad hoc bodies in planning see the second chapter in Volume I. Also, changes in local government structure and boundaries, which are currently being formulated, are bound to have implications for people's sense of belonging to the particular administrative subdivision created to govern the area in which they live. The organisational structure will, no doubt, influence people's likelihood of involving themselves in local decision making and public participation. The role of the people is a subtext to many chapters. The issues arising are gathered together and reflected upon in the last chapter.

The development process

Development and developers

The development process was explained in the second chapter of Volume I. A brief explanation will now be given, to set the scene for newcomers to the subject. Figure 2.2 shows the process of property development. Individual contributors present their own versions of how they understand this process from a planner's perspective.

3 Obtaining planning permission

Representing client in submitting outline application, followed by negotiation and planning gain consultation, or inquiry
Local authority and central government 'planners' determining the application may also be surveyors
Also private surveying practices act as consultants to local authorities in statutory plan preparation

Town planners
Lawyers
Economists
Architects as design controllers
Community groups

6 Letting and management

Agency role in letting disposing of units (GP)
Property management (GP, QS)
Property maintenance (BS)
Overall financial management, portfolio revisions (GP)
Legal issues, rents; rate reviews with District Valuer (GP)

Property agents
Maintenance engineers
Retail managers
Arbitrators and lawyers

2 Decision to develop

Development advice (P&D, GP)
Feasibility studies (P&D)
Location analysis (P&D)
Site finding (GP)

Town planners
Architects
Market researchers
Design consultants
Property agents

5 Building design and construction

Liaison on design with user groups (GP)
Liaison on planning controls (P&D)
Costing, procurement, tendering (QS)
Project management (QS)
Involvement in building team in many specialist roles (BS, QS, GP)

Architects
Planners
Accountants
Civil engineers
Structural engineers

1 Analysis of property investment situation

Review of property portfolio (GP)
Existing portfolio management (GP)
Examination of future trends (GP)
Property market analysis (GP)

Accountants
Financiers, bankers
Economists
Stock market specialists
The developer as client

4 Site development

Investigating land rights, covenants as constraints on development (GP)
Monitoring land transfer, site analysis and setting out (LS)
Landscaping liaison (LA)
Design consultation (GP)
Consumer research (GP)
Occupancy prediction (GP)

Civil engineers
Landscape architects
Highway engineers
Architects and planners
Lawyers

Fig. 2.2 The process of property development, showing the sequence and aspects of the process. Different divisions of surveyors contribute in an archetypal example of a new scheme for a developer as client. Contributing professions other than surveying are shown in italics. GP General Practice, P&D Planning and Development, LS Land Surveying, LA Land Agency, *MS Minerals*, QS Quantity Surveying, BS Building and Surveying divisions of the Royal Institution of Chartered Surveyors. *Adapted from Greed (1992).*

This account is given from a broader perspective putting more emphasis on the role of the private sector, and also the wider construction industry context. There are a range of books which give further details on the process from a private sector viewpoint. Such books emphasise the commercial dimensions, including the funding, valuation, estate management and marketing and disposal aspects of the process (Grover 1989; Lavender 1990; Stapleton 1986; Scarrett 1983; and Cadman and Austin-Crowe 1991). There are many different views and definitions of the development process and the implementation process. The following account is intended as a starting point for further thought by the reader. The stages in the production of a development by a private sector developer will now be outlined, to draw out the role of the different professional groups in the process. Because there are different views on this subject, and the nature of the sequence, it is important for readers to hold a critical perspective at this stage in the study of the subject and to develop their own views in the light of the material presented in the following chapters. This is particularly so for mature students who may already have worked in the world of construction, property and planning, and who have their own insights and experience of the situation.

Firstly, therefore, it is worth defining development and developer, although it is fully acknowledged that individual contributors will return to these themes, and take them further in the various chapters (especially in the following chapters by John Allinson and Jim Claydon), but there is a need to give an initial explanation. Development is defined in planning law under Section 55 of the 1990 Town and Country Planning Act:

> The carrying out of building, engineering, mining, or other operations in, on, over or under land, or the making of any material change in the use of any buildings or other land.

(as reiterated and discussed further in more detail in Part II). Therefore development means two main activities. Firstly, the development of new buildings and other works, that is, operations, and secondly, the change of use from one land use to another. A planning application form from the local planning office must be completed and submitted in the hope of obtaining planning permission (or refusal). However, in the wider world of property, development can mean the process of construction, as in 'undertaking development'; the likely financial return, as in 'this site has development potential'; and the product, that is, a building, scheme or project, as in 'office development'.

Developer also has a variety of usages. Whereas Cadman and Austin-Crowe (1991) believe that valid definitions include the property company who put a scheme together, the investor financing the scheme and/or the builder; Lavender (1990) argues that the term developer should usually be reserved for the property development company itself, or the investor on whose behalf they are operating. Therefore, the developer is the individual or organisation who initiates a construction project, not the builder, designer, user or planner. A major role of the developer is that of bringing funding, or at least financial backing to the development. The scheme may be directly financed by the developer, or backed by pension funds, insurance companies, trusts and other financial bodies. As stated in Volume I, the chief purpose of undertaking development in the private sector is to get a worthwhile return from the scheme. Questions relating to meeting human need, improving the environment and making cities more functional are secondary considerations, important only insofar as they affect site potential, and likely markets. However, it should not be assumed that all developers are necessarily from the private sector. As will be seen in the following chapters, public sector bodies, and especially such bodies which have recently been 'privatised' but still retain a quasi-public role, such as the National Health Service, may operate as developers. In the past, local authorities, new town development corporations and other governmental bodies initiated development. Nowadays, in view of many years of government cut-backs, and changing political attitudes towards the role of the public sector, it is only special ad hoc public sector planning bodies which have the funding and power to undertake development themselves, such as urban development corporations (UDCs) as in the case of the Bristol Development Corporation. Even so, they are expected to give more attention to providing enabling infrastructural development to generate either private sector development, than necessarily to act as property entrepreneurs in their own right. Also, as will be illustrated in later chapters, the public and private sector sometimes act together as developers. One example is the regeneration of inner city sites, where the local authority has the necessary statutory powers and authority to develop, and the private sector has the money – two of the most vital ingredients.

Development stages

In this introductory summary the process will be outlined from the private sector developers' viewpoint, but later chapters will provide the mirror image by describing the process from the planners' viewpoint, and in much more detail at that. The process was previously summarised in *The Process of Property Development* in Chapter 2 of Volume I page 33, which is reproduced again, for convenience in this present Volume as Figure 2.2. It should be noted that the authors have received a range of feedback on Figure 2.2, some positive, some negative. But they believe it still stands as a valid thumbnail sketch of the process, although the sequence might vary according to the site under consideration, and in the changing world of professional practice different actors might undertake different tasks. Indeed, it is often said that 80% of the work that property professionals undertake is in no way related to their original training, or job description!

Before deciding to develop, the would-be developers are likely to carry out a feasibility study as to the potential catchment area and turnover of the scheme. This may involve drawing on the specialist skills of a development surveyor and property researcher, possibly using the in-house expertise of one of the large London companies of chartered surveyors, who produce property market analysis reports. (In fact property research, and the related growth in methodological approaches are now a major area of professional activity; future volumes are intended to cover them in more depth.) Informal property research mainly occurs on the grapevine; surveyors phone up their colleagues to find out the going rate for certain sites and the way the wind is blowing for development potential. Much decision making still depends on initiative and hunches, as is the case in most speculative investment activity! The surveyors, who are advising the developers (their clients) as to the viability of the site in question will also need to consult with the local authority planners to find out the overall policy for that area, and to find out what the planners will countenance in terms of types, mixes and range of land uses and building forms. It is likely that in large or controversial schemes, planning consultants for the developers will produce a planning brief setting out the proposals as a basis for negotiation. The local planning authority may have already have drawn up its own development brief or policy statement as to what is acceptable in the area, particularly if they are located in an area such as parts of London where there is already demand to develop, and site finders are scouring every square inch of the territory looking for development potential. The question of what is finally agreed as acceptable to be put on that site, depends very much on the relative aptitude of the planner and the developer in exercising negotiating skills and overall bargaining powers as to who holds the best hand of cards. It is likely that matters of planning gain will be discussed early on, both with the developer offering and the planner requiring certain social and amenity related elements in association with the proposed development. Obviously, the process which determines who gets what, where, why and how is highly politicised and this is illustrated in the various case studies, particularly in Part V, where the community and minority groups are likely to be politically disadvantaged and less likely to be heard than the powerful property development companies.

On large-scale developments it is likely that such preliminary discussions will take place over several months, only when the planners and developers are clear where each other stands, and have possibly reached some sort of middle ground as to what might be acceptable on the site in question will the developers submit a planning application. In determining (deciding) a planning decision, the planners need to look not only at the detailed nationwide planning controls of planning law but also at central government policy statements, and especially at the implications of city-wide and local level plans. However, the process is not that clear-cut, and often there will be other factors to take into account, not least the influence of the local councillors, that is, the members who sit on the local planning committee and make the final decision. They have the power to reject the advice of their planning officers, although increasingly nowadays this is less likely in view of recent case law, and various television documentaries which have exposed perceived corruption among the members of certain planning authorities. Nevertheless, planning is a very political process, both because it is dealing with matters where, perhaps, millions of pounds are involved, and also because it affects the way in which people live their lives, through the shaping of the built environment.

There is often a great deal of suspicion and distrust directed at the planners from among the general public because the system often seems to be secretive (Reade 1987). Often decisions about development appear to be based on secret negotiations between planners and developers, so that third party interests, in particular those of the residents who live in the area, are excluded. This theme variously manifests itself in many different chapters, especially in those by J. Askew and L. Davies. Indeed, the question of whether 'planning [really] is for people', and if so, who these people are, what they actually want from the planning system and how planners find out what they want, will be revisited in the last section of the book, as nowadays they are key issues relevant to the implementation process. This book is chiefly concentrating on implementation from the overall planning and development perspective. The more detailed aspects of design and layout will be explored in a later volume, centred around the issue of urban design and local planning. But in the real world, the implementation process does not stop with the giving of planning permission; other runners take up the baton from the planners, such as the architects, construction professionals and civil engineers, who actually design and build the development. There is also a multitude of detailed design factors, costing considerations, legal constraints and site-related factors which need to be taken into account. A vast army of people at professional, supervisory, trade and manual levels swing into action to create the development, as explained in the second chapter of Volume I (and see Ball 1988; Dolan 1979).

When the development is built, it has to be let or sold in order for the investor to reap the reward of his or her efforts. There is no denying that some buildings seem to increase in value, even in a recession, by simply standing there empty as investments in the property portfolio, without any humans creating wear and tear and maintenance problems. However, changes in the rating of empty commercial buildings have put paid to this particular strategy. Following letting and disposal, the building and site has to be cared for and managed. Again this is the job of the surveyor (Cadman and Austin-Crowe 1991; Scarrett 1983; Stapleton 1986). There are the maintenance aspects to be considered, but beyond this caretaking role, there are all the other invisible financial and legal matters to deal with, such as rent reviews, property management and future policy development. As explained in Volume I, the process goes around in a circle, because once built and occupied, it is likely there will be a need for new planning applications for change of use or expansion, and eventually for major refurbishment, even redevelopment; the process starts all over again.

Mapping the process: CISC

Purpose

This section will set the role of the planner within the wider context of the construction professions, as been by a recent 'mapping' exercise on the construction industry. It is fully acknowledged that many planners do not like being referred to within this category, as part of the construction industry. But for the purposes of the establishment of a lead body to supervise the mapping exercise, undertaken in order to establish standards for National Vocational Qualifications (NVQs), planning, architecture, aspects of housing, general practice surveying, valuation and estate management have all been put within this category. This is in order to place the role of the planner (Fig. 2.3) from the CISC exercise (CISC 1993) which maps the main functions of the construction professions, all of whom have to be involved in order to achieve development. There are more than two million people working in the construction industry, producing development, and planners are but one group among many. Readers may be able to locate some of the aspects of the implementation process within the map, as described in the case studies of this book. Appendix 2 contains the list of functional elements relevant to town planning.

Functions

Figure 2.3 is a simplified version of the *Functional Map* which summarises diagrammatically the main areas of construction activity. Area A is the area concerned with planning, and it is put first because it includes all the strategic decision making and policy making activities which decide that development should take place in the first place. The main CISC diagram and its explanatory pages (located in Appendix 2) break down the functions into more detailed statements. In summary A = planning: B = design; C = construction; D = costing and control; E = financing; and F = management. Readers are advised to consult the original document to appreciate the full breadth and scope of the exercise (CISC 1993 and revised CISC 1994). In fact the report consists of several hundred pages. The map is organised diagrammatically like a matrix. Each element within each function is further disaggregated into detailed activities, and the report outlines the range indicators for each activity. Further material has subsequently been produced which specifies process and product evidence required to show the satisfactory undertaking of each specified activity within the map. Those readers interested in this field should check with their college or with CISC as to the most recent documents available.

The editor has been a long-standing member of the working group developing the map in respect of function A, planning. The full description of function A is 'Formulate strategies and policies for the development, improvement, and use of the environment.' However, functions A and B of the map include town planning components, being broadly parallel to the development plan (policy and strategy) and the local plan (design and lay-out) respectively. The diagram and the following pages of further detail at the end of this chapter are from a penultimate draft of the CISC document and are produced with kind permission of Richard Larcombe, the development director of CISC, who welcomes their inclusion to present the map to a wider readership, including future members of the professions currently studying on built environment courses.[1]

Implications

Undoubtedly there are problems with the nature of the CISC/NVQ exercise and these are discussed more fully in Appendix 2 in a polemical critique intended to give the reader a sense of current debates over the scope and nature of the functions and the ethos of the built environment professions. Some of these issues will no doubt be resolved by the time this chapter is published. Although there are criticisms, the project must be praised greatly for attempting to map the unmappable and to provide an up-to-date picture of the scope and structure of the British construction industry. CISC has tried, for the first time in Britain, to provide some sort of structured mapping of a very complex set of professional groupings and activities, which grew up in a somewhat ad hoc organic manner without any centralised state planning or centralised regulation, as in the case in some other advanced Western countries. Readers might find it worthwhile to try to produce their own map to see the processes, products and professionals involved. The aim behind CISC, and the wider NVQ exercise, is apparently to increase productivity and efficiency and to enable the subsequent harmonisation with other professional bodies within the European Union. Already some engineers have the designation EurIng (European engineer/ingénieur) and surveyors EurGeo (European surveyor/géomètre).

The CISC/NVQ approach might be used to make the implementation process more efficient or successful, a theme which will be returned to in the final chapters after readers have seen from the case studies how many variables are involved in achieving implementation. But do town planners want to subscribe to this NVQ concept of efficiency and competence? Will such standards lead to faster and cheaper implementation, and a speeding up of the whole development process? Can one speed up and make more cost-effective something so complex? Will this lead to the leaving out of the social

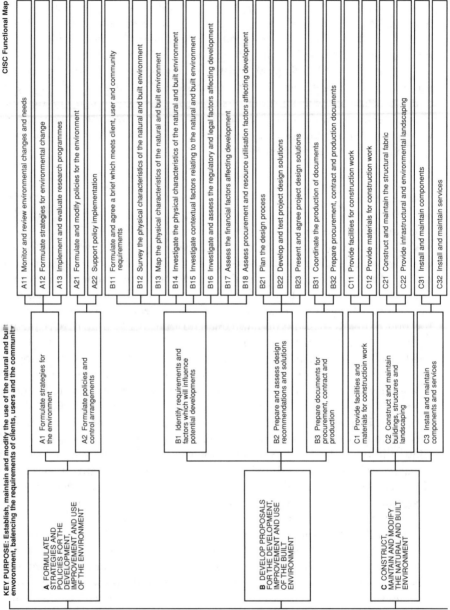

CISC Functional Map

KEY PURPOSE: Establish, maintain and modify the use of the natural and built environment, balancing the requirements of clients, users and the community

A FORMULATE STRATEGIES AND POLICIES FOR THE DEVELOPMENT, IMPROVEMENT AND USE OF THE ENVIRONMENT

A1 Formulate strategies for the environment
- A11 Monitor and review environmental changes and needs
- A12 Formulate strategies for environmental change
- A13 Implement and evaluate research programmes

A2 Formulate policies and control arrangements
- A21 Formulate and modify policies for the environment
- A22 Support policy implementation

B1 Identify requirements and factors which will influence potential developments
- B11 Formulate and agree a brief which meets client, user and community requirements
- B12 Survey the physical characteristics of the natural and built environment
- B13 Map the physical characteristics of the natural and built environment
- B14 Investigate the physical characteristics of the natural and built environment
- B15 Investigate contextual factors relating to the natural and built environment
- B16 Investigate and assess the regulatory and legal factors affecting development
- B17 Assess the financial factors affecting development
- B18 Assess procurement and resource utilisation factors affecting development

B DEVELOP PROPOSALS FOR THE DEVELOPMENT, IMPROVEMENT AND USE OF THE BUILT ENVIRONMENT

B2 Prepare and assess design recommendations and solutions
- B21 Plan the design process
- B22 Develop and test project design solutions
- B23 Present and agree project design solutions

B3 Prepare documents for procurement, contract and production
- B31 Coordinate the production of documents
- B32 Prepare procurement, contract and production documents

C CONSTRUCT, MAINTAIN AND MODIFY THE NATURAL AND BUILT ENVIRONMENT

C1 Provide facilities and materials for construction work
- C11 Provide facilities for construction work
- C12 Provide materials for construction work

C2 Construct and maintain buildings, structures and landscaping
- C21 Construct and maintain the structural fabric
- C22 Provide infrastructural and environmental landscaping

C3 Install and maintain components and services
- C31 Install and maintain components
- C32 Install and maintain services

D INITIATE, RESOURCE AND CONTROL THE DEVELOPMENT, IMPROVEMENT AND USE OF THE BUILT ENVIRONMENT
D1 Initiate projects for the development, improvement and use of the built environment
D11 Secure contracts for supply of professional services, works, goods and materials
D12 Implement and coordinate construction projects
D2 Procure, deploy and control resources for projects
D21 Procure, deploy and control material resources
D22 Procure, deploy and control plant and equipment
D3 Control projects for the development, improvement and use of the built environment
D31 Control project costs, quality and progress
D32 Coordinate and control individual, community and environmental safety
D33 Implement policy and statutory control arrangements
D34 Determine the resolution of disputes
E FACILITATE THE USE OF PROPERTY, SYSTEMS AND SERVICES
E1 Facilitate investment, appraisal, agreements and use management relating to property
E11 Facilitate investment in property
E12 Appraise and value property
E13 Progress and determine property transactions and agreements
E14 Manage the use of property
E2 Operate and maintain systems and services
E21 Operate systems and services to meet operational requirements
E22 Assess the performance of systems and services
E23 Maintain required levels of availability and reliability in systems and services
F CONTRIBUTE TO THE COMPETITIVENESS AND OPERATIONAL EFFECTIVENESS OF ORGANISATIONS OPERATING WITHIN THE BUILT ENVIRONMENT
F1 Procure, deploy and control resources within the organisation
F11 Develop, monitor, control and improve strategies for the procurement and deployment of organisational resources
F12 Procure, deploy and control financial resources for projects
F2 Develop and implement strategies for recruiting, developing and enhancing the performance of human resources
F21 Develop and implement strategies for the development of human resources
F22 Develop and implement strategies for recruiting and enhancing the performance of human resources
F3 Develop, monitor and improve organisational products, services and systems
F31 Develop, monitor, control and improve strategies for enhancing the quality of products or services available from an organisation
F32 Develop, monitor, control and improve information systems

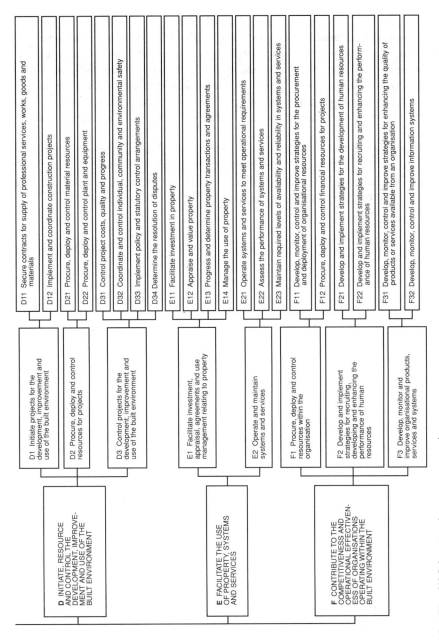

Fig. 2.3 The CISC functional map summary diagram

and other less quantifiable objectives which planners seek to achieve in the course of the implementation process? Recall from Chapter 1 how, paradoxically perhaps, some of the greatest achievements of town planners have been in what has not been built, or in successfully doing nothing, waiting and waiting, riding out the storm over a particular site; hardly an image of professional competence within the CISC world-view. Whether planners want to or not, it is rumoured that in the long term, particularly in view of CCT privatisation of some of the functions of planning (over 50% in some offices), that evidence of competence at the appropriate level might be required for professional indemnity insurance (PII) or for some new European test of professional competence. This trend ties in with the move towards regulation of professional practices, such as through BS 5750 *Practice Management Standards* (as well as the European standard on management performance EN 29001 and International Standard 150 9001). Further discussion of CISC *vis-à-vis* town planning within the context of the powerful construction industry is given in Appendix 2.

[1] Acknowledgment and thanks go to Richard Larcombe, development director of CISC, for permission to use extracts from this document and to reproduce Figure 2.3.

PART II

THE LEGISLATIVE AND PROCEDURAL FRAMEWORK

INTRODUCTION

The purpose of town and country planning is to intervene in the processes of land and property development in order to achieve an outcome which is socially, or environmentally, preferable to the results which the unfettered processes of the private market would produce. Part II explores the procedural and legislative context that provides the framework within which the implementation process operates. This chapter sets out to describe the process in which planners intervene, the mechanisms they use and the consequences of their actions. The first section of the chapter describes the nature of the development process. This is because the authors believe it is crucial for planners to develop a better understanding of the means by which property is produced. The second section is concerned with the role of the planners in the process, and it also explains their tools. Although these tools include legislation, they also comprise planning skills, experience and training as practitioners. The legislation and statutory instruments themselves are described, including their application to some special cases such as listed buildings and conservation areas. In Chapter 4 other controls on the development process are considered, such as the statutory requirements to conform to building, fire, health, safety and wider legal constraints. In each chapter, attention is drawn to the financial aspects of regulation compliance. As will be explained, such regulations can help or hinder the effective planning and regulation of the built environment, and can hamper the implementation process from the planners' viewpoint. Towards the end of the book, this theme will be taken further, in a discussion of the limitations on the powers of planners to implement principles of good planning.

Chapters 5 and 6 discuss the role of the planners in shaping the development process beyond just giving planning permission. Particular attention is given to the means of implementing socially and environmentally beneficial planning policies. These include planning agreements, that is, the extraction of planning gain from developers; the production of development briefs; and participation by the planners in full-scale development partnerships. To give some historical perspective to the whole question of such state intervention by the planners within the free market development process, the final chapter concludes with a broader reflection upon the compensation and betterment question, which runs right through postwar planning; the debate about planning gain is its modern manifestation. Land that is given planning permission for a certain type of development acquires a value in line with this permitted use, which may be much more than the value for its current use. This increase in value, or betterment, has resulted through no direct efforts of its owner. Governments, having accepted the need for planning, have subsequently wrestled with the apparent injustices, the gains and losses to different individuals, which have resulted. Discussion of these issues, especially the betterment debate, and its current manifestation in the question of planning gain, runs throughout the chapters as an important theme, variously illustrated by the case studies. Planning is for people, as the adage goes, and therefore, planners seek to use their control powers over physical land use and developments in such a way as to obtain wider social and economic implementary spin-offs.

The processes outlined are not as straightforward as they might appear, and indeed the time-scale may be protracted when major differences of opinion occur over the nature of site development. Also, the process is not necessarily fair or neutral in that certain groups of players have more power, or at least more knowledge, than others. In particular, residents and community groups may feel that the whole process occurs over their heads and in spite of them. A related ongoing concern is the limited rights and representation of so-called third party interests in the process. This group includes the ordinary people, shoppers and commuters who may use the area and make their home in it. Neither landowners of the site in question, nor members of the local government hierarchy, third party interests may have little voice, although in theory at least the development in question may be marketed as being for their benefit. Clearly there are both losers and gainers.

Chapter 3

THE PROCEDURAL CONTEXT

John Allinson and Jim Claydon

The development process

Definitions

There are as many views of development as there are actors in the process. These include, among others, landowners, occupiers, bankers, builders, architects, planners, surveyors, estate agents, local government officers and engineers, not to mention property developers, whose views on what should be achieved are likely to be highly diverse. However, if each individual is to be effective in participating in the process, they need to have a clear idea of its stages and who is likely to be involved. In order to understand the sequence it is useful to define the development process as follows:

> The means by which land and property is transformed into a more profitable or socially beneficial purpose.

It is clear from this statement that this particular section is not concerned with describing unintended changes or the deterioration of land or property, although sometimes this does result. But most authors would agree that the process of transforming land and buildings follows a predictable pattern. However, it is rare, for example, that building of two identical houses actually follows exactly the same process. With complex office development, retail uses and redevelopment, the peculiarities of the product render each development unique.

The simplest descriptive models of the development process describe a sequence of events which starts with the identification of a site and finishes with the use of the completed building. Such a sequence is described in Cadman and Austin-Crowe (1991) and involves key stages of site acquisition, design and costing, certification (including planning permission), evaluation and implementation. A more sophisticated model was produced by Barrett, Stewart and Underwood (1979) and is represented in a pipeline diagram (Fig. 3.1). It is useful to study this in some detail as it gives an indication of the complexity of the process as well as a feel for its dynamic nature.

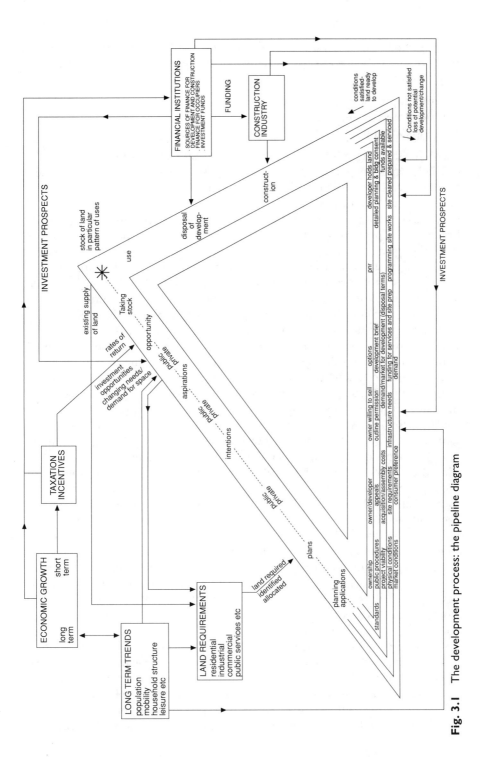

Fig. 3.1 The development process: the pipeline diagram

The pipeline diagram

The pipeline diagram consists of two main elements. Firstly, the process itself is represented by means of a triangular pipeline shown passing through three critical stages:

(1) Development pressures and prospects
(2) Development feasibility
(3) Implementation.

Secondly, the diagram shows a series of external factors which influence the efficiency and capacity of the pipeline. These include economic and social trends, government fiscal policy and the health of the construction industry and financial institutions. Each of these external factors has the effect of either accelerating the demand to produce property, or putting a significant brake on the process by acting as a disincentive to developers. The pipeline itself represents a more detailed description of the property development process, and starts with an individual public or private sector organisation taking stock of its property needs and opportunities. This is translated into an aspiration to develop which is then crystallised into an intention through a plan of campaign. In other words, property development is subject to the same process of decision making as most other policy areas. However, with property, the expression of that decision eventually emerges as a planning application. To the developer this is the beginning of one of many concurrent tests of the feasibility of his/her aspirations. These tests are indicated in the diagram by a series of parallel (roughly concurrent) procedures which will inform the developer of the likely success of their proposition.

Of course, to develop land one needs an interest in that land. (In the distant past, this was not always so. Unscrupulous developers could get planning permission on other people's land without telling them. Tales abound of wicked developers buying land from innocent widows for a song then making millions.) For clarification, having an interest means that one must either own the land or have some other legal right to its development. In real property and planning law, land includes the site and anything which is built upon it (e.g. as used in the title of Circular 13/87 *Changes in the Use of Buildings and Other Land*). Developers will set out either to own or to take an option on land which they have identified as having development potential.

Planning permission is one of a number of hurdles to certification which the developer will need to surmount; that is, the developer will need formal approval from a range of other statutory bodies. For example, the developer will need to conform to the requirements of the building regulations; to conform to any restrictive covenants over the way in which the land can be used or developed; and to receive fire, health and safety certificates. These factors are considered more fully later in Part II, and are illustrated in the case studies, for example, in Robin Tetlow's account of the development of a difficult site in Bristol.

The developer will also wish to test the proposal's viability, and here a particular use of the word is intended. It may be feasible to build a property on a piece of land from the point of view of ownership, certification, physical conditions and such like, but only if the proposed scheme passes the test of economic viability, will the developer be prompted to go ahead with the project. Hence the developer (or the valuer advising the developer) will assess the costs of building and borrowing, against the likely return on that building when it is completed. Developers will only be convinced that the project is viable if the return on their outlay will be greater than on some other investment and will compensate them for the enormous risks involved in property development. (Editor's comment: This aspect cannot be over-stressed, as the profit motive, or the obtainment of a reasonable return from the site, is what powers the whole property development process, not whether a development is good, needed or useful.) Part of that assessment involves market research on the feasibility of the development in question, in that particular location, at a predicted, specific date in the future when the building would be envisaged to be completed. This is a highly speculative assessment. Finally, as part of the feasibility, the developer must be assured that it is physically possible to build on that particular site and provide the building with the necessary services.

Should all the above tests prove successful, the developer may decide to move on to the implementation stage by contracting a builder or construction company to construct the building. This requires considerable supervision of both the contract and the plans until finally the property is complete. However, this is not the end of the process. It is only when the developer sells, or lets the building to a user/occupier, that the process is complete; this is the point at which the developer obtains a return on the investment. Even this sophisticated pipeline model hides the enormous complexity in the details of the process, in particular, the specialised nature of this assembly process in the property industry. Unlike other manufactured products, buildings take a long time to put together, involving many individuals and skills, and require very substantial financing. Each product (each building) is unique, at least in its location, if not in many other respects too. These characteristics of the development process are specific to buildings and they pose tremendous risks to developers who need to be skilled in their judgement of opportunities and risk as well as skilful managers of people and organisations.

Other models of the development process

In recent years a number of researchers have sought to investigate and describe the forms that the development process might take, producing a variety of alternatives to the above account.

For example, Gore and Nicholson (1991) identify four different categories of model:

(1) *Sequential description models* describe the development process in terms of its constituent events and show the inputs required at each stage. The pipeline diagram is a sequential description.

(2) *Behavioural models* focus on the actors in the development process, their relationships, their aims and their responsibilities.

(3) *Models of production based analyses* present the economic signals indicating effective demand for, and supply of, built floor space as reflected and expressed in market prices, yields and rents.

(4) *Structures of provision models* are rooted in urban political economic theory. This type of model focuses on an analysis of the processes of production of the built environment through consideration of power relations between the representatives of capital, labour and owners of land. Indeed, in most models describing the development process, such economic and market factors are central considerations.

The authors conclude that there is no such thing as a universally applicable model but that different types of model offer different levels of understanding. In general, they advocate the development of structures of provision, that is, models which emphasise the social and economic processes as well as the physical processes involved. In a similar vein, Healey (1991) also identifies four groups of model, and in a subsequent paper (Healey 1992) proposes a new institutional model, embracing four different levels of analysis, in an attempt to incorporate the benefits of the perspectives of the four different types of model identified above. The function of this chapter is not to develop these ideas further but to alert the reader to the potential complexity of understanding the forces which drive and shape the development process. However, through the processes of plan making and planning control (development control), town planning forms one of the most crucial and complex components, and is therefore considered in greater detail. Having looked conceptually at the development process, the next section will provide essential background material on the legislative framework of systems for plan making and development control.

Plan making

The Town and Country Planning Act of 1947, and all subsequent town and country planning acts – the most recent main planning act is the Planning and Compensation Act of 1991 – charged local authorities with the function of producing plans for their areas (also see Fig. 2.1). The current distribution of responsibilities is as follows:[1]

(1) *Structure plans*: broad statements of policy and intent at a strategic level, produced by county councils in England and Wales, and regional councils in Scotland.

(2) *Local plans*: specific policies and proposals for local areas, showing proposed land uses in considerable detail, normally produced by district councils.

[1] Items 1 and 2 comprise the two-tier planning system, whereas item 3 represents the newer unitary (one-tier) system.

(3) *Unitary development plans*: essentially a combination of structure and local plans, comprising Part I (the strategic level, similar to a structure plan) and Part II (the specific level, similar to a local plan). These are produced by the unitary planning authorities, that is by the London boroughs following the abolition of the Greater London Council and the metropolitan districts, the six metropolitan counties being abolished along with the GLC in 1986.

So that plans may be produced, planners need to assess what is needed in the plan area in order to develop appropriate policies. This book aims to deal more directly with implementation rather than the policy making process *per se*. But planners' actions in the implementation process are inevitably informed by perceptions of what they want to achieve – policies. Also many of the more social and environmental dimensions of planning gain conditions undoubtedly relate back to planning policies, as will be illustrated in the case studies. Later chapters return to the question of policy, that is, what planning objectives, be they latent or obvert, are informing planners' implementary activities, although the policy issue does crop up before then.

The plan making process may be encapsulated in the old recipe: survey, analysis, plan. In fact, these three little words cover vast worlds of theory, methodology and differing opinion on how plans are actually made. In general, plans are produced after surveys of the areas to which they apply have been undertaken. These surveys highlight the main planning issues in those areas (for example, concerning derelict land, green belt, conservation). Topics which should be investigated were originally specified in the *Development Plan Manual* (Department of the Environment l972b) and, more recently and flexibly, in *Development Plans: Good Practice Guide Note* (Department of the Environment 1992a). The surveys are published by some local authorities in separate documents, which can prove extremely useful and are usually held in good planning library collections. There are also likely to be a series of reports and policy papers devoted to specific policy areas.

These, and the subsequent draft plan, will form the basis for extensive public consultation throughout the stages of production of a plan. All affected and interested parties will have the opportunity to make comments, objections or representations. These inputs from the public will undoubtedly influence the final plan because a planning authority is obliged to take into account the representations received in drawing up the plan. Anyone can make representations about development plans; they do not have to have a valid legal interest in the land in question, as is the case in many planning appeal situations concerning planning decisions over a particular development on a certain piece of land. Section 33 of the 1990 Town and Country Planning Act sets out requirements for public participation for structure plan production, s.39 for local plans, and s.12 for unitary development plans (participation is discussed in more detail in Chapter 18 in the context of people and planning).

Having produced the first draft of a plan, the local authority places it on deposit; it makes it available for inspection at certain locations in the area. Further representations may be made during the on deposit period. These are considered at a public local inquiry (for a local plan) or, selectively, at an examination in public (for a structure plan). Representations are aired by interested parties, and the ensuing examination, argument and debate will inform the local authority's amendments and modifications to the plan before it is finally adopted and becomes law. After adoption, plans are kept under review. As statements of development intent for their areas, plans form the frameworks for development control therein by the local planning authority. The intentions expressed in the plans will guide local authorities in their decisions on planning applications, and will advise private property developers on what sorts of development will be allowed and where.

The 1991 Planning and Compensation Act made a number of important changes to plan-making procedures. The first and probably the most important change, which affects the status and consideration of the development plan in the context of the implementation process, is that local planning authorities are now obliged to 'have regard to the provisions of the development plan' first and foremost in deciding planning applications. Before this act was passed, the development plan was to be only one of the material considerations that may inform local planning authorities' decisions. Thus the 1991 act affirmed the primacy of development plans in importance in development control. The second change brought about by the 1991 act is the requirement of all district councils to produce 'district wide' development plans; that is, plans covering their entire areas. The intention is for the whole of the country to be covered by an up-to-date 'planning background' – that is with a set of adopted plans – and thus with a reliable and definite statutory development climate.

Readers may have noticed that no mention of approval by the Department of the Environment was made in describing the stages of plan preparation. This is because the third change was the removal of the requirement for structure plans to be approved by the secretary of state for the environment before adoption by the county council, as was the case for the last twenty years under the 1971 Town and Country Planning Act. Following an examination in public, a county council can now proceed to full adoption; this is a step which grants a degree of local autonomy and removes a major source of delay. Notwithstanding, structure plans are still required by law to conform with national policy and regional guidance as expressed by central government in planning policy guidance notes (PPGs); and the Department of the Environment must be consulted on the plans through the normal mechanisms. A complete list of all PPGs and other statutory directives mentioned in this volume are listed in the *Source Material* section at the end of the book. In conclusion, it is difficult to overemphasise the importance of the development plan as a framework for development decisions. Property developers are certainly well aware of its importance; many will seek to make representations on any plan before it is adopted, and make special efforts to be present at a public local inquiry or an examination in public.

Planning control

Development

This section explains the development control function of local authorities more fully than the account in Volume I, in Chapter 2 and the development control Chapter 10. However a fuller account is given here which will be of value both to newcomers to the subject and those who have already read Volume I. All development requires planning permission. The Town and Country Planning Act of 1990 defines development as

> the carrying out of any building, engineering, mining or other operations in, on, over or under land, or the making of any material change in the use of any buildings or other land.

There are clearly two parts to this definition. The first part is the carrying out of operations, defined very broadly. However, there are certain exclusions. Maintenance and improvement works which affect only the interior of a building or do not materially affect the exterior of a building are expressly excluded. So is use of land for agricultural purposes.

The general development order

Even taking such exclusions into account, the operation of a system which sought to control *all* development would be a Herculean task. In particular, there are certain minor, but frequently occurring, types of development which make no significant impact on the environment and should not properly fall under such a system of control. Thus, the Town and Country Planning Act of 1990 also allows the secretary of state for the environment to make a general development order (GDO) specifying classes of permitted development, that is, development for which planning permission is deemed to have been granted. The General Development Order was revised in 1988, and there have been procedural, and other, amendments in 1995; and loss of exemption of permitted development rights in some instances owing to the effects of EU environmental impact assessment regulations. Changes are detailed in the Town and Country Planning (General Development Procedure) Order 1995 and the Town and Country (General Permitted Development) Order 1995. (See list 1, Part VIII Government Publications at end of book). It is important for the reader to check the most recent changes as planning law is constantly being modified, and as stated in Volume I, the most reliable source of information is to consult the *Encyclopaedia of Planning Law* (Grant 1995) a loose-leaf publication which is frequently updated. The classes of permitted development include such items as development within the curtilage

Table 3.1   The use classes order

Class	Description
A1	most uses as a shop;
A2	use for the provision of financial or professional services;
A3	use for the sale of food or drink for consumption on the premises, or hot food for sale off the premises;
B1	the "business use" class: use for an office other than those in A2; for research and development; for any industrial process that does not cause detrimental noise, vibration, smell, fumes, etc.;
B2	general industrial use;
B3–B7	use for various special industrial purposes;
B8	use for a storage or distribution centre;
C1	use as a hotel or hostel where no significant element of care is provided;
C2	use as one of various kinds of residential institutions;
C3	use as a single dwelling-house, for habitation by a family or not more than six residents living together as a household;
D1	use as one of various kinds of non-residential use, such as the provision of medical or health services, education, art galleries, museums, etc.;
D2	use for assembly and leisure, such as cinemas, swimming baths, concert halls and so on.

Source: DoE, 1987a

of a dwelling-house, within certain limits (Part 1); minor operations, including the erection of gates, walls, fences, subject to certain height restrictions (Part II); and works to provide access, drainage and other infrastructure (Parts IX–XVII). Chapter 10 of Volume I also provides a summary of the General Development Order and the use classes order (see below). These permitted development rights conferred by the GDO may be removed by the local planning authority through the mechanism of an Article 4 Direction. These are applied to certain sensitive areas and have the effect of requiring that planning permission be obtained for all development, including the above works.

The use classes order

The other statutory instrument facilitated by the 1990 Town and Country Planning Act, and which a potential developer needs to be aware of, is the use classes order (UCO). This document divides the uses of buildings into a number of classes. Change of use within these classes is a permitted development (that is, it does not require planning permission). Change of use between these classes does require planning permission. In this way, the planning system exerts control over the way in which the built environment is used. This is important because some changes of use can be seen to have an enormous environmental impact, for example, change of use from a dwelling-house to a hot food shop. The classes are given in Table 3.1.

Some land uses are not included in any use classes (such as theatres or funfairs): these are regarded as *sui generis*, that is, in a class of their own. Thus, change of use, *from* or *to* such a use would always receive planning permission. In many cases, this is a matter for professional judgement as to where they fall. The designation of such a use will obviously determine whether planning permission is required for any change in use. Without this element of discretionary judgement, the planning control process would prove purely mechanical, and there would be little room in the process for the utilisation of the professional expertise and judgement of the professional planner. Between certain classes, it can be seen that changes of use would have little or no environmental impact, and these are expressly permitted by Part III of the GDO; for example, from A3 to Al or A2, from B2 or B8 to B1, from B2 to B8. The UCO was last revised in 1987, and, again, the reader is advised to check whether there have been any further updates.

Applying for planning permission

Anyone intending development as so defined must apply to the local planning authority (most usually the district council) on the requisite forms, giving details of the proposed development (normally illustrated on maps and plans) and including the necessary fee. Outline approval or detailed approval may be sought. An application for outline approval will give broad, general details of the proposed development and will seek approval in principle. It should be followed up within three years by an application for detailed approval, giving full details of floor space, building materials, scale and configuration of buildings, access, servicing and so on. Detailed approval may be sought without first applying for outline approval; in this case, it is usually termed an application for full planning permission. The local planning authority will then consider the application, having regard to the development plan in force for the area of the development; to the outcomes of consultations with other interested parties, including the highway authority where applicable; and to other material considerations. It will then recommend one of three courses of action:

- Approval
- Refusal (there is a right of appeal against this to the secretary of state)
- Approval with conditions (again, there is a right of appeal)

The final decision normally rests with the elected members of the planning committee, although minor applications are in some authorities decided by the officers on the basis of delegated powers.

A developer needs to be aware of matters likely to influence a local planning authority's decision; they include:

(1) The statutory planning background for the area, as enshrined in the adopted local plan and structure plan.
(2) Any informal planning guidance that may have been issued for the area, such as development briefs, guidelines or policy documents.
(3) Whether the site is in a conservation area or includes any listed buildings (see below).

(4) Planning history of the site and area as expressed through earlier development control and appeal decisions.

The local authority's decision must be made within eight weeks of having received the planning application; there is a right of appeal against non-determination within this period (Town and Country Planning Act of 1990). Full planning permission lapses after a period of five years if no development has begun within this time.

Listed buildings

Special planning regimes apply to environmentally sensitive buildings or areas, for the purposes of controlling development rather more strictly. Some buildings are regarded as of special historical or architectural interest and these may be listed by the secretary of state under the Planning (Listed Buildings and Conservation Areas) Act of 1980. Procedure here is governed by the Town and Country Planning (Listed Buildings and Buildings in Conservation Areas) Regulations of 1987. This is a protective measure, so the planning regime for such buildings is more restrictive than for non-listed buildings. Listed buildings are either Grade I (exceptional interest), Grade II* (of more than special interest; also known as Grade II starred), or Grade II (of special interest). Lists are compiled by the secretary of state and records may be inspected at the offices of the local authority.

The planning regime differs with grade of listing. Grade I listed buildings comprise 1% of the total and are regarded as of exceptional value, possessing both interior and exterior features worthy of retention. Grade II listed buildings will usually possess only external features worthy of retention. It is an offence to demolish or alter any listed building without first obtaining listed building consent (in addition to any planning permission that may be required). Alteration may be defined more rigidly here than by the GDO; for example, the painting of the exterior of a listed building may be taken to constitute an alteration. Protection also extends to work to the interior of the building, if it affects its special character, and to structures within the curtilage of the building, for example, walls, railings, outbuildings and paving. The local planning authority also has a duty to protect the setting of listed buildings; that is, the surrounding environment. Thus it may be found that the planning regime is more strict in such areas.

The procedures for obtaining listed building consent are similar to those for obtaining planning permission; application is made to the local authority on the requisite form. The applicant is required to advertise the application, including posting a notice on the land in question. English Heritage, a government body, must also be informed where the building is a Grade I or Grade II* listed building. In making its decision, the local authority will take into account the views of national and local conservation groups; its overriding concern will be the maintenance of the special architectural or historical character of the building. The local planning authority must inform the secretary of state if they are minded to give consent to the listed building works; he or she may then call the application in for decision. The demolition or alteration of a listed building without consent, or in breach of conditions imposed in a consent, is an offence punishable by fine and/or imprisonment. A defence of this action may be possible where it can be proved that the works were urgently necessary in the interests of health and safety or for the preservation of the building, that they were the bare minimum needed and that the local planning authority was informed in detail of the justification of the works as soon as was reasonably practicable. In addition, the local authority may issue a listed building enforcement notice, specifying the restoration of the building to its former state or the execution of other works.

Conservation areas

Whole areas of the built environment may be of special architectural or historical interest and thus may be worthy of extra control. The local planning authority may designate these as conservation areas under the Planning (Listed Buildings and Conservation Areas) Act of 1980. The planning regime is more strict in these areas, with procedures being governed by the Town and Country Planning (Listed Buildings and Buildings in Conservation Areas) Regulations of 1987. Local planning authorities must also produce special plans for such areas. These will include policies and proposals aimed at preserving and enhancing the character and appearance of the areas. The local planning authority is required to advertise any application that affects the character or appearance of the conservation area. With certain exceptions, demolition of any building or part of a building within such an area requires special conservation area consent; a condition may be applied here, preventing demolition until the contract for redevelopment is placed. Planning control in conservation areas also extends to trees and advertisements. Since it is sometimes difficult to draw a definite boundary to such areas, sites just outside conservation areas may also be affected by a stricter planning regime.

Conclusion

In this chapter the reader has been given a basic background on the nature of the planning framework, in terms of plan making and development control, from a local authority planner's perspective. Although Volume I has already dealt with some of these issues, the emphasis was much more upon the individual applying for permission for small-scale development, perhaps a kitchen extension, and it was pitched towards the beginner. In contrast, the authors have attempted in this chapter to set the discussion within the context of the world of property development, and to relate the processes to large-scale development, in order to provide background to the case studies.

Chapter 4

OTHER STATUTORY CONTROLS

John Allinson

Non-planning controls

In this chapter the objective is to outline the range of other controls which affect the development process and the likelihood of successful implementation of planning policy. These controls derive both from public sector governmental law and private sector real property law (concerned with land and rights over land). As stated in Chapter 2, these controls are not only hurdles to be overcome in the planning process, but as will be explained in later chapters, they can act as helps or hindrances to the implementation of wider planning policy, particularly if the planners have little control or influence over the jurisdiction of other statutory authorities' policies which affect the design of the built environment, such as in matters relating to the internal layout and design of buildings. In this chapter (and in the book as a whole) the emphasis is upon the place of planning within the property development process and broader construction context. The specific role of central and local government in implementing current planning policies, and details on alternative methods of implementation by means of specific financial and spatial programmes, for example, by the use of Enterprise Zones, City Challenge, single regeneration budget, and EU incentives and controls, will be explored in depth in the next volume of this series. This exploration will be within the context of investigating the different types of planning (social, economic, physical and environmental) and the means of imposing planning policy in Britain. This chapter does not focus on the wider economic planning context, the financial costs of regulation compliance for the developer in relation to the hurdles which must be overcome.

Building control

A major legislative hurdle that has to be cleared by the prospective developer is the Building Regulations. No one may carry out any building operations (including the installation of works and fittings), make structural alterations (internal or external) or make any material change in the use of buildings without complying with the Building Regulations. As will be seen in later chapters these hurdles cannot always be cleared, as they may act as inhibitors or limitors of good design and implementation of intelligent planning policy. In Britain, responsibility for the control of the built environment is shared by a confusing array of municipal and central government departments, whose functions have grown up somewhat haphazardly over the years. There are actually conflicts between fulfilling both planning and building regulation controls, particularly in respect of conservation areas. Likewise, it can prove remarkably difficult to implement the smallest change in the built environment, be it a dropped curb for the disabled or better lighting for security purposes, if the function in question falls outside the jurisdiction of the local planning authority and instead rests with the highways or city engineers department.

Purpose

The overall intention of the Building Regulations is to ensure quality and safety in the built environment. The power to make regulations governing building operations is vested in the secretary of state for the environment by Section 1 of the Building Act of 1984. They may be made for the following purposes:

(1) Securing the health, safety, welfare and convenience of people in or about buildings and of others who may be affected by buildings or matters connected with buildings.
(2) Furthering the conservation of fuel and power, a key issue in view of the current emphasis upon sustainability and green issues in planning.
(3) Preventing waste, undue consumption, misuse or contamination of water. Quality, as far as the Building Regulations are concerned, is judged in terms of the creation of a safe, healthy and convenient built environment which promotes conservation and prevents waste.

The Building Regulations were last revised wholesale in 1985, although they are selectively updated every year. Also some might say they are selectively applied nowadays in view of various moves to privatise their administration on a contract basis, and the general growth of Compulsory Competitive Tendering (CCT) of local authority functions. In these times of streamlining and cost-cutting of public services, the importance of the Building Regulations must be stressed. The price paid for this may be calculated in terms of training and employment costs (of building inspectors and support staff), and in terms of the extra costs imposed upon the construction industry in complying with regulations. But many would argue that it is money well spent and its worth cannot be calculated merely in financial terms.

Scope

The Building Regulations apply to a wider area of building activities than the Planning Regulations, although their scope appears to be similar:

- The design and construction of buildings
- The material alteration of a building
- The provision of services, fittings and equipment in or in connection with buildings
- The making of any material change of use in the building

An extension to an existing building is regarded as a new building, and is covered by the regulations as such. A material alteration is defined as an alteration that would adversely affect an existing building with regard to structure, means of escape from fire or internal fire spread. The removal of a supporting wall would be a clear case of this; and normally would not constitute an action governed by planning controls.

On the other hand, material change of use in the Building Regulations is interpreted rather more liberally than in the UCO. It is defined as

- Change of use to a dwelling
- Provision of a flat
- Change of use to a hotel or institution
- Change of use to a public building
- Change of use from an exempted to a non-exempted use (see below)

Certain classes of buildings, such as small porches, sheds and buildings used for mining operations, are exempt from the regulations. In certain other cases, such as small greenhouses, detached garages and carports, exemption may be claimed from most of the provisions of the regulations, although in these cases, particulars and plans must still be prepared and submitted, and local authority approval obtained before work is commenced.

Intention

The Building Regulations seek to ensure quality of buildings by specifying methods of construction and types of materials to be used. Flexibility is ensured by the use of 'deemed to satisfy' provisions. These operate by first specifying a standard of performance, and then specifying a mode of construction or type of material that meets that standard. If this mode or material is used, the standard shall be deemed to have been satisfied.

Content

The Building Regulations contain three comprehensive schedules, the most important of which is Schedule 1, giving technical requirements as follows:

A: Structure, covering:
    loading
    ground movement
    disproportionate collapse

B: Fire, covering:
    means of escape
    internal and external fire spread

C: Site preparation and resistance to moisture
    includes drainage

D: Toxic substances
    includes cavity insulation

E: Resistance to the passage of sound

F: Ventilation

G: Hygiene

H: Drainage and waste disposal

J: Heat-producing appliances

K: Stairways, ramps and guards

L: Conservation of fuel and power

M: Facilities for the disabled

(The Building Regulations, 1985, Department of the Environment)

The Building Regulations themselves contain no technical details: these appear in a set of thirteen 'Approved Documents' (A to M), which refer to British Standards and Codes of Practice. These are designed to give practical guidance on how the requirements in Schedule 1 may be implemented; for example, types of materials to be used, size of joists, depth of foundations and layout of drains. Use of certain materials or components is deemed unsuitable by the Building Regulations. It should be noted that Documents G and M will be returned to in Part VI because they particularly affect access to the built environment for minority groups.

Procedures

The regulations are enforceable by district councils, similarly to the planning controls, and require developers to apply for consent and deposit with the local authority particulars and plans giving details of all proposed work and/or changes of use. A fee is payable; this is assessed on the basis of the estimated value of the work. The local authority has a period of five weeks in which to approve or reject the application and plans. This may be extended to two months by written agreement. If the local authority does not decide the plans in this period, they are deemed to have been approved. If the developer commences building work without the necessary Building Regulations approval, he may be required by the local authority to alter the work to comply with the regulations at his own expense (Building Act 1984, s.36). The plans must be approved by the local authority it they are in accordance with the Building Regulations (and unlike with planning controls the local authority has no discretion here). If there is any contravention, however small, with either the Building Regulations or other controls in the Building Act of 1984, the local authority may

(1) Reject the plans (there is a right of appeal to the secretary of state against a rejection).
(2) Pass the plans subject to necessary modifications (if requested by the applicant).
(3) Dispense with or modify the regulations to ensure that the plans comply (there is a right of appeal to the secretary of state against a refusal of the authority to use these powers: s.8 and s.39. 1984 act).

Approval lapses if the development has not begun within three years. Approval may be given in stages; the local authority must then require further plans to be deposited prior to the commencement of new stages. Work may commence after the applicant has received approval, and given the local authority 48 hours notice of commencement. In order to facilitate the application of the Building Regulations, the developer must also give the following notices to the local authority:

• 24 hours notice of the covering up of any foundation, concrete, dampproof course or any other material laid over a site
• 24 hours notice of the covering up of any drain or private sewer subject to the regulations
• 7 days following the laying of any drain or private sewer
• 7 days following the erection of any building
• 7 days following the completion of any other work

The local authority building inspectors will visit the development at intervals during construction (governed by these notices) to ensure compliance, and will issue a Certificate of Final Completion when the development is completed.

Other controls

Other controls are vested in the local authority under the Building Act of 1984; these may be described as public health considerations. They are sometimes referred to as the linked powers, as they are related to, but not part of the Building Regulations. They are applied at the same time as the application of the Building Regulations and are as follows:

(1) No building may be constructed over a public sewer, except with the consent of the local authority in consultation with the water authority.

(2) Satisfactory provision must be made for drainage (including roof drainage).

(3) Sufficient and satisfactory provision must be made for closet accommodation.

(4) The local authority must be satisfied that any offensive material filling the site of a planned building has been removed or rendered harmless.

(5) Satisfactory means of storage of refuse and access to the building for its removal must be provided.

(6) Satisfactory exits and entrances must be provided for certain kinds of public buildings. This may involve consultation between the local authority and the fire authority. Special provisions apply to some buildings under the Factories Act of 1961 and the Offices, Shops and Railway Premises Act of 1963.

(7) A wholesome water supply must be provided for a house.

(8) The height of some chimneys may be controlled.

(9) In the case of a conversion of a building into one or many dwellings, the local authority is given discretionary powers to ensure that each separate dwelling is provided with sufficient food storage accommodation and a bathroom with a bath or shower and hot and cold running water.

Where these conditions are not fulfilled, the local authority may either reject the plans or dispense with the need to comply (at its discretion). There is a right of appeal against rejection to the local magistrates court.

Contravention

Contravention of the Building Regulations is a serious matter! It may be made with or without knowing. Contravention is likely to be discovered through regular inspection, and may be enforced by

(1) A notice, served by the local authority, requiring that the contravening work be altered in order to comply with the Regulations (1984 act, s.36).

(2) Criminal proceedings for a fine (Public Health Act of 1961, s.65).

Real property law controls

Restrictive covenants

Developers not only have to overcome the hurdles of public sector legal regulations, such as planning and building controls, they also need to take into account private land law, that is, the effects of real property law. Therefore, a self-respecting developer will be aware of the necessity to check on the existence of any restrictive covenants on land or property that is earmarked for acquisition and development (Riddall 1993), and the consequences and financial implications of this for the proposed development; or alternatively the costs involved in modifying or discharging any covenants.

Restrictive covenants are any legal devices that restrict the use of land or property. Positive covenants require the carrying out of certain works on land or property. Covenants are governed by general real property law, including the Law of Property Act of 1925, but are generally more difficult to enforce, unless backed up by other statutory controls. The development control system, through its use of planning conditions and planning agreements can impose both restrictive and positive covenants. In this chapter, restrictive covenants apply to terms in the freehold or leasehold tenure of a plot of land or a property that restrict the use of the land or property and/or the carrying out of certain works or activities on or in the land or property. Restrictive covenants generally run with the land; that is, they are enforceable against successive owners, and thus can be imposed on successive developments. This makes them a useful device for local authorities in restricting the use of land and buildings when they own the freehold. These restrictions may be more than could be achieved through planning law. Note that the 1991 Planning and Compensation Act strengthen the powers to impose positive covenants within the ambit of unilateral agreements to ensure performance (enforcement) of planning gain *inter alia* against successors. (Again note that the legal use of the word 'land' in this chapter, includes empty fields, and building sites, but also property, buildings and development.)

Scope

Restrictive covenants may prevent alterations to a property; they may require that a property remains in a certain use (e.g. as a single dwelling-house); they may prohibit certain uses of a property (e.g. for business use); they may prevent subletting or subdivision of properties. Some restrictive covenants date from Victorian and Edwardian times. They may be completely outmoded today, but they still exist and they are still enforceable unless specifically extinguished or modified. For example, estates composed of Victorian villas with large back gardens were often covered by a restrictive covenant which prevented their subdivision into smaller plots, to maintain the low density and thus the property values and tone of the area. Nowadays, although such areas might have gone down socially, such covenants might form a deterrent to developers seeking to undertake high density residential infill. However, it may be possible to extinguish the covenants, especially if no successors in title (owners and others with a legal interest in the land) seem particularly concerned about ensuring their enforcement.

Leases

Restrictive covenants embodied in leases are somewhat clearer than those embodied in freeholds. There is no doubt about their enforceability, nor usually about the reason for, or relevance of, their existence. The lease-holder will also normally be well aware of, and in agreement with, them when he takes on the tenure. These covenants may prevent certain works *per se*, or allow them only with the consent of the landlord. This consent may not be withheld unreasonably, nor charged for unless the works are structural, or involve the diminution of the premises, or involve the landlord in legal expenditure. These are implied terms of all leases.

Existence of covenants

How does a property owner know of the existence of a restrictive covenant? It will be contained in the deeds of the property, and should have been revealed on its purchase. Covenants created after 1925 are registrable land charges and will thus be contained in the Land Charges Register at Plymouth or (for registered land) at the Land Registry. They are revealed through the search procedure, at the Land Charges Register or the Land Registry as above. Covenants created before 1926 are not registered in this way, although on registered land they will usually be shown up on the register at the Land Registry, but must be notified to the purchaser. These are two separate registries, distinct from the Local Land Charges Register which gives information on other relevant matters, such as road widening that would affect a piece of land, as well as planning and real property law issues. For example, the Local Land Charges Register also contains details of conditional planning consents. Also the local planning authority is required to keep a register of planning applications (Section 69 of the 1990 Town and Country Planning Act), which is open to the public and may be consulted without charge. (See Volume I, p. 185 for more details relevant to individuals submitting applications.)

Enforcement

For a covenant to be enforceable, it must be

(1) Assigned to a defined plot of land.
(2) Entered into for the benefit of that land, and be capable of benefiting that land.
(3) Enforceable by some person, either the original owner of the land (and covenantee), or his/her successor.

If there is any doubt about these points, a prospective developer or purchaser may apply to the Chancery Division of the High Court for a declaration as to whether the covenant is enforceable, and if so, by whom (Law of Property Act of 1925, s.84, as amended by the Law of Property Act of 1969). Restrictive covenants on freeholds are enforced by means of injunctions preventing a landowner/developer from carrying out works that are restricted by the covenant. In some cases, it is possible to settle out of court, which would involve the owner/developer in paying a sum of money to the covenantee. Proceedings under the Chancery Division are civil proceedings, not criminal proceedings.

Restrictive covenants on leaseholds are enforceable by the landlord through the remedy of forfeiting the lease. Thus the first steps in deciding whether a restrictive covenant is truly restrictive upon a proposed development would probably be to determine if it is enforceable according to the above conditions. Another possible course of action may be to take out indemnity insurance against the possibility of a covenant being enforced. Finally, the owner/developer may seek to have the covenant modified or discharged. This is described below.

Modification and discharge

Restrictive covenants may be modified or discharged by the Lands Tribunal (Law of Property Act of 1925, s.84, as amended) on one or more of the following grounds:

(1) By reason of changes in the character of the property or the neighbourhood, or other material circumstances, the restriction is obsolete, or its continued observance would impede the reasonable use of the land without giving substantial benefits to anyone.
(2) All persons of full age and capacity entitled to the benefit of the restriction have agreed to the discharge or the modification requested.
(3) The discharge or modification would not injure any person entitled to the benefit of the restriction.
(4) The continued existence of the restriction would impede some reasonable user of the land, where the restriction does not secure any practical benefit or is contrary to the public interest, or (in either case) money would be an adequate compensation for any disadvantage. The Lands Tribunal is required here to take account of the development plan and local development control decisions.

An application for a covenant to be modified or discharged is a comparatively simple process if it is uncontested. The requisite form is filled in; a small fee is paid upon application and upon hearing, and the Lands Tribunal makes a decision; this may involve the payment of compensation by the developer to the covenantee. There is an alternative provision for application to the county court for the discharge or modification of covenants relating to the conversion or subdivision of houses. This is even cheaper and more straightforward and is covered under s.610 of the 1985 Housing Act (previously by s.165 of the 1957 Housing Act). The county court is also the forum for application of a developer for an order permitting certain works which may be prevented by a restrictive covenant but are nevertheless necessary to comply with other legislation.

Factories Act and Offices, Shops and Railway Premises Act

Finally, there is the substantial body of health and safety legislation for the developer to consider, all of which may have financial implications as to construction standards. The Factories Act of 1961 and the Offices, Shops and Railway Premises Act of 1963 lay down certain standards that must be complied with in all such buildings, whether converted or newly constructed. Some of the most important considerations are as follows:

(1) *Space standards*: minimum space standards are laid down to prevent overcrowding. In both cases, these amount to 400 cubic feet per person (unless the ceiling is lower than 10 feet in the case of offices, shops and railway premises; then a figure of 40 square feet of floor space is specified).
(2) *Temperature*: in rooms where work carried out does not involve severe physical effort, temperatures of 60 (or 60.8 for offices, shops and railway premises) degrees Fahrenheit must be maintained after the first hour. There is scope for relaxing this according to type of room or work carried out.
(3) *Ventilation*: effective and suitable provision must be made for the circulation of fresh or purified air. All fumes and dust must be rendered harmless.
(4) *Lighting*: sufficient and suitable lighting (either natural or artificial) must be provided where people are working or passing.
(5) *Sanitary conveniences*: sufficient and suitable private and segregated conveniences must be provided. They must be adequately lit and ventilated.
(6) *Washing facilities*: adequate and suitable facilities for washing must be provided, including hot and cold running water, soap and towels or other means of drying.

Fire precautions

Further safety regulations, those related to fire, are covered by the Fire Precautions Act of 1971, which requires that a fire certificate, issued by the fire authority, is required for all premises covered by the act. These are as follows:

• Hotels and boarding houses where sleeping accommodation is provided for more than 6 persons.

- Factories, offices, shops and railway premises in which more than twenty persons are employed at any one time or more than ten persons are employed other than on the ground floor.
- Buildings containing two or more such premises where the same characteristics are observed.
- Factories where explosives or highly flammable materials are stored.

The act requires that the premises should contain

- reasonable means of escape, capable of safe and effective use
- reasonable means of firefighting
- reasonable means of giving warning in case of fire

The extent of the fire precautions necessary is normally at the discretion of the fire officer. Since the precautions may have a major implication on the design of the building, the fire officer should be involved at an early stage in the design and construction process.

Other factors

Conflict or harmonisation

There are many other regulatory factors which affect the likelihood of successful implementation of planning policy. In addition to the actual regulations outlined above, a range of British Standards covers certain aspects of building design, types of materials and provision of public facilities, a topic which will be returned to in later chapters. Some such standards (and some of the regulations above) clash with principles of good urban design upheld by the planners. Indeed there is always likely to be an element of contradiction and confusion among the different fields of legislation and policy making, all of which have grown up at different times for different reasons under different bodies.

There is talk of some sort of harmonisation of all the various aspects of codification and regulation affecting the built environment. It is likely that even if this does not happen nationally, it will eventually happen within Europe, as part of the ongoing programme of European Union legislative harmonisation (within which there are at least nineteen different planning systems and as many different building regulation systems as there are federal and administrative divisions within the member states). Over and above all this, it should always be borne in mind that in respect of local government financial constraints, there are some quite strict regulations, limits and rate-capping rules hidden away in the various local government acts, which may mean that a particular local authority is not allowed to spend money on some public facility or some physical design element within the built environment, even if the local plan or urban design guide produced by the planners recommends that it does so. Likewise, even if some developer makes a generous planning gain offer, the local authority may not be able to accept it because of the rules of local government finance, as explained in Volume I, p. 238. Such agreements must be directly linked to the planning permission or they will fall foul of the Local Government and Housing Act of 1989, which requires 50% of capital receipts (such as inducements from developers not specifically related to the development site) to be set aside to repay current debts. Similar rules apply in respect of certain categories of monies, or offers of enhanced design standards, highways matters or better facilities, in respect of pedestrianisation schemes, landscaping and amenity provision. This is because of complex rate-capping regulations which can limit the provision of environmental amenities and social facilities and thus reduce the likelihood of effective implementation of wider planning objectives (Ainsbett 1990).

Social infrastructure

Town planners may specify in their structure, unitary and local plans, that in order to plan areas in a balanced manner, social facilities such as schools, health centres and sports facilities should be provided. But, these land uses do not come directly under the power of the planners. They are dependent upon the will of other public and private sector bodies for their provision. Before health, education and similar public bodies were privatised, it was arguably easier for each of them to liaise with the others, as they were all in a sense on the same side, part of the tool-kit of the Welfare State. In the past, local authorities often developed strategic management policies which were interdepartmental in concept. In order to plan for an area and to deal with its health, housing, education and social services, it was realised that coordinated policies were the most effective. Nowadays, the situation is more patchy and complex; Chapter 6 considers the National Health Service.

However, the situation never was ideal; back in the heyday of the new towns, during the 1960s, the planners had huge powers under the auspices of the New Towns Commission and the individual new town development corporations, but they still had little direct control over ensuring that a new town would be provided with adequate schools and health facilities. The problem seemed to be one of phasing, in that, for example, hospital building budgets and programmes operated by the then local health authorities, did not necessarily tie in with the influx of new town population, many of whom were young families with children. Nowadays, particularly in relation to inner city initiatives such as City Challenge, and the Action for Cities programme (under the 1986 Housing and Town Planning Act), there have been attempts in dealing with so-called problem areas to coordinate housing, planning and social policy to a degree where possible. As will be seen in Chapters 12 and 13, the planning consultant responsible for the development of an inner city development site sought to draw on inner city funding in order to implement aspects of the scheme. It would seem that housing legislation, especially legislation related to improvement grants, and inner city policies are a particular fruitful means of public funding in seeking to achieve implementation. But housing law brings hurdles of its own; consult the *Encyclopaedia of Housing Law* (published in a loose-leaf format similar to the *Encyclopaedia of Planning Law*) for the current situation, as housing is a rapidly changing field of legislation.

Physical infrastructure

In order to achieve development, the site in question must be provided with, and linked up to infrastructural services. In view of the current trend towards privatisation, a whole new ball game has emerged in respect of negotiations with erstwhile statutory providers of gas, water (sewerage and drainage) and electricity. But many of the statutory powers remain, albeit somewhat amended; powers which enable the funding, construction, laying and subsequent maintenance of the various pipes, conduits, sewers and drains along which such services flow. It is extremely expensive to provide such services and to provide roads to and within a site – a crucial factor in assessing site viability. It can no longer be assumed that the local authority, or some other statutory body will pay for all this (indeed it never was). It has been common practice for Section 39 of the Highways Act of 1980 to be applied, which enables a developer to undertake the construction of roads (or to fund their construction) in return for the local authority adopting and maintaining them as public rights of way. Alternatively, developers have made advance payments to the local authority, under Sections 219 and 228 of the Highways Act, before sites have been released for development. Sections 38 and 228 have allowed for an element of negotiation over highways gain (rather like planning gain). But nowadays, local authorities are less willing to commit themselves to major ongoing maintenance, and in some areas there is a trend towards expecting the developer to be financially more forthcoming. Readers are advised to check the New Roads and Street Works Act of 1991 and the *Encyclopaedia of Highways Law*, which gives updates on all these issues. Even at the height of the property boom in the mid 1980s some major bulk house building projects on greenfield, out-of-town sites (and therefore at a distance from existing main sewers and road connections) did not take place because of the costs of roads and other infrastructure. It used to be said in the days when surveyors and engineers dominated town planning that, in the final analysis, town planning comes down to sewers and drains, and it still rings true today.

European factors

There is an ever increasing range of legislation and directives emanating from the European Union (EU). There are now requirements for environmental assessment to be undertaken on certain larger categories of development (Fortlage 1990). EC Directive 85/337 on this has to be incorporated into the relevant legislation of each member state. In the case of England and Wales they are administered through the 1988 Town and Country Planning (Assessment of Environmental Effects) Regulations No. 1199. The overall emphasis upon environmental protection and sustainability policy within town planning has also been strengthened by the 1990 Environmental Protection Act, and is manifest in the content of various recent PPGs such as PPG 13 on Transport, which is clearly concerned with environmental pollution from motor cars. The EU provides various grants for regional development and certain urban programmes, a situation that constantly grows and evolves. Details of some such projects and research funding from the EU is to be found on Euronet, a Europe-wide computer information network.

Conclusion

This chapter has covered the hurdles of certification that a developer must clear throughout the feasibility and implementation stages. Towards the end, it gives some indication of the ensuing conflicts, constraints and inconsistencies. In theory, all these hurdles are intended to ensure a good quality built environment – a built environment that is safe, attractive and durable. Do not assume that, once the hurdles are surmounted, planners and related public authorities have no further role beyond certification. There are many ways in which town planners are involved throughout the process of implementation, as illustrated in the case studies. The next chapter introduces ways in which planners are likely to be involved in the development process, working with developers and monitoring follow-through, to implement planning policy and to obtain compliance with the conditions of permission, especially for planning gain agreements.

Chapter 5

PLANNING GAIN

John Allinson and Janet Askew

Planning gain: definitions

This chapter pursues further the role of the planner in the development process with particular reference to the question of what means are available to the planner to get benefits from the development and thus to implement the wider social and environmental objectives of planning. Particular attention is given to the role of planning gain as a means of achieving such policies, with extensive reference to examples. (The nature of the policies and objectives in question will be discussed in other chapters.)

Although the powers to undertake planning by agreement have existed since 1932 (Keogh 1982), in recent years, planning gain has come to be applied to the practice of negotiating additional facilities, or gains, for the community when the development of large sites is being discussed. In a review of planning gain the Property Advisory Group (PAG) argues that bargaining for planning gain 'is unacceptable and should be firmly discouraged' (PAG 1980). As a result, the government published Circular 22/83 *Planning Gain: Obligations and benefits which extend beyond the development for which planning permission has been sought*, subsequently replaced by Circular 16/91 *Planning and Compensation Act 1991: Planning Obligations*. Check the list of Circulars in the Reference Section at the end of the book.

Planning gain was defined as

> a term which has come to be applied whenever, in connection with a grant of planning permission, a local planning authority seeks to impose on a developer an obligation to carry out works not included in the development for which permission has been sought or to make some payment or confer some extraneous right or benefit in return for permitting development to take place.

The latter part has been cited by many as a corruption of the planning process – the implication being that an unacceptable development might be permitted merely because of the amount of planning gain offered by a developer. Circular 22/83 reiterates this point, stating that a 'wholly unacceptable development' should not be permitted because of any extraneous benefits offered. The circular also guards against local authorities' attempts to extort unreasonable benefits from developers. A test of reasonableness is urged, namely, Is the gain fairly and reasonably related in scale and kind to the proposed development? It has been said that developers are more likely to use planning gain as a sweetener, than local authorities are to initiate demands for extraneous benefits (Fordham 1991). Nevertheless the view held by many, especially in the private sector, is that local authorities actively attempt to extort illegal gains. The Royal Town Planning Institute published a paper on planning gain (Byrne 1989) giving a balanced overview of the pros and cons of the practice. Despite the above examples, planning gain is defined by most commentators as an alternative development land tax, with some town planners advocating an explicit price or lump sum of cash to pay for local improvements, or a percentage figure applied to developers' profits, rather like the old betterment levy. Byrne recognised in 1989 that new legislation on compensation and betterment was unlikely, and therefore the system relied upon planners and developers to negotiate to develop infrastructure and environmental improvements, a view put by Claydon (1991) and considered in Chapter 9. Fordham (1993) suggests that planning gain cannot be defined at the outset, but is only defined at the eventual outcome after lengthy negotiations on its nature, scale, phasing and distributional effects. Therefore it cannot be specified or predicted as a fixed proportionate amount of development costs, as in the case of taxation levies on land.

Again, the concept of planning gain is best expressed by Circular 22/83.

> Whenever, in connection with a grant of planning permission, a local planning authority seeks to impose on a developer a positive obligation to carry out works not included in the development for which planning permission is being sought, or to make some payment or confer some right or benefit, in return for permitting development to take place.
>
> (Department of the Environment 1983)

The philosophy of planning gain lies in the view that by granting planning permission, the local planning authority is conferring great increases in land value; and in return the community, which essentially created these values, is entitled to a benefit, or planning gain. The process of securing planning gain is enshrined in legally binding agreements between developers and local planning authorities. The legal power facilitating these is contained in Section 106 of the 1990 Town and Country Planning Act, hence their common name, Section 106 Agreements. These enable development proposals to be handled in a more positive manner than through the essentially negative mechanism of development control.

Planning gain can take a variety of forms (as explained in Volume I, p. 35, and in detail in the various chapters in this volume). A local planning authority might seek certain benefits from the developer, through negotiation, such as additional contributions towards infrastructure, amenities, social facilities and landscaping, in return for a better planning permission than might otherwise have been expected. For instance, a developer might be allowed to build at a higher density overall if a certain portion of the land were allocated for a small public park. It should he stressed that this is not a bribe to individual planning officers but for the benefit of the community. However, at the height of the property boom in the 1980s, in the case of sites in great demand in high value areas, developers would compete with each other offering the planners sports centres, crèches, even the construction of a whole primary school in one instance to get the favour of the planners. Of course, planning gain did not work well in areas where no developer wanted to build, and the main instances of the phenomenon were to be found in London and the South-East, and to slightly less extent in Avon. But, legally speaking, planning gain should be concerned only with land use and development, that is, with physical planning. Anything else is strictly *ultra vires* (outside their legal authority) (Greed 1993: 237 ff.). However, planning authorities are in a stronger position to bargain for planning gain, and to impose additional conditions on the planning permission for development, if they can claim that the adopted planning document for the area contains policy statements which require social and amenity provision as an integral part of a development proposal. In the 1990s, recession followed the decline of the property boom, and developers became less willing to accept what were seen as unreasonable planning conditions, conditions likely to challenge their legal validity. Any planning condition must be for a 'genuine planning reason' (Morgan and Nott 1988, 139). Any planning gain agreements must be 'for restricting or regulating the development or use of land' and must be 'reasonable' (Circulars 22/83 and 16/91).

Circular 16/91 cites the following as 'reasonable' subjects for planning gain:

(1) *Specification of uses* is probably the most common subject of planning gain. It covers such items as an element of residential use in a commercial proposal, or low cost housing in a residential development.
(2) *Dedication of land and building for public use* includes making part of a development site available for public open space or for road improvement. Larger developments may include such community uses as libraries or sports centres.
(3) *Improvements in environmental quality* cover landscaping and boundary treatments that would improve the appearance of a scheme.
(4) *Off-site infrastructure provision* includes roads and sewers. Such contributions are common in a climate of reduced public expenditure; they are often favoured by the developer, local authority and statutory undertaker, alike, as they help a scheme go forward.
(5) *Cash payments* are acceptable in certain circumstances and are often proposed by the developer. They should be related in scale to the development and should be used to provide gains that are linked with the development in some way.

Local authorities are urged by the government (Circular 16/91) to apply the following tests of reasonableness when seeking planning gain:

(1) Is it necessary to allow the development to proceed?
(2) Is it related to the development in terms of land use and timing?
(3) Is it reasonable in terms of scale, quality and timing of provision?
(4) Does it offset the loss of an amenity or resource present before the development took place?

The Planning and Compensation Act of 1991 significantly altered the framework of planning agreements through the introduction of Planning obligations. These came into force in October 1991 and enable planning gain to be promised by anyone having an interest in land. The significant difference from planning agreements is that obligations may be unilateral (from the developer); effectively, a developer can name a planning gain in a planning application. The main use of planning obligations is projected to be at appeal, where there are planning objections that an obligation can solve, but to which the local authority does not agree; at an appeal, the inspector may grant planning permission with the obligation.

Profit and people

The prevailing economic conditions will always set the context for development. Planners need to take this factor fully into account because it fundamentally affects their likely level of success in attempting to produce plans which are realistic and capable of being implemented. During the 1980s, the planning system, especially its power to control and influence development, was reduced by a number of legislative measures 'through a strategy of consistent incremental erosion' (Thornley 1990). The nature of government guidance and advice (through Circulars and PPGs) reflected a more property market-led approach to planning. For example, Circular 22/80 *Development Control: Policy and Practice* and PPG 1 *General Policy and Principles* stressed the concept of presumption in favour of development, when determining planning decisions. Both reiterate the fact that many aspects of a development are to be determined by the market, and not controlled by the local planning authority. This is reinforced by legislative measures introduced in the early 1990s, such as the Planning and Compensation Act of 1991. The current governmental perception of planning has clearly had an impact upon the implementation of planning policy and upon the way in which development occurs.

Economic and social gains

There is a wide range of benefits which can be negotiated, but as will be seen from the following examples, what counts as legitimate planning gain provision is open to wide interpretation. Examples of planning gain include roads, environmental works, affordable housing, jobs for local people, sports centres, major infrastructure (e.g. flood prevention) and public open space (Byrne 1989). At Canary Wharf in London's Docklands, the developer (Olympia and York) agreed to pay £2.5 million into a fund for training, and to ensure that two thousand local people would be employed. At Broadgate (City of London), the proposal for 3.5 million square feet of office space offered to provide eight training places in banking and finance (Coupland 1989). As can be seen, the provision might be purely physical and infrastructural development or it might be social provision. Social provision is based on more shaky legal grounds. Agreements, for non-physical development provisions, such as training or child care supervision are difficult to enforce, especially when definitions are loosely worded, but some would argue that they are a very crucial method for local authorities to promote economic and social development. In general, however, economic gains, such as training, take second place to highway and social gains (Macdonald 1993). Examples of social gains include low cost housing either within a private development, with a percentage set aside for affordable housing, or as an addition to the development receiving planning permission. In the latter case, supermarket developers have been the main providers. Such schemes are also difficult to enforce. One of the main problems is how to retain low cost housing as just that in the long term when the original developer has long since moved on. Subsequent occupiers, or successors in title, may have no wish to enforce the requirements, or maintain the agreement (see Chapter 5). Positive covenants, enforceable through unilateral planning agreements, and control over tenure and occupancy, through the management practice of housing associations, may be means of resolving these problems, particularly in respect of residential development.

Once the principle of housing has been approved by the planning authority, planning legislation does not generally allow for control of the price, tenure or nature of the occupancy of housing. In the case of a Sainsbury supermarket in Camden, the 'low cost' housing, built in association with the supermarket, was eventually sold off, at its inflated market value, negating the gains to the community (Coupland 1989). Although low cost housing remains a common demand by local authorities of house builders, there is scant evidence that such social provision is taking root, even in large residential developments (Milne 1992). However, PPG 3, 'Housing' (1992) reinforced the principle introduced in Circular 7/91, 'Planning and Affordable Housing', of creating protected categories of low price housing, even controlling the tenure and occupancy qualifications by means of housing association management to keep the housing from increasing its value and being sold off. However, marrying these principles of affordable housing provision with planning gain, negotiation is a complex matter, albeit tried by some rural authorities and in some inner city areas. Town planning is strictly concerned with physical land use and development matters, and seeking to control such social matters as property tenure or the nature of its occupants may be seen as *ultra vires*.

Retail development has been seen as a major source of planning gain, as developers' profits have been high, particularly on out-of-town retailing sites. It may be significant to the level of provision of planning gain that Tesco has decided no longer to develop out-of-town stores (*Planning Week*, January 1994), and concentrate instead on the development of smaller, inner city stores. Inevitably, these developments will pose more problems than those encountered on greenfield sites, creating less profit and less opportunity for planning gain that is related in scale and kind to the development. No doubt, a contributory factor in this decision was a change in policy direction by the Department of the Environment, under John Gummer, to discourage out-of-town development in 1994, as reflected in the draft PPG 13 on transport. Possibly within inner city locations the demands for planning gain will be greater, because of greater need for social and amenity provision to serve the surrounding residential areas in which such schemes are likely to be located. For example, several supermarket chains have been looking at the development potential of playing-fields and other areas of public open space, often the only undeveloped areas left in heavily built-up locations. On part of such sites, supermarket chains have offered to build improved, more user-intensive types of sports facilities and recreational centres, in order to compensate for the development of the rest of the playing-fields.

Community facilities, such as sports centres, health centres, schools and child care facilities have all been the subject of planning gain agreements. Some of them might have been brought about as a result of political pressure from members of the council. When public funding of community facilities is almost non-existent, the provision of a play area, for example, might tip the balance in favour of a particular political candidate in a marginal seat. It is possible to see how such gains could corrode the concept of objectivity and the neutrality of the planning officers negotiating over a major planning application. They might find themselves under excessive political pressure.

Many of the examples of planning gain include commitments which are remote from and unrelated to the actual development which receives planning permission. However, incidences of this are not perhaps as frequent as is often imagined, according to the 1992 DoE survey on the use of planning agreements (Burton 1992; Fordham 1992). It was found that there was very little evidence of non-planning objectives being obtained through planning agreements. But such planning gains should normally be related to the development of the site in question, and be relevant to planning, as otherwise it might be argued that the requirements are *ultra vires*, this being particularly the case when gain relates to wider social and economic objectives, rather than to physical land use and development related provision. Possibly the testing of the legality of the gain imposed will not arise if the developer is willing to go along with it, in order to achieve development, and nobody else raises any legal objections.

Planning obligations

The general acceptance of the practice of planning gain (Fordham 1993) may have resulted in the decision of central government to cancel Circular 22/83 and replace it with Circular 16/91 *Planning and Compensation Act 1991: Planning Obligations*. It reiterates (Annex B2) that the term planning gain has no statutory significance but 'rightly used, planning obligations may enhance development proposals.'

The 'misleading and imprecise' term *planning gain* (Circular 16/91) is not used in policy guidance from central government; the term *planning obligation* is preferred. It is argued that Circular 16/91 takes a much more relaxed view of planning gain, acknowledging that the public sector no longer provides many things which it used to. Circular 16/91 allows for much wider claims on developers that would otherwise be possible (Fordham 1991). The test of reasonableness remains in Circular 16/91, reiterating that planning obligations must be reasonably and fairly related to the development applied for, both in scale and kind. Where intending developers have challenged local authority demands for planning gain, the secretary of state has adhered to the principle of Circular 16/91, and rigorously applied the test of reasonableness, as in an appeal by AMEC, Cherwell, 1994 (Rees 1994). In that case, highway improvements were demanded, and ruled by the secretary of state to be unreasonable.

Recent case history

Recent case history has generated confusion in defining planning gain. Although the government seems to remain committed to the test of reasonableness in scale and kind of planning gain, court decisions seem to contradict the spirit of Circular 16/91. In *R v. Plymouth City Council and Others*, gains including a £1 million contribution to infrastructure for an industrial site elsewhere in the district, and £800,000 towards a park-and-ride scheme, were offered by Sainsbury in an attempt to persuade the local planning authority to grant planning permission for two supermarkets. This the local planning authority did, and the decision was challenged in the High Court by the Plymouth and South Devon Co-operative Society Ltd. The challenge was dismissed, and it was held that the planning gain packages were material considerations to be taken into account by the local authority when considering the planning application. In the case of *Tesco Stores v. Secretary of State, West Oxfordshire District Council and Others*, an offer of funding for a river crossing was dismissed by the Secretary of State (as unreasonable and unrelated in scale and kind to the development), but the decision was overturned in the High Court with the so-called Plymouth case cited. The effect of this may mean that any offer made by an applicant has to be taken into account in determining planning applications. The question now asked is what happens to government policy as a result of this decision. It would seem that the boundaries of planning gain are hugely extended and the principles of Circular 16/9I are under question (Rees 1994). There are others who would question whether or not the government ever had a coherent policy, and these recent court decisions are bound to add weight to their arguments. In fact, in many areas of ambiguous central government policy on planning matters, it is often case law and planning precedent which shapes and sharpens the interpretation of inadequate policy statements.

Despite the continuing provision of facilities by the application of the planning gain principle, as stated above, the term remains an informal one and has no basis in planning law. Fordham (1993) argues that planning gain has reached maturity, becoming an acceptable term in common usage. Various bodies (County Planning Officers Society, London Planning Advisory Group) have urged the Government to allow for the negotiation of planning gain from all large-scale developments. Many others consider that such a course of action might be necessary by local authorities under severe financial restraint to help fund social infrastructure (Byrne1989). But there is limited empirical evidence on the practice of planning gain (Healey, Ennis and Purdue 1992), and it may be that an examination of planning gain agreements of the 1980s will show that many were not successful in achieving their aims – affordable housing is an example frequently cited.

Planning gain and plan implementation

The whole concept of planning gain is widely used in local plans as a means of implementing much sought-after public facilities and infrastructure works. Also it would appear that the new unitary development plans (UDPs) which, as explained in Chapters 2 and 3 combine the features of the old development and local plans, also feature policy statements requiring planning gain. Many UDP policy statements include a shopping list of preferred gains (Healey, Ennis and Purdue 1992). The requirements, usually located in the appropriate policy topic section in the plan statement, include demands for low cost housing, environmental improvements child care facilities, transport and infrastructure improvements and employment training (Milne 1992). Such lists may cause the DoE to consider how to police the new development plans, especially where the newer term *extraneous benefits* is slowly superseding *planning gain*, thus avoiding legal criticism (Millichap 1991). But, how relevant is planning gain in a recession? In a recent survey (Healey, Ennis, Purdue 1992) of the new round of local plans and unitary development plans, most plans were found to make reference to planning gain, both directly and explicitly. Some references occurred in implementation sections, others as policy statements. Plans acknowledge that, with limited finances, local authorities have a new role as enablers or facilitators of development, rather than providers. However, if the developers are not coming forward to develop, because of the recession, the window of opportunity for planning gain negotiation will not be opened. The theme of alternative possibilities, when planning gain 'fails', will be returned to in the case studies.

Not only is planning gain subject to the effects of the economic situation, it is also dependent on the social and cultural attitudes and priorities of those involved in approving and implementing plans. Another survey of the London Unitary Development Plans (London Women and Planning Group 1991) again illustrates the type of lists present in the new plans, but from the perspective of women. The London plans originally surveyed in this study were in different stages of completion, some adopted, some still out for consultation. A later update of the study (London Women and Planning Forum 1993) found that some such policies had met with more success than others, indeed there seemed to be a significant difference of opinion and lack of continuity among the different inspectors as to what was, and what was not, acceptable policy. But overall it was found there was a tendency for social policies related to child care facilities, accessibility policies and women-and-planning policies to be seen as *ultra vires* by the DoE. Likewise, other investigations have found that planning gain requirements related to the needs of ethnic minorities do not fare very well.

In contrast, policies which required affordable housing seem to feature in most of the unitary development plans, and have not been ruled unacceptable. They appear to be seen in a favourable light, by some inspectors at least, and this includes policies that require 25% of new housing schemes to be affordable housing. However, there are other indications that attempts to use plans to include policies for affordable housing (as is the case with child care and women's issues) are being erased, and local authorities will be asked to include them as guidance only. Guidance is an extremely ambiguous concept in planning, with little legal strength when it comes to appeal. Therefore, such guidance policies will carry no statutory weight, and any gains will depend upon the negotiating powers and skills of the local authority, and the economic conditions prevailing at the time. In contrast, the London property fraternity was recently led to believe, or so it is rumoured, that the DoE preferred clear statements of social provision policy within relevant borough plans instead of untidy mixtures of ad hoc planning gain agreements and conditions of permission, cobbled together during negotiations. According to the DoE, ad hoc planning gain agreements were bound to lead to appeal if the developer had second thoughts. This forms part of a wider debate about the place of social policy statements in development plan documents, especially for an equal opportunities agenda. This theme will be taken up by Linda Davies in Chapters 16 and 17, and will be returned to in the concluding discussions on the sort of policies people and planners want to see implemented through the planning process.

Although the situation is extremely patchy in the London boroughs in respect of the social policy uses of planning gain, elsewhere in the country, other types of planning gain are making more progress. The new city-wide Local Plan for Bristol does not make heavy demands on developers (Bristol

1993a). Punter (1990) considers that Bristol City Council has demanded planning gain in the past in the way of good design, and various examples prove this to be true. However, as explained in the section on the economy in the Bristol plan, there is also specific reference to planning agreements and obligations in relation to training, the provision of facilities for the disabled and child care. In the housing section, the plan outlines aspirations for affordable housing, for example, to be achieved by negotiation. Regarding recreation and leisure provision, there is an acceptance that the city council will not be able to fund any new facilities, and a reliance on the private sector to provide these uses. Apart from those directly provided by private means, some suggestions are made to relate provision to housing development, e.g. for children's play areas. This context is of relevance to the case study of Canon's Marsh.

Disadvantages of planning gain

In conclusion, certain disadvantages inherent in planning gain may be identified. Planning gains can only be provided when development occurs, and when the economy allows development to boom. Even then, it is relevant to ask exactly how advantageous is the practice of planning gain to the local residential and business community. Various conclusions can be drawn from the experiences cited above and can be applied to a consideration of the value of planning gain.

(1) Planning gain agreements are inequitable. Gains are only achievable in areas of development pressure, where there is the potential for profitable, large-scale development. There are vast areas of need where planning gain agreements will not be able to occur, e.g. on deprived outer housing estates, in rural areas or in the marginal areas. It may be that in these areas, community need is as great as in the inner city, and yet the use of the private sector to contribute to public facilities will be available.

(2) The system of negotiating for planning gains is corrosive to the neutrality of the local planning authority, and indeed to democracy itself. This can occur when a local planning authority negotiates under political pressure for planning gains, which can then be channelled into politically marginal wards. It would be naive to assume that this does not happen, especially now that local authorities do not have the finance to provide the type of facilities already mentioned. Provision of a play area, for example, could tip the balance at a local election.

(3) The very character of planning gain agreements is one of secrecy. Negotiations are held behind closed doors between developers and planning officers. The developer will want to disclose as little information as possible relating to the financing of the development, or where the burden of any planning gain agreement will fall. The planning officer is

unlikely to have been trained in commercial valuation appraisal, and in any event will not have access to the profit potential of the development. The gain is only as good as the negotiator, leading to many inconsistencies between local authorities, and even within an authority.

(4) There is a question of the actual benefit of the gains to the local community. For example, in a large scheme there might be a case for infrastructure, such as strategic roadworks, which do not really benefit the local community. In that case, it might be the Department of Transport siphoning off large amounts of money for roadworks which are of very limited local value.

(5) Because of the system of negotiating for planning gains, commercial viability has been heightened as a material consideration at appeals. Too stringent a negotiator can be held to be acting unreasonably if the overall viability of the total package is threatened. This may ultimately undermine the objectivity of the town planner.

(6) Surveys have shown that compliance with planning gain agreements is scanty, and enforcement is difficult. Experience shows that local planning authorities are short-staffed with regard to the normal function of enforcement – Bristol, for example, only follows up enforcement in the case of complaint. Failure to deliver the products of a planning gain agreement cannot be the subject of enforcement action, and unless local authorities are prepared to use the courts, the agreements may never be implemented.

Chapter 6

PUBLIC AND PRIVATE COOPERATION OR CONFLICT

John Allinson and Janet Askew

Introduction

The last chapter demonstrated that the use of planning gain can prove a viable means of providing additional funding in order to implement wider social and economic policies in the course of site development. Largely as a result of the funding crisis in local government, many local authorities have come to depend upon the private sector for the provision of public facilities. But the possibilities for plan fulfilment remain uncertain, and the likely level and nature of provision imprecise, because local planning authorities have to rely upon their own powers of negotiation when dealing with private sector proposals for large-scale development to achieve the required outcomes. Nowadays, negotiation is a key factor in the implementation process (see Chapter 9).

Although a significant factor in achieving benefit for the community from the development process, it should not be assumed that planning gain is the only means of doing so. Therefore this chapter will consider alternative means of bringing about development that satisfies the objectives of the planners, utilising resources from both the public and private sector. Planning gain and the other methods discussed in this chapter are all means of righting the balance; they seek to ensure that the community receives benefit rather than loss from the development process. To give a historical perspective and an opportunity for more reflective analysis, the second half of this chapter is a wider discussion of the compensation and betterment context, which has dogged the story of town planning from (at least) 1947. The compensation and betterment debate has effectively been concerned with the same issues that relate to planning gain: how to get back from the developer, and return to the community, some element of the profit that has been made as a result of development to fund necessary social and infrastructural provision.

The local government finance context

The public sector can no longer afford to provide houses, parks, industrial units, play areas, recreational centres or swimming-pools. With some creativity, alternative means of funding and implementation have been investigated; planning gain is just one. Central government has currently employed a number of measures to control and reduce local government spending, resulting in local government underfunding and thus the shelving of proposals for public projects and social facilities. Local public sector finance has also seen a number of changes in the way local government collects its money locally. Rates were abolished and replaced by the community charge, or poll tax, a system whereby everyone contributed on an individual rather than household basis (regardless of income or assets). Poll tax's unpopularity, and the related difficulties of collection, led to the introduction of another system, known as council tax. Each year, central government has cut the grant it gives to local government for local expenditure. In addition there are new powers for central government to cap the spending of local authorities (i.e. to prevent the imposition of high council taxes). Yet in spite of all these changes, local planning authorities are still required to prepare development plans that include provision for a wide variety of land uses and controls for all types of development. Traditionally (when the planners and local authorities were more powerful) these proposals were made without proper consideration of land values or land ownership. It is open to question whether this blinkered attitude is nowadays appropriate to the preparation of development plans, in view of the reduced powers and limited funds available to local planning authorities. It creates particular problems for construction of new infrastructure to service new development.

Partnership

Partnership schemes may be seen as having great potential in bringing the two sides, public and private, together for their mutual benefit. Possibly the greatest involvement that a town planner can have with the development process is through a development partnership. Under a development partnership, different parties collaborate to share common objectives and common endeavours (Ratcliffe 1978). The objectives would be to ensure a certain development is implemented. The partners will usually be from public and private sectors. The public sector may supply the town planner, highways engineer, environmental health officer and/or architect. In some cases the land upon which development is to take place may be in public ownership under the control of the local authority. The private sector may supply the property developer, the financial institution and the tenant of the completed property. There may also be a role in the development partnership for community groups or charities. The way to understand partnership is through two key questions: What abilities, benefits, skills and inputs does each party contribute to the partnership? What benefits, objectives and outputs does each party seek from the partnership? The property developer may, for example, contribute development expertise in order to ensure the scheme is implemented. The developer may seek a guaranteed profit and a secure programme of work. The local authority may contribute planning permission, other statutory consents, grant aid, infrastructure, the land necessary for development and a wider environmental perspective. The authority may seek the accordance of a development scheme with a local plan or a comprehensive scheme for which it would never have the resources nor expertise, for example, a new shopping centre and arts/entertainment facility. The charity may bring detailed knowledge of the needs of a particular social group, and may seek the satisfaction of certain social objectives. The financial institution brings the finance and seeks a return on that finance.

All of these objectives and contributions are focused in the implementation of a particular development scheme. They will obviously determine the roles of each partner, and will affect the way they act, behave and negotiate. A good test of the appropriateness of a partnership is to ask what would happen without such an arrangement. Local authorities generally do not have the finance or the expertise to implement their own plans (Harvey 1992). Private sector property developers can offer these attributes, but left to their own devices, would not necessarily create developments for the benefit of the community; leisure centres are notorious loss-makers.

The involvement of the town planner is important throughout the development process, not just when planning permission is needed. Planners should deal with other property development professionals to ensure that planning objectives are met. With continuing cutbacks of local authority expenditure since the mid 1970s, Partnerships have become more attractive for local authorities as ways of achieving development. Between 1976 and 1982, one-third of all factory units built by local authorities were based on partnership schemes (Fothergill, Monk and Perry 1987). But according to the Property Advisory Group, under successive Conservative governments in the 1980s and 1990s, the local authority's role in partnership schemes has been reduced to that of facilitator and land assembler (PAG 1982).

Ideologically, there has been some opposition from the government to the principle of public bodies becoming involved in development; this was best left to the private sector. Notwithstanding, there has always been an enthusiasm for partnerships between the local authority and the private sector property developer. For the local authority they can provide a way of harnessing the energy of the property developer in order to implement plans; for the developer they can give a measure of security in a field that is notorious for its exposure to risk. Overall, it is difficult to talk about any definitive model of partnership. So much depends upon the circumstances of development and the parties involved. In recent years, there have been new forms of partnership, which may not include local authorities.

The urban development corporations of the London and Merseyside Docklands, and subsequently many other run-down city areas, followed their regeneration objectives through assembling land and pump-priming private sector investment; thus operating in exactly the way that the Property Advisory Group proposed. Success was sometimes spectacular (Allinson 1988). The government's new Urban Regeneration Agency, which changed its name to English Partnerships on launch in 1993, is charged with pursuing similar objectives to the development corporations, but across England as a whole. Partnership, as the agency's name suggests, is the key to its operation. Partnerships are sought with the public, private and voluntary sectors, with the aim of promoting the development of vacant, derelict and contaminated land, thus stimulating local enterprise, creating jobs and improving the environment (Minton 1993 in *Planning Week*). The objectives remain the same as ever; the partners and procedures change. What English Partnerships does not have is more money; it is simply a new way of managing and dispensing existing budgets. It should be noted that local government finance, economic planning and the role of current 'special area' target policies (such as the various inner city programmes) as means of implementing town planning policy, *vis-à-vis* the urban policy maker's perspective will be discussed in the next volume of this series, where the emphasis will be more upon planner's planning, as against the planner within the developmental process.

Development briefs

More effective uses of the resources that are available, greater understanding between the developer and the planner and, therefore, potentially less conflict may be achieved by use of the development brief:

> A summary statement of the authors policy position on development matters relating to a site and/or premises.
>
> (RTPI 1990b)

A development brief is a non-statutory document setting out the development intentions for a certain important site in a locality. It is usually produced by a local authority prior to the granting of any planning permission on the site, and yet provides a useful method of setting guidelines for the development process after the granting of permission. It has a dual function, informational and promotional. A development brief's informational function is to provide details of the site, its location, its surroundings, its constraints to development, its statutory planning background, past planning history, its current and historic use. From this function alone, it can be seen that a competent and comprehensive brief is an extremely useful document! It provides information that would otherwise take many hours and may be too costly to accumulate. A development brief's promotional function is to set out the aims and objectives of the local authority as to how the site should be developed. This may be both general and specific, covering such topics as land use, design standards, mix of developments, scale, distribution and massing of buildings, permissible building materials, access points and so on. It would almost certainly include in outline or detail, the types and amounts of planning gain that the local authority seeks from any developer. By its very existence, a brief promotes development interest in a site and often ensures its objectives are met.

Compared with a local plan, a brief is distinguished by its site-specific nature and its relatively detailed concern with certain types of implementation. One of the main advantages of a development brief, as opposed to a statutory local plan, is that it can be produced quickly. A brief need not go through the various procedures of consultation and draft production required for a local plan. But it may go through some of them or summarise their outcome. A brief is, however, no substitute for a statutory plan, and one of its main requirements is to summarise current statutory planning policy, views echoed by the Department of the Environment.

> Development Briefs are no substitute for a proper plan, though they may be useful ways of providing supplementary advice on site-specific or other detailed matters not appropriate to the plan itself.
>
> (Department of the Environment 1992a)

Since development briefs are concerned with implementing a certain development on a specific site, they should, after production, form the basis for the submission of one or more planning applications from interested property developers. This step may come after detailed negotiation between the developer and the planning authority. But briefs cannot themselves automatically ensure that a development takes place. A completely unrealistic set of ideas for a site will not be implemented simply through the production of a brief. Ideally, a brief should not be over specific; it should leave room for flexibility and the acceptance of a range of development proposals. A development brief should be replaced if it has not led to development within a reasonable time period, or if it is overtaken by events such as the production of a new plan or changing economic circumstances.

Other considerations

In each of the methods identified in this and the last chapter, the planner may require other skills and management techniques in order to ensure that the planner's viewpoint is clearly stated. The form of the development is precisely agreed and the developers are kept to that agreement. Negotiation is an important component in this process, as discussed in Chapter 9. The planner's role does not finish at the approval stage; it continues through mechanisms such as planning gain, partnership agreements and development briefs, so the planner is likely to have an ongoing participatory, monitoring and enforcement role in relation to the completion of the development in question.

Gain or loss: compensation or betterment

In this concluding part of the chapter, the intention is to link the current agenda about planning gain and about other methods of obtaining community benefit with deeper historical debates about compensation and betterment. It is important to understand how these issues go to the heart of a planning system that is fundamentally based upon the concept of state intervention, and thus interfering with the so-called natural property market situation for better or worse.

A gain for the developer or the community?

The last chapter and the first half of this chapter may have given an impression that developers are really quite generous people in agreeing to planning gain, or in cooperating with the planners in partnerships or over mutually acceptable planning briefs. But they may still be gaining more than they lose. In the case studies, Janet Askew maintains that planning gain cannot be seen as a form of betterment levy or community benefit tax, or as an additional land tax because, in reality planning gain only ever goes a small way towards making up for the potential losses to the community caused by the development for only commercial uses. Fordham (1991) comments on this concept of planning loss: 'due to the result of development there is a net loss within a given category of infrastructural capacity available to the existing community.' He sees it as the role of planning gain to minimise such loss created by development. Planning gain, it is argued, should be seen as a reasonable part of the cost of the development, not an additional unfair tax on the land value. Indeed the developer might actually benefit financially from offering planning gain, as described below.

Jowell (1977) has argued that planning gain is the achievement of a benefit to the community that is negotiated, and is therefore not commercially advantageous to the developer. However, it could be argued that a developer would be unlikely to engage in, or cooperate with, the practices of planning gain, and the negotiating process which goes with it, unless it were commercially advantageous. In one such case, the developers of a new shopping centre in Bristol (The Galleries, Broadmead, mentioned in the Bristol Chapter 10) sought permission to use an adjacent public park (Castle Park) for alternative surface car parking to replace shoppers' parking spaces lost during the duration of the redevelopment. This was to allow the development to be completed (and therefore let) in a shorter time, allowing the rents to be reaped earlier. The rehabilitation and restoration of the Castle Park was presented to the people of Bristol as a planning gain, as the developers were offering a sum of money to relandscape it. It is doubtful whether this was indeed a gain to the community, who actually lost a valuable green space for some three years. Other examples exist where planning gain, presented as a benefit to the community is largely advantageous to the developer. This might include, for example, the provision of landscaped space around a building, which might increase its attractiveness to potential leaseholders and ultimately its rental value.

Debates and definitions

The debates about planning gain and planning loss may be seen as a modern extension of a historical debate about land taxes, and specifically about whether developers should be taxed on the increase in value achieved because of obtaining a favourable planning permission, and whether the community should be compensated for such loss of amenity caused by the imposition of development upon their area. It is important to air these issues in this book to give the reader a wider perspective on the debate. All of the procedures described above seek to exert control over the free market in order to make it perform in a more equitable and acceptable way; control mechanisms have as their target a better quality of practice and result. However, the intervention of the state in a free market has both intended and unintended results. One such result is betterment:

> Any increase, realised or unrealised, in the value of property or land, due to the possibility of an alternative use.
>
> (Town and Country Planning Act of 1947)

All governments that accepted the need for state intervention, have wrestled with the concept of betterment. The great betterment debate is a theme running right through twentieth-century town planning (and as a subtext right through this book); the planning gain controversy is its modern manifestation. The argument for betterment is as follows. Land may have more than one value. Its most obvious value is the value for its current use, its current use value. There may be a host of other values for alternative uses. Some of these alternatives may be more feasible than others; town planning controls may make some alternative uses completely impossible. Many may be lower than the value of the land in its current use. For example, no one would seriously propose the purchase of an office block in central London then turn it over to scrap metal processing. That plot of land can be much more profitably used to house an office block; this particular alternative use value is lower than the current use value. On the other hand, there may be alternative uses that are more profitable than the current use. Not only do these give rise to betterment, they also have the effect of encouraging development interest and thereby changing the environment in which we live. This interest and these changes come about when there is a desire to realise a betterment value. Realised betterment would be an increased value that is translated into money on the sale of the land or property. Unrealised betterment would be value that remains locked in the land.

Land values and town planning

Since the planning system seeks to allocate land uses, it fundamentally affects land values. Yet while the system has almost total control over land uses, through the mechanisms described above, it has no control over their values. Consider the following. A farmer owns a plot of land just outside a thriving town. He uses it as rough grazing. Its value as such is around £1,000. Time elapses and the town grows to almost surround the plot of land. The farmer sees his opportunity and applies for planning permission for housing development on the site. This is granted by the local planning authority in accordance with its development plan. The site's value as housing land is many times greater than its value as agricultural land. In fact, it is now worth £350,000. The farmer sells the land to a housing developer and takes a profit, or betterment, of £350,000 − £1,000 = £349,000. The farmer has realised this profit simply by holding his land and, in the fullness of time, applying for planning permission. The creators of the vastly increased value are the community that have caused the town to expand and place a development value upon the farmer's land, and the planning system, which has permitted this site, in preference to others, to be developed for housing. In this example, the farmer has done nothing to receive such rewards; by historical accident perhaps, the land he owns has just happened to be in the right place at the right time. The planning system has effectively conferred these rewards but it has not the power to enjoy even a share of them. In fact, by inflating them, it may have ensured that prior and subsequent development proposals are based not on considerations of local need but on considerations of what makes the most money for the private purse. In other words, what is betterment levy for the farmer may be seen as compensation to the community.

Betterment triggers

The discussion on the ethics of betterment is almost as old as the history of land ownership. Betterment has been defined as an increase in value of property or land, through the possibility of a more profitable use. The increase in value is achieved through this possibility, and *not* through any works that the landholder has carried out. In the example above, the plot of agricultural land has remained a plot of agricultural land. The increase in value has been achieved through an event completely external to its existence: the granting of planning permission, the expression of an interest by a potential purchaser, even the construction of an adjacent motorway or a ring of encircling housing estates.

It is worth examining each of these potential betterment triggers in turn. Firstly the granting of planning permission. This represents a conferral of development rights from the state to the individual. A planning application is considered by a group of democratically elected representatives of the locality. On the basis of advice from its officers, the group makes a decision to approve or refuse (or approve with conditions). This decision will be guided by the provisions of the development plan and by other material considerations, such as representations received from affected parties through the consultation stage. Design, layout, scale and appearance of development will be important; the local authority will generally be looking to achieve a development which blends into the local environment, and is appropriate alongside surrounding countryside or buildings. The local planning authority will not, and cannot, be guided by any consideration of the effects of their decision on the value of the land. This is not a proper planning consideration. But, at the stroke of a pen (the pen that writes 'approved' on the planning decision notice), the value of the land can be increased as much as 350-fold. The actions of the public (in the guise of the local planning authority) have enormous financial consequences; yet these consequences cannot form considerations in guiding these actions.

Secondly, the expression of interest by a potential purchaser. The potential purchaser would entertain hopes of obtaining planning permission through a similar process as is outlined above. These hopes would be reflected in the price that the purchaser paid to the owner. It may not be quite as high as the value of the land for the projected alternative use, due to the possibility of not obtaining planning permission. Nonetheless, the interest in the land must have been inspired by a belief that the planning permission would probably be obtained. Another source of interest may be an attraction to the land's unique character, for example, its location or its surrounding environment. In this example, the seller of the land has done nothing at all other than to become the owner of the land, perhaps by canny foresight or by historical accident. This has led to the achievement of profit for no outlay.

Thirdly, the construction of a motorway or encircling housing estates. The construction of a motorway, or any similar major infrastructural development, is financed directly out of the public purse, yet it confers huge increases in the values of land in its environs. It is not uncommon for developers to purchase sites along the lines of projected motorways as soon as their routes are announced (Goodchild and Munton 1985) in the hope that these can be developed for uses which benefit from such a location; for example, out-of-town shopping centres, warehouses and industrial parks. Clearly, not all sites will be available for these purposes (the planning regime is all-important), but the potential benefit of fast motorway access and its consequence for the value of surrounding land cannot be denied. Plans for a light rapid transit system in Bristol at the end of the 1980s turned this concept on its head: projected increases in land values surrounding the route of the light rail system were designed to pay for the system itself. A similar idea would be a motorway tax levied on landowners along the route of a planned motorway; the tax would help to pay for the road. Without such a tax, private landowners can enjoy increases in land values that are brought about by public expenditure.

The role of the planning system

It is important to note that the original town and country planning system, as designed in 1947, had two essential aspects; firstly, the nationalisation of development *rights* (our familiar and broadly accepted system of development control) and secondly, the nationalisation of development *land*. Not only did the new system bring with it a 100% betterment levy (the development charge) but it also envisaged that the vast majority of new development would take place on publicly owned land. The 1947 Town and Country Planning Act gave local authorities the power to acquire land 'to achieve the proper planning of an area.' Overwhelmed by the postwar baby boom and a population explosion that simply hadn't been foreseen, this vision did not come to pass. It may be argued that at a time of desperate need for rebuilding, complicated measures to extract development value and take land into public ownership were entirely misplaced; they simply acted as a dead hand on the market. This was the rationale for their removal from the town planning system by Conservative governments of 1951–1964. The 1947 act was followed by a number of attempts by subsequent Labour governments to address this issue: the 1967 Land Commission, the 1976 Community Land Act (CLA) and the 1975 Development Land Tax Act (DLTA). The Land Commission was a quango empowered to deal in and make available development land in the right place and at the right time; it was also required to collect a betterment levy of 66% of realised increases in land values. The Community Land Act had similar intentions, but it gave these powers to local authorities, who were required to consider acquiring land that came forward for planning permission, or changed hands. The Development Land Tax Act was the means by which the treasury collected varying proportions of betterment. Both the CLA and the DLTA were parts of the Community Land Scheme, which envisaged eventual complete nationalisation of development land. All of these measures were removed by subsequent Conservative governments.

Political dimensions

Part of the problem is that these measures have always come into existence at the wrong time. During a property boom, when large private gains are made from buying and selling land (such as 1961, 1972 and 1988), the political stakes are high and there is agreement that something should be done. But by the time legislation reaches the statute book, the property industry is in slump, land prices are falling and there is simply no need for a system of profit-sharing or public land acquisition. In fact, such measures may even help to depress the market. So they are stripped away, and there follows a property boom. That these measures did not have time to prove themselves is fairly clear; what is perhaps a little more surprising is that, just before their death, they began to operate in the way people had intended. The

Community Land Act, for example, was moving into the black in some areas in 1979, when it was repealed. Consider what might have happened if the Community Land Act and the Development Land Tax Act had been in existence during the property boom of the late 1980s. Certainly Chancellor of the Exchequer Nigel Lawson would not have been able to argue that development land tax cost more to collect than it produced in revenue (House of Commons 1985). Additionally, with powers (and finance) to acquire and trade land, local authorities may have been able to harness the massive energy of the property boom and direct it towards providing developments that the community needed.

The issue of betterment is inherently political and the attempts to tax it must be seen in this context. Public sharing of private gains is a central plank of Labour party policy (and indeed general socialist policy); the taxing of betterment is an aspect of public sharing. Conservatism does not generally accept this view and submits that to give this role to the state is to set it to perform a task beyond its powers and responsibilities (Cecil 1912). Public sharing of development land is absolutely fundamental to socialist principles and utterly at odds with conservative views. It is, therefore, difficult to see an end to the game of political football that has been played over the past fifty years. Indeed, rumblings were heard during 1989/90 as we approached the 1992 election; Clive Soley MP, Labour spokesman on the environment, stated that land nationalisation would be included in his party's election manifesto, and the Liberal Democrats also put forward some ideas (*Planner* July 1989a). A future Labour (or Liberal Democrat) government would almost certainly try to implement such a measure. In the same way, a future Conservative government would repeal it. At present, without any measures to involve the public sector in the development of land or the consequent realisation of profits, we are left with the essentially ad hoc system of planning gain and the non-specific capital gains tax, unrelated to planning. Neither can be viewed as a specific and powerful means by which local authorities can deal in land markets. Notwithstanding, it would repay town planners to be ready for the next time around and to put some thought into making attempts to recoup betterment work. It is up to the readers to relate this section to their current political situation and to consider how the treatment of compensation and betterment (or more likely planning gain) helps or hinders implementation.

Conclusion

In Part II the interpretation and description of development as a process of linked events has been considered. This has led to a consideration of the ways in which planning authorities, and the public sector generally, can influence this process: through certification and regulation, which control the standards of practice and the output from the process, and through more direct involvement in the process itself, with local authorities adopting some of the approaches and objectives of the private property developer. The consequences of public intervention in the development process have been considered through a discussion of the effects of planning decisions on land values. Unlike building regulations and development controls, there is no widely accepted solution to this problem, despite the attempts of successive governments. Yet still it seems the key to a built environment for society's needs will come through a deeper understanding of the development process, a deeper understanding by local authorities. This involves an appreciation of the pressures on property developers; of their objectives and responsibilities; and of the way they seek to fulfil, respond to or achieve them. Only by understanding can local authorities hope to capture the enormous energies of property development and turn them to socially beneficial outcomes. In the words of Nigel Moor (1983):

> The planner must first understand the development process and then harness its dynamism to his own goals.

Part III

Resolving Conflict

INTRODUCTION

The development control system is bound to be a source of conflict, and dissatisfaction, particularly when the planning authority does not give permission to the developer, or imposes conditions that are seen as unacceptable. Planning authorities may find that certain landowners or users may ignore the decisions and flout the requirements made in respect of development control, or they may not perform the conditions attached to the permission. Part IV looks at ways of dealing with conflict within the planning system.

Having described in detail the nature of the appeals and inquiries system in Chapter 7, John Allinson uses Chapter 8 to consider other means of conflict resolution, possibly less adversarial or litigious. Appeals and inquiries can be very expensive and wasteful of resources to all concerned. As mentioned in Volume I, some developers have become adept at using the system (Creed 1993, 36–38; and see Chapter 10). For example, the various case studies give examples of developers putting in more than one application at a time, so that they can appeal if all are not dealt with in the specified time-scale. From the local authority planners' viewpoint, such procedures are time-consuming, and in these days of cut-backs, no one wants departmental resources tied up for weeks at a time on some interminable planning appeal. However, it must be admitted that planners, as members of the local government bureaucracy, also operate all sorts of strategies for slowing things down; the situation becomes a war of nerves and attrition on both sides. Nevertheless, the government is constantly suggesting ways of speeding up and streamlining the planning system, such as the DoE's consultative document *Streamlining Planning*) and there is concern among both the public and private sectors for more efficient ways of producing development without the need for acrimonious legal proceedings, because of the workloads involved.

Chapter 9 approaches the question from a wider perspective, looking at the role of negotiation in resolving potential conflict in the first place and as a tool of effective implementation essential to all planners. Negotiation has a key role in the case studies of Part IV. Negotiating permeates all human activities and relationships; town planning is no exception. Chapter 9 looks at the unique circumstances of town planning negotiations, the particular procedures that create negotiating opportunities and the special skills of effective negotiators. Planners in all aspects of their work will find themselves negotiating with applicants, politicians, residents, consultees and within their own organisations. Every aspect of the planning process requires planners to exercise their skills as negotiators, in order to achieve wider social and environmental goals from the development process initiatives of others. Chapter 9 explores these influences on the negotiating activities of town planners. It is argued that because planners have limited access to the power and resources which direct the development process, they have to be especially effective negotiators in order to achieve their desired influence on the built and natural environments. Chapter 9 continues a theme introduced in the chapters on appeals and inquiries: how to find alternative means of resolving conflict and bringing about development, that is, achieving implementation without having to resort to expensive and time-consuming quasi-legal proceedings. Evidence of negotiation at work is illustrated in the case studies, such as the developments of York Gate, Canon's Marsh and King's Cross. One's view of negotiation in the planning process depends on one's position, be it developer, resident or planner. Some positions appear to have more power and may be nearer to holding a winning hand.

Circulars, PPGs, regulations, orders and acts of Parliament are collected in the relevant lists in Part VIII: Source Material. Additional DoE references (such as reports and research studies) are found along with other books and reports in the main bibliography section.

Chapter 7

APPEALS AND INQUIRIES

John Allinson

Appeals and inquiries: philosophy

The right of appeal

In any statutory process there should be a right of appeal to a higher authority against a decision that is perceived to disadvantage an individual or an organisation. In town planning, the statutory process takes away an individual's right to do what he or she likes with his or her land or property; essentially, development rights are nationalised into a system of development control. An individual has the right of appeal to the higher authority of the secretary of state for the environment if they perceive a decision to be disadvantageous. The individual could be anybody from a householder to a large consortium of builders. For example, an individual might appeal against a refusal of planning permission for proposed development; the imposition of conditions that are deemed to be onerous or unreasonable; or simply the non-determination of a planning application within the statutory eight-week period following registration. A fictitious case study will be used to illustrate some of the issues arising from the appeal system, centering on the refusal of an application for the development of a new country town by the local planning authority, Dimwold District Council. In this case the individual appellant is a consortium of local developers called Alliance Developments Ltd.

An appeal is properly seen as an administrative rather than a truly legal process. It is part of the statutory system of town and country planning, and yet its basis does not rest within civil or criminal law. Its purpose is to enable information to be examined and shared in order that the higher authority can reassess a planning decision. This may involve an opportunity for objectors and supporters of the proposal to be heard. All are treated similarly, both in their rights to appeal and in the procedures followed for hearing and deciding the appeal. Hence the process is intended to be essentially democratic in nature. Appeals are not won or lost, tempting though it is to use these terms. They are allowed or dismissed. If an appeal is allowed then the proposed development may go ahead, with or without conditions. If the appeal is dismissed, then the planning authority's original decision to refuse the proposal, or impose certain conditions on the proposal, is upheld. Appeal rights and procedures operate to three basic principles (Heap 1991): fairness, openness and impartiality.

Planning appeals

Following the refusal, or permission subject to unacceptable conditions, or non-determination of a planning application, the applicant has a right of appeal. This is made to the secretary of state for the environment within six months of the date of the planning decision, or within six months of the date when the planning application should have been decided (Town and Country General Development Order of 1988 and see Circular 10/88 *Inquiries and Appeals Procedure Rules* abbreviated title). Alliance Development's new country town application has been refused by Dimwold District Council, and they have appealed against the refusal. The original planning applicant then becomes the appellant. The appeal is normally heard by the secretary of state's representative, the government planning inspector, (Town and Country Planning Act of 1990), who will take into account submissions supporting the proposal or the local authority's decision. These submissions come from the appellant, the local planning authority and (in certain circumstances) any interested third parties. In this example, the third parties the Griftonshire, the relevant county planning authority; Keep Dimwold Green, a local environmental group; the farmer of Outfields Farm and Westwold Gravels Ltd., the owners of the site; and a local residents group. All have views about the proposed development, views which may be important to the inspector when considering and assessing the proposal. Furthermore, these authorities and interested groups are *entitled* to appear at the Inquiry (Sections 65 and 66 of the 1990 Town and Country Planning Act). Also see the Town and Country Planning (Inquiries Procedure) Rules of 1992.

There are three different procedures for hearing appeals: the public local inquiry, the informal hearing and the written representations procedure. They differ considerably in their characters and are covered in detail below. The secretary of state (or more usually, his or her representative, the inspector) may allow, dismiss or vary any part of the planning authority's decision; the application is considered as a whole, and as if it were submitted for the first time (Town and Country General Development Order of 1988). In due course, the decision from the appeal is communicated to the local planning authority, the appellant and any interested third parties. Thereafter, certain mechanisms can be used to contest points of law through the courts, but in general terms, the decision of the Inspector or the secretary of state is final. Conflict over the proposed development is taken to be resolved, and there the matter rests.

Aims of the appeal mechanism

The underlying aims of the appeal mechanism are firstly, to bring impartiality to bear on a contested decision; secondly, to encourage debate from the contesting parties, and (in certain circumstances) from other parties that are affected by a development proposal; and thirdly, to gain information which will help to reassess the contested decision. The procedures by which appeals are heard and decided are designed to accord with these three aims. These procedures have been with us since the birth of the town and country planning system in 1947, so an observer might conclude that they have served us well, or at least that no better means has been found. In the example, the appeal decision and the public inquiry discussions will be watched closely by other developers as they may give an indication of government thinking on the new country towns issue; they may even establish precedents. The appeal procedure is a useful gauge of government policy. It is important to keep the above aims in mind at all times. The aim of gaining information is particularly relevant when the public local inquiry procedure is considered. It will not necessarily be the best arguer who wins the day; and however much cross-examination sessions appear like exercises in confrontation, the inspector is only interested in the information that emerges from them!

Background

Current legislation

It is important to remember that a local planning authority has a duty to permit an application for planning permission unless, in the words of the Department of the Environment's PPG 1 *General Policy and Principles*, 'it raises demonstrable harm to an interest of acknowledged importance.' This is spoken of as a presumption in favour of allowing an application. Applications are decided by the local planning authority having regard to the development plan, the results from any consultations and any other material considerations. According to the Planning and Compensation Act of 1991:

> Determination shall be made in accordance with the plan unless material considerations indicate otherwise.

This statement apparently gives primacy to the approved development plan in deciding applications. What happens where there is no development plan? The situation is less clear. This is Dimwold District Council's problem in the example. The council is working on the production of a local plan which places the site in a green belt, however, it is only in draft at the present, and the statutory planning background is the town map, produced in 1955! This is by no means a rare situation, despite the government's avowed intention that all planning authorities should produce district-wide local plans and thus remove such ambiguities (Planning and Compensation Act of 1991).

The application has, however, been decided in accordance with the current draft plan, which is a far more relevant indication of local authority policy and the needs and character of an area than the town map. The applicant's right of appeal against the refusal of a planning application, or a permission subject to unacceptable conditions, or the non-determination of an application within the statutory eight-week period following registration, is enshrined in the General Development Order of 1988. The right of appeal lasts for six months from the date of decision (or in the case of non-determination, from the date when it should have been decided). Appeal is made to the secretary of state for the environment, on the correct forms, available from the National DoE Inspectorate, based at Tollgate House in Bristol.

An appeal constitutes a copy of the original planning application (together with plans, drawings and location maps), together with the appellant's submission as to why the application should have been allowed. The local authority's response consists of its reasons for refusal of the planning application, together with elaboration on these and responses to the appellant's case. Dimwold District Council's reasons for refusal of the new country town application centre around the intention to designate the site green belt; the identification of sufficient housing and industrial sites to satisfy future demand elsewhere in the district (as outlined in the approved county structure plan); the desire to preserve an important scenic backdrop to its major settlements; the concern that the new country town's shops would detract from the district's existing shopping centres (again, in conflict with an approved structure plan policy); and the fear of the generation of an unacceptable volume of traffic. Both parties to an appeal are offered the written representations procedure, governed by the Town and Country Planning (Appeals) (Written Representations Procedure) Regulations 1987 (See under list of Regulations and Orders in References) and DoE Circular 11/187 *The Town and Country Planning (Appeals) (Written Representations Procedures) Regulations.*

If the secretary of state (or the government inspector) considers it appropriate, a public local inquiry (PLI) may be held. The rules of procedure for PLIs are enshrined in the Tribunals and Inquiries Act of 1971 (s.11); and two sets of inquiries procedure rules as outlined below. The Tribunals and Inquiries Act of 1971 enables the Lord Chancellor to make rules of procedure for inquiries. The Town and Country Planning (Inquiries Procedure) Rules of 1992 apply to appeals and inquiries where the decision will be made by the secretary of state. The Town and Country Planning (Determination by Inspectors) (Inquiries Procedure) Rules of 1992 apply to appeals and inquiries where the decision has been delegated to an inspector appointed by the secretary of state. Another important set of regulations is the Town and Country Planning (Determination of Appeals by Appointed Persons) (Prescribed Classes) Regulations of 1981, 1986 and 1989. (DoE, 1981, 1986, 1989) (See under Regulations and Orders list in References) enable the wholesale determination of appeals by inspectors and thus greatly enhance the importance of the latter set of procedure rules (Heap 1991). Then there are the Town and Country Planning (Appeal) (Written Representations Procedure) Regulations of 1987, applying where the appeal is to be heard through written representations. Some 98% of appeals are now determined by inspectors. Those that remain (by advice of the Prescribed Classes Regulations) in the secretary of state's jurisdiction are as follows:

(1) Residential development of 150 houses or more
(2) Proposals for development of major importance having more than local significance
(3) Proposals giving rise to significant public controversy
(4) Proposals which raise important or novel issues of development control
(5) Retail developments of over 100,000 square feet
(6) Proposals for significant development in the green belt
(7) Major proposals involving the winning and working of minerals
(8) Proposals which raise significant legal difficulties
(9) Proposals against which another government department has raised objections
(10) Cases which can only be decided in conjunction with a case over which inspectors have no jurisdiction, so-called linked cases (Department of the Environment 1986)

Clearly, the new country town Proposal will be decided by the secretary of state in person. The rules of procedure govern the way in which appeals are heard and decided, and the ways in which the various mechanisms for their decision are conducted. They are important, and it is important to follow them. If they are not seen to be followed correctly, then the decision on the appeal may be challenged in a court of law.

Appeal procedures

The most commonly used method for dealing with appeals is the written representations procedure, often called written reps. Under this procedure, the appeal is basically conducted through exchange of documents. Written statements of case and supporting documentation are prepared by the appellant, the local planning authority and any parties that have made representations about the original planning application. The submissions, which may include maps, plans and photographs, but not video or audiotapes, are then sent to the inspector, who considers them, makes a site visit and seeks further clarification on any issue deemed necessary. On the basis of this consideration, the inspector decides the appeal.

The written representations procedure is relatively cheap and speedy, and therefore popular; some 83% of appeals are decided in this way (Department of the Environment 1993). On the other hand, it is a cold procedure; cases are presented, and the case of either side may take account of the issues raised in the other's submission, but the procedure does not allow

Table 7.1   Appeal decisions by procedure

Year	% Written reps appeals allowed	% Inquiries appeals allowed
1988/89	31.8	40.0
1989/90	27.7	41.0
1990/91	32.4	40.9
1991/92	35.7	44.4
1992/93	31.6	49.0

Source: Planning Inspectorate, 1993

for the contesting of points or the airing of arguments face-to-face. It is perhaps relevant to note that appeals heard through the written representations procedure have a slightly poorer chance of success than those heard through public local inquiries (Table 7.1).

The other two methods available for hearing appeals involve face-to-face contact between the parties involved. The more common procedure is the *public local inquiry*, which is attended by the appellant, the local planning authority and any other bodies which may be appropriate to the determining of the appeal, such as affected local residents and amenity groups, bodies responsible for providing infrastructure and local landowners. Cases are put by both sides; cross-examination of each side by the other is an integral part of the procedure; expert witnesses and legal advocates may be used to support cases. The inspector makes a decision based on the information obtained through the inquiry. In the example, this procedure will be used to decide the appeal.

An important difference between public inquiries and the other available procedures is the ability of the inspector to hear evidence from *interested third parties*. As well as the appellant and the local planning authority, the following parties are entitled to appear at inquiries (by virtue of the Inquiries Procedure Rules of 1992).

(1) The relevant county councils
(2) The relevant national park committee if appropriate
(3) Any joint planning board, if applicable
(4) The development corporation of a new town or urban development corporation
(5) Parties who have made representations at the planning committee stages (including the community or parish council)
(6) The Historic Buildings and Monuments Commission if exercising planning functions
(7) Certain other bodies exercising planning functions
(8) Any other person who has served a [valid] statement of case
(9) Any parties whom the secretary of state for the environment requires to be present (at his discretion, for example, neighbours, local amenity groups

(Town and Country Planning (Determination by Inspectors)
(Inquiries Procedure) Rules of 1992)

It would seem a somewhat arbitrary choice as to who or what organisation is called upon, although standard custom and practice has developed over the years. But the chances of acceptance are higher in cases where there has been a significant departure from the current development plan, another accepted policy or national planning regulations, and where the third parties in question are specifically focusing on this disparity.

The *informal hearing* is less common, although it is becoming more popular. It is private to the appellant, the local planning authority and the inspector. Third parties or other bodies which may be affected by the appeal are not allowed to attend. At an informal hearing, representatives put their cases and each side is permitted to cross-examine the other. Why are they called informal? Certainly there is less formality of proceedings than at a public local inquiry, but also certain powers are available to an inspector at a public local inquiry but not at an informal hearing (Telling and Duxbury 1993): the requiring of evidence under oath; the power to subpoena witnesses; and the power to require the production of documents (Local Government Act of 1972 and Town and Country Planning Act of 1990). Both the public local inquiry and the informal hearing involve the prior production and exchange of written statements of case in similar ways to the written representations procedure. But the procedures themselves differ markedly. They both require the attendance of parties (and the inspector) in a certain place at an arranged time. They both allow the testing and analysis of argument by each side through the mechanics of cross-examination. They have a slightly higher rate of success than written representations. On the other hand, in terms of staff time, premises hire, fees, documentation production and so on, they are obviously more expensive. They also tend to be more time-consuming in preparation, execution and subsequently decision. In choosing the written representations hearing and inquiry procedures, an appellant needs to weigh up the increased chance of success of the inquiry with the greater cost. For the local authority, the inquiry presumably loses on all counts – it is expensive as well as risky! Both appellant and local authority are likely to choose their appeals route in accordance with the importance of the proposed development and the issues at stake.

Appeals procedures

Procedure prior to consideration

The procedures prior to the consideration of appeal are designed to ensure the fullest and earliest exchange of information. The starting pistol to the appeal procedure is the receipt by the Department of the Environment of the appeal against a planning decision. If the appellant has agreed to the written representations procedure, the appeal submitted initially to the DoE will include the appellant's case for why the appeal should be allowed. The local planning authority will be notified and are required to notify in turn any parties that made representations at the application stage. These include

(1) Those who have responded to publicity regarding the landowners application for planning permission (1990 act, s.65).
(2) Those landowners or agricultural tenants who have responded to notice served upon them regarding another party's application for planning permission on their land (1990 act, s.66). Members of this second group are commonly referred to as Section 29 parties because of their rights under s.29 of the 1971 act (now see s.70 and s.71 of the 1990 act). See Volume I, p. 184 on Certificates A–D as to ownership or other interests in the land which are required to be submitted with any planning application under s.66 (and s.27 to s.29 of the 1971 act).

Any representations from these parties are passed to the inspectorate, who sends the planning authority a questionnaire requesting certain details about the application and the decision. The planning authority returns the completed questionnaire to the inspectorate and sends a copy of this, and all other documents that have been exchanged, to the appellant. This may constitute the planning authority's case in its entirety. However, the authority is entitled to submit further representations, and the appellant is entitled to respond to these representations. The appellant may not agree to the written representations procedure; or he/she may agree, but the DoE may consider it necessary to hear the appeal by means of the public local inquiry or informal hearing. In these cases, an inquiry or a hearing will be held; whether it is an inquiry or a hearing will be at the discretion of the DoE. An appellant cannot demand that inquiry be held. In either case, the appellant has a little longer to prepare his/her case (Figure 7.1).

The DoE will notify the appellant and the local planning authority of the holding of an inquiry or a hearing. The date of the inquiry or hearing should not be less than twenty-eight days nor more than twenty weeks from the date of notification. If an inquiry is to be held, other interested parties (the Section 29 parties referred to above), such as those that have made representations at the planning application stage, should also be notified. In the example, local residents and environmental groups like Keep Dimwold Green will be notified and will choose whether to attend the inquiry to air their views.

The local planning authority must serve a written statement of any submission that it intends to put forward at the inquiry or hearing no later than six weeks after the date of notification of the appeal, and no less than four weeks before the inquiry or hearing. This is sometimes called the Rule 6 statement as it arises from Rule 6 in the Inquiries Procedures Rules of 1992, and will include brief details of the local planning authority's case. The appellant must do the same no later than nine weeks after the date of notification. The appellant's case will normally be based on why the planning application should not have been refused (or conditions should not have been

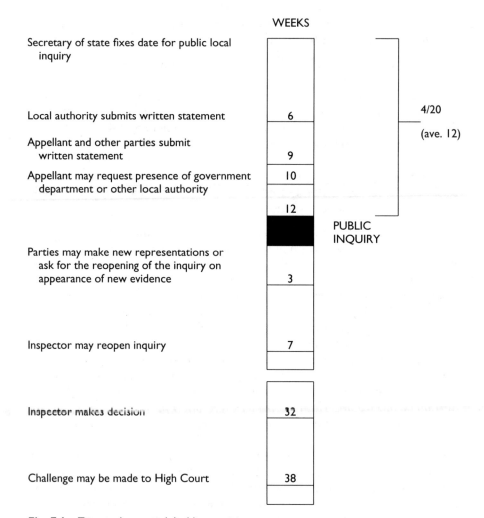

WEEKS

Secretary of state fixes date for public local inquiry

Local authority submits written statement — 6

4/20

(ave. 12)

Appellant and other parties submit written statement — 9

Appellant may request presence of government department or other local authority — 10

12

PUBLIC INQUIRY

Parties may make new representations or ask for the reopening of the inquiry on appearance of new evidence — 3

Inspector may reopen inquiry — 7

Inspector makes decision — 32

Challenge may be made to High Court — 38

Fig. 7.1 Time-scales: appeals/public enquiries

imposed). The local planning authority's case will seldom go beyond a full justification of the reasons for refusal.

In the example, Alliance Developments may seek to argue that the proposal is entirely in accordance with the current statutory planning background, as the appeal site was designated white land (Volume I: 174) in the 1955 development plan; that the proposed development is of a high scenic quality and may actually improve the appearance of the area; that the proposed infrastructure works will be more than adequate for the volumes of traffic generated; that there are insufficient housing and industrial sites of the required quality to satisfy demand in the district; and that the proposed shopping centre would be used by the new inhabitants of the country town, and thus would not take custom away from the old shopping centres.

The written statements are circulated to either side, to the inspector and, in the case of an inquiry, to other interested parties. They are subsequently worked up into full proofs of evidence, which are comprehensive summaries of cases. These are similarly circulated no less than three weeks before the date of the inquiry or hearing. The Inquiries Procedures Rules of 1992 also require that a written summary accompanies any proof which is over fifteen hundred words long. It is this summary which will normally be read out at the inquiry, not the full proof of evidence. It is important to realise that the appellant does not, in his/her proof of evidence or written statement, need to justify the proposed development. This is after all an appeal against refusal of a planning application. The appellant's case will therefore usually rest upon the reasons why the refusal is untenable; in planning jargon, why the proposed development does not 'cause demonstrable harm to interests of acknowledged importance' (PPG 1, *General Policy and Principles*). In the example, the interests are those of the inhabitants, shopkeepers and business executives of existing settlements in the district; and the interests of those who enjoy the countryside likely to be taken by the proposed development. If this can be successfully argued, then the appeal is won. The local planning authority, on the other hand, must obviously argue that the proposed development *does* cause demonstrable harm.

In the example, Alliance Developments will no doubt seek to reassure the Inspector that their proposed development will not take any important open land (in fact, part of the site is occupied by a derelict gravel works); that the production of the green belt plan is still some distance away and firm boundaries have not yet been set; that the development includes all the necessary transport infrastructure; and so on. They may marshall surveys of landscape quality and traffic to support their case. Dimwold District Council will seek to place maximum emphasis on the key reasons for refusal, perhaps the availability of land supply and green belt protection issues. The aforementioned changes recently made to the public inquiry rules of procedure aimed at, but have not succeeded in, speeding up and simplifying the process through earlier exchange of written material and through the requirement that longer proofs of evidence must be summarised for reading at inquiries (1992 rules). The 1991 Planning and Compensation Act (s.18) also introduced a facility for an appeal to be dismissed if the appellant is guilty of undue delay.

Procedure at consideration

For the written representations procedure, the inspector will read the submissions of each side to the appeal, consult any supporting documentation, make a site visit and then make his or her decision or recommend a decision to the Secretary of State. The public local inquiry or informal hearing is obviously much more involved, but the structure is quite straightforward

(Mynors 1987). The inspector begins by introducing the proceedings, the appellant presents his/her case, the local planning authority replies, in the case of an inquiry any third parties have their say, the appellant makes a final statement, and after a site visit, the proceedings are closed. Presentations at inquiry or hearing normally take the form of an introduction to the person presenting them (together with brief career details), a description of the appeal site and the development proposal, and an argument as to why the appeal should be allowed or dismissed. The presentations can include matters of fact and opinion (MacCoubrey 1988). Within their cases, they will usually include references to local planning policy, government policy as expressed in circulars and guidance notes and a clear identification of the planning issues.

Presentations may be carried out by the appellant or the chief planning officer in person; but they are more usually carried out by expert witnesses that offer specialist advice on matters relevant to the proposal. The local planning authority or the appellant may call any number of expert witnesses to give presentations to support the case. For example, Dimwold District Council may wish to call the local development control officer for information on the detailed planning issues; the county highways department for the traffic impact of the proposal; and the environmental health department for specialist advice on the environmental effects of the proposed development. The appellant (Alliance Developments) may use a planning consultant as an expert witness to examine the overall planning issues such as land supply, green belt and statutory background. The planning consultant may in turn call an environmental consultant for advice on how certain works may not harm, or possibly even improve, the environment of the development.

Examination or cross-examination of witnesses by either side is permitted; this may be carried out by other expert witnesses, or by a specially trained legal advocate. For a good discussion of the differences between an expert witness and an advocate, see MacCoubrey (1988). The advocate could be a barrister (for the rich), a solicitor (usually one specialising in planning law) or a town planner. The aim of cross-examination is to draw out further information for the benefit of the inspector in deciding the case. Each side will usually seek to draw out information that is supportive to its case, looking for the weak points in the case of the other side and stressing the strong points in its own case. Alliance Developments may lay the stress on the current statutory planning background (including the old town map) and the land supply issues, while steering clear of the forthcoming green belt plan and the traffic congestion/environmental arguments. Dimwold District Council's cross-examination will be structured in exactly the opposite way. It is *not* the aim of cross-examination to ridicule or embarrass the person being examined. In fact, the inspector is likely to take a fairly dim view of this (Keeble 1985). Third parties, that is Section 29 parties, are invited to put their case for or against the proposed development. They can call expert witnesses, conduct cross-examination and be cross-examined in exactly the same way as the appellant and the local planning authority. For them the inquiry is likely to be a rather more unusual environment than for the appellant or the local authority. The inspector may visit the appeal site before, during or after the inquiry; this visit can be unannounced and unaccompanied if it is before or during the inquiry, but it must be communicated to the parties to the appeal if it is to take place after the inquiry, in which case it will usually be accompanied. Further argument is not permitted during a site visit, but this does not stop parties seeking sometimes to make subtle points regarding noise and traffic congestion, for example.

Procedure after consideration

The inspector will then consider all of the evidence and make his or her decision, or recommend a decision to the secretary of state for the environment. The inspector (or the secretary of state) can allow or dismiss an appeal, respectively upholding the position of the appellant or the local planning authority. Or the inspector may change the local authority's decision in some other way, for example, by adding or removing conditions to the approval. Having made a decision, the inspector gives written notification to the appellant, the local planning authority and any parties who have made representations at the inquiry or have specifically asked to be notified of the decision. This may take some time. The average time taken for an inspector to decide an appeal is around seventeen weeks for one heard through written representations, and thirty-nine weeks for one heard through a hearing or inquiry (Department of the Environment 1993). The inspector *may*, however, give an indication of the likely decision at the end of a hearing or inquiry. The inspector's decision letter does not usually go beyond three or four sides. It will include clear and supporting reasons for the decision. Generally, inspectors' letters are broken down into a number of sections.

Firstly, the planning application and decision will be described in detail, including a site description and the planning application number. In the example, the land includes Outfields Farm and Westwold's gravel workings in the District of Dimwold. Secondly, the inspector will describe the issues as he or she sees them. In the example, the inspector will no doubt draw attention to the forthcoming green belt plan, to the land supply issue, to the traffic congestion issue, to the environmental issues and to the likely competition with existing shopping centres. The letter will then discuss each of the issues at length, paying due regard to the arguments aired at the inquiry, hearing or through the written representations (by both sides and all parties), and due regard to local planning policy and government policy. All of these are important in determining the final decision. Next will be given the decision or the recommendation to the secretary of state for the environment, together with any conditions. Usually there will be a rider, in which the inspector states that he or she has considered all of the other matters raised in the appeal, but that none of them outweighs the factors considered in the determination.

What, then, should be the correct decision in the example? It will depend largely on the planning issues thought to be most relevant, and also of course on government guidance. In cases such as this, where major national issues are at stake, the way in which the decision is expressed will be of paramount importance. It should also be realised that the inspector's letter will make a *recommendation* which may, or may not, be followed by the secretary of state. The inspector may recommend allowing the appeal with conditions that require that certain environmental works and safeguards be carried out as part of the development; thus acknowledging the importance of this issue but effectively dismissing the other reasons for refusal (green belt, congestion, land supply and so on). The decision letter in this case would need to say precisely why they were not felt to be valid reasons for refusal. On the other hand, the inspector may recommend dismissing the appeal since the proposal conflicts with current (statutory) structure plan policies on shopping, industrial and residential land supply; and with current (non-statutory) local plan policies on the green belt. The former is likely to carry the most weight since it contravenes a statutory document rather than a simple statement of intent (the draft local plan).

Or the inspector may recommend deferring the decision pending the outcome of the forthcoming inquiry into the green belt plan. Major proposals may have a significant impact not only on how the green belt is drawn but on how future applications within the locality are determined. The inspector may deem it appropriate to consider such an application at the same time that he or she considers the whole of the green belt; and thus postpone the decision until this time. Any prior decision may effectively pre-empt the local plan inquiry. I think that this is the most likely outcome of the example. It would of course mean more work for the developer and the local planning authority, and the inspector for the local plan inquiry may not be the same as the inspector for the appeal! But, in many ways, it would be more logical to deal with the application in this way. The secretary of state's decision letter may give some hints as to the inspector's thinking on the main planning issues raised at the inquiry and this will no doubt be of great interest to both sides in their preparations for the local plan inquiry.

Finally, the letter will deal with any application for costs which has been made by either side. These may be awarded where the inspector is satisfied that either side has been put to unnecessary expense by the 'unreasonable, frivolous or vexatious' behaviour of the other party (Parliamentary Costs Act of 1865). The inspector's (or the secretary of state's) decision on appeal is final. It may only be challenged through the courts on a point of law, for example, if the inspector is thought to have exceeded his or her powers in some way (that is, acted *ultra vires*), or if the procedures for hearing appeals are not believed to have been complied with. Applications must be made to the Queen's Bench of the High Court within six weeks of the decision date;

complaints about procedure may also be made to the Council on Tribunals or to the Parliamentary Ombudsman. These bodies may only consider points of law; they are not empowered to look at the planning merits of a decision. Neither are they empowered to make a new decision; they simply strike the decision down and refer it back to the inspector or the secretary of state in order that correct procedures may be followed. The decision that results from these correct procedures may be identical to the one originally challenged. The relevant difference will be that it has been reached through the correct procedures.

Conclusion

The appeals and inquiries system is fairly complex, time-consuming and expensive. However, it is also highly structured, legalistic and increasingly formal in nature, which may or may not have its advantages depending on the nature and financial means of the appellant. In the following chapters, alternative ways of dealing with differences of opinion are discussed, in particular other types of public hearing which may be seen as less like a court of law.

Chapter 8

ALTERNATIVE APPROACHES TO RESOLUTION

John Allinson

Existing workloads

Numbers

As can be seen from the following figures, there are huge numbers of planning appeals requiring vast amounts of money and time. Tables 8.1 and 8.2 impart some of the main characteristics of appeals and their outcomes. A vast majority (81%) are decided through the written representations procedure; an even bigger majority (98%) are decided by inspectors. Informal hearings now exceed public local inquiries in importance; and the chances of an appeal being allowed are slightly higher at a public inquiry than through written reps (Table 7.1).

Table 8.1 Appeals decided 1992/3

Procedure	Numbers Decided	%
Written Reps	14,409	80.8
Public Inquiry	1,339	7.5
Informal Hearing	2,084	11.7
Total	17,832	100

Table 8.2 Determination responsibilities

Determined by:	Numbers	%
Secretary of State	296	1.7
Inspector	17,536	98.3

Source: Planning Inspectorate, 1993

Table 8.3 Appeals received

Year	Appeals received	% Change over previous year
1988/89	28,659	+27.4
1989/90	32,281	+12.6
1990/91	26,692	−17.3
1991/92	22,121	−17.1
1992/93	17,959	−18.8

Table 8.4 New Forest D.C.: numbers and costs of appeals

Procedure	Number	Average cost	Total cost
Written reps	185	£100	£18,500
Inquiry	64	£700	£44,800
Hearing	55	£140	£7,700
Total	304		£71,000

Table 8.3 shows another characteristic that is worth noting; appeal numbers rise and fall in a cyclical pattern. The number of appeals received rose by 88% between 1983 and 1990, and has since fallen back to its lowest level since 1985. The recession of the early 1990s, and the accompanying fall in the number of development proposals and submitted planning applications is one of the main factors in contributing to this fall.

Notwithstanding, it is still true to say that a local authority will deal with hundreds of appeals every year; appeals make up 65% of the Planning Inspectorate's casework by volume (Department of the Environment 1993). The workload involved in preparing for and fighting appeals is not spread evenly. For the appellant, it is a once-for-all, or at least an infrequent, occurrence. He or she can spend much time and many resources in preparation; indeed, the issues at stake would normally warrant it. For the local planning authority, however, an appeal is only one of up to ten that it may have received in a typical week; as well as one of many other duties and responsibilities that it is charged to carry out. It simply may not have the time, the resources or the staff to give it the same attention that it received from the appellant. At the height of the development boom, the New Forest District Council carried out a study of the numbers and costs of appeals over a typical year (Johnson 1990). The results are given in Table 8.4.

Costs

The appeal-related costs represent costs over and above those that an authority would have to meet in any case, for example, staff costs. It is also true to point out that costs can rise astronomically for the larger public inquiries or those that use legal advocates outside the employ of the local authority. In any event, it can be seen that the appeal process represents a substantial cost for the local planning authority, and by implication, the council tax payers. In this example, public inquiries can cost seven times as much as written representations. It is thus true to say that the process of contesting planning decisions through appeals costs a great deal of public money.

Alternatives

The planning inquiry commission

Over the years, various governments have explored alternative ways of deciding appeals, partly in response to the growing numbers of appeals and the increasing time taken to reach a decision, and partly in response to concern that the appeals procedures are used to decide issues far beyond their capability. These concerns were becoming evident as long ago as 1967. The government's 1967 White Paper *Town and Country Planning* (see under list of Command Papers, 1967) echoed widespread dissatisfaction with the public inquiry mechanism and sought an alternative for 'wide or novel issues of more than local significance.' The alternative, which is still on the Statutebook, was the planning inquiry commission. This was to have three to five members, was to be set up by the secretary of state and was to operate as an expert committee advising the minister on the issues at stake in a proposal which raised 'considerations of national or regional importance' or 'unfamiliar technical and scientific aspects' (White Paper, 1967 ibid.). The best way of understanding the brief of a planning inquiry commission is to think of it as a small Royal Commission bolted on to a public local inquiry (House of Commons 1968). The first part of the inquiry would be carried out by the commission. It would examine the broad background to the proposal by considering evidence from all sides. It would, unusually, be empowered to identify and recommend alternative sites for a development proposal, although the processes by which it would do this are unclear. Would the developers be canvassed as to the suitability of the proposed alternative sites? Would the landowners be consulted? Would any subsequent planning application be refused by a local planning authority that did not agree to the alternative site selected? Would there then be another planning inquiry commission into the alternative site?

The second part would be a public local inquiry following the normal pattern of presentation of cases and cross-examination. Following this, the planning inquiry commission would present its report and recommendation. Despite many proposals which would seem to have been ideally suited to the use of a planning inquiry commission (such as the nuclear reactor proposals at Windscale, Cumbria, in 1978, Sizewell B, Suffolk, in 1983/85 and Hinkley Point C, Somerset, in 1988/89), the procedure has never been used. In its evidence to the House of Commons Environment Committee in 1985/86 (House of Commons 1986) the government cited several reasons for its non-use.

Firstly, it felt that the decision would effectively be made after stage 1, thus pre-empting the public local inquiry in stage 2. Secondly, it felt that duplication would occur between stages, as it was difficult to draw a clear line between national and regional considerations (which should be examined at stage 1) and local ones (which should be examined at stage 2). Finally, it felt that existing public local inquiry procedures were flexible enough to allow major considerations to be debated. Perhaps the closest we have ever come to using a procedure resembling the planning inquiry commission (Cullingworth 1988) was the Roskill Commission, which was established in the mid 1960s to examine three potential sites for the proposed third London airport. At a cost of over £1 million, and over two and a half years (Cullingworth 1988), the Roskill Commission, who had themselves spent £750,000 in the preparation of their cases (Hall 1992), used sophisticated techniques of cost-benefit analysis to conclude that Cublington in Hertfordshire was the ideal site. In the teeth of fierce local opposition, the commission's recommendation was promptly rejected by the government. The site initially decided upon by the government (Foulness, or Maplin Sands) was the one considered the least suitable, or the most costly, by the commission, but had been the government's original choice *before* the work of the Roskill Commission (Ravetz 1986). Stansted, the site that eventually became London's third airport, was not even considered by the commission. It has been suggested by Edwards and Rowan-Robinson (1980) that this unfortunate experience may have coloured the picture for the use of the planning inquiry commission.

Another possible answer to the non-use of the planning inquiry commission is the apparent threat to government policy that it presents; if an expert commission appointed by the government recommends a course of action contrary to government policy, the potential embarrassment to the government is clear (Edwards and Rowan-Robinson 1980). It must either change its policy or quash the recommendation of its own experts. The remaining worry with the public local inquiry is that the government decides major issues in advance. According to Cullingworth (1988), during the first Stansted Inquiry, the secretary of state for trade said, 'Stansted has really chosen itself.' Halfway through the Sizewell B Inquiry, the government authorised the Central Electricity Generating Board to spend £12 million on advance orders for the proposed nuclear power station.

The examination in public

Another procedure that has been used to examine different sides of an issue or number of issues is the structure plan examination in public (EIP). Slightly different from a public local inquiry, its brief is to investigate selected matters to assist the secretary of state for the environment in his or her consideration of a structure plan. The 1991 Planning and Compensation Act enables county councils to approve structure plans without recourse to the government, so more recently the EIP has been for the advice of the county council. The EIP is a large step away from the quasi-judicial appearance of a public local inquiry; the atmosphere is (or should be) one of balanced, rational discussion of a limited number of issues. The examination is led by a

Table 8.5 Planning inspectorate staffing, 1993

Employee category	Numbers
Grades 3/7 (office based)	23
Inspectors (salaried)	241
Administrative (inc. casuals)	372
Total	636

Source: Planning Inspectorate, 1993

panel with an independent chair; the county council decides on the matters that shall be examined and invites interested parties to submit evidence. The panel then reports to the county council, which considers this report in its production of the structure plan. It is difficult to see how an EIP would be appropriate for examining purely local issues at appeal, but its philosophy of choice and debate of key issues in a discursive frame may be thought of as suitable for some of the larger proposals currently dealt with through the local inquiry mechanism.

A review of existing arrangements

Notwithstanding other ideas about the correct way to deal with appeals, it does appear that the current procedures of written reps, public local inquiries and informal hearings, outlined in the last chapter, will remain with us for the foreseeable future. But they could still be subject to review and change. In fact, there have been a number of important changes recently. Firstly, the DoE Planning Inspectorate was greatly expanded in the late 1980s. Some twenty-five salaried and nineteen contract inspectors were newly recruited in 1987 alone. The recruitment target for 1992/93 stood at twenty inspectors, although this was revised downwards as workloads continued to fall, and in the event, only three new inspectors were recruited. The staffing levels of the inspectorate in March 1993 are shown in Table 8.5.

Expansion is intended to improve decision time-scales. An emphasis is placed on shorter reporting; the inspector is required to be selective in reporting only the factors and arguments that bear upon his or her conclusion. Secondly, the inspectorate was launched as an executive agency on 1 April 1992. Significant performance targets for 1992/93 were as follows:

(1) To decide 80% of written representations within twenty-two weeks
(2) To hold the average unit cost (per appeal) below £706
(3) To achieve a 2% efficiency improvement in gross running costs over those in 1991/92

All of these targets were achieved. New targets for 1993/94 include deciding 80% of written reps appeals within nineteen weeks; holding the average unit cost below £690; and achieving a 3% efficiency improvement over 1992/93's running costs (Department of the Environment 1993). The Planning

Inspectorate is confident it can achieve these more demanding targets. Thirdly, there have been several important changes to the rules of procedure. The main ones were identified in the Town and Country Planning (Determination by Inspectors) (Inquiries Procedure) Rules of 1992 and the Town and Country Planning (Inquiries Procedure) Rules of 1992 both produced by the Department of the Environment (and listed under Regulations and Orders in the Reference Section). The points identified are as follows:

(1) Earlier and fuller exchange of written statements is required. Dates for exchange are fixed forward from the notification date rather than backwards from the date of the inquiry (if there is one).
(2) It is planned to arrange 90% of public local inquiries to start within eighteen weeks of the appeal.
(3) The appellant as well as the local planning authority is now required to give a written statement of submissions.
(4) Other parties who plan to appear at a public local inquiry may also be required to produce written statements.
(5) Specific provisions are made for pre-inquiry (and pre-informal hearing) meetings, with a more formalised exchange of information enabling better programming.
(6) The inspector is given the express power to lay down a timetable for a public local inquiry or hearing.
(7) For major inquiries, the secretary of state is to provide statements of relevant matters, and the main parties are to provide fuller pre-inquiry statements.
(8) The use of statements of agreed fact, and generally taking written statements as read, is encouraged at inquiries.

Other possible ideas for further changes to procedure include the awarding of costs against the losing side in an inquiry (this would follow legal practice and would presumably represent a deterrent to appeal); charging for appeals (in the same way that planning applications are charged for); requiring that an appellant obtains leave to appeal, instead of it being an automatic right; or the issuing of an instant appeal decision after the end of an inquiry or a hearing (Planner September, 1989b). Almost all of them would increase the speed of decision making, but Chief Planning Inspector Stephen Crow cautions against sacrificing democracy on the altar of speed.

> Improvements in output and efficiency . . . are not the whole story. The Citizen's Charter rightly demands high standards from the Public Service.
>
> (Department of the Environment 1993)

Conclusion

The system of appeal against planning decisions is based on fundamental principles of democracy, openness and fairness. Everyone has the right of appeal against a planning decision that they consider to have harmed their interests. Aside from the costs of preparing and presenting a case (which may be substantial), there is no direct cost for making an appeal. The appeal is heard by an impartial, independent arbitrator who will consider the case as if for the first time. The appellant may prepare his or her case at any length and cost that is considered appropriate. This may involve calling key expert witnesses to explain certain points (or the entire case) and legal advocates to carry out skilful presentation and argument. The appellant may cross-examine the local planning authority and any other party to the appeal, in order to support his or her case (or expose the weaknesses in the case of the opposition). Appellants need to be prepared to face cross-examination themselves. Given the many rights open to an appellant, and the number of procedures through which these rights are exercised, it is perhaps no small wonder that appeals remain popular. Put simply, the appellant has nothing to lose; in fact, there is a one-in-three chance of winning. Having received a planning refusal, or an approval with onerous conditions, who would not appeal?

Small wonder that appeals take a long time to be heard and decided. Proper procedures must be correctly observed, perhaps painstakingly so. If they are not correctly observed, then one or other side could (quite justifiably) claim they were disadvantaged. Rights and procedure are at the centre of the appeal philosophy. Of course, everyone (especially appellants) would like appeals to be decided more quickly, and everyone (especially local planning authorities) would like there to be fewer of them. But any move to achieve these objectives must not lose sight of the central philosophy of rights and procedure. If such a move took away these rights (e.g. the necessity of obtaining leave to appeal, or the losing side paying all costs) then it may be considered improper. If such a move was not based on sound procedure (e.g. the issuing of instant appeal decisions) then it would be open to challenge through courts of law. The consideration leads us back to where we began: fairness, openness and impartiality lie at the heart of the appeals process. To date, we have found no better way of maintaining them than current appeals procedure: written representations in most cases, public local inquiries in a few cases and informal hearings in a small but growing number of cases. This is not to ignore other procedures or to gloss over imperfections in the current system as it struggles to cope with an ever increasing tide of appeals.

The system of planning appeals has proved particularly robust. Its basic principles have remained the same since the birth of the planning system. Certainly there have been changes, and change will continue to cope with rising numbers of appeals, increasing pressures on staff and longer turn-around times. The efficiency of the appeal system has undoubtedly been improved through changes. But these changes have not been accompanied by the development of new procedures to cope with major new issues, such as nuclear power station development. Nuclear power stations are hardly local, but they are still dealt with through public local inquiries. Desmond Heap (1991) has described the appeals procedures as part of a system of natural justice that is, in many ways, the envy of the world. And it is undoubtedly true that some sort of forum for discussion of major development issues is better than no forum at all, as was the case in the development of the Channel Tunnel. Thus importance and presence of the appeal and the procedures, for hearing the appeal, will continue; one can only hope these procedures will be subject to continual review and improvement, but perhaps without large-scale change. The pressures they impose upon those who deal with them, the DoE Planning Inspectorate and the local planning authority, will of course continue.

Postscript

In all these debates, the arguments seem to centre around the needs of the planners and the developers, especially in respect of planning applications, but also to a considerable degree in the case of development plan preparation and subsequent inquiry procedures. The process often comes across as a two-sided fight, even though there is space for third party interests. But many such interests are official bodies or consultative groups. Many would argue that the people who live or work in the area in question should also have more say, and a right to representation in the initial planning application stage as valid third party interests (long before matters reach the appeal stage), even though they may not actually have any legal interest in, or rights over, the land in question. This third element has been particularly strong in relation to nuclear plant inquiries. This issue re-emerges throughout the case studies of Part V, and is seen as being linked to the wider public participation in planning debate. It is also considered in the last two chapters of the book.

Although this chapter has chiefly concentrated on planning appeals, inquiries and their alternatives within the realms of town planning, other statutory bodies, such as the Lands Tribunal, also seek to resolve conflict over land matters. The role of professional arbitrators is also important in dealing with a range of professional and legal disputes in the wider world of the property professions and construction industry, whose activities also impinge on town planning. Finally, town planning practice and individual town planners are themselves becoming increasingly privatised through the operation of compulsory competitive tendering (CCT), and planning departments are becoming more commercially minded. In the future, it may be that town planning practice will become more litigious (as in North America), in which case civil actions could become commonplace, not against entire departments but against individual planners. Professional indemnity insurance (PII) is already a major overhead and an absolute necessity in the private sector property professions; increasingly it may become essential for town planners as well.

Chapter 9

NEGOTIATIONS IN PLANNING

Jim Claydon

Definitions and concepts

Negotiations occur when two or more parties attempt to reach an agreement. It is important to distinguish the terms *negotiation* and *negotiating* from other similar concepts. *Bargaining* involves the trading of benefits but is only one means by which negotiations may be undertaken or may be a part of the process. *Compromise* occurs when two or more parties accept agreement at a level below their preferred outcome for the sake of agreement. Again this should be seen as a mechanism which may be part of a negotiating process. *Mediation* and *conflict resolution* involve the active participation of disinterested third parties in the process of negotiation and through their objective and creative input enable the interested parties to reach agreement (preferably a superior agreement) which might otherwise not have been possible.

Town planners engage in negotiation involving bargaining and compromise and will at times act as mediators attempting to resolve conflicts in which they have no direct interest. The distinction of these terms is more than a semantic exercise, it is important that practitioners recognise their role and the possibilities which it presents to them in achieving their objectives. Negotiating is not an arbitrary process and neither are negotiating skills innate; the process is predictable and manageable and the skills can be learned and improved upon.

At the simplest level, successful negotiation involves

- the identification of individual interests
- an exchange of information
- the exploration of solutions
- agreement

There are two distinct schools of thought as regards the achievement of best results. The first, exemplified by Kennedy, Henderson and Penrose (1980) concentrates on the performance of the negotiator. By adopting certain tactics and following set procedures, negotiators are able to ensure the best deal for themselves. If all parties follow this approach the outcome should be satisfactory to all participants. This approach contrasts with that of

Fisher and Ury (1983) in which the parties to negotiation seek to identify one another's interests and see their resolution as a mutual problem. The advocates of this approach, known as principled negotiations, are critical of Kennedy's positional bargaining approach, because it portrays negotiations as involving trade-offs from an optimal aspiration until some satisfactory midpoint is reached. They argue that in some circumstances the principled approach can lead to agreement which is more beneficial to both parties than could have been achieved through the compromises of positional bargaining.

The role of negotiations in town planning

Town planning as a function of local government has long been recognised as an activity concerned with implementation, but where resources and powers are limited. Development planning is essentially a coordinating and allocating activity, whereas development control is exercised through the certification of the development proposals of other agents. Inevitably these activities bring planners into contact with actors and agencies who have the power and resources which planning authorities lack. It is through the successful harnessing of the attributes of the planning authorities and the other actors that implementation of development occurs. It is the author's contention that successful implementation is dependent upon successful negotiations among these interested parties. There may be great complexity in achieving satisfactory outcomes because of the variety of actors/agencies involved in negotiations: the two tiers of planning authority, the various departments of central government, the providers of public utilities and the multifaceted private sector (as illustrated by the case of York Gate in Part IV). To add to the difficulties, individuals acting on behalf of each of these agencies operate to different objectives, within different time constraints, with differing degrees of discretion and with different sets of values (both personal and organisational). Some see the solution to these difficulties in giving planners more legislative power and/or financial resources. However, unless there is a complete restructuring of society, local authority planners working in a mixed economy will always be dealing with private sector developers, and unless the centralisation of government is accelerated to a greater degree, there will always be a need to reconcile the interests of a variety of governmental agencies. What is more, recent government circulars seem to have emphasised the greater need for planners to concern themselves with negotiation. Circular 2/86, *Development by Small Businesses* advocates 'informal discussions at an early stage between potential applicants and planning officers,' reiterating advice previously given in Circular 1/85 on planning conditions.

Statistics on successful appeals (see Chapter 8) suggest that planning authorities would be well advised to seek negotiated modifications to applications rather than refusing the application outright and inviting an appeal. According to Circular 38/81 *Planning and Enforcement Appeals*, 'consultation and negotiation between parties ... can often resolve difficulties more quickly and cheaply than appealing.' Planning gain now remains as the only means of abstracting community benefit from private initiatives, and despite ideological reluctance in government, Circular 16/91 on planning obligations suggests 'it may be reasonable to seek to enter into a planning obligation by an agreement with an applicant which would be associated with any permission granted.' Such agreements can only be achieved through negotiations and the processes of bargaining involved in negotiating have been the subject of considerable interest among planning commentators. Consequently, Jowell (1977) has suggested that planning has moved from a judicial technical model to a bargaining model. In fact, development control as a whole may best be understood as a negotiation process. In other words, the function of development control is to weigh the merits of a number of competing claims on development proposals for a particular piece of land. Weighing of the merits is inevitably undertaken through verbal and written communication, a process of negotiation.

Negotiation in public and private sector planning

Town planners in practice find themselves constantly negotiating with colleagues, clients, seniors, politicians, members of the public and representatives of other organisations. Their ability to be effective is constrained by a variety of factors such as organisational structure and procedures (Sheldon and Claydon 1990) as well as their own skills and knowledge. The importance of negotiating is probably better recognised in the private sector than in local authorities. Planners in consultancy or development companies understand that for their clients to achieve their development aspirations, they must persuade local planning authorities to accept their proposals. This is achieved through participation in the development plan and development control processes. Planners working for planning authorities are frequently perceived as being more reactive than proactive, that is, dependent on the initiatives of others, a belief reinforced by the erosion of power and resources from local authorities over the past twenty years. Equally, government advice has emphasised the administrative nature of the task of planning authorities and emphasised efficiency and speed in plan preparation and development control (as in the draft consultation paper *Streamlining Planning* issued 14.12.93 (DoE 1993, December).

However, the development planning and development control processes provide considerable opportunities for planners to negotiate improved outcomes to land and property proposals. Indeed, it has been argued that negotiation represents an important means of policy implementation. Barrett and Hill (1981) concluded that if we recognise a situation in which one agency is seeking to influence others over which only limited control may be exercised, then it is necessary to think in terms of negotiation and compromise rather than coordination and control. According to Barrett and Fudge (1981) it is appropriate 'to consider implementation as a policy/ action continuum in which an interactive and negotiative process is taking place over time between those seeking to put policy into effect and those upon whom action depends.' In other words, the view that implementation means putting policy into effect is too simplistic and unreliable as a model of the real world.

Development plan preparation

Development Plan preparation consists of drawing together the varied interests of public and private agencies in an attempt to allocate land and devise policy for the foreseeable future. In the process there are considerable opportunities for negotiation and consultation (Fig. 9.1). As the plan preparation process progresses, the opportunity for open negotiations decreases as policies get firmer.

With development plans, access to the process and knowledge of procedures assumes considerable importance for outside bodies wishing to engage the local planning authority in negotiations about sites and policy. The most privileged organisations are those invited to comment at the early stages of the process. For example, the House Builders Federation, representatives of the private sector who might participate in a joint residential land assessment exercise, have considerable opportunities to negotiate. From the local authority planner's point of view, the incentive to negotiate is to attempt to ensure the production of an effective plan. The process of negotiation enables the local planning authority to achieve a consensus among competing interests and a commitment to the proposals from agencies with the power and resources to implement the plan, for example, with the highway and water authorities.

Development control

The frequency of negotiations

Development control is a task undertaken by small teams of officers in local planning authorities. They advise planning committees on the decisions they should make on planning applications made by applicants and agents. Research on development control sections Claydon (1991) has shown that negotiations proliferate in their day-to-day activities. Table 9.1 illustrates the passage of two contrasting planning applications through their own negotiating history, taken from the research referred to earlier in this chapter. Application A was a major city centre application for a new retailing develop-

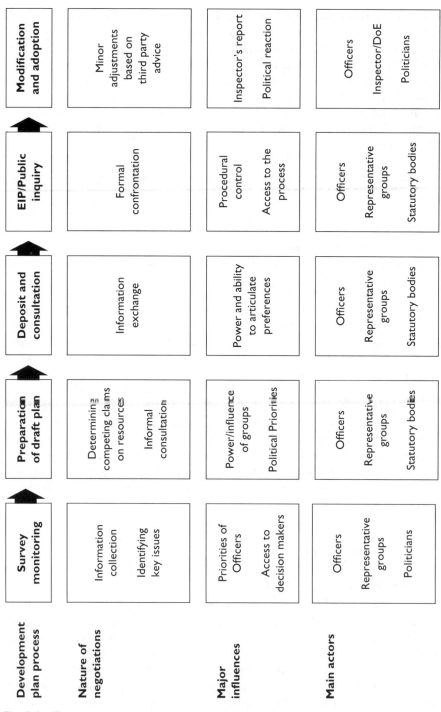

Development plan process	Survey monitoring	Preparation of draft plan	Deposit and consultation	EIP/Public inquiry	Modification and adoption
Nature of negotiations	Information collection Identifying key issues	Determining competing claims on resources Informal consultation	Information exchange	Formal confrontation	Minor adjustments based on third party advice
Major influences	Priorities of Officers Access to decision makers	Power/influence of groups Political Priorities	Power and ability to articulate preferences	Procedural control Access to the process	Inspector's report Political reaction
Main actors	Officers Representative groups Politicians	Officers Representative groups Statutory bodies	Officers Representative groups Statutory bodies	Officers Representative groups Statutory bodies	Officers Inspector/DoE Politicians

Fig. 9.1　The development process and negotiation

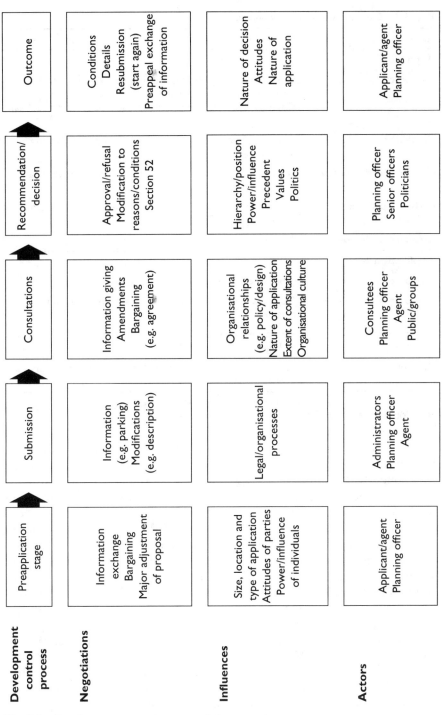

Fig. 9.2 Development control as a negotiation process

Table 9.1 Case study examples of negotiation

Stage	Negotiating activity
Application A	
Pre-application	Extensive meetings among Head of Policy, Listed Buildings Architect, Head of Development Control, City Engineer and County Highways. Developer represented by Architect from large practice
Consultations	Limited importance because of extent of pre-application negotiations
Recommendation/decision	Defer subject to more detailed negotiations, but acceptance in principle
Revised application	Further negotiations between developer's Architect and Head of Development Control
Recommendation/decision	Approval
Application B	
Pre-application	Landowner and agent meet case officer
Consultations	Objections from City's Architectural Consultant and neighbours
Recommendation	Refusal recommended and subsequent meeting of case officer and agent
Decision	Site visit followed by refusal with an invitation to re-submit an alternative scheme

A = Central city shopping development involving listed buildings
B = Householder application for development on area of adjoining land

ment in the heart of an historic city. It involved the redevelopment of listed buildings and was clearly contentious and complex from the outset. Consequently the applicants, advised by their consultants, decided to negotiate with the planning authority in advance of the submission of an application. This demanded extensive involvement from within the local authority, the county highways authority and the developer's team. It also took several months. But once agreement had been reached on the proposed scheme, the application was processed relatively straightforwardly, and subject to an amendment on details, it was approved by the authority. Application B was for the construction of a single dwelling by a housebuilder on adjoining land, which on the face of it should have been a simpler scheme. The applicant and their architect met with the case officer prior to submission but failed to respond to the advice given. Following submission of the application, a number of objections emerged which subsequently led to its refusal, even though development of the site was accepted in principle. The applicant was consequently faced with two alternatives: an appeal against the decision to refuse permission or submission of an amended application. A summary of the process is shown in Figure 9.2. It illustrates the process of development control, the potential for negotiations, the influences on those opportunities and the role of key actors in each phase. This too is based on research and on observations of planning officers over a period of some months and involving selected applications.

For many applications (generally larger ones) negotiations occur from the point of initial contact between the applicant/agent and the authority. The nature of negotiations at this presubmission stage will vary considerably according to the character of the proposal. While for some applications the interaction may constitute little more than an exchange of ideas, for others (again generally those of a large and complex nature) quite significant multi-agency negotiations may occur with bargaining and compromise leading to the submission of a proposal very different from that originally conceived of and being assured of a very different response from consultees as a result. Following formal submission of the application a series of parallel processes occur which may involve negotiations with the applicant, neighbours, consultees, councillors, representatives of the public or interest groups and people within the planning department.

Mediators or provocateurs?

The officer's site visit provides an opportunity not only to contact the applicant but also any neighbours who may have objected or may potentially do so. Planning officers may here be acting as mediators or provocateurs, inviting support for their position on the proposal. In negotiations with consultees the planner may well operate on behalf of the applicant, as a mediating agent unless (as may be the case with major applications) the applicant has undertaken individual negotiations with the consultees in advance. Within the department the planning officer is involved in negotiations whose outcome will depend a great deal on office procedure and hierarchies of power as well as the merits of the case. For example, the relevance of a policy issue can be an important factor only if the policy section has influence and access to the decision-making process or if case officers (or their supervisor) choose to make it so.

One very important feature of the negotiating process in development control is the position of the case officer in terms of the organisational hierarchy. If case officers are delegated responsibility and power to make recommendations to committee, their negotiations carry a greater degree of certainty than if they are constantly having to premise opinions by reference to a superior. In reality, this may vary from case to case and is subject to committee approval, so the planning officer always enters negotiation as an agent for the authority with responsibility but not complete power of decision. Negotiations beyond the committee stage are dependent on the outcome of the recommendation. However, further negotiation is a strong possibility in all cases: on details, on a resubmission or prior to an appeal.

Implied in this account of negotiations in development control has been the recognition of factors of influence on the negotiators, such as the organisation structure or power relations between applicant and officer. But even where officers operate within the same authority, research indicates there is a different approach to negotiations. It seems that individual professionals express their own objectives and values in their dealings with applicants, so they may well arrive at different decisions or recommendations. The weight to be attached to aesthetic criteria as opposed to policy matters; the manner in which policy is to be interpreted; the importance of impact on neighbours and public dissatisfaction with schemes may be awarded higher or lower priority according to the preferences of the particular officer handling the case.

Professional values and assumptions

Professional socialisation

Of particular interest is a subject previously studied by Underwood (1981), the question of where the professional values actually come from, values so prominent in the negotiation process. Obvious sources, such as education and training, are important but each department would also seem to have its own culture, which suggests agreed standards of good design, appropriateness of use, density and so on. It is also interesting that local authority planners have been found to spend little time preparing for negotiations or contemplating strategies for obtaining acceptable outcomes/agreements. This contrasts with the more systematic approach, frequently adopted by large private sector organisations, and could lead to development control officers being at a considerable disadvantage. Surprisingly, although the development control officers themselves recognise negotiating as an important activity for them, they may have little training in negotiating skills, nor are the demands of negotiating recognised by the organisational or procedural arrangements of their authority.

The need for planner as negotiator

To be effective in their work, town planners need to be skilled at negotiating and should be given the opportunities to practise. Recent literature in Britain and North America has given guidance on the qualities needed for planners to be more effective. According to Forester (1989), planners who ignore those in power 'assume their own powerlessness.' Among the solutions to the problem of their potential powerlessness, Forester proposes strategies for mediated negotiations. He envisages planners engaging in the tasks of negotiating and mediating to address power imbalances which threaten the quality of local planning outcomes. Benveniste (1989) addresses a similar set of issues, also in the American context and sees effective planning as the management of change. He notes that young planners are 'ill equipped to deal with the complex dynamics of networking, coalition building and negotiation.'

In the British context, Thomas and Healey (1991) consider 'the planner as intermediator' as one of the models for the profession in their examination of the role of the planner in practice. From Sheldon and Claydon (1991a) research, 'the involvement of development control officers in negotiations with applicants was surprisingly limited, with case officers involved largely in the collection of information from a number of different sources'. They also noted that the development control process is typified by the involvement of a large number of actors, some more important than others.

> A key aspect of development control work involves the collation of the views of these different actors. (ibid.)

Consequently Sheldon and Claydon conclude that there is a key role for development control officers to reduce conflict among actors and in so doing bring about improvements to the development proposals. Similarly the role of forward planning officers provides opportunities for reconciling the conflicting interests of key actors. The impediment to exploiting these opportunities has also been explored (Sheldon and Claydon (1991b). They concluded that organisational procedures can have a significant effect on the outcome in as much as they restrict the opportunity for effective negotiations. Circumstances highlighted by the authors which appeared to inhibit effective negotiating are

- A series of two or more case officers on a particular site or application, resulting in lack of continuity.
- Limited responsibility delegated to the case officer to determine his or her own recommendation on an application.
- Poor working relations with consultees and other sections of the same department; this leads to difficulties in determining corporate objectives upon which to base negotiations.
- Failure to allocate sufficient time to preparation for negotiations, often due to the difficulty of accommodating negotiations within the routines of the control section, but also due to underestimation of preparation time.

Other authors have studied the role of the planner as negotiator, often concentrating on explicit examples associated with achieving planning gain. For example, Elson and Payne (1992) studied planning obligations for sport and recreation, concentrating on the knowledge and preparation necessary for negotiations. Healey, Purdue and Ennis (1993) researched development impacts and obligations; they advocate a more systematic approach to negotiations based on predetermined scales of obligation in relation to specific types of development. However, the activity of negotiating in planning is far more extensive than those specific (and relatively rare) occasions when the authority and an applicant are attempting to determine the details of a plan-

119

ning agreement. It is in the day-to-day work of planners that opportunities to negotiate are more frequently wasted – when dealing with more mundane applications and routine consultations in devising development plans. Sometimes even, opportunities are lost through a failure to recognise the benefits and potential mutual interests that exist.

Conclusion

This chapter has examined the negotiating opportunities offered to planners by planning practice. Where these opportunities occur, planners may be able to achieve gains for their clients which would otherwise be lost if they were to adopt a strict administrative view of their role. Effective planners need to be skilled negotiators, recognising and utilising opportunities when they occur, and even seeking out opportunities to negotiate with those who may be able to offer the power and resources to achieve planning objectives. It is by the means of negotiation that planning can achieve better environments and can limit the impact of new development. Negotiation should be seen as the essential implementation skill.

PART IV

THE PROCESS IN PRACTICE

INTRODUCTION

This section presents a series of case studies drawn from the Bristol area. Chapter 10 provides information about the nature and planning of Bristol, and the surrounding county of Avon to provide a context for the case studies. Its more discursive style allows it to play devil's advocate, to air misgivings about planning policy and to express opinions which are not necessarily held by all of the other contributors. This approach is intended to offer the reader a more critical approach towards policy matters and towards the objectives of the implementation process. Some of the statutory planning procedures described in this volume can appear very cut and dried, especially when hidden beneath the bureaucratic surface of planning. But below that surface, there is likely to be a seething mass of different opinions, held by the planners, the public and the politicians. As discussed in the final chapters, by answering the question, What do we want? we discover the policies that should be implemented through the planning processes we have described. In particular, Chapter 18 confronts the reader with some alternative proposals on how cities might be planned and designed; it may be useful to look at this chapter after reading Part IV, to compare ideals with realities.

Chapters 11 and 12 are a case study of the York Gate site in Bedminster, on the edge of the central area of Bristol. On this 'difficult' site, the planning consultant, Robin Tetlow, worked to gain planning permission, originally for office development. Chapter 11 considers the wider context of the potential for office development on the site in relation to national, regional and city-wide levels. It discusses implications for the viability of proposal of the planning policy framework, and the related governmental levels of the planning from which they emanate, namely, the national, regional, county, city and local levels. The organisational structure of the planning system is an important factor to take into account, especially in Bristol, where both county and city levels of planning hurdles have to be surmounted. Chapter 12 discusses the process of development in order to illustrate its complexity. Robin Tetlow is a director of the Oldfield King consultancy group and a busy practitioner. He quotes mainly from government circulars, PPGs and statutes as well as from *York Gate: A New Approach to Bedminster* (Oldfield King 1989) produced by his own consultancy. Future developments may be published in the Oldfield King newsletter *Outlook* (Oldfield King 1994).

Chapter 13 is a case study by Jennifer Tempest, responsible for advising a local health trust over the disposal and development of National Health Service land. She, too, takes a somewhat different viewpoint from a local authority, even though health trusts were created out of public bodies. In Chapter 14, Janet Askew describes the development situation in Canon's Marsh, a dockside location in the centre of Bristol. Janet Askew begins Part V with a chapter on the King's Cross site in London, and she compares it with Canon's Marsh. The case studies illustrate the complex factors that influence development decisions, and the changes in pace over the years. The description of the planning situation in Bristol also provides a vehicle for drawing attention to some of the broader planning issues of national concern to planners and public alike. On these issues people are deeply divided.

The chapters in this section demonstrate that, while dealing with the machinations of the public sector, consultants also have to be aware of what is going on in the private sector world of property development. The site is subject to the effects of the varied conditions of the market. The ever changing financial climate will affect the choices of the owners and investors who give the scheme their backing, and the fortunes of the building firms and contractors who take responsibility for turning the proposals into bricks and mortar. In a sense, the planning consultancy might be seen as an interface between the respective worlds of the public and private sectors, each with its own agendas, time-scales and objectives. In fact, the development of one relatively small site can be suprisingly complex. The whole approach to these case studies reflects the importance of consultants in the implementation process, consultants working on behalf of private sector developers to find and apply the relevant sections of planning policy and planning law. If necessary, such policy statements also form the basis of argument on appeal, to strengthen and justify the case for development. The case studies give good illustrations of the different hurdles identified in Part II, all of which have to be overcome in order to produce development, including the different certifications from the various levels of planning authority .

Chapter 10

THE BRISTOL AND AVON CONTEXT

Clara Greed

Planning and land use characteristics

Bristol is a major provincial city in the south-west of England with a population of around half a million (it depends on where you draw the boundary of the city, on geographical or administrative bases). Over a million people live in the whole of Avon including Bristol, and the county of Avon comprises 520 square miles or 1,347 square kilometres (Fig. 10.1). The city of Bristol contains a population of 376,146 (1993). Bristol is a relatively short journey from London along the M4 motorway, or less than a ninety-minute journey by train from Parkway Station or Temple Meads. Bristol was already established as a major city and port, prior to the Industrial Revolution, and was the gateway to the Americas for such explorers as Cabot. Much of its wealth was based on the infamous trade triangle between Africa, Britain and the West Indies along which slaves, spices and sugar were transported. The mercantile wealth is reflected in the central area, historic dock development and surrounding warehouses. It is expressed, in bricks and mortar, in the elegant Georgian development in Clifton and other parts of the inner city. The whole of the central and inner areas of Bristol are covered by a patchwork of urban conservation areas, and Bristol is increasingly, along with Bath, a major tourist destination.

During the nineteenth and first part of the twentieth century the manufacturing base of Bristol grew apace. Through its proximity to the docks, Bedminster, the area discussed by Robin Tetlow, became an important industrial centre with many factories, including the Wills Tobacco factory. Indeed, Bedminster (Fig. 10.2) has many of the characteristics of a Midlands or Northern inner suburb of a factory town, with its small terraced houses and obvious industrial past. However, the area is also skirted by several rows of good quality Georgian housing that dates from earlier affluence around the port developments. Some of the central area of Bristol was bombed during the Second World War, and nowadays the main mass-market, central shopping area of Broadmead constitutes a 1950s postwar reconstruction, which in the 1980s was substantially pedestrianised. More recently the Galleries shopping centre was built in Broadmead, an enclosed, multilevel shopping centre

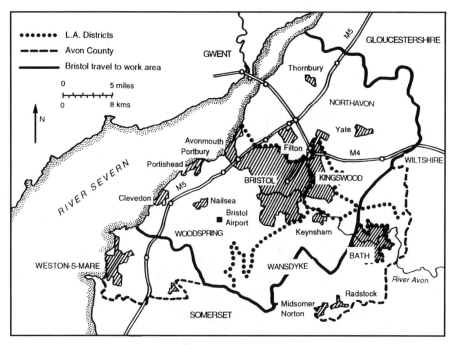

Fig. 10.1 Avon: administrative boundaries

on the sloping site previously occupied by the old Co-op department store, a site referred to later in the book by Linda Davies. In the postwar period, many of the residential areas surrounding the centre, which had not been bombed, were threatened by so-called slum clearance. During the 1960s, when many modern office blocks were built, there was great pressure to demolish anything that was old. But eventually the pendulum swung back towards protection and conservation of Bristol's historical architectural heritage; areas such as Clifton have been preserved for posterity. Punter (1990) in his book *Design Control in Bristol, 1940–1980* gives a detailed account of the development of the urban conservation movement in Bristol.

The historical docklands area of Bristol penetrates right into the centre of the city. However, most shipping nowadays goes to Avonmouth, boats having long outgrown Brunel's lock gates at Cumberland Basin, where the River Avon runs into Avon Gorge beneath the Clifton Suspension Bridge (also built by Brunel). Dockland sites have been redeveloped, and old warehouses refurbished adjacent to the central area. One of the first to be refurbished was the Arnolfini, formerly a tea warehouse and now an art gallery. On the other side of the harbour, the Watershed consists of another arts centre, a row of tourist shops and a restaurant. A colleague from Sydney, Australia, no doubt accustomed to an enormous harbour, overlooked the entire Bristol docks and dismissed them in a single query, 'Where's the rest of it?' In fact, an amazing range of buildings and uses is packed into such a small area.

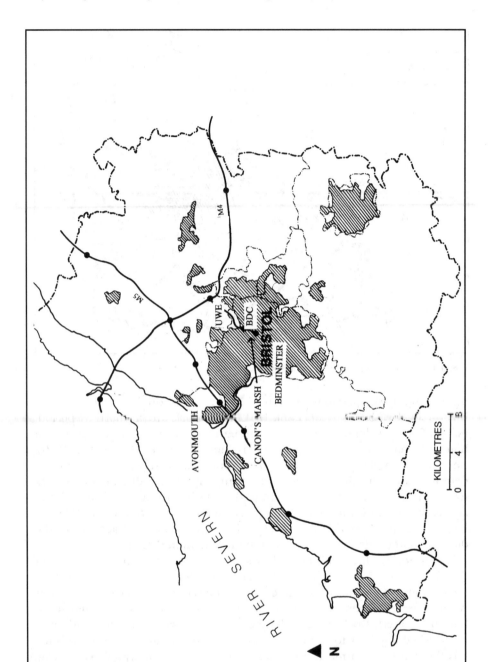

Fig. 10.2 Bristol location map: sites referred to in case studies

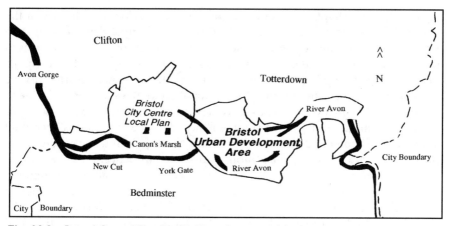

Fig. 10.3 Bristol Central Planning Divisions (not to scale)

The Canon's Marsh site is one of the remaining 'vacant' dockside areas where the choice of planning policy still hangs in the balance. Debates over Canon's Marsh reflect in microcosm so many of the key planning issues and conflicts concerning future policy for Bristol as a whole; some of the issues are set out above (Fig. 10.3).

Canon's Marsh

The Canon's Marsh site is located a short distance from the cathedral, and College Green is one of the few dockland sites which has not yet been developed. At present, this site is used for car parking for commuters (at £4 per day). There have been many proposals for this so-called disused, vacant site, including arts centres, housing and an Olympic-size swimming-pool. But many hard-pressed commuters would say it is not disused; they believe it provides vital car parking for the central area offices. Indeed, there appears to be conflict between tourist/arts/conservation proposals and office/central business district/commuter pressures on all the dockside sites. But according to Janet Askew, the planning authority is not taking a strong lead in sorting out the nature of site development on Canon's Marsh. Long periods of uncertainty, inaction and a somewhat negative approach to development are highlighted in her case study. This contrasts starkly with a surprising *volte-face* in allowing development on the site relatively recently, in the form of the Lloyds Bank European headquarters complex. This scheme took place although it went against all the reasons previously given to keep office development off the site. Undoubtedly Lloyds was quite a catch for Bristol because the bank had looked at several other European cities, including waterfront sites in Amsterdam. The location of the Lloyds offices on the site also illustrates the increasing competition between demands for the extension of central area business district.

Janet Askew's chapter concentrates more on the background history of the planning policy attitudes in relation to this site's potential development than upon a substantive description of exactly what was to go on the site in terms of site layout. This is to demonstrate the complex processes and uncertainty involved in planning implementation. In the past, planners appeared to have far more power than they do today, often manifested in the power to decide to do nothing. The marks of this past period of control over the city, for better or worse, are manifest in the site history of many central area locations, including York Gate (Chapters 12 and 13). There has been great interest among local people about the future of the Canon's Marsh site, with a variety of viewpoints being expressed. Some want to keep it as car parking, especially those commuting in from outside the city to work in the central area offices, although it seems to the editor at least, that this is often seen as an unworthy non-use by some planners. Indeed, it is significant that Lloyds Bank made sure they had their own car park, bringing into use previously disused land, so its workers would not have to compete for spaces with the users of the public car park. Bristol City Council employees working in the council-house (town hall), including those in the planning and highways departments also have their own protected car parking area on Canon's Marsh, currently located under and around the large railway shed. This is seen as somewhat hypocritical bearing in mind the restrictive measures they have introduced for the general public, and the high daily charges to use the Canon's Marsh car park. Proposals to scoop up all the surface parking and put it in multi-storey car parks on the site, thus freeing the ground for other uses, have been considered from time to time. Architecturally this is considered problematic, particularly if the future of the land bounded by the waterfront, College Green and the cathedral is to be the subject of comprehensive urban design planning, possibly to open up townscape vistas across the whole area. Such vistas have not been glimpsed since medieval times, when it really was a marsh and the canon stood in his cathedral tower to watch the ships as they came up the river.

Other groups within the city have favoured different uses, such as housing. There is some resentment, especially among inner city working class communities, about lost opportunities back in the history of the site. Some of the docklands were previously under council ownership and might have been developed for social housing back in the 1970s. But this has been seen as non-revenue producing, an uneconomic waste of a good site, in view of the extremely high land values which developed there in the 1980s, and the pressure on public bodies to dispose of valuable land assets to make up for cut-backs in their funding. Youth groups and sporting interests have long argued for better sports and swimming-pool facilities in the centre, and again Canon's Marsh was proposed as an ideal site for such facilities. Many years ago there was talk of relocating to Canon's Marsh what was then Bristol Polytechnic, now the University of the West of England, but eventually it was relocated on a decentralised, out-of-town site. In summary, the debates about the site reflect the wider Bristol agenda, which revolves around conflicting priorities in respect of urban conservation, housing provision, car parking and transportation, office development and leisure uses. In particular, differences of opinion are marked between commuters seeking parking space; residents of the urban conservation areas seeking to protect the quality of their location; and residents (or would-be residents) of the adjacent, formerly working-class housing areas seeking cheap housing and local employment. Some of the key planning components identified in the debate will now be considered more closely, namely, transportation, overall city structure, conservation and social pressures in Bristol.

Transportation plans

The motor car is a major issue affecting all aspects of planning for Bristol, site-level or city-wide. Car ownership in the Bristol area is higher than the national average, not necessarily because of affluence but because of the somewhat poor bus services in the urban region, and the far-flung, semi-rural nature of many of the hinterland settlements. Traffic and car parking problems abound. Of late there have been various attempts at transportation strategies such as Park and Ride, shortened to PRIDE, as emblazoned on the sides of buses serving these routes. Badgerline (now called First Bus), a private bus company, took over the running of the main bus routes in Bristol and Avon following privatisation, and although there is considerable liaison between the bus company and the local authorities, obviously neither Bristol nor Avon have direct control over public transport, and they have no specific government funding for this purpose. This has affected their chances of implementing effective land use/transportation policy. However, Bristol has been famous for several unsuccessful attempts to introduce a metro (mainly promoted in association with the private sector). A metro is a light surface commuter railway system that can be used to alleviate traffic problems; the Bristol metro was known as the ATA (Advanced Transport for Avon). There is a range of other policies intended to discourage car use as set out in 1993 in the consultation document *Transport Plan 1993–2013* (Avon 1991a), including traffic calming, further parking restrictions and road pricing. None of them are popular with non-planners (or even some planners) because there is no viable alternative means of transport, especially for those living further into the county, outside the area some commuters now call Fortress Bristol. Avon as the county authority is the strategic highways and transportation authority, whereas Bristol City is the local parking authority for the city district.

City structure and decentralisation

The emphasis upon decentralisation accompanied by restrictive land use zoning, moving both industry and housing out to greenfield sites, was a feature of postwar town planning throughout Britain). It has no doubt contributed towards, if not created, the transportation problems Bristol now faces. In contrast, office development was for many years the subject of centralising policies, which enforced high central area land values. From the 1960s onwards, Bristol became an increasingly popular location for office decentralisation away from London. But more recently, office development too has begun to relocate in out-of-town locations. For example, a business park was built at Aztec West, near the motorways to the north of Bristol and adjacent to a massive new area of housing development at Bradley Stoke, which stretches from the motorway across to Parkway Station. The University of the West of England (UWE) is itself decentralised in this vicinity, located at Frenchay. This location may be bad for students (and lecturers) as it is miles from anywhere, with no local banks, shops or facilities beyond what is provided by the Students' Union, and it requires a car or adequate bus service to reach. Ironically, while many decentralised in order to escape the congestion of the central area, now the out-of-town locations themselves are becoming overcrowded and clogged with traffic and parking problems. The locality around UWE is gradually being taken over by other decentralised users and new high technology firms, including Du Pont, Hewlett Packard, several insurance companies and imminently the Ministry of Defence administrative offices, currently under development. Years ago, when the decision was first made to relocate, there were planning proposals to create a new second city centre in the Frenchay area to the north of Bristol, with a proper local infrastructure and public transport linkages. Over the intervening thirty years or so this became transmuted into a car oriented out of town growth area. Apparently, one of the reasons for the decision was that one of the more influential councillors owned farm land up there. Major developmental decisions are by no means always the result of rational decision making, but are the result of the capricious choices made by individual personalities, with long-term sub-optimal results.

Retail development decentralisation is also taking place, centred around Cribbs Causeway, near the M4/M5 motorway intersection to the north-west of the conurbation. Recently, for example, there were proposals for Lewises, one of the main department stores in Broadmead, to relocate there following in the wake of many large furniture stores and the electricity showroom. Interestingly, no food outlets have yet appeared at Cribbs Causeway. But there is talk of turning it into a new centre in its own right, particularly if the local government reorganisation effectively separates the north of Bristol from the south. On the other hand, there has been a rash of out-of-town applications for hypermarkets and yet more Tesco stores. Although it is understandable that those with cars want to shop where they can be assured of a parking space and later opening hours, there is serious concern about this trend. Those without cars, be they elderly, young, poor or disabled, have their options severely limited if one has to have a car to get anywhere. In the case of food shopping, it could have serious implications for people's survival, where bus routes and helpful neighbours are non-existent. More broadly, the current trend towards decentralisation undoubtedly increases motor traffic, and is therefore bad for congestion of the environment and fundamentally goes against the principles of logical, economic, sustainable, green development. It will be interesting to see whether PPG 13 stems the flow.

Urban conservation

In Bristol some would argue that the city went through a veritable anti-urban phase in the postwar period, in which traditional central area manufacturing and industrial uses (not office and retail development) were discouraged because of some misdirected desire to clean up the city. This was accompanied by an emphasis on demolition and extinguishment of so-called nonconforming uses such as one might find in the industrial heart of the city around the docklands. Along with this attitude went a disdain for anything old, with large areas of housing development being condemned for slum clearance, including areas such as High Kingsdown, or allowed to run down, such as Hotwells; both are now conservation areas. The urban conservation movement which developed in the 1970s might be seen as a reaction. It would seem that the city planners went from one extreme to the other, swinging from a demolition/decentralisation hit-and-run attitude to planning, to an overprotectionist/conservationist mentality, neither approach necessarily benefiting sites such as Canon's Marsh.

In particular it is amenity and conservation interests which have been prominent in discussions over Canon's Marsh. Yet, ironically, one of the reasons Bristol was so slow in encouraging development of the site was because of its rather rigid conservation policy which did not allow much flexibility. Conservation is a hot potato in Bristol, but conservationists are not a unitary group; there are many viewpoints on how conservation policy should be applied. Perhaps some of the conservation groups are somewhat elitist and protectionist in outlook, whereas other so-called conservation groups are really community groups in all but name, seeking to ensure a well-balanced, well-planned city, which takes into account all the social and economic considerations as well as the more visual and design factors. Much of the discourse of the planning agenda in Bristol since the late 1970s has been couched in terms of conservation language. Indeed, it has become an effective vehicle of complaint among pressure groups, who in other cities might package their demands in other terminology, such as a concern with transport or economic issues in order to get taken seriously by the planners. But until recently, other issues have received possibly less 'space' than conservation; issues related to the more social agenda of town planning, such as meeting demands for women-and-planning policies (Little 1994). Nevertheless, the emphasis upon urban conservation has generally been seen as doing more good than harm. In particular, Bristol is nowadays seen as an attractive city, and therefore a magnet to firms and individuals wishing to relocate. Planners have been in a strong position to require high standards of design in central area locations because of the strength of urban conservation policy measures, for example, a mosaic of protective urban conservation areas covering the whole of the city centre.

Social problems

Although Bristol is relatively prosperous and has become a white-collar city, compared with its blue-collar past, there are still strong socio-economic contrasts among its population. In the inner city, prosperous gentrified areas such as Kingsdown are found in close geographical proximity to deprived areas such as St. Pauls. A range of detailed case studies of different parts of Bristol have been undertaken from a more sociological perspective such as the work of Bassett and Short (1980) which gives attention to the class dimensions of urban structure, an important issue in what some see as a deeply divided city. It is also worth consulting publications by the School of Advanced Urban Studies (SAUS), effectively a graduate planning school, and a part of Bristol University. Attempts have been made to research and plan deprived areas such as St. Pauls (Bristol 1985); these are carried through into current planning documents for Bristol (Bristol 1993a), but they still seem somewhat separate from the main policy areas pursued. Occasional reference to policies from this plan, especially social and access policies, will be made in future chapters. One senses that, apart from giving attention to the more newsworthy deprived areas, such social planning activities are somewhat marginal to the main thrust of emphasis on urban conservation, with less attention being given to the more mundane, day-to-day needs of the ordinary people of Bristol. There are very clear demarcations in wealth and poverty within the city (Bristol 1985).

Areas in Bedminster were still struggling with the effects of planning blight brought on by a previous generation of planning policy in the 1960s and 1970s (see Chapter 11). In areas like St. Pauls in the inner city ring to the north of the city centre, male, black, unemployment might be 60% in some streets; and female unemployment although lower, is reduced only because women get low paid jobs in the retail and service sector. The trapped inner urban old and poor in St. Pauls may have little time for the residents of the gentrified conservation areas bordering on their territory (Bristol 1985). Clearly new development, or indeed refurbishment of older properties, should not intrinsically be taken as an indicator of a better urban life for everyone, although in terms of implementation achievements and public relations, new development always looks good. Instead, one needs to consider who lost their homes, who was relocated or who was compulsorily purchased when development took place. This is illustrated in the discussion on the establishment of Bristol Development Corporation (BDC) towards the end of this chapter (BDC 1990). And while some areas have become gentrified by middle-class groups, in parallel with the growing extent of the city's urban conservation policy, other groups have been displaced to poorer areas or are homeless; Bristol has a high rate of homelessness for such an apparently prosperous city.

There has been a growing trend on the part of the present government over the last ten years to target run-down inner city residential and industrial areas by the creation of enterprise zones (EZs), urban development corporations (UDCs) and a whole range of other more social initiatives such as City Challenge, the emphasis being upon private sector enterprise (Volume I, pp. 136–138). Some would argue that central government is tightening its grip on local authorities through such policies and getting them to compete with each other for money that should rightfully be theirs in the first place, were it not for rate-capping and other local government cut-backs. Undoubtedly, the nature of what is on offer in terms of central and local government finance, the relationship between the two, and who holds the purse strings are major factors in shaping the chances for the implementation of planning policy objectives. Bristol has competed for a variety of special status initiatives. Run-down areas such as Hartcliffe, a council estate to the south of the city, and St. Pauls, an inner city area, are apparently not generally seen as bad enough to warrant the sort of funding provided by City Challenge to some Northern cities and inner areas of London. In fact, Bristol planners have sought to monitor social deprivation in these areas (Bristol 1985). Bristol as part of the South-West is seen by many, often falsely, as an affluent area throughout, whereas Avon is still seen by some as a place for holidays, not as a potential area of urban deprivation or rural homelessness and unemployment. Interestingly, certain more rural parts of the subregion are currently being considered more favourably in respect of EU funding.

The Bristol Development Corporation Area

Although Bristol has not been particularly successful in having its social problems and needs recognised in respect of the poorer areas of the city, it has somewhat paradoxically acquired an urban development corporation (UDC), namely, the Bristol Development Corporation (BDC), but has not been eligible for an EZ or for special regional status (BDC 1990) (see Fig. 10.3). The Bristol Urban Development Area (BUDA), is the same as the BDC. The BUDA area runs east from Temple Meads Station along the River Avon besides Totterdown. Current typical developments in the BUDA include a fourteen-screen cinema, Burger King and a central industrial park at St. Philips (covering only one small section of the site); in Spring 1994 it was 85% let. There is also some classier development being undertaken at

Temple Meads and Kingsley Village in the western corner of the site. The BDC initiative has generally not been particularly welcomed either by Avon or Bristol City. This is because the local planners and developers were already making considerable progress, working their way along from the revitalised central docklands area, upstream. The area designated would most likely have been redeveloped in any case, without central government stepping in. Indeed the BUDA area is comprised of mainly derelict and run-down old industrial areas, such as around St. Anne's Board Mills, and land backing on to the Totterdown area. But it avoids some of the more needy areas, stopping short of Bedminster (as explained by Robin Tetlow) and also keeping deftly away from areas such as St. Pauls.

It would seem that both Bristol and Avon are frequently united in relation to their attitudes to the policies emanating from the BDC. The BDC is funded from central government and was established to be completely separate; it is not answerable to either the county or city authorities. The BDC does not have to obtain planning permission from either authority to carry out development, an apparently ideal world for itself, at least in terms of effecting fast implementation of policy. The reason for this was to create an entrepreneurial organisation intended to speed up the planning process, similar to the idea behind the new town development corporations, which also existed in splendid isolation from the administrative area in which they were located. Ironically, while local government finance is being cut back, money is available to the BDC for development, especially of initial infrastructure; the idea is that after pump-priming has occurred they will become financially competitive without subsidy.

The BDC has its own agenda and plans for the development of the area; a key feature is the development of a spine road to facilitate access to the more remote parts of the site. Unfortunately, this spine road was not seen as tying in with Avon County's highway policies, nor did it seem to connect particularly to Bristol City's traffic policies, indeed the new road appeared to encourage more traffic to come into the city, but once there it would not link up rationally with existing city-wide networks and transportation strategies. Ideas of grandiose road building, including elevated highways, have the feel of 1960s, Los Angeles, no longer fashionable or politically correct in Britain. The BDC was truly dubbed the cuckoo in the nest. There were also fears at the beginning that all this emphasis on new dynamic development would undermine the city's commitment to conservation policy, but it would seem that the BDC respects this policy, has carried out a detailed survey of all historically significant features in its area and is apparently committed to conservation itself, blending the old with the new. The BDC proposals, far from facilitating local Bristol based development, seem to have done little for all the York Gate proposals of this world waiting for the opportune moment to develop when the surrounding road network or development climate becomes more favourable to the site in question. Indeed, some have described UDC policy as using a sledgehammer to crack a nut, or as the proverbial bull in a china shop, riding roughshod over existing schemes, previous hope values, local businesses and small-scale grass roots development projects.

The situation became particularly heated when it was realised that existing housing would have to be demolished to improve access to the BDC area. Likewise some small factory units, to which local businesses had been relocated, owing to a previous redevelopment scheme by Bristol, were now to be demolished because they were in the way of the new road system. It was ironical that, in order to revitalise the inner city, existing businesses and industries which were already being 'revitalised' had to be disturbed. Nowadays it would seem that different levels of planning, those administered at the local government level and those funded at the central government level, may potentially be in conflict. However, in the case of the Bristol BDC, as time has gone on, it might be said that confrontational attitudes have softened somewhat and that more of the local community, businesses and property fraternity have been drawn under its spell. In order to make progress, some *modus vivendi* needed to be established, requiring considerable negotiation and adjustment to take place on all sides. Ironically, in view of the current property recession and further government cut-backs, which are now even affecting UDCs and other such enterprise projects, it would seem that little more development potential is going to be achieved by making the area a UDC at vast expense than would have occurred if the area had been left in the hands of the 'local' local planning authorities.

Relevant statutory plans

In the case studies, references are made to the various plans and planning policy documents which have governed planning policy in respect of the sites under discussion. Some of the documents mentioned by individual authors are only referred to in general terms; they are not specifically referenced. This is because they are now virtually unobtainable, having long since been superseded; perhaps one dog-eared copy languishes in some reference library, although in its time it may have shaped the fortunes of whole areas. In summary, prior to 1974 Bristol City had produced a series of development plans under the 1947 Town and Country Planning Act, mainly consisting of zoning maps with some additional policy documents and policy review material in the late 1960s. In 1974, following local government reorganisation, the development plan function – to produce a modern structure plan – was handed over to Avon, which subsequently produced a series of Avon structure plans (Avon 1980). Generally speaking, these structure plans have taken many years to go through the approval and revision procedure and some quite major changes in policy direction have occurred over the years, particularly when there has been a change of political masters.

As will be explored in relation to York Gate, there is an uneasy relationship between Avon and Bristol over a whole range of planning matters. This is because the planning functions are split according to the two-tier system explained in Chapter 2. Following imminent local government reorganisation, in 1996 major planning functions will return to Bristol City and it will again be responsible for the production of its own autonomous development plan, as was the case before the previous reorganisation in 1974. In anticipation of this change, Bristol has over the last couple of years produced two substantial documents: the *Bristol Local Plan* (Bristol 1993a) and the *City Centre Draft Local Plan* (Bristol 1990). Town plan making requires the creation of effective planning units; two questions are fundamental: where to draw the boundaries and how large to make each area. The administrative county of Avon covers much of the commuter catchment area of the conurbation. Yet there are instances of people commuting from much further afield to Bristol; and people from Bristol regularly commute to London. Yet, there are also people who live their whole lives within one little area of Bristol and seldom stray outside the conurbation. Some of the case studies, especially those related to the packaging of policy within development plans, may cast more light on the problem of how large an area to take as an appropriate planning unit.

As explained in Volume I (p. 28 ff.), local authorities, in the interim, also prepare a range of non-statutory *ad hoc* plans which are 'adopted' by the local planning committee and eventually incorporated in subsequent revisions in the development plan. Grant (1990, 148) has commented that the government puts limited weight on such bottom-drawer plans when it comes to appeal, but in the case of Bristol, where urban change and expansion has been rapid, such innovative plans, reports and policy statements have formed an important component of written policy. A particular problem has been that county authorities are meant to produce their structure plan in time to guide the districts (including Bristol City) before they produce their own local plans. In fact Bristol City surged ahead, producing a collection of impressive local plans through the 1970s and 1980s, while Avon plodded along with its more traditional land use based structure plan. And Bristol City was a pioneer in urban conservation, producing policy documents covering many separate conservation areas, and later combining some of the key principles into a design guide format. Bedminster has been covered by a local plan since the late 1970s and part of it is subject to conservation area policy; statements from these policy documents were used effectively in negotiations over the Bedminster site (Bedminster 1980 and updates). But it should also be borne in mind that Avon as highways authority and county planning authority sometimes had its own, somewhat contrasting, ideas about the future of the area. Over the years, there has been a considerable amount of planning blight and concern over road widening, affecting the development potential of key sites in the area and the lives of its residents.

Rural and subregional environs

Other factors to look out for in the case studies are policy references in relation to rural and urban fringe sites, particularly in the chapter by Jennifer Tempest on green belt development proposals. Although much of this book centres on urban issues, Avon is a suprisingly rural county, incorporating areas formerly part of Somerset or Gloucestershire. The whole of Avon may be seen as a tourist destination in its own right, especially the city of Bath. Avon is a gateway to the South-West and to a wide range of seaside towns and holiday resorts, such as Weston-super-Mare. It has motorways and rail routes running into the Deep South West to Devon, Dorset and Cornwall; others lead into Wales. In summer, there are even paddle-steamer services. Although the population of South Wales, in particular Newport and Cardiff, are geographically close to Bristol, there appears to be a major psychological and cultural division, perhaps accentuated by the high toll charge on the Severn Bridge. Historically, South Wales has been a strong industrial area subject to a quite different set of government policies, regional economic grants and development objectives. The Welsh Development Agency (WDA) is responsible for a massive programme of reclamation and restoration of areas ravaged by years of mining, slag-heaps and heavy industrial activity. In contrast, the Avon area is not the subject of any special regional policy or grants, but the Bristol Development Corporation has been established to help regenerate the inner area of the city and does receive government funding.

Conclusion

The planning situation in Bristol has been presented, perhaps partly from the viewpoint of a devil's advocate, in order to highlight the complex problems of site development and implementation. Any new scheme or road programme is bound to affect other surrounding sites and schemes, rather like throwing a stone into a pond and watching the ripples move outwards. Whether the Bristol situation is typical or unique is for readers to judge on the basis of making comparisions with other cities. Various contributors cite the work of Professor Patsy Healey, who has written on the situation in Newcastle upon Tyne. Indeed, comparisons between Bristol and Newcastle, at opposite ends of the country, might prove fascinating as a research study to gaining insights on the North/South divide. Both cities are important provincial 'capitals' but are arguably quite different. Healey points out that some of the more economically depressed regions of Britain never experienced the great pressures for development that occurred in London and in prosperous provincial cities such as Bristol during the property boom of the 1980s (Healey 1993). Therefore it was less likely that planners in Newcastle could extract planning gain from developers to the extent possible in Bristol.

She comments that cities such as Newcastle looked more to the planners than to the private market in seeking the revitalisation of the city. Implementation of planning policy should not be dependent upon trends in the property market. According to Healey, the situation in Newcastle indicates that consistent local urban planning policy can be a steadying influence, helping to level out the helter-skelter of troughs and highs which occur in an unregulated property market and thus preventing sudden, opportunistic policy decisions which might later prove regrettable. Effective implementation should be planner-led not developer-led.

Chapter 11

YORK GATE: CONTEXT

Robin Tetlow

A difficult site

The York Gate site is located on the outer edge of the central area of
Bristol to the east (Fig. 11.1) It is virtually a corner site, located beside a
major roundabout, at the convergence of a high street, serving an inner
city local district, and several major commuter routes into the centre. The
consultants became involved with this site from approximately 1987, when
the intention was to seek approval for office development across the
whole site. This was subsequently revised, and by late 1994 housing development was completed on part of the site. The York Gate site is
approximately 1.8 hectares (4.5 acres) in area; it comprises the site of a
derelict glue factory and some disused buildings, together with numbers
42–64 York Road.

Numbers 42–64 York Road comprise unoccupied houses in urgent need
of refurbishment. They are very run-down, but potentially a very elegant set
of buildings which form part of a Grade 2 listed late Georgian terrace
(built between 1790 and 1802) which originally continued along the whole
of York Road. York Road is an important secondary traffic route which runs
besides the New Cut. The New Cut is part of the river/canal system which
feeds the docks in the central area; it was built by prisoners from the
Napoleonic War. Across the cut there is a collection of high-rise council
flats, which in recent years have been refurbished somewhat colourfully.
There are relatively few examples of high-rise in Bristol, compared with
similar sized cities. It has been suggested that these flats have potential for
privatisation as occurred in the London Docklands, but they are currently
serving an important social need, they are relatively quiet and they are not
characterised by crime or vandalism. The overall impression is somewhat
seedy, but the area has great potential because of its proximity to the
centre. Indeed, several other sections of the terrace further along York
Road are now being refurbished, mainly by housing associations, whereas
other sections remain derelict.

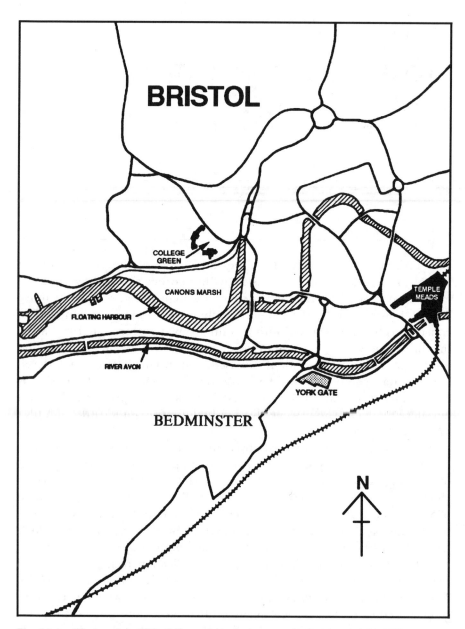

Fig. 11.1 The location of York Gate within Bedminster (scale approx 1:20,000)

The socio-economic context and the office market

The national context

Since the original trigger for development was for office provision, because of a perceived demand for more office space near to the centre of Bristol at the time of the property boom in the 1980s, the first section provides a discussion of the office development context which generated the demand for office development in the first place. The growth of the office function is an ongoing trend, an expression of the evolution of industrial societies from a manufacturing base to a service-dominated economy during the course of the twentieth century (Cowan 1969). In this process the following factors have been important:

- The expansion of transportation and public utilities as auxiliary services in the movement of industrial goods. The related expansion of administrative organisations and services.
- The expansion of finance, insurance and professional services caused by the mass consumption of goods and growth of population.
- The expansion of the personal services sector as people have higher marginal increments of disposable income to spend on business and insurance.
- The expansion of health and education services as these become fundamentally important to the quality of life, and more recently the introduction of internal markets and privatisation to such services.
- The expansion of the financial and business sectors of the British economy, nationally and internationally.
- The growth of white-collar workers, middle-class and professional groups, increased incomes, home and car ownership and consumer expenditure.

It would seem that office development is always a good bet and likely to be required in spite of temporary troughs in demand. However, even this cannot necessarily be taken for granted in view of the great strides that have been made in telecommunications, especially telecommuting (in which people work at home or in neighbourhood-based modem-linked centres). This chapter argues that there is still a need among particular sectors of the business community for certain types of central area office provision. (Goddard 1975; Price and Blair 1989: Ch. 9, Finance and Property Development)

Regional economic policy

Office expansion has been increasingly concentrated in regional centres such as Bristol. This has, in part, been because of previous government policies which restricted growth in London and the South-East and encouraged relocation to the provinces. Also Bristol itself has moved from being a primarily manufacturing based city towards becoming an administrative and financial services centre. Bristol has also actively sought to make itself an attractive location by promoting arts and leisure facilities and pursuing high quality urban conservation policies, such as the strategies encapsulated in the regeneration of the central area docklands (see Chapter 14). The trend of office expansion in Bristol has manifested itself as pressure for central area development and as development of out-of-town office parks and hi-tech developments such as Aztec West near to the M4/M5 motorway intersection to the north-west of Bristol (Massey *et al.* 1992). Research has shown that as a city becomes larger it accumulates office space at a greater rate than it acquires population (Daniels 1975; Bell 1974), so there is always likely to be a great deal of demand.

City-level trends

In spite of outward location trends, particularly in the case of new computer related development in the high technology sector, offices are still probably the most important centripetal (inward moving) force in urban development at a time when centrifugal (outward moving) trends in retailing, industry and population are characteristic of most metropolitan areas. However, this centripetal movement is countered by the undoubted erosion in the accessibility of major metropolitan city centres through congestion and parking problems. In particular, Bristol City Planning Department has operated a somewhat restrictive parking policy within the central area. Also as the redevelopment of the docklands continues, areas such as Canon's Marsh, which for many years provided essential commuter parking, are no longer going to be available for this function. Significantly, there are somewhat higher parking allowances for new development in the inner ring immediately surrounding the centre; this ring includes the York Gate site.

There are definite signs that some office functions are being decentralised to out-of-town locations, but the need for accessibility and the effects of agglomeration economies are still important to many key businesses which depend on traditional face-to-face contact within the central area. With increasing specialisation of certain sectors of office activity, such as those related to financial services, there is still a demand for sites that enable a high degree of interdependency, interaction and linkages. There are other less tangible factors at work, possibly tradition and familiarity with central area locations, but the fact remains that office functions continue to generate high-level values especially in central areas. Sites such as York Gate, just within walking distance of the centre but not subject to the stricter planning and parking controls of the central business district, are potentially ideal sites for office development. Readers of Volume I will no doubt recognise the York Gate site as a classic example of a site in the zone of transition. According to the Chicago concentric zone theorists, it is a run-down zone of lodging-houses and working-class housing that is being colonised by expansion of the central business district (Volume I, p. 218).

Although there is ongoing demand for office floor space, the take-up and the level of provision tend to be characterised by peaks and troughs. The imperfections of the land market in general are especially pronounced in the particular case of the office market. The supply of office space is a cyclical process which responds to the economic climate. The office market is more sensitive to economic fluctuations than any other sector of the economy. In the city centre, physical space constraints are bound to cause a shortage of development sites. This is especially so in the case of Bristol, where most of the central area is also covered by conservation area policy, strict parking controls and a range of policies which have sought to modify land use mix beyond exclusively office development. However, there is also evidence that the most prestigious companies will always pay large sums of money for the right site in metropolitan areas, regardless of the state of the general market, consequently fuelling high central area land and rental values. The office market is never in equilibrium and periods of high demand are often followed by gluts. Office development potential is also linked to demand and supply factors in the wider construction industry, in terms of demand for labour, skills and building materials. It is significant that when the property market began to decline in the late 1980s, demand continued in Bristol well after London was gripped by recession. However, there is a direct relationship between the office market and inner city decay, as illustrated by this case study. York Gate's location on the edge of the central business district gives it marginal development potential. Before considering the site development history it is necessary to consider in more detail the ways in which the planning system has affected the development potential of this particular site, as manifested in the various levels and in the different policy statements.

The planning policy framework

National policy and guidance

Before dealing with the progress of the planning application, it is necessary to look at the different policy statements from the various levels of the planning system, statements that affect the potential nature of the development. On the York Gate site, the consultant needs to consider the adequacy of the planning framework, the opportunities it offers, the problems of decline and the demands for development. The planning policy context is constantly changing; the application for mixed development was being considered in late 1980s when the planning policy statements were putting greater emphasis upon the needs of businesses, especially small businesses, and there were attempts to make the planning system less onerous for developers, as illustrated by guidance from a range of circulars and planning policy guidance notes.

Government circulars and planning policy guidance notes (PPGs) had increasingly emphasised the presumption in favour of development (Circular 22/80, *Development Control: Policy and Practice 14/85*, and PPG 1 *General Policy and Principles*) Circular 14/85 *Development and Employment* and the White Paper *Lifting the Burden* (1985, Cmnd No. 9517) stressed the need to provide the right balance between 'the needs of development and the interests of conservation.' The White Paper reiterated a basic principle of planning law, namely, that permission should be granted unless there are 'sound, relevant and clear-cut reasons for refusal.' It further added 'there is always a presumption in favour of allowing applications for development, having regard to all material considerations unless that development would cause demonstrable harm to interests of acknowledged importance.'

Government advice, at the time of initial development discussions, made it clear that local plans should be only one material consideration in the determination of planning applications. DoE Circular 14/85 'Development and Employment' stated that development plans:

> cannot be expected to anticipate every need or opportunity for economic development that may arise. They should not be regarded as over-riding other material considerations, especially where the Plan does not deal adequately with new types of development or is no longer relevant to today's needs and conditions – particularly the need to encourage employment and to provide the right conditions for economic growth. (Paragraph 5).

Although changes in government policy, as reflected in the Planning and Compensation Act of 1991, have subsequently modified the above so there is now a general presumption in favour of the development plan – towards a plan-led planning system – there is as yet no clear evidence that this change of attitude has had a fundamental effect on the operation of the development control system.

Planning Policy Guidance Note 4, 'Industrial and Commercial Development and Small Firms', refers to the vital role of industrial and commercial development in the expansion of the economy and of employment. This was also emphasised in Circulars 2/86 *Development by Small Businesses*, and 13/87, *Changes in the Use of Buildings and Other Land*.

> Development should be prevented or restricted only where this serves a clear planning purpose and the economic effects have been taken into account. Development control must avoid placing unjustifiable obstacles in the way of any development especially if it is for industry, commerce, housing or any other purpose relevant to economic prosperity.
>
> (PPG 4, para 2)

Circular 16/84, and PPG 4 *Industrial and Commercial Development and Small Firms* (previously 1988, revised 1992) also emphasise that full use should be made of potential employment sites in inner city areas and recommend flexibility over their permitted uses. Paragraph 12 of PPG 4 states that policies intended to prevent speculative building are seldom justified. For a planning consultant seeking to develop a difficult site, these policy statements are all-important negotiating points in dealing initially with the relevant planning authority and they provide potential defences in any subsequent appeal, should the application for change of use and new development be rejected.

The change in the Use Classes Order of 1987 introduced a new B1 business class at the same time as it swept away many of the old Victorian uses by an overall modernisation and simplification of its categories. The new B1 (Table 3.1) allows for more modern 'office' uses and mixes of such uses, which reflected the impact of modern computer based technology in the office and manufacturing workplace. This is particularly important in the case of Bristol, at the end of the Golden Corridor of microchip manufacturers and hi-tech offices alongside the M4 (Massey et al. 1992). In Bristol, the more visible of these developments are to be found in the office parks and the out-of-town locations.

The creation of B1 was to reflect the greater blurring and complexity of definitions. B1 includes all office uses not serving the general public, R&D uses and any industrial process which could be carried out in any residential area without detriment to amenity. The use classes order also includes an unrestricted right to transfer from B2 (general industrial uses) to B1. The overall effect is to introduce more flexibility within employment uses. The site of the derelict glue works on the York Street location, was previously used for industrial purposes. If the factory were still standing, there would be a right to use it for B1 purposes. DoE Circular 8/87, *Historic Buildings and Conservation Areas* (now superceded by PPG 15, *Historic Buildings and Conservation*) gives advice on the policies and procedures concerning listed buildings and conservation areas in England. 'New Uses for Listed Buildings', Paragraph 19 of Circular 8/87, helped to argue the case for new uses at the York Street site on the grounds that they 'may often be the key to their preservation.'

> In many cases it must be accepted that the continuation of the original use is not now a practical proposition and it will often be essential to find appropriate alternative uses.

In general, the emphasis was on both flexibility and practicality in making decisions on listed building applications. The circular was favourable to office development or any other use which retained the character of a listed building. This reflects the purpose of conservation policy which is not to turn buildings into museums, at great cost and no financial return, but rather to see them as part of the living fabric of the city, as buildings lived in and worked in, just like any other buildings, as discussed in Volume I, Chapter 9, on 'Urban and Regional Conservation'. This is particularly important in the case of Bristol, because the whole central area, and much of the surrounding 'inner city' ring around the centre is now completely covered by a patchwork of conservation areas containing many listed buildings.

The Bristol planning policy framework

TWO-TIER SYSTEM

The conurbation of Bristol is subject to two planning systems. Avon County Council is responsible for producing the structure plan, that is, the main development plan, a county-wide document which sets out the large-scale, policy statements in respect of the main land uses (as specified originally in the *Development Plan Manual* (Department of the Environment 1972b) now updated in the *Good Practice Guide* (Department of the Environment 1992a). The City of Bristol lost its historical city powers following local government reorganisation in the early 1970s; strictly speaking it is a second-tier local district planning authority. (The two-tier system of local government was explained in Chapter 2, of Volume I, and see Fig. 2.1 of that chapter). Obviously there is likely to be some difference of opinion between two such major planning authorities, especially over strategic land use and transportation matters, particularly considering the development plans since the war had previously been produced by Bristol City (under the 1947 Town and Country Planning Act). It was important that negotiations over the site satisfied representatives of both levels, county and city, not only in respect of town planning matters, but also in dealing with Avon as highways authority. This situation may not exist much longer as the future of the County of Avon is being considered by the Local Government Boundary Commission as briefly explained in Chapter 6.

COUNTY STRUCTURE PLAN POLICY

The planning policies of relevance to the development of the York Gate site were those set out by the Avon County Structure Plan (incorporating the first alteration and second alteration as approved by the secretary of state in 1989) and guiding development between 1985 and 1996. As a starting point, Bristol was earmarked in Policy E2 of the Avon Structure Plan as a major employment centre, essential to the continued growth of the economy of Avon. But detailed employment policies did not reflect the B1 category established in the Use Classes Order of 1987 and offices were separately identified. Bristol was subdivided into various areas in Policy E15. The site was not included in the Bristol Central Area where 185,000 square metres of office floor space was proposed. Instead, it fell just out of the central zone, into the Bristol Inner/Suburban Area where 25,000 square metres of office floor space was proposed. In Policy E16 it was emphasised that where office development was proposed in conservation areas, or if it affected a listed building, it would be expected that the developer would make a positive contribution to conservation (conservation gain). By April 1990 the total supply of office space in the Bristol Inner/Suburban Policy Area was 122,973 square metres. This was calculated by adding up developments completed since 1985, sites under construction and sites with planning permission.

The 'limit' of 25,000 square metres, therefore, had already been breached by 400%. Although 42% of the total consisted of schemes merely with planning permission, that is, they had not yet been built, it is clear that in practice the structure plan policy had been of little significance in controlling the office market and had already been discredited by the time the York Gate application was entered (incorporating a further 13,000 square metres of office space).

It is important that the secretary of state in his approval letter of the original structure plan in 1985 (Avon 1980 contains the original policy documents) noted that the panel had expressed concern that the figure for the provision of gross floor area for office use in Bristol Central Area in Policy E15 was so unrealistic that it was below the figure of valid or implemented permissions (para 4.4). Later he 'notes that the County Council consider that a substantial increase should be made in the inner and suburban Policy Areas of Bristol' (para 3.8, secretary of state's approval letter of the first alteration to the Avon Structure Plan, Dec 1988). Although he decided not to modify the policy, he 'would wish the County Council to keep the position under review and if necessary submit further alterations.'

Local planning framework

It is significant that the site was included within the area covered by the Bedminster Local Plan adopted by Bristol City in 1989, rather than in the area covered by the draft city centre plan published later the same year. The site in fact lies adjacent to the boundary of the two plans. The local plan (Bedminster 1980) identified eight key sites that required special policies because the city council believed that land use controls alone would not be adequate to provide proper guidance for the future. Among the eight key sites were

The site of the former glue works, Bedminster Parade and York Road: a major objective of the city council was the ongoing redevelopment of the site with high quality buildings, in sympathy with adjoining historic buildings. The land use policy was that housing, shopping, or industry together with ancillary offices would be acceptable. But any proposal had to accord with a set of planning criteria.

Numbers 42–64 York Road: the major objective of the city council was to retain and rehabilitate these listed buildings. The presumption, therefore, was in favour of residential development. Any proposals had to accord with a specified set of planning criteria for the area.

The concern to ensure the retention and rehabilitation of the listed buildings, numbers 42–64, was first set out in the York Road study carried out by Roger Wilson in 1984. Its purpose was

to put forward a firm programme for upgrading the historic buildings and finding suitable uses for the associated derelict land in York Road.

It is significant that the York Road study emphasised the advantages of utilising the site of the former glue works for offices. It pointed out the good access to the city centre and major roads, the adequate population for a workforce close by, the good shopping facilities close by and the potential for providing suitable car parking. The concept of the proposals is similar to that envisaged by Roger Wilson. It was recognised in the adopted Bedminster Local Plan that there has been a large drop in industrial employment and, although Bedminster has less severe problems than other areas of Bristol, there is a recognised need to bring employment to the area south of the River Avon. The city council expressed its major employment objective:

> To secure a continuing role for Bedminster as a source of employment for people living over a wide area. Despite the general trend towards a fall in the total number of jobs in the inner city areas, the City Council believes it was vital that jobs continued to be available in these areas. This will enable more efficient use of limited land resources and keep work journeys short.

The council preferred any new employment created in the area to be of manufacturing type and 'to contribute positively to the creation of a better living environment.'

In relation to offices, the plan stated that since sufficient land is available for the foreseeable future in Bristol Central Area, there was little reason to contemplate large-scale office development in Bedminster at that time (para 4.5.1). In the light of recent demand, this assumption was highly questionable. The planning framework was complicated by the designation of 900 acres of land within Bristol Central/Inner Area as part of the urban development corporation. The development corporation were approving office sites within the Bristol Urban Development Area (BUDA) and the employment policies were independent of structure plan allocations. Bristol City Council had stated that a policy of restraint should be adopted in respect of part of the central area falling within the BUDA. If consents were granted for excessively large office schemes within the BUDA this could effectively use up the structure plan floor space allocation, starving the rest of the central area of office investment. There was, however, a large element of uncertainty associated with the BUDA proposals. A revised land use strategy had recently been published in August 1990, but given likely delays in the construction of the north–south link road, crucial to the success of the whole BUDA, it was likely that many of the proposals of the development corporation would not be capable of implementation until 1995 at the earliest.

The next chapter discusses the actual process of development on the site, highlighting the problems, themes and issues which became central to that process.

Chapter 12

YORK GATE: PROCESS

Robin Tetlow

The time factor

In this second chapter describing the factors involved in the development of the York Gate, the account centres on describing the specific problems related to the application to develop this site, highlighting the trade-offs, delays and complexity of factors which came into play in determining the final form that development on this site was to take (cf. Ambrose and Colenutt 1979). When the site was first considered for development, during the 1980s property boom, there was so much pressure for development that many otherwise marginal and somewhat unattractive sites were being drawn into development. But its complexity made the development process so lengthy that even in 1994 only part of the site has been completed. If development had been achieved in the late 1980s, it is likely that a much more ambitious solution, covering the entire site, would have resulted. As it happened, this was not possible. At present, only part of the site has been developed, but the potential is still there for the future.

Originally there had been talk of public subsidy, aimed at the social re-vitalisation of run-down inner city areas, being made available for the site to enable its regeneration, but nothing came of this. For example, when the Bristol Development Corporation area came into being in 1989, under national urban development corporation policy, the boundary did not extend to cover this area. Claims for funding on environmental and urban conservation grounds also did not materialise. For example, grants from English Heritage and the Department of the Environment were not forth-coming, owing to other priorities. Ultimately, any planning solution has had to stand on its own, in commercial and funding terms. The most promising strategy likely to yield a financial return was to develop the site for offices, although at the height of the market in 1989, residential development for sale was seriously considered for the whole site as an appropriate use. As to possible retail development, the site is located at the far end of an existing (but somewhat declining) secondary shopping centre in Bedminster. It was not an attractive site, being somewhat off the beaten track and heavily trafficked. Another development eventually took place

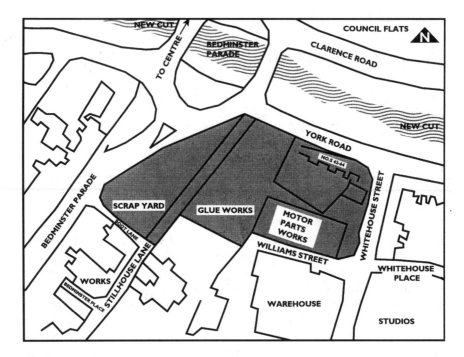

Fig. 12.1   Sketch of site before development (scale approx. 1 : 25,000)

only a short distance away on the other side of the main roundabout in the late 1980s, namely, an Asda supermarket which was to occupy the equivalent corner site on the other end of the high street. What happened around the site and its relationship with other adjacent developments in the immediate vicinity undoubtedly affected the way in which the York Gate site was perceived in terms of development potential. The possibility for development to occur on this site was directly linked to the wider planning framework and to planning policy at regional, county, city-wide and local plan level.

The evolution of the application to develop the site

Explanation of illustrations

This section looks in detail at the implementation process in relation to York Gate, or rather at the implementation of at least part of the original proposal. Figure 12.1 gives a sketch plan of the site before development, Figure 12.2 shows an outline plan of the proposals used in a publicity leaflet, Figure 12.3 shows cuttings of some of the publicity the site attracted and Figure 12.4 provides an artist's impression of façade refurbishment.

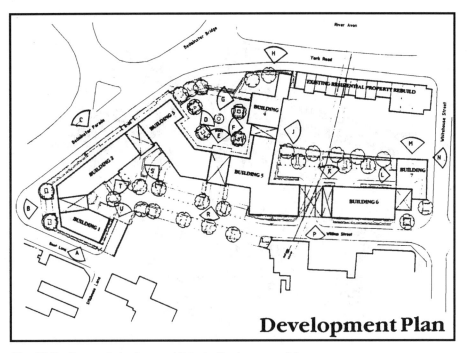

Fig. 12.2 Proposal plan from publicity leaflet (not to scale)

Ownerships and opportunities

Following the initial events which led to the dereliction of the site, successive owners have speculated that it might ultimately prove suitable for office development. Such factors have included the effects of war damage (for example, the glue factory was destroyed in 1941); blighting of the site over the years through a range of road widening and previous planning proposals; and structural or economic decline in the area, as factories and businesses have closed down, changing the character of the local economy. Owners have held on and done nothing in anticipation. In the early 1970s the land values would have been relatively low, but as time has gone by they have gradually increased. Bedminster itself, and the nature of its residents, have changed over the years. The original increases in the land values were because of a perceived demand for more office space, adjacent to the centre of Bristol, a demand heightened during each commercial property boom over the last twenty years.

By 1981 the Bedminster Conservation Area had been declared, including this site, and previous road widening schemes had been dropped, but they had taken their toll in blighting the area, so much so that most of the properties along York Road were uninhabitable. In the 1980s Bristol City Council was itself unsuccessful because of the complex multiplicity of land ownerships on the site, and in particular, because of the tenacity of one

151

Fig. 12.3 Press cuttings about the development

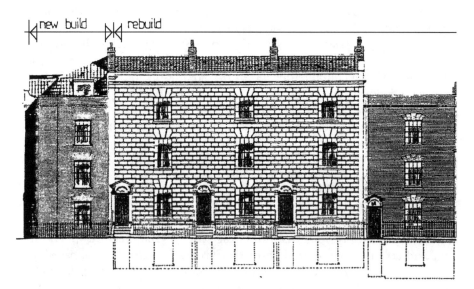

Fig. 12.4 Artist's impression of refurbished façade

such owner, a Mr. Smith. In September 1985 the city council agreed to grant planning permission with conditions subject to a legal agreement for the erection of a major retail warehouse store and ancillary loading facility and 420 car parking spaces on two upper levels on the rear of the site. The conversion/restoration of the listed York Road frontage as housing formed part of the proposed legal agreement. The application remained technically undetermined because the legal agreement was never signed.

There are three principal reasons for this. Firstly the landowners were never in control of 42–64 York Road and both the planning authority and the developers were unable to deal successfully with a single landowner who was. Secondly there was the subsequent planning permission for, and development of, a retail superstore by Asda less than 100 metres away, across the roundabout, in Bedminster Parade; this reduced the commercial attractiveness of such a development on this site. The application had been made by a commercial property developer, Helical Bar, but there was never any clear interest from a retailer; it was a purely speculative initiative. Thirdly there were insuperable difficulties in agreeing design details. This was hardly surprising bearing in mind the utilitarian design of retail warehouses in the mid to late 1980s, which was in obvious conflict with the conservation area/gateway status of this site.

A change of circumstances

The turning point came in early 1987 with the acquisition from various owners of 42–64 York Road by D.F.W. Golding Ltd., a building company based in Hereford. This was the first time that the terrace had been substantially in one ownership. Permission was granted for the refurbishment of the terrace in 1988, and in the same year Golding was taken over by Bellway plc, a well-established housing and commercial developer based in Newcastle and looking to extend into the south. The additional resources of Bellway were to prove significant because it was clear that cooperation was still needed between the owners of the front and the rear of the site if progress was to be made.

Fundamentally the condition of the terrace was such that, whatever the state of the housing market, it could not be refurbished without cross-subsidy; the cost of restoring the Bath stone façade to three of the units alone was £300,000. Ultimately Bellway bought out the interests of Helical Bar and by mid 1989 the whole site was substantially under their control, although there were still three small parcels controlled by Bristol City Council. The housing market was then at its peak, and sketch schemes were prepared for housing across the whole site. But soon, offices became the preferred option, and a detailed planning application for 15,000 square metres of B1 space was submitted in April 1990.

Infrastructural problems

In the meantime, 42–64 York Road continued to deteriorate, and in September 1989 no. 42 collapsed into the road on to a family in their car! Fortunately no one was injured. Subsequently, York Road was closed for three months while Bellway Homes, in cooperation with Bristol City Council and English Heritage, agreed and implemented a schedule of works to make the terrace safe and preserve the façade. Avon County, as highways authority, and Bristol City, as traffic authority, both played a significant part in the negotiations on the future of the site. Its location was significant in terms of traffic flows into the centre, various road widening schemes and related compulsory purchase proposals figuring in the history of the site. Other local and county departments were involved in relation to the infrastructure of the site. The site was already served by Victorian sewers in need of renovation, such as the famous Malago sewer, which ran under part of the listed row of houses. In the case of the listed buildings, particularly in view of their somewhat precarious condition, the relevant building, fire, conservation and safety regulatory authorities kept an eye on the site, both in terms of the maintenance of existing properties and land, and in relation to proposals for future development (refer to Part II on the range of certificates). And bodies responsible for provision of services on the site were involved, not least because a high pressure gas main runs underneath.

As to environmental health considerations, there was concern that the operation of a tannery on the site many years ago might have caused contamination. Detailed ground tests revealed that this was unlikely to prove a major problem.

There was also the question of car parking provision on the site. Although this area allowed a somewhat more generous parking allocation than central area sites, it was still a problematic issue. In addition to office development, there was also the possibility of residential development on the site as a result of refurbishing the listed terrace and/or providing additional housing elsewhere on the site, possibly from a housing association housing. Normally, there are strict requirements for residents' parking (Volume I, p. 204) with at least one off-road parking space per dwelling-unit, and at least one other shared between two dwellings. It has been found, in respect of negotiations on other sites, that in the case of social housing provision, especially for the elderly and disabled, lower requirements are acceptable, such as one parking unit only per dwelling or less in some instances. Paradoxically, while on-site parking is often welcomed by occupants, too much allocation for parking space uses up valuable space for the developer which could be used for more intensive development. A social housing component, or for that matter other forms of planning gain (as described in Part II) are useful negotiating tools, as the trade-off might be a more amenable planning permission in relation to the proposed dominant office use of the site. At the detailed site layout and design level, much thought has to go into what can actually be put into a site of 1.8 hectares once parking, landscaping, access and planning gain considerations have been accommodated.

The proposal

The proposal put forward was for a series of terraced blocks of no more than four storeys in height with a gateway feature incorporating principal towers at the corner of York Road and Bedminster Parade. It was proposed to refurbish and convert 42–64 York Road and to incorporate a new-build element at the end of no. 64, adjacent to Whitehouse Street, to create thirty-seven flats. The existing façades would be repaired and integrated, as far as possible using traditional materials. Thirty-seven car parking spaces were to be created to the rear of the terrace. The majority of the site was to be developed for B1 use. It was envisaged that the total office floor space to be created would be approximately 15,000 square metres (gross) consisting of seven self-contained units. The majority of the parking was to be tucked under the buildings. A total of 350 car parking spaces were to be provided for the commercial element, including 59 surface spaces and 292 underground spaces, and a further 37 spaces for the residential component.

It was envisaged that all the B1 floor space would be allocated to office space. The need for a high quality design along the main frontages acted as a major constraint. It was intended to create a public area at the junction of York Road and Bedminster Parade in the form of an elevated plaza. The plaza would incorporate a fountain and colonnade together with newly planted trees and associated landscaping. The architecture had its own identity but made reference to the differing materials, styles and building forms found to the west in York Road and to the east in Bedminster Parade. Mansard roofs, gables, dormers, familiar window forms and building materials were to be used to provide a form of development which humanised the scale of commercial development and acknowledged its location in a conservation area.

The basic design principles of the proposal were as follows:

- The creation of a high quality scheme, particularly along the frontage which would form the gateway to Bedminster.
- The function of the plaza as a public space.
- The need for the residential and commercial elements to have their own identity within a comprehensive whole.
- The creation of a strong design feature on the corner of Bedminster Parade and Boot Lane.
- The creation of a simple but compatible design to the new buildings along William Street to allow flexibility of use.
- The maintenance of good pedestrian access, including the integration of the public footpath at Bedminster Bridge.
- The need to provide for the disabled.

Access was proposed via Boot Lane and William Street with egress via William Street only for the office/retail uses. Boot Lane is one-way only. Stillhouse Lane would remain open for private traffic only beyond the entrance to the site. A new and separate access would be created adjacent to Whitehouse Street, approximately 35 metres from the York Road junction. Bellway was prepared both to dedicate land and to contribute towards road improvements at the junction of York Road and Bedminster Parade, required by Avon County Council as part of its programme of road improvements for the inner circuit road network. This was to be the subject of a legal agreement.

The negotiation process

The negotiations were protracted. Key considerations were the consultation carried out by Bellway in advance of the application, and the priority it placed upon early determination. Advantage was taken of expedited procedures so that all statutory consultees were approached directly. An A3 illustrative brochure was distributed selectively to key decision makers. Smaller leaflets (quoted in this chapter) were distributed widely to the general public (Oldfield King 1989). Exhibitions were held at Bristol City Council and the local Asda supermarket. A public meeting was held and considerable interest was shown by the media. Bellway had submitted duplicate applications and this allowed the possibility of an appeal against one of the applications after eight weeks, on the grounds of non-determination. This possibility of an appeal formed a backcloth to the negotiations over $2\frac{1}{2}$ years, but no appeal was ever lodged, consequently relations between the parties were often delicately poised. Over the months, meetings were held and gradually a better understanding of each others position developed. Ultimately Bristol City Council resolved to approve the application in January 1991 but it was not until October 1992 that all matters relating to the s.106 agreement had been resolved and the planning permission could be issued.

The main issues of negotiation

The issues that were negotiated between the parties can be summarised as follows:

- *Overall quantum*: the overall quantum of development, principally the floor space.
- *Overall mixture*: the overall mixture of uses within the development, i.e. the balance between housing, retail and commercial uses.
- *Urban design*: the quality of the scheme as a whole, its relationship with the surrounding area and the interrelationship of the various uses.

- *Traffic generation*: there was some question as to whether the traffic generated would warrant contributions to the improvement of the adjacent Bedminster Bridge roundabout. The traffic survey showed that this would not be justified.
- *Public space*: there was considerable debate regarding the detailed layout and design of the public plaza area.
- *Car parking*: the city council were keen to keep the on-site car parking to a minimum, whereas the developer was advised by its consultant surveyors that the relatively high level of car parking was an important selling point.
- *Access*: the city council were keen to keep vehicular and pedestrian access separate and to cater for the disabled.
- *Phasing*: the council were keen to control the phasing via the s.106 agreement, to ensure the terrace was refurbished before the commercial development was begun. But this inevitably had flow implications for the developer.

The actors in the negotiation process

The negotiation process was multidimensional and included a number of interests:

1   *The developer*: Bellway was keen to obtain planning permission as quickly as possible with as few restrictions as possible for as commercial a scheme as possible.
2   *The local residents*: York Road Residents Group saw the scheme as an opportunity to improve their environment and to enhance the value of their properties. They were keen that the application be approved as soon as possible.
3   *Avon County Council as highway authority*: in the initial stages the highway authority still had visions of the terrace being demolished to enable major road widening; ultimately, however, more modest improvements were secured. Relations between Bristol City Council and Avon County had always been difficult since the creation of the latter in 1974. In 1994 it was proposed that Avon should be abolished and that a unitary authority be created for Bristol in its place.
4   *Avon County Council as landowner*: the county council held small pieces of land adjacent to the highway which were important in the detailed negotiations, since Avon was still in a position to prevent implementation of a scheme that was deemed satisfactory by Bristol City Council.
5   *Bristol City Council as planning authority*: Bellway and its consultants always argued that the proposal accorded with the adopted Bedminster Local Plan. The city council took a different view, but eventually referred it to the secretary of state and advertised it as a departure. This difference of perspective manifested itself throughout the negotiations, as did the weight to be accorded to 'other material considerations.'

6   *Bristol City Council as landowner*: the small areas left under the ownership of the council, areas which they had agreed to sell to Bellway, were an effective bargaining chip and ultimately from a commercial point of view the council were able to profit from the ransom situation they held. At times there was tension between the planning and estates perspectives within the Council.

7   *Conservation interests*: these were articulated by English Heritage and the Urban Design Section and the Conservation Panel of Bristol City Council as well as city-wide conservation groups. Detailed negotiation regarding the façade of the terrace proved problematical. In 1992 the façade was demolished, thereby reducing development costs considerably, but during the negotiations on the overall planning application, listed building consent to demolish the terrace was effectively used as a bargaining chip. Wide-ranging opinions were expressed about the overall design of the whole scheme.

8   *Political interests*: several members of Bristol City Council and Avon County Council and local members of parliament became actively involved in the determination of the application. There was concern among local Labour members that the type of employment proposed did not accord with the traditional manufacturing base of Bedminster. Ultimately there was all-party support based on the overall regenerative impact and the 650 jobs likely to be created.

The section *The Road towards Planning Permission* at the end of the Chapter details the main stages in the negotiation process.

Implementation: the present situation

The protracted negotiations between the parties eventually did result in planning permission, but by October 1992 the commercial property market, as well as the residential market, was in decline. Bellway has not been prepared to speculate on finding an end-user. The availability of additional unexpected funding from the housing corporation in late 1992 and the introduction of Bristol Churches Housing Association to Bellway by Oldfield King who specialise in social housing work enabled them to acquire the existing terrace and associated residential land for the development of thirty-seven flats. This has both secured the future of the listed terrace and enabled the provision of such need social/affordable housing in the area. This was completed in late 1994, and one of the key planning objectives for the site has at last been achieved. But in 1995 the majority of the site still remains derelict and a blight on the area.

The property market remains depressed. Furthermore, alternative city centre sites and inner city office sites will have become available in the Bristol Urban Development Corporation area. Out-of-town locations, particularly to the north of Bristol, have proved increasingly attractive. Bellway has not been prepared to speculate in finding an end-user under such market conditions. Other alternative uses have again been considered, and screening by advertising hoardings in this prominent site location has provided a useful source of interim income to help cover the costs of holding the land.

In planning terms, this site can only be viewed as a long-standing problem justifying positive enabling action. Market forces have not enabled the satisfactory redevelopment of the whole site, nor has the planning process. The policies of the approved development plan were demonstrated to have been overtaken by events, but when a window of opportunity arose during 1990, it was apparent that various authorities could not respond quickly enough for implementation to occur in tandem with the aspirations of the developer and the vagaries of the market cycle. No central government subsidies were available to assist implementation. The planning authority may with some justification argue that the quality of the eventual scheme was all-important; better to have no development than a poor development. But bearing in mind the long history of dereliction on this site, there was ample time for the planning authority to have formulated a clear and realistic negotiating position. It is hard to avoid the conclusion that the negotiations were protracted by fruitless posturing of the two parties, who never sufficiently trusted each other to achieve anything positive. The planning authority could also argue that perhaps Bellway never intended to develop the site and that all along their main objective was to improve the land value before selling it on. The precise truth of the situation will never be clear. Watch progress!

In the meantime, since the development plan will be the primary consideration in the determination of any future planning application, Bellway has sought to influence the emerging Bristol City Local Plan to ensure that it has maximum flexibility to respond to future market circumstances over the plan period (up to the year 2001). The local plan will be subject to an inquiry in early 1995 and is likely to be adopted during 1996.

Conclusion

This site graphically illustrates the complexities and difficulties of implementing town planning and picks up on a number of themes introduced in other chapters. In particular, the case study has demonstrated the interaction between economic, social, political, geographical, financial, technological and urban design issues in the development of a site. It also demonstrates the interaction of different levels of plan making, as instrumented through the different local planning authority levels and other policy-making bodies, such as the highways authority. It has also shown how long it often takes to achieve development. During the course of the planning and implementation process, the original plan is likely to be revised several times, so the end result might be somewhat different or less complete than originally envisaged. Urban areas throughout Britain are littered with sites having similar stories to tell: stories of endless years of negotiation and modification; stories of backers, builders and developers changing direction; stories of planning authorities changing their policies and minds; and stories of local residents campaigning, or growing apathetic, as the years roll on. The development process is not a tidy, complete, instant process but a highly complex business.

Here are some key factors in the achievement of development:

- The state of the land and property market.
- The importance of land assembly and ownership.
- The difficulties that are often inherent in the redevelopment of inner city sites.
- The importance of urban design issues in a conservation area containing important listed buildings.
- The influence of and interaction between the development plan framework and national planning guidance.
- The evaluation of alternative development proposals for the site.
- The process of negotiation of planning permission, including the involvement of other bodies and local residents.
- The differing roles and perspectives of the various agencies and actors in the negotiation of the planning permission.
- The political dimension.

The road towards planning permission

1 Apr 1990	Meeting with planning officer, Bristol City Council (BCC) to present application.
2 Apr 1990	Submission of detailed planning applications and listed building applications in duplicate with full supporting statement to BCC; press launch; meeting with York Road Preservation Group/York Road Residents Association (follow on to press consultation).
5 Apr 1990	Expedited consultations by applicant with Avon County Council (ACC), British Gas, Bristol Civic Society as per general development order.
11 Apr 1990	Further planning fees requested by BCC, as well as further information before application can be registered.
20 Apr 1990	Dispute between parties over planning fees (£3,515 at stake) still unresolved. Despite informal support from the Department of the Environment, Bellway has no alternative but to send money in order for application to be registered.
27 Apr 1990	Applications registered (normally takes two or three days after submission).

May 1990	Exhibitions organised in BCC planning department; BCC area office at Zion Hall, opposite the site; and at Asda in Bedminster Arcade. One hundred A3 brochures distributed to help decision makers. Two thousand smaller leaflets distributed to the general public.
9 May 1990	BCC formally request environmental statement under the Town and Country Planning (Assessment of Environmental Effects) Regulations 1988.
14 May 1990	Oldfield King/Bellway appeal to the secretary of state against the request for an environmental statement.
17 May 1990	Meeting with William Waldegrave MP (Conservative member for adjacent constituency and also a Cabinet Minister).
23 May 1990	Department of the Environment upholds the appeal against the need for an environmental statement.
31 May 1990	Correspondence indicates frustration and impatience on the part of Bellway. As the application has been lodged for eight weeks, there is a mention of the possibility of appealing one of the duplicate applications.
6 June 1990	Letter from BCC indicating considerable sensitivity to criticisms of delay and negative attitude.
7 June 1990	First reaction from BCC to the application, setting out the following concerns:

- predominance of office development
- rigid design
- traffic generation
- relationship of offices to listed buildings/proposed residential use
- car parking
- functioning of the public space

In summary, the scheme was deemed unacceptable. But BCC did agree to a meeting.

11 June 1990	Further detailed information requested by BCC.
13 June 1990	Bellway decides to delay appeal on non-determination of second application, pending meeting of 26 June 1990.
25 June 1990	Public meeting organised by Bellway held at Hilton Hotel, Bristol. Attended by sixty persons representing a range of interests. Reaction in press described as 'mixed' but support given by local residents.
26 June 1990	Meeting held with BCC.
27 June 1990	ACC formally request full traffic generation study; first indication of this arose on 19 June 1990.
29 June 1990	Following meeting of 26 June 1990, letter from BCC setting out detailed points of concern:

- scale of development
- land use
- design
- flexibility
- traffic

Tone of letter conciliatory. Talked of 'mutual co-operation' to achieve development of this 'important site'.

4 July 1990   Conciliatory reply to BCC letter of 29 June 1990 by Oldfield King. Stated that there was no intention of an appeal and sought to address as many of the issues as possible.

26 July 1990   Meeting with Dawn Primarolo MP, Labour member for Bristol South.

16 Aug 1990   Revised plans, revised supporting statement and traffic study submitted to BCC. Scheme reduced to 13,000 square metres of offices; important design changes; other detailed points incorporated, e.g. pedestrian links and provision for disabled.

20 Sept 1990   Meeting with Urban Design Section to resolve matters of conservation interest. Negotiations on other matters delayed for a month due to principal planning officer's commitments at a public inquiry.

9 Oct 1990   Full set of further revised plans submitted to BCC in preparation for meeting of 18 Oct 1990.

18 Oct 1990   Meeting with BCC recommended new application should be submitted incorporating all the agreed changes, this to be determined on 19 Dec 1990. Bellway refused to withdraw current applications in the interim.

24 Oct 1990   Letter from BCC confirming outcome of meeting of 18 Oct 1990. Reaffirmed commitment to negotiation and to 'see an early start on site.'

26 Oct 1990   New application lodged with BCC.

31 Oct 1990   New application registered.

6 Nov 1990   Meeting with ACC following lack of response to traffic study. Basic assumptions of traffic study altered. ACC also objected to changes to the frontage to Bedminster Parade requested by BCC, despite raising no objections previously.

12 Nov 1990   Letter from Oldfield King to Dawn Primarolo MP and leading councillors of ACC and BCC regarding difficulties created by ACC.

13 Nov 1990   Letter from Oldfield King to ACC complaining about handling of application.

28 Nov 1990   Apology received from ACC.

30 Nov 1990   Further meeting with BCC. Fine points of detail agreed.

6 Dec 1990   Late objections received from Bristol Royal Society for the Blind, who speculatively acquired adjacent site and sub-

mitted a subsequent planning application for a day centre. Previous consultation had taken place.

12 Dec 1990	Bellway organises a press conference to further promote proposals.
14 Dec 1990	ACC Planning Highways and Transport Subcommittee resolved to request meeting with BCC to ensure their 'objections' could be resolved, objections related to Bedminster Parade frontage.
17 Dec 1990	Further minor amendments agreed with BCC.
18 Dec 1990	Front-page headline in the *Bristol Evening Post*: Fury at Delay on £40m City Facelift Bid. Article cites ACC decision.
19 Dec 1990	Consideration of application by BCC delayed to 2 Jan 1991.
2 Jan 1991	On the basis of a comprehensive· officer's report recommending approval, the Planning and Traffic Committee of BCC resolved 8–1 (one Labour councillor against) to grant detailed planning permission subject to several caveats, including

- advertising it as a departure from the Bedminster Local Plan
- a comprehensive s.106 agreement
- a requirement for a report-back by officers on various detailed points
- a comprehensive list of conditions

7 Feb 1991	Further meeting with BCC to resolve detailed matters.
13 Feb 1991	Ad hoc joint committee of BCC and ACC finally resolved differences between the two authorities.
22 May 1991	BCC Planning and Traffic Committee advised of satisfactory progress in resolving matters of concern at meeting of 2 Jan 1991. The advertisement of the departure resulted in no action by the secretary of state to call in the application.
7 Oct 1992	After extensive negotiations during which the possibility of an appeal again briefly emerged, BCC Planning and Traffic Committee approved the terms of the s.106 agreement. Delay exacerbated by interim departure of principal planning officer dealing with the application. Signing of s.106 agreement finally created a planning permission which enabled the following to be triggered:

- completion of purchases of small parcels of land from BCC
- completion of purchase of land from ACC
- various highway closures which could not easily be implemented until there was an actual planning permission

1993–5	The process continues.

Chapter 13

THE PLANNING SYSTEM AND THE NATIONAL HEALTH SERVICE

Jennifer Tempest

| The National Health Service |

What is a chapter on the National Health Service (NHS) doing in a book about town planning? Firstly, it looks at the relationships, past and present, between the functions of the Department of Health (separated from the Department of Health and Social Security in 1988) and the Department of the Environment. Secondly, it focuses upon the organisation of the NHS. The NHS is a very significant holder of land on behalf of the secretary of state for health. Thirdly, it considers how the position of the NHS in relation to town planning has changed in recent years, particularly as it differs from other central government organisations because it now needs to obtain express planning permission for development, almost as if it were a private sector developer. This chapter provides an interesting set of examples of the interrelationship between the NHS and the planning authorities in achieving implementation of development. In particular, it shows how the gaining of a valuable planning permission, for change of use or building, prior to the disposal of NHS land can significantly increase the value of that property. The chapter gives further illustrations of the use of planning gain, this time being offered by a former public sector body for the social good.

The National Health Service came into being in 1948 and was at the heart of postwar welfare state provisions for the creation of a more equitable society

> to ensure that in the future every man woman and child can rely on getting . . . the best medical and other facilities available, that their getting them shall not depend on whether they can pay for them or any other factor irrelevant to real need.
>
> (Ministry of Health 1944)

The examples cited in this chapter are based on experience in England (outside London) where the NHS is currently structured into regional and district health authorities, NHS trusts and Family Health Service Authorities (FHSAs). Different organisational arrangements are applicable in London, Scotland, Wales and Northern Ireland. The NHS is the largest employer in Europe – over one million staff across the United Kingdom (HSJ 1993). One consequence of the size, duration and purpose of the NHS is that it holds very significant tracts of land and buildings which represent a major capital asset to the service. In common with other central government departments, the NHS benefited for many years from Crown Immunity in respect of the system of town and country planning. This meant that developments on NHS land – building new hospitals or altering existing NHS property – did not require the permission of the local planning authority. The relevant NHS organisations needed only to consult with the local authority on their proposals but they did not need to seek express planning permission.

Although this situation offered certain advantages to the NHS in avoiding the need to obtain planning permission, there were also disadvantages. When the NHS needed to dispose of land and buildings which were no longer required, they were not able to obtain planning permission for alternative uses or for redevelopment. This potentially hampered its ability to obtain the best value for assets upon their disposal, as the obtainment of planning permission for development is frequently the best means of determining best value. It was addressed by the Town and Country Planning Act of 1984, which introduced provisions for government departments to seek planning permission on land intended for disposal. From 1984 until 1991 the NHS benefited from the dual advantages of not requiring permission for their own developments and being able to seek permission on redundant sites intended for disposal. In 1991, the Crown Immunity of the NHS was removed so that permission was required for all development. The special provisions relating to Crown Land are described below. But in March 1994 the Department of the Environment announced proposals to remove Crown Exemption.

Crown Land and development

Under the provisions of the Town and Country Planning Act of 1971, the Crown was not bound by planning legislation. This meant there was no legal obligation upon government departments, including the Department of Health, to obtain planning permission for their developments. In recognition of the desirability of government departments disposing of surplus land and thereby obtaining capital receipts for disposal, the Town and Country Planning Act of 1984 introduced arrangements under which the Crown could seek planning permission in respect of land intended for disposal.

The Crown's general immunity from planning control is continued in the Sections 293–302 of the 1990 Town and Country Planning Act. (But on 10 March 1994 an announcement was made by the DoE on the lifting of this immunity.) The NHS exemption from planning control had already been removed by the provisions of the National Health Service and Community Care Act of 1990. Apparently following on the NHS model, the secretary of state for the environment announced in July 1992 that the government was planning to abolish general Crown Immunity, although limited exemptions would remain in respect of national or prison security and trunk road proposals (Grant 1992). A DoE consultation paper issued for comment in November 1992 further explained possible changes in the provisions relating to Crown Land against the background of the government's aims of more open government and greater accountability (Department of the Environment 1992b). Planning Minister David Curry announced that as soon as a legislative opportunity arose it was intended to remove Crown Exemption from the planning system so that in future all Crown bodies should be required to apply for planning permission, listed building consent, conservation area consent and scheduled monument consent in the normal way (Department of the Environment 1994b).

Notwithstanding the change in status of Crown Land, the health service has for some time recognised the potential development value of some of its surplus real estate and made use of the provisions of the 1984 act to apply to local planning authorities for permission for non-health related developments in an effort to enhance and establish the value of its land. Such land can then be sold and the capital realised can provide a very valuable contribution to new capital projects for health care purposes. The National Health Service has undergone radical change in the past decade, both in its structure and in its care policies. These changes have influenced the interaction between the NHS and the town planning system. Some of these changes have brought the service into contact with the town planning system in ways previously unknown to public bodies. Perhaps more remarkable is the way in which the town planning system has reflected and accommodated some of the changes in care policies within the NHS. The interaction between the NHS and the planning system may be seen as a two-way process.

National Health Service reform

In 1989 the government issued the *White Paper Working for Patients* (Department of Health and Social Security 1989) which set out proposals for radical reform of the service. These proposals, subsequently enacted in the National Health Service and Community Care Act of 1990, introduced the internal market into the NHS, allowing health authorities to trade with one another, with self-governing hospitals, with other services (NHS trusts) and with the private sector. Responsibility for NHS property holdings, as a consequence of these reforms, will no longer be concentrated at the levels of regional and district health authorities, but will increasingly be devolved to individual NHS trusts as operational land is transferred to the trusts when they are set up. The Audit Commission (1991) reported that the reforms in the structure of the NHS would have a profound effect on estate management in the NHS. By Spring 1994, the government had set in motion further reforms initially to halve the number of regional health authorities and greatly reduce the staff employed at regional level. Further change to the structure of the NHS is likely and it is intended that regional health authorities will be abolished in 1996. Estate departments within regional health authorities have been responsible for the disposal of surplus land and buildings. Future arrangements for such disposals have yet to be clearly defined. In any new arrangements, it must be hoped that the NHS does not lose its advantages of obtaining best value for its land assets by seeking planning permission for alternative uses prior to disposal.

Changes in health care policy

A consultative document *Care in the Community* (Department of Health and Social Security 1981) estimated that fifteen thousand mentally handicapped people and five thousand of the mentally ill need not be living in hospitals if suitable care facilities were available in the community. The Griffiths Report (Griffiths 1988) was aimed towards speeding up the process of providing care in the community and closing large institutions which traditionally provided long-term care. Replacement facilities tend to be in the form of small, domestic-scale units in the community providing rehabilitation and long-term accommodation. New acute care units providing short-term care and treatment are often now associated with large general hospitals. The closure of large institutions and other specialist units for which there is no longer a health care need (such as chest hospitals or tuberculosis and isolation hospitals) has left the health service with large buildings in substantial grounds for which there is no health care need.

The responsibility of disposing of these properties – redundant land and buildings – currently rests with regional health authorities. The Audit Commission (1991) pointed out that the NHS should regard all property assets as a dynamic resource because needs for property will change as the pattern of health care changes. Changes in clinical practice have tended to reduce the length of time a patient stays in hospital. Day surgery is becoming increasingly important and avoids overnight stays in hospital. Consequently, the numbers of beds required by acute hospitals has reduced. At the same time, mental illness and mental handicap hospitals, which provide for long-stay patients have been closing and continue to close in favour of patients being cared for in the community. The NHS has undertaken a large number of estate utilisation and rationalisation studies to try and ensure that the space within buildings which are costly to build and maintain is put to the most efficient use, another effect of introducing internal markets into the NHS.

The NHS estate

In 1991, when it published *NHS Estate Management and Property Maintenance*,

167

the Audit Commission valued NHS land and buildings in England and Wales at about £25 billion. Each year £400 million of major new building schemes are completed and £500 million is spent on maintaining existing premises. In 1991 the NHS was estimated to occupy nineteen hundred hospitals in England and Wales as well as many smaller buildings such as day hospitals, clinics, health centres, staff accommodation, ambulance stations and administrative offices. These premises occupied somewhere in the region of 40 million square metres of building space on 20,000 hectares of land. In April 1991 the *Health Service Journal* reported that land sales in English regional health authorities were likely to fall significantly short of Department of Health estimates as a result of the continuing property slump (HSJ 1991). Receipts of around £200 million instead of the originally predicted £300 million were likely. Failure to meet land sale targets affected capital programmes and therefore the ability to fund new capital projects to provide health care facilities.

The fragmentation of the NHS estate and the proliferation of NHS trusts, each responsible for their own landholdings will make comprehensive planning of the overall estate increasingly complex. Each trust will be directed by market forces and the demand for the services they provide. The ability of individual trusts to understand and work effectively within the town planning system will inevitably vary and will take some time to evolve.

Interaction between the NHS and the planning system

Planning permissions

At present, the NHS comes into direct contact with the town planning system in the following broad ways:

- Seeking planning permission to carry out new health care developments.
- Seeking planning permission for new uses for redundant land and buildings prior to sale.
- Making representations upon the content of development plans, both in respect of health care/community policies and policies affecting surplus land.

These contacts are illustrated in the case studies later in this chapter. However, there is evidence of other links between the NHS and the operation of the planning system, links reflected in central government planning policy and regulations.

Links between NHS and DoE policy

The radical changes in the delivery of health care and in particular the increasing importance of care in the community has been reflected within the operation of the town planning system. The Town and Country Planning Use Classes Order was the subject of major review in the late 1980s culminating in the adoption of the Town and Country Use Classes Order of 1987. This order introduced for the first time a use class relating to dwelling-houses.

Class C3 dwelling-house

Use as a dwelling-house, whether or not as a sole or main residence,

- by a single person or by people living together as a family, or
- by not more than six residents living together as a single household (including a household where care is provided for residents).

Class C3, newly introduced in 1987, clarified the position in cases where unrelated residents live together as a single household, including small group homes for disabled and mentally disordered people living in the community rather than in institutions. There had previously been doubt about the appropriate classification of uses involving residential care (Grant 1993). This change to the use classes order is further explained in the Circular 13/87 *Changes in the Use of Buildings and other Land* issued at the same time. This refers to the number of appeals which arose from determinations under what was s.53 of the 1971 act and has now been superseded by s.192 of the 1990 act. More significantly:

the single household concept will provide more certainty over the planning position of small group homes which play a major role in the Government's community care policy which is aimed at enabling disabled and mentally disordered people to live as normal lives as possible in touch with the community.

(Circular 13/87, para 27)

The significance of this policy is that it directly links the Department of Health's policies (which are essentially social policies) with those of the land use based town and country planning system. The new class was introduced despite a very significant number of objections to it during consultations and illustrates a special relationship between health service policy and that of the Department of the Environment. Outside the NHS there are other instances of social policies impinging upon land use planning policies. In the area of housing provision, for example, national planning policies provide scope for local authorities to seek a proportion of 'affordable housing' (PPG 3, *Affordable Housing*, DoE 1992) in new developments and to allow housing for local needs in rural areas on sites where open market housing would not normally be permitted.

Editors comment: Some experts have commented upon the implications for care in the community projects of splitting C1 hotels and hostels into two separate categories. The divison was intended to restrict the tendency for some seaside hotels to become hostels for the homeless in the wintertime, but it may affect other categories of hostels. Once again, social policies impinge on land use policies.

Redundant hospitals in green belts

Another example of this special relationship, again linked to the policy of care in the community, is in the guidance given by the DoE on the redevelopment of redundant hospitals in green belts. Normal planning policy for the green belt is that only a specific range of uses are acceptable in the green belt. This would include recreation, leisure, cemeteries and institutions standing in substantial grounds. Government policy is set out in PPG 2 *Green Belts* and in circulars. An update of PPG 2 *Green Belts* was subsequently issued for consultation in March 1994. More specific government guidance in respect of redundant hospitals in green belts is contained in a Circular (12/89). The guidance was first issued in Circular 12/87, *Redundant Hospital Sites in Green Belts: Planning Guidelines,* now superseded by Circular 12/91. The guidelines are intended to assist local planning authorities in preparing policies for the future use of redundant hospital sites in green belts and in dealing with planning applications for their future use. This guidance states that first priority should be given to securing acceptable green belt uses which would occupy the existing buildings, and then to other uses which could utilise the existing buildings. If no such use can be found, local planning authorities can consider other uses, including redevelopment of the site for purposes which would normally be contrary to green belt policy, for example, employment and residential development. This can have a significant effect on land values.

This government policy is a specific recognition of the need to assist the NHS in the disposal of hospital sites which have become redundant through the implementation of the care in the community programme and other changes in health care policy. The redundant institutions, released by health authorities and NHS trusts when patients are cared for within the community, can represent a substantial capital asset to the NHS. If this asset can be turned into cash – usually by disposing of the site to a developer – the money can then be invested in more appropriate health care uses, such as new acute hospitals and rehabilitation facilities. Although there is a need for sensitivity in respect of any proposed development within a green belt area, the view has been that provided the proposed development does not exceed the footprint of existing development, it should be looked upon reasonably (the footprinting principle). But despite the increased flexibility in planning policy for redundant hospitals in the green belt, the first priority remains disposal for other acceptable green belt uses. If there is no market for such uses, without the benefit of the flexibility offered by the circular, these sites would be a liability rather than an asset. Where the guidance in the circular does allow redevelopment to be considered, the extent of the new development must be no greater than the footprint of the existing development. Footprint development is generally taken to mean replacement of the ground floor area of the existing building and therefore differs significantly from floor area, which would refer to all floors of a building. Local planning authorities may display a reluctance to allow redevelopment in the green belt despite the NHS demonstrating that no suitable use can be found for redundant properties.

There has been a recent indication that central government policy in respect of redundant hospital sites in green belts may change as reflected in the new draft PPG 2. The DoE is considering the introduction of special provisions for the reuse and redevelopment of existing employment sites in green belts, where these sites are identified in local plans, and cancelling the provisions of Circular 12/91 which are specific to hospital sites (and see PPG 2 *Green Belts* revised version, 1995).

Development plans and health policy

This chapter focuses predominantly upon the contacts between the NHS and the town planning system in relation to NHS-owned land. There is a case, however, for NHS bodies seeking involvement in the development plan process if land use based policies affect issues of health policy. An example of this is the Sandwell Unitary Development Plan in the West Midlands where the Sandwell Health Authority has commented and objected to the policies of the plan and defended these objections at the public local inquiry into the plan. Among the authority's stated reasons for becoming involved in the plan-making process was its belief that national imperatives in health care policy, such as community care, The Health of the Nation and the Children Act, can only be delivered effectively within a safe environment with sound infrastructure (Middleton and Pulford 1993). The unitary development plan (UDP) provided the health authority with the opportunity to point out the potential health drawbacks of certain policy statements and proposals for the natural and built environment within the borough. According to Middleton and Pulford, the objections lodged related to

- The mechanism for control of industry operation in residential areas.
- Overreliance on the ability of the market mechanism to supply housing for people with disabilities.
- A perceived weakening of protection for green space.
- The threat of out-of-town shopping centres to local shopping, local communities and people without cars.
- A perceived threat to health of redeveloping land close to old mines and refuse tips.
- The intention to scrap plans for a bus/tram interchange station and the attendant loss of better public transport facilities.

Middleton and Pulford also point to the changing role of health authorities since the advent of NHS trusts which means that health authorities are no longer involved in the direct management of health care services. One of their enhanced roles is therefore that of advocates of health care policy and

171

health promotion using whatever means are appropriate, including direct involvement in town planning.

Case studies

The NHS and the development process

The case studies below illustrate how the NHS must act as developers and become deeply involved in the development process if they are to utilise the system of town and country planning to best advantage, both for health care developments and in the disposal of surplus sites.

Coney Hill Hospital, Gloucester

Coney Hill Hospital (Fig. 13.1) dates from 1884 and occupies a site of some 45 hectares (110 acres). The hospital is some 2.5 kilometres east of Gloucester city centre, and although much of the hospital site is open land, the site as a whole is now contained within the developed area of the city. The South and West Regional Health Authority (SWRHA) began planning for the closure and disposal of this hospital site in 1989; the hospital is scheduled to close in 1994. The SWRHA appointed a team of consultants to advise it and to act on its behalf in seeking planning permission to redevelop the site prior to placing it on the open market. The SWRHA is itself acting as agent for the NHS, a public body, so it is legally obliged to obtain best value for any assets that it sells. Where land is to be disposed of for redevelopment, obtaining planning permission for alternative uses is frequently the best means of ensuring the best value can be obtained. Proposed sales in some regions must be sanctioned by the district valuer (who works for the Inland Revenue).

The team of consultants appointed by the SWRHA included town planning and development consultants, legal advisors, highway and infrastructure consultants; and marketing advisors. Landscape consultants were later brought into the team, and specialist advice was sought from ecologists and archaeologists. Counsel's advice was also sought at key stages in the process when it was thought that it might be necessary to appeal against the local planning authority's failure to reach a decision. This list gives an indication of a typical team required when seeking planning permission for a major development. The health authorities concerned had kept the local authorities informed about the hospital development programme and the local authorities were therefore aware of the likely closure of Coney Hill Hospital during the early 1990s. According to the draft local plan for the city, published in 1988, land at Coney Hill Hospital was suitable for the development of up to five hundred houses, and a landscaped park was needed to serve the wider area.

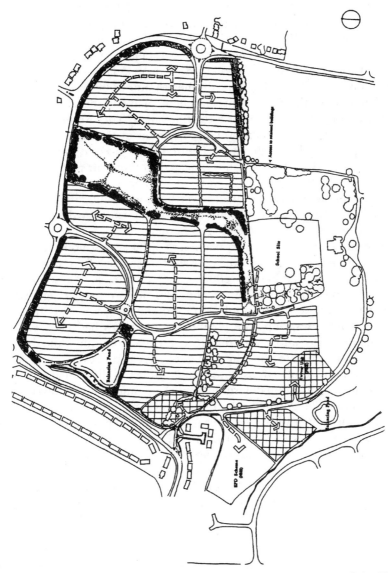

Fig. 13.1 Coney Hill Hospital, Gloucester. Reproduced by permission of the Planning Practice. (Scale approx. 1 : 6000.)

Key: ▦ proposed residential development; ▦ affordable housing;
 existing landscaping; ◼ proposed structural landscaping;
┌╌╌╌┐ cycleway; ┌╌╌╌┐ footpath.

Without consulting the site's owners, the city council prepared a draft planning brief to propose certain guidelines for the development of the site, but it also purported to designate a large part of the site as a landscape conservation area. The regional and district health authorities submitted a planning application to develop the whole of the NHS-owned land at Coney Hill (except for a small area for new health care developments). This application was submitted just before the issue of the planning brief, upon which they were consulted in the same way as any other consultee. In other words, no special consultee status was conferred on them as landowners.

After considerable negotiations, the health authorities accepted that during the period of the current development plan, the development of five hundred houses on their site was a realistic target. They were nonetheless at variance with the city council over the question of the balance of the site, which the planning brief effectively required to be given to the city as public open space. The health authorities objected to the draft planning brief on the grounds that the open space was considerably larger than required for such a development and there had never been any public right of access to the land. The planning brief was nonetheless confirmed by the city council's planning committee with this requirement intact.

The health authorities lodged a planning appeal against non-determination of their planning application but followed this shortly afterwards with a revised planning application on a reduced site area capable of accommodating some five hundred houses. A second appeal was lodged against non-determination of the revised application. Both appeals were eventually withdrawn. In both cases, duplicate planning applications had been submitted which allowed negotiations with the city council to continue while the health authorities entered into the often lengthy appeal process. The process of lodging duplicate applications, often called twin tracking, means an appeal can be lodged against non-determination at the same time as allowing applicants to attempt a negotiated solution with local planning authorities. These manoeuvres have met with the disapproval of central government because it considers such tactics wasteful of time and money within the inspectorate. Considerable work goes into arranging inquiries, but appeals are often withdrawn before the hearings open. To try and discourage such tactics, there are now increased application fees for duplicate applications and penalties in the form of costs for parties who withdraw appeals at a late stage.

After considerable negotiation and the conclusion of an agreement under Section 106 of the 1990 Town and Country Planning Act (elements of which could be described as planning gain), planning permission was granted for the development, together with open space provision within the site sufficient to satisfy the requirements of the development itself. There was no requirement affecting the balance of the development site. Other matters covered by the agreement included the provision of a site for a primary school, a contribution towards its construction and contributions towards off-site highway improvements. In July 1991 the deposit version of the local plan was published, in which land at Coney Hill was designated as a landscape conservation area. The health authorities duly objected to that designation and subsequently argued their case at a public local inquiry in July 1993. The inspector's report recommended substantial changes in the council's pro-

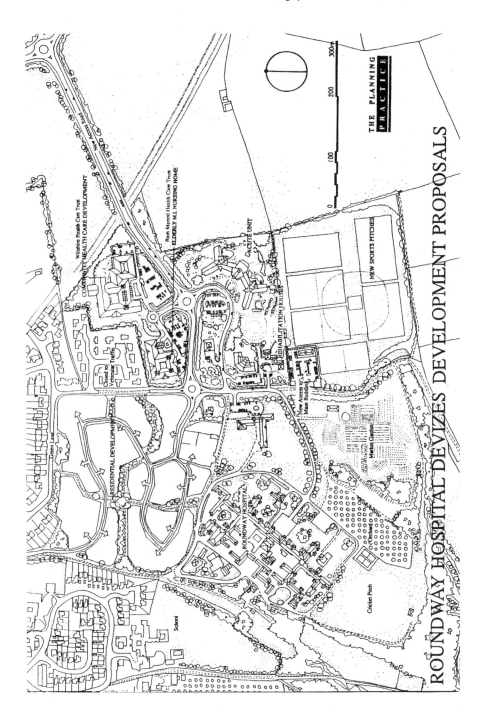

Fig. 13.2 Roundway Hospital Development Proposals

posed designations for consideration by the council. If the NHS and its estate is to some extent treated as a special case by the planning system, at least insofar as community care and redundant hospitals in the green belt are concerned, then it must also be aware that planning authorities may seek to take advantage of the public aspect of their nature and seek additional public goods, which might not be required of more conventional developers. This case study demonstrates that, even where public bodies are dealing with one another, there can be a tense relationship and negotiations can be extremely lengthy. It is vitally important to distinguish those areas where agreement exists or agreement is likely to exist from those areas where compromise is unlikely to be achieved without some form of arbitration.

Roundway Hospital

Roundway Hospital (Fig. 13.2) is a large institution with main buildings dating from 1840. It was the original county asylum for Wiltshire and is included in the statutory list of buildings of special architectural or historic interest (Grade II). NHS land holdings in the area amount to some 70 hectares (170 acres) and include the existing hospital buildings, land leased to a local farmer and land leased to the local town council for playing-fields. The hospital site lies on the south side of the town of Devizes some 1.2 kilometres from the towns market-place.

Similar to Coney Hill, Department of Health policy to close large long-stay institutions for psychiatric patients means that the majority of Roundway Hospital will be empty by 1994/95. Replacement facilities will be required in the form of acute units, units for the elderly, rehabilitation houses and day care. The district health authority and latterly NHS trusts decided that some of the surplus land would provide an ideal location for these facilities, offering the opportunity for phased transfer of facilities and shared staffing, while in the longer term providing a new site, effectively unrelated to the existing institution and its associations. Achieving this development would mean building upon the playing-fields leased to the town council. The health authorities and trusts recognised that given the formal arrangements in place and the level of use of these playing-fields, development would only be acceptable if alternative facilities were made available. Furthermore, the adopted local plan contained a policy stating that these playing-fields should not be developed for non-sporting activities.

Long-term planning on the part of the health authorities had meant that, as long ago as 1985, they had sought active involvement in the local planning process and successfully negotiated a reduction to a suggested designation of the whole of the hospital site as an area of minimum change. Under this designation, the local planning authority policy would have resisted change and hence new development. The designation in the approved local plan was a reduction upon that previously proposed, extending over the listed building and its immediate setting, whereas the whole of the developed part of the site was included within the built-up limits of the town.

The professional team assembled by the regional health authority included town planning and development consultants, solicitors and highway consultants. Later in the development process, when new health care facilities were being planned and costed in more detail, the trust appointed a further team of architects, landscape architects, quantity surveyors, structural and civil engineers, services engineers and interior designers. Two planning applications were submitted. The first sought outline planning permission for a new community hospital, mental health care facilities and a new access road to serve the development. The second application submitted concurrently, was for permission to change the use of agricultural land to sports pitches which would allow the existing playing-fields to be replaced with new ones.

The applications had considerable support from the officers and elected members of the district council, although this did not mean they passed through the development control system without difficulty. Indeed, it took some eight months to achieve a planning permission for the health care developments and six months for the permission to replace the playing-fields. In both cases, legal agreements had to be concluded – in the former case with the county council as highway authority to ensure that the new access road would be provided at the appropriate stage in the overall development. The legal agreement with the district council was concluded to secure the provision of the new sports pitches prior to the existing pitches being redeveloped for the new mental health care facilities. Outside these planning agreements other agreements had to be concluded. The first involved securing an option agreement to provide a new road access into the development site because the existing access was not adequate to serve a community hospital as well as a mental health care unit. Although the NHS could use compulsory purchase procedures, it was concluded that a negotiated solution was preferable. New lease arrangements had to be put in place with the tenant of farmland (needed for the new playing-fields) and the town council to secure the existing playing-fields for the new development.

All these agreements had to be coordinated to allow the development to commence in the summer of 1993. The first work on site was the laying out of the new playing-fields as the agreements with the district and town councils required that these be ready for play before the existing playing-fields were taken for hospital development. Parallel with the planning and other legal agreements under negotiation, discussions were taking place regarding the transfer of land from the regional health authority to the trusts and the attendant responsibilities regarding the commitments given in the Section 106 agreements. The application for the health care developments did meet with objections from those local residents who would be most directly affected. Some residents overlooked the playing-fields or open spaces that would be developed with hospital buildings. Objections from people affected in this way are fully understandable. The local planning authority then had to weigh these objections against the benefit of providing new health care facilities.

The local planning authority accepted the need to develop a previously undeveloped part of the NHS estate in Devizes to provide necessary health care in modern facilities. At the same time, sports pitches have not only been safeguarded for the local population, they now have a much more permanent basis. However, the local planning authority has yet to plan positively for the vacated and redundant site which the new development will create. The regional health authority has therefore needed to adopt a more confrontational approach with the district council in seeking to secure the redevelopment of this substantial area.

The existing hospital buildings occupy more than 20 acres of land, and this land is identified by the local planning authority as being within the framework of the town. Indeed, it has been shown as such in a local plan of more than ten years standing. The regional health authority considers this land could be redeveloped to provide housing. The draft local plan, published in April 1993, has allocated greenfield sites elsewhere and on the edge of the town for new housing, while not making any comment upon the future of the existing Roundway Hospital site. According to the draft policies in the plan, the development of the greenfield sites as proposed will allow developers to fund part of a new road system around the west of the town. The proposed road is not included within the highway authority's transport policy programme and is therefore essentially a district-level proposal. In due course, and through the local planning process, the local planning authority will be asked to justify its stance that developing greenfield sites to provide a road is preferable to redeveloping a redundant site within the existing framework of the town. The regional health authority has therefore submitted representations to the district council objecting to the draft local plan and seeking amendments to its housing policies and allocations. The council has considered these representations and has not modified its position in relation to the redundant hospital site. It will therefore be necessary for the regional health authority to consider lodging formal objections to the local plan when it is placed on deposit if the health authority wishes to secure the best value for the land prior to any disposal.

Conclusions

The NHS has benefited from the operation of the town and country planning system in a number of ways. Firstly, in terms of developments for health care purposes, health authorities had long enjoyed Crown Immunity and did not have to become directly involved in the need to obtain planning permission. The NHS lost its Crown Immunity in 1991. Secondly, since 1984 the

NHS, in common with other holders of Crown Land, has been able to seek planning permission upon sites intended for disposal. In addition, some of the policies of the Department of Health have been reflected in land use planning policies, thereby making it easier for the NHS to implement its own policies. A clear example of this is in the implementation of the Department of Health's care in the community policy, where changes to the use classes order have simplified the provision of small homes within the community for NHS patients and the realisation of capital from the sale of redundant hospitals in green belts has been facilitated by specific policies and guidelines to local planning authorities. The Department of the Environment is now suggesting changes in policy on the future of existing employment sites in the green belt, including redundant hospital sites (PPG 2 *Green Belts* draft revision, 1994). This could offer greater flexibility not only to other government departments with major landholdings affected by changes in government policy, such as the Ministry of Defence, but also to other privately owned sites. It is likely to become increasingly important that sites, including those of hospitals, are clearly contained within the provisions and proposals of local plans, in line with the government's increasing emphasis upon a plan-led system of town and country planning.

There remains a significant gap in the policy framework at central government level in relation to existing redundant sites in rural areas that are not designated green belts. Such sites tend to be dealt with by local planning authorities on an ad hoc basis. There will be increasing pressure from landowners and their advisors to ensure that such sites are addressed in the context of development plan policies. In some instances the time-scale for the closure of institutions and installations will be relatively short, so the local planning process may prove too inflexible to allow the future of such sites to be properly planned. But without central government guidance, each local planning authority may address such sites in a different way. There currently exists specific government policy guidance to assist local authorities and the NHS when the site is a redundant hospital in a green belt. But there is no specific guidance when a redundant hospital is in a rural area that falls outside a green belt. Arguably, the policy provisions applying to green belt situations are the minimum which the NHS could expect to gain from development of the site, but local planning authorities may propose that only development normally allowed in the countryside is applicable. For example, at Tehidy Hospital, in Cornwall, the district council has refused a variety of planning applications to convert the existing buildings to new uses. They have done this despite the fact that two of the main buildings are listed and therefore every effort must be made to secure their retention. A marketing campaign in the absence of any planning permissions has not attracted any potential purchasers and now the health authority must consider submitting further applications, if necessary pursuing them to appeal. The stance taken by the local planning authority is that no use will be acceptable unless it is clearly and directly beneficial to the local community. In contrast, Plymouth

Health Authority has secured permission to convert an unlisted redundant hospital within the Dartmoor National Park into some one hundred dwellings. This permission followed a dialogue and negotiations with the local planning authority spanning some five years and involved the submission of several planning applications.

Policy frameworks to deal with large redundant sites are incomplete and fragmented. Outside the context of redundant hospitals in green belts, there is little formal policy guidance above development plan level and even this guidance proves inconsistent and incomplete. The NHS must continue to develop a close involvement in the planning system at all levels. Development plans, in particular local plans, need to reflect aspirations both for health care uses and the development potential of redundant sites. The NHS at a central and regional level must be aware of the nature and potential effect of emerging central government planning policy and the policies contained in development plans. Close coordination between the Department of Health and individual NHS trusts will be essential if the value of the NHS estate is to be retained and enhanced for the future provision of health care. Individual NHS trusts must be aware of the importance of local plans and the consequent need for clear forward planning of their own estate, so they can seek effective involvement in the development plan process.

Chapter 14

CASE STUDY: CANON'S MARSH

Janet Askew

Introduction

How is a major mixed development achieved on a large-scale inner city site? In this chapter and the next, two case studies are selected to investigate how development occurs; both have been the subject of much debate about the level and necessity for planning gain; neither have the benefit of a statutory local plan, both have been the subject of planning briefs. The consideration of these two major sites, one in Bristol, one in London, reveals much about the development process, and the interaction between the public, developers and the local planning authority, as well as their aspirations. The two case studies at Canon's Marsh and King's Cross illustrate emerging trends in attitudes towards major development. In Chapter 10 there is an introduction to the Canon's Marsh location in the historic docklands area of Bristol.

Canon's Marsh: a site of unique importance

Canon's Marsh is a centrally located site forming part of Bristol's central docklands area (Fig. 10.3). The site comprises some 33 acres of land (almost ten times as large as the site chosen by Robin Tetlow in Bedminster). The majority of the site is derelict, following the decline of the traditional docks function in the city centre. The traditional functions of the city centre cover a wide area in Bristol. Canon's Marsh lies close to the city centre, between two shopping centres, Broadmead and Queen's Road, Clifton. To the north of Canon's Marsh is Bristol Cathedral and its associated open space, which it shares with the council-house, town hall to Bristol City Council. To the east lies Queen Square, its Georgian expanse, now mainly occupied by offices. Queen Square adjoins King Square, an important area for entertainment, restaurants and night-life. Running through and adjacent to the central areas of Bristol is the so-called Floating Harbour, which was once the main port, linked with maritime and commercial activities alongside the docks. Many of

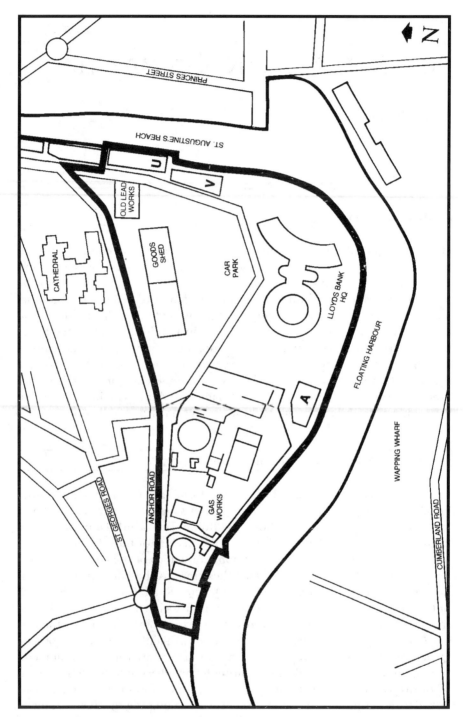

Fig. 14.1 Canon's Marsh – existing plan and site boundary (not to scale)

the buildings and sites that once performed that function now stand derelict, or have been turned into a museum, an art gallery, cinemas, cafes, restaurants and housing. One of the largest undeveloped dockside sites is Canon's Marsh (Fig. 14.1).

Bristol was one of the first British cities to realise the touristic, residential and commercial value of its derelict docks. During the 1970s and 1980s much redevelopment and refurbishment occurred in and around Bristol Docks and the adjacent Floating Harbour. Former warehouses near the city centre were converted into cinemas and arts centres; an exhibition centre and an industrial museum were established in disused warehouses. Shops and cafes were provided along the waterfront; the tourist potential of the SS *Great Britain* (Brunel's steamship) was recognised; upmarket housing was built. Despite all this activity, Canon's Marsh remained undeveloped. Until 1987, the site was dominated by huge tobacco bonds occupying 6 acres of prime land on the waterfront. These were subsequently blown up in a controlled explosion which made the national television news. The remainder of the site has come to be used as a commuter car park with fourteen hundred spaces. It clearly serves an important function in a city where parking is an acute problem and where car ownership is among the highest in Britain. At present, Bristol City Council employees have their own protected parking area at Canon's Marsh; Lloyds Bank provided car parking in association with its offices; there is a public pay-and-display car park and an area for coach parking. At Christmas, the area is used as a Park-and-ride site to feed the main shopping centre of Broadmead (approximately half a mile away). The council has considered using the site for multi-storey car parking. There was a suggestion to use the former tobacco warehouses, but their structure did not allow vehicle turning space.

Central to this debate is the importance of car parking on a city centre site. Both Avon County Council and Bristol City Council have attempted to restrict the provision of parking in the city centre. There is a very low requirement to provide car parking spaces on new schemes. In one case, a new office in Prince Street, Bristol (another central location) the main issue of contention between Bristol City Council and the developers was the developers' requirement for more car parking space than the council was prepared to allow. It was part of the council's policy to restrict the use of cars in the city centre, where many vehicles were parked all day. Bristol city centre has more private dedicated car parking spaces than it has public spaces. In the meantime, car parking has become an important interim use for many pieces of unused land. Car parking releases some value from derelict, blighted or unused land, with minimum effort and investment by landowners. During a recession, demand for offices may be low but demand for car parking remains very high. This has also happened at King's Cross in London.

The western end of the site is occupied by a disused gasworks, with gasometers and derelict buildings. Along with the surrounding land, they are contaminated mainly with arsenic from past industrial activities on the site.

183

Also related to the docks, a range of other sheds are to be found along the waterfront, some occupied with small boat-building workshops further along from the site. A large disused goods shed and redundant lead works lie near the northern boundary of the site. Bristol City Council is the main land-owner, along with British Gas, British Rail and formerly Imperial Tobacco (who later sold its land to Lloyds Bank for development overlooking the waterfront).

Planning history

The unique importance of Canon's Marsh as a development site has long been recognised by Bristol City Council. To date, Bristol City Council has no statutory local plan, a fact which has created some uncertainty in the city, and a poor relationship between the city council and potential developers (Punter 1990). A city docks plan was published in 1980, when the first of many attempts to market the site for development was made by employing consultants. The city council's enduring aspiration for the site was that it should be used for leisure and recreation. Hillier Parker, the first consultants, recognised that any proposals had to be financially viable, despite the recession of the early 1980s. The tobacco bonds buildings (a local term for bonded warehouses) were recognised as a constraint to any development. As a result, they dismissed the idea of leisure uses, suggesting that non-profit uses (i.e. leisure and recreation) should be avoided. Furthermore, it would not he possible for the commercial elements to support the cost of leisure facilities (Hillier Parker 1983). Thus from an early stage, the possibilities for planning gain were ignored. It is hard to imagine now, but there was a phase when developers were somewhat cautious about committing themselves to docklands sites in Bristol and it took quite a while for the momentum to build up then take off in terms of market demand.

Planning brief

In 1984 the city council's first brief for Canon's Marsh (Bristol 1984) was rigid regarding the physical layout of the site (Fig. 14.2). It lacked imagination and suggested retention of many existing features, presumably in the name of conservation policy. It did not view the site as a whole and made no proposals for the key waterfront site occupied by the tobacco bonds. Dockside schemes offering a tourist mixture of uses were becoming popular in North America and were beginning to influence planners. Particularly influential were schemes in Boston and Baltimore, on the eastern seaboard of the United States, and the emerging tourist attraction of Covent Garden in London. The planning brief was adamant in stating that office development was completely unacceptable on the site, and that its main use should be leisure and recreation, including hotels, cafes and speciality shopping.

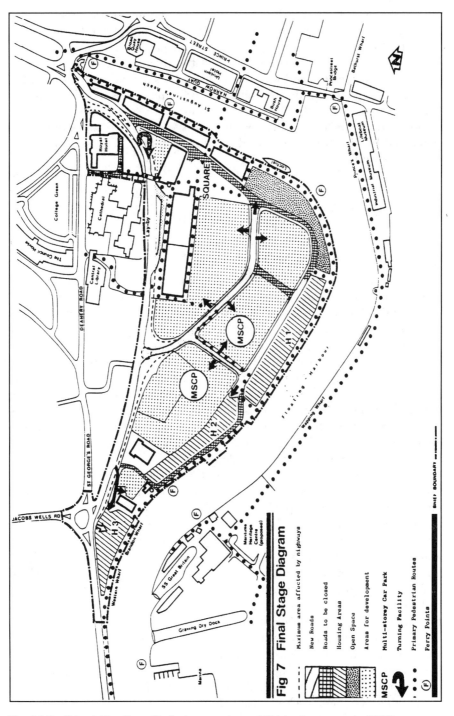

Fig. 14.2 Bristol City Council's final stage scheme 1984 (scale approx. 1 : 8000)

One of the main failings of the brief was that it did not address the issues of land ownership or the dominance of the tobacco bonds. Bristol City Council failed to recognise the importance of its own position as the prime land-owner on the site. This gave the council the financial leverage to form a partnership with other landowners and developers for the redevelopment of the site. Their failure to do so resulted in the value of the council's land not being realised. Ironically, the tobacco bonds were sold in 1986 and later demolished to create a prime development site. The land was immediately purchased by Lloyds Bank on condition that planning permission could be obtained for offices.

Although demolition of the bonds had always been seen as a constraint to development, the promise of offices on the site, allowed the cost of demolition to be absorbed.

Lloyds Bank proposal

The proposal was for some 210,000 square feet of office space. The grant of planning permission represented a complete volte-face by the planning committee and the city planning officer, as all previous briefs had rejected any office development at Canon's Marsh. The scheme was presented to the public as part of a conspiracy (Punter 1990), which would involve the inclusion of Canon's Marsh within a newly designated urban development corporation, thus removing control of this important site from the city council. Some commentators wondered if this would be such a bad thing, since nothing had happened on the site despite so much development interest. The advantages described by the council to justify the decision were job creation, demolition of the bonded warehouses and the opportunity to pump-prime the site, opening the way for further development.

The intention of Lloyds was to develop the prime site at Canon's Marsh in isolation to any other proposed uses at Canon's Marsh. A crescent-shaped building was proposed for phase 1, enclosing an 'amphitheatre' alongside the water, which it was agreed the public could use for one hundred days per year. (There are now two circular 'crescent' buildings on the site, one by the waterfront and one built behind it). Punter wondered if this space would be 'merely a monument to the power of major financial institutions.' Good design and the quality of the building were proclaimed as planning gain, as had happened in the past with schemes in Bristol. In 1976, the particular relationship between office development and conservation policy was outlined in a report to the planning and traffic committee. Office development could go ahead if there was a possibility of obtaining an adequate conservation gain, or if it 'would make an outstanding contribution to the environment which could not otherwise be achieved.' At the time of the Lloyds proposal, the local paper reflected a high level of debate. There were objections from the public, from professional town planners and from architects.

It is hard to imagine the creation of a more difficult building form for subsequent architects to respond to.

(Punter 1990)

And so it was that Bristol City Council permitted the best site at Canon's Marsh, the waterfront site, to be developed without any regard for what might happen elsewhere. It's principal basis was a hope of pump-priming to open the way for further development. Some seven years later, nothing else has happened.

Other schemes and plans

Certainly, at the time of the Lloyds application, development interest was high, probably because it coincided with the peak of the property boom. Comprehensive schemes were submitted, some even taking account of Lloyds' desire to site offices on the site, but the Council seemed to reject them all, and none came to fruition. In November 1988, LDR International Ltd., another group of consultants, was employed to create a plan for Canon's Marsh (LDR 1990), but without reaching agreement about cross-subsidising land values. Engaged by some of the landowners, LDR was required to cost any of its proposals, and its work is significant for two reasons. Firstly, LDR applied a completely new concept called parcelisation (see Fig. 14.3). Although new to Bristol, it is reminiscent of the approach within the Isle of Dogs Enterprise Zone in London Docklands. LDR divided the land into a number of parcels; inside each one was a mixture of uses which allowed for cross-subsidy within the parcel. Secondly, LDR included the south side of the Floating Harbour, namely, Wapping Wharf. The main proposal was for offices (36%), with residential uses (26%) and leisure uses (38%). Bristol City Council had not officially updated its 1984 brief, which still stated that office development was unacceptable, and as a result, the proposals by LDR were rejected. Three new principles had been accepted:

(1) Development plans for Canon's Marsh should include land at Wapping Wharf.
(2) Offices may be necessary for viable development.
(3) There should be cross-subsidisation of land values over the whole site.

Because the LDR scheme had succeeded in interesting all the landowners at Canon's Marsh, demands were made for a new planning brief, prepared with proper public consultation, which would include a development framework for the whole area. As if to close the door on past mistakes, and to create a new image, the area was renamed Harbourside, and the city council engaged a development facilitator to promote the partnership between landowners and to find a developer or the means of financing the development.

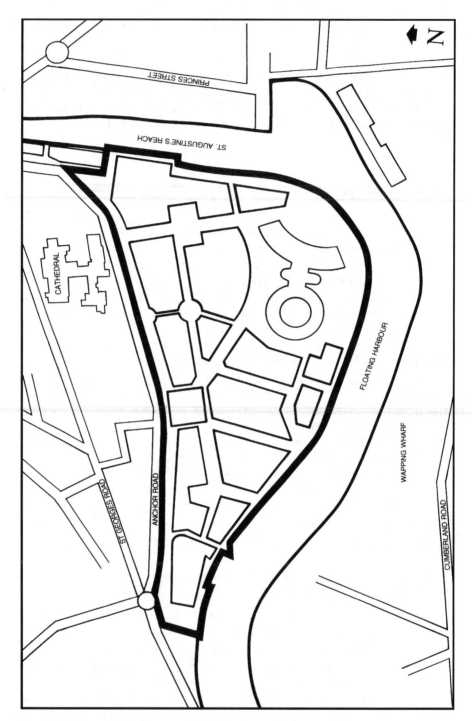

Fig. 14.3 Canon's Marsh – example of 'parcelisation' (not to scale)

Yet more consultants

Following some work by a group of local architects, called the Concept Planning Group, a new consultant's brief was drawn up by the city council in 1993 to employ yet more consultants, Drivers Jonas. It could be argued that this brief (Bristol 1993b) was better defined than previous briefs for the area. Its specific objectives included a mixed use comprehensive approach, viability phased over a number of years, major recreational and cultural facilities for Bristol and more general objectives relating to employment, urban design, access, etc. Significantly, the objectives state that each solution must be 'capable of being implemented by each landowner acting alone.' And all solutions had to undergo financial appraisal. According to a 1993 press release from the city council, a centre for the performing arts (CPA) will be a key element of the proposed development. The Council acknowledged the need to create a special Harbourside fund, of initially £1 million.

Regrettably, the plan produced by Drivers Jonas for Canon's Marsh in 1994 consists almost entirely of an office park comprising some 600,000 square feet of office floor space. Drivers Jonas estimated the need for £6 million of public money to be put into the scheme over six years (*Planning*, 25 March 1994, No. 1061, p. 27). Drivers Jonas and Hillier Parker were but two of the firms of private consultants and chartered surveyors involved in producing plans for the site. The consultants suggest that the office element would release some surplus value to contribute towards the CPA, now emerging as a proposal alongside the waterfront to the east of Lloyds Bank. The Concept Planning Group has suggested that waterfront land to the west of Lloyds should be used for housing, and the offices could be built along the main Canons Way. There is also some consideration of potential grant aid, especially for the CPA. A draft outline plan for the CPA includes all sources of public funding and grant aid which might be available. Funds are to be gathered from six sources: the Arts Council Millennium Fund; the National Lottery; the Urban Regeneration Agency; the European Union; the value of the council's land in Harbourside; and the value of the land currently occupied by the Colston Hall, a concert venue owned by the city council in the centre of Bristol (on a site unrelated to Harbourside). The funding of an important public facility returns partly to be the responsibility of the public sector.

There would appear to be no theory of development behind the Drivers Jonas plan. It neither includes the principle of parcelisation nor takes account of land cross-subsidy, so necessary at Canon's Marsh, where land clearly has different values. The Drivers Jonas plan cannot be described as comprehensive, since the office blocks could be developed in isolation from each other and from the other uses on the site. There is no flexible development framework, along the lines suggested by Wrenn (1983) and considered in the very next section. Instead, the Drivers Jonas plan depends very much upon the notion that use of land for offices will produce high values, which in turn depends upon an increased demand for office floor space. In Bristol there are considerable areas of vacant office floor space; current claims suggest 10 million square feet.

A catalogue of failed plans

The history of Canon's Marsh represents a catalogue of failed plans and proposals. Development interest has been high in Bristol since 1945 (Punter 1990), and Canon's Marsh has long been recognised as a site of unique importance. It certainly represents a massive development opportunity, standing as it does in the centre of Bristol, located in the successfully developed and renovated city docks. It could be argued that the city council has never taken the necessary lead in promoting development. In his book *Urban Waterfront Development* Wrenn documents the situation in America. This is important because of American influences, especially on Bristol, where examples in the United States are regularly cited. He stresses strong leadership by local government, and his case studies of successful redevelopment schemes of urban waterfronts, show a need for a waterfront development plan, a financial strategy and a phasing programme. More cooperation between public and private development interests is considered to be the way forward in America.

> The best waterfront plans are specific enough to provide a framework for development, yet flexible enough to respond to dynamic factors influencing project implementation.
>
> (Wrenn 1983)

Various conclusions can be drawn from the case study of Canon's Marsh:

1   The city council was not prepared to take the lead either as a landowner or as the planning authority. As the main landowner, the city council utterly failed to take a lead in the redevelopment of the site by urging the formation of a landowners consortium, or by forming a partnership with private sector interests to redevelop their part of the site.

2   The city council rejected many proposals for development. Some took the form of preapplication approaches by the developers, others were in the form of interested parties and local architects putting forward plans, ideas and proposals for the site. Some schemes were rejected because they were considered to be unrealistic and incapable of being implemented; others were discounted for more minor reasons, such as not complying with some existing brief for the site. Development opportunities were consequently missed during the property boom of the mid 1980s.

3   There was a failure to guide potential developers when developer interest was being shown in the site, and a failure to harness expressions of professional interest by local architects and other local expertise. An

analysis of the numerous plans produced by consultants must lead to a conclusion that time and money has been wasted, especially as none have succeeded in promoting development on the site.

4   In permitting the Lloyds offices, the city council accepted a type of development that had been vigorously denied for many years, making a mockery of their planning and development briefs for the site. They prematurely provided a road into the site without any regard for the future uses or urban form of the site, which in the end allowed Lloyds to locate at Canon's Marsh without contributing anything to infrastructure costs. The latest plans for the site use Lloyds as a precedent for the location of further office development.

5   During the boom years of the mid 1980s, planning gain did not feature in any of the city council's plans or any of their briefs to consultants. This meant they did not come to terms with the possibility of cross-subsidy as a way forward. Although in 1984 they did not agree with a comprehensive plan for the whole area, they failed to understand the difference between a masterplan approach, which would have been rigid, and a development framework or concept, which would have been sufficiently flexible. The Deposit Bristol Local Plan (Bristol 1993a) wants to achieve a 'comprehensive approach to the planning and redevelopment of Harbourside.'

6   In its latest plans for Harbourside, Bristol City Council recognises that the proposals for leisure and recreation, in particular the centre for the performing arts, will not be implemented by the private sector alone. Public sector finance is back on the agenda, with a list of various sources for funding, although other cities are certain to be tapping the same limited sources. There is also some reliance upon the economics of the market-place, and this might prevent the performing arts centre from going ahead under its latest proposals.

PART V

PEOPLE, POLICIES AND POWER

INTRODUCTION

Community issues

In this part, the emphasis shifts from site development towards a consideration of the needs of the wider community who might benefit from the development, and the chances of achieving satisfactory development by means of planning gain, by negotiation and by imposing conditions on planning permissions. A longer introduction is provided in this section to provide a social context to the issues under discussion.

The last chapter provided a case study of the problems of the development of Canon's Marsh in the centre of Bristol. The planning authority was presented by Janet Askew as not taking a strong lead in respect of site development on Canon's Marsh, and not liaising with community interests, or taking the opportunity to obtain socially and environmentally advantageous development. This contrasts starkly with the proactive and innovative role taken by the planning authority in the case of King's Cross, where a much higher level of community involvement is in evidence, as described by Janet Askew in Chapter 15. Comparisons between approaches adopted on the two sites are drawn out in the latter part of this chapter. The situation at King's Cross is not resolved and the process continues. In her conclusion to Chapter 15, Janet Askew puts forward interim proposals for using the land positively to the benefit of the community.

In an article 'Visionary Plan Derailed?' (*Estates Times* 8 April 1994, p. 15 of its London Midtown Survey) the site is referred to as a 'poisoned chalice' and there is discussion as to how much of the original vision can survive under a more commercialised environment with denationalisation of British Rail, and ownership passing to what is now called Union Railways. But, according to a report in *Planning Week* (28 April 1994, p. 3), Camden subsequently decided that office-led development on the site would not go ahead, giving a further boost to the prospects of implementation of the community interim use initiative. Michael Edwards' account of King's Cross is also of relevance (Edwards 1992). Readers are strongly advised to check the current development situation.

Equal opportunities and planning

Chapters 16 and 17 move further along the social spectrum in considering the opportunities that planning might offer for the implementation of equal opportunities policies. Such policies are borough-wide, thus the examples presented by Linda Davies are not limited to one particular site, as opportunities for compliance may occur wherever application for development occurs. Linda Davies draws on her extensive experience in England and Scotland to move the book further into the realms of people and planning. But she remains cognisant of the processes introduced earlier on.

> In all their professional activities, members [of the Royal Town Planning Institute] shall seek to eliminate discrimination on the grounds of race, sex, creed, religion, disability, or age, shall seek to eliminate such discrimination by others, and to promote equality of opportunity.
> (From the *Code of Professional Conduct*, RTPI, 13.4.94: Para 2)

During the course of their professional duties, not least in their involvement with the implementary process, town planners have a duty to promote equal opportunities and to eliminate discrimination against minority groups. Chapters 16 and 17 therefore consider different aspects of the relationship between equal opportunities issues and town planning. They present national data and the findings of a region-wide study undertaken by Linda Davies (1993) in respect of 'planning and ethnic minorities' in the south-west of England.

Chapters 16 and 17 together cover three topical issues: planning for ethnic minorities, planning for the special needs of women and planning for the disabled. These three policy areas combine to cover perhaps the most important aspects of equal opportunities in the planning profession. Examples are drawn from a range of development plan documents with particular emphasis upon the London boroughs (Fig. 16.1) and the South-West. The implications of current planning practice in the equal opportunities field are considered together with some pointers for future policy formulation.

As explained in Chapter 2, the development plan, whether it be the structure plan in the shire counties, or the UDP in the London boroughs and larger metropolitan areas, provides strategic policy direction. The policies developed should, in turn, be reflected within the local plans and through development control decisions within the implementation process. The role of development plan policy statements as a means to enable planning-for-people, and thus as a negotiating tool in extracting planning gain, has already been introduced by Janet Askew. Under the British planning systems (including Scotland), all applications for development are considered against the relevant policies of the adopted development plan. The implementation of any development, therefore, will be strongly influenced by these policies. It has been found that equal opportunities issues are given prominence in the format of many of the new-style development plans in London, but are also found to a lesser degree in some of the traditional structure and local plans in the South-West. To a greater or lesser extent, many development plans nowadays incorporate equal opportunities policies. In fact, this national variability and patchiness reflects the generally unsatisfactory and ambiguous nature of government guidance. It also reflects the different levels of commitment to equal opportunities from individual local authorities and the varied politically informed perceptions of the role of planning policy in society.

What is a minority?

One still comes across planners, men and women, who ask: *Is there really any need to plan separately, or differently, for minorities?* More worryingly, one still hears comments which suggest some are not convinced of its importance: *There aren't many of them in any case, so why should they receive special treatment; they should fit in with all the rest!* Or more tellingly: *Why should they have all the resources? We will lose out.* In fact, everyone benefits.

These issues must be faced as they affect planners' perceptions of who and what they are planning for. Such assumptions must inevitably affect their choice of objectives in plan making, and inform their priorities and perceptions of success in undertaking the implementation process. The development process, and the end-product – what is built – can appear somewhat peopleless and not particularly user-friendly. This is especially true if the other professional groups, such as surveyors, engineers, lawyers and construction managers, dominate the implementary process, as they are chiefly concerned with cost factors, planning appeals, technical matters and engineering constraints. Planners are one of the main groups in the development process who can push for a more socially aware approach to design and development, and can promote the needs of the residents. But if the planners' perceptions of the people they are planning for, people who will use the ensuing development, are limited then it is no wonder that residents and community groups are often so dissatisfied with the results of the planners' efforts.

This is noticeable in respect of race, gender and disability issues, but even in the past, when some 'socialist' Neo-Marxist planners made much of the fact they were 'planning for the working classes', they often seem to see such groups in purely workerist or sentimentalised terms. Indeed, many of the mainstream (malestream) 'urban sociology' and 'urban politics' books (Dunleavy 1980; Pickvance 1977; Pinch 1985; and even in respect of Bristol, Bassett and Short, 1980), in spite of all their emphasis on issues of class and power, seem by today's standards amazingly peopleless, with no mention of the problems of the disabled, women, children or the elderly, and how human beings *uze* cities. I choose *uze* purposely to distinguish it from *use* in the sense of land use. Greed (1994) makes the same distinction because there is a whole different world-view in seeing town planning as being to do with *land uses* as against being a matter of how people *uze land*. When people uze land they uze the developments, streets and buildings thereon, all of them included in the legal definition of 'land' (see Part II and Circular 13/87). This different perspective is undoubtedly reflected in much of the work of the women-and-planning movement, and in disability policies.

Planning is for people, but who does *people* include? How many are women? Ethnic minority? Disabled? Numerically it was found that the number of ethnic minority people in some areas was quite small, especially in some of the local authority areas investigated within the South-West in Linda Davies' research. But ethnic minority groups made up significantly large proportions, over one-third, even one-half, of the population of some London boroughs. This is also the case in some parts of the Midlands. National minorities they may be, but in these areas of concentration, the people in question are clearly *not* minorities. The two groups next to be considered are spread rather more evenly throughout the country. Women can hardly be called a minority group when they represent 52% of the population, according to the last census. Also, except for a few separatist feminist communities, some schools and some religious institutions, one is unlikely to find whole settlements composed exclusively of women, or men for that matter. People tend to come in varied mixtures of age, gender, class and ethnicity, all living in the same urban or rural space. In fact, one might argue that people are more likely to be sorted on the basis of class in most urban areas, still a valid point (as stressed in Bassett and Short 1980) but incomplete without the other dimensions of inequality, including those of race, gender, disability and age.

In fact, women are an integral 'half' of all human communities. It should be remembered, for example, that 50% of all ethnic minority groups are female, with the figure reaching 55% in the case of the Afro-Caribbean population (at least half of whom are over the age of 30). This contradicts the frequent media stereotype of young, black, deviant males. Numerically the most typical black person in Britain is probably a middle-aged woman who is likely to work in the service industries, such as the health service. Indeed, one of the ongoing women-and-planning debates is whether one should, or could, plan separately for women's needs when they share the same urban space (houses, streets, towns) as men. Planning is for people. Traditional plan making seldom disaggregated people on the basis of personal characteristics; all were seen as human beings likely to have similar needs and town planning requirements. But many have shown how 'planning for all', where 'all' is male, white, car-driving, middle class and young to middle-aged can seriously disadvantage everyone who falls outside this stereotype.

As to the numbers of disabled, it is hard to be exact, although Linda Davies does give some figures. It depends on what counts as disability. Again, there is a popular stereotype that the disabled consist only of people in wheelchairs. This somewhat narrow view has no doubt restricted the emphasis of much planning policy; as Linda Davies found in her research, the issues that predominate are transport, mobility and access. Indeed, the provision of an occasional ramp or dropped kerb seems to epitomise the lack of imagination in some local authorities. Many show a very limited understanding of the full range of disabilities and the varied needs they create. All the same, every ramp is appreciated.

Also it must be borne in mind that Britain has an aging population; many but by no means all disabled are also elderly. This trend will put increasing demands on the town planning system to provide for those who perhaps can no longer drive; need more public transport; like plenty of seats and benches along the way; cannot tackle steps; require frequently placed public conveniences; and have their own particular shopping, leisure and even recreational interests which are very different from those of able-bodied youngsters. Concomitant shifts are required in land use planning priorities. In particular, many are suggesting that possibly more close-knit, higher density cities, in which land uses are integrated together and not zoned apart, will prove more convenient for the forthcoming less mobile population of the future, as well as being more environmentally friendly and requiring less car use. The end of Chapter 17 considers some guidelines (originally developed for the CISC exercise described in Chapter 2) on how to ensure the planning process complies with equal opportunities objectives. The reader can find out more about changing demographic patterns in Britain by consulting *Social Trends*, produced annually by the Office of Population, Census and Surveys (OPCS 1994).

Envoi

After reading Chapter 17, refer to Appendix 3. This material was originally prepared for the CISC mapping exercise (Chapter 2) and incorporated as an appendix in the RTPI draft equal opportunities policy statement (RTPI 1994b). Appendix 3 seeks to present guidelines on how to ensure that minority groups gain full representation throughout the planning policy implementation process. Chapter 18 and especially Chapter 19 continue this theme. They consider how socially oriented policies might best be packaged to appear acceptable and valid, and thus increase their chances of implementation) in a planning system which so often has ruled them *ultra vires*. Indeed, the professional culture and the world-view of the policy makers is bound to influence which considerations are seen as worthy of inclusion, or exclusion, from the implementation process, particularly in the white, male dominated, middle-class built environment professions (see Chapter 9; Greed 1991, 1994).

Chapter 15

CASE STUDY: KING'S CROSS

Janet Askew

| Two sites compared |

Two-thirds of this chapter paints a fascinating picture of the King's Cross railways lands site; the final third draws lessons from King's Cross and from Canon's Marsh. The history of the King's Cross development is very different from Canon's Marsh; throughout the process, both community and local authority play a much stronger role.

The King's Cross railway lands comprise some 134 acres (Canon's Marsh was 33 acres, York Gate was 4.5 acres), large parts of which are derelict and underused, but possessing the commercial potential for redevelopment (Fig. 15.1). This is located at

> the interface between central business-district type activities and an old established inner city working class community.
>
> (Parkes and Mouawad 1991)

The site extends northwards from two stations, King's Cross and St. Pancras. It includes vast areas of railway lands and goods yards, and is crossed by the Regents Canal. The northern part of the site is used as a depot for receiving imported aggregates by rail for processing into concrete. The site is surrounded by residential communities, although there is only a relatively small amount of housing on the site itself. Parts of the southern area of the site are designated as conservation areas and are dominated by the Grade I listed station buildings of St. Pancras and King's Cross. The railway lands contain

> A unique assemblage of dramatic mainline rail termini and attendant support services . . . (standing) as a testimony to the Victorian architectural and engineering innovation and panache which was to so solidly shape the destiny of King's Cross and London over the succeeding century.
>
> (Parkes 1990)

Planning history

In 1988, when Camden Borough Council produced a community land planning brief for the site, they failed to realise, or predict, its true commercial

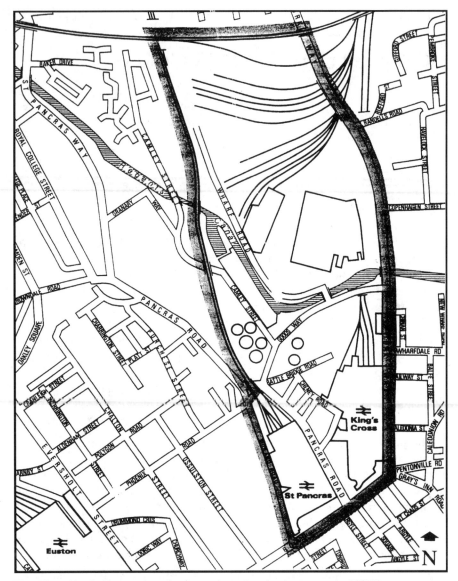

Fig. 15.1 King's Cross railway lands: site boundary (scale approx. 1 : 10000)

potential. It was recognised that regeneration was necessary and the brief realised that the development of the railway lands provided

> an unprecedented opportunity for the local community, developers, landowners, the local authority and other public agencies to demonstrate how large-scale, inner city regeneration can be accomplished through cooperation, not confrontation.
>
> (Camden 1988)

Unlike Bristol's brief for Canon's Marsh, Camden Borough Council's 1988 brief for this area of land promoted a 'comprehensive approach' to the development of the land. The council would only allow new uses on the site, dependent upon how they would fit into a 'comprehensive package or master plan.' A further, and later significant objective was that local people should be protected against any adverse social and environmental impacts of large-scale commercial activities. The brief was to provide

> A strong incentive ... for the developer to come forward with a scheme which respects the industrial heritage of the site, which encourages diversity, and which strikes a proper balance between the interests of strategic and local community and commerce.

> (ibid 1988)

Channel Tunnel terminal

It is doubtful whether, some five years later, the community would consider Camden Borough Council had been loyal to their objectives. In 1989, the London Regeneration Consortium (LAG) and British Rail submitted a planning application in outline to Camden Borough Council for the development of the railway lands. This was largely prompted by the proposed use of King's Cross as a low-level Channel Tunnel terminal and new rail passenger concourse. The concourse depended upon a strategic decision by the government, and despite uncertainty around the route of the Channel Tunnel rail link and its London terminal, plans were prepared. The application was for 5.86 million square feet of offices (57% of the total floor space); 1.6 million square feet of residential uses (16%), 0.2 million square feet of industrial uses (2%); 0.3 million square feet of shopping uses (3%); 0.36 million square feet of cultural uses (3%) and 0.1 million square feet of hotels (1%). The remaining 18% was car parking, storage, plant, etc, all underground. The scheme, prepared by Foster Associates, includes a central park surrounded by offices buildings of between seven and ten storeys, and two office towers of forty-four storeys, each as high as the NatWest Tower in the City of London. To accommodate the underground terminal for the Channel Tunnel, the southern part of the site would be a vast construction site, necessitating the demolition of many buildings and whole streets around King's Cross. It was immediately clear that the proposed scheme did not meet the objectives of Camden Borough Council's brief, i.e. for a development that allowed the local community to 'participate fully' and for a scheme that would provide substantial benefits for the existing community.

The 1987 statutory local plan presumed against increases in speculative office development schemes and in particular at King's Cross. British Rail had pointed out at the local plan inquiry that the only way to fund improvements to the mainline stations was by using any available land for office development. To overcome this objection, the borough council resolved to discuss with British Rail other methods of funding improvements to the stations. In submitting the application, British Rail clearly had no regard for the policies adopted in the Camden Borough Plan, nor for the desires of the people who lived within and adjacent to the site. Surveys of those people indicated that the preferred choice of development on the site was overwhelmingly housing, mainly low cost housing. It was clear that the submitted scheme dominated as it was by offices, was intended to maximise returns for British Rail and other owners of the land (including National Freight Corporation, British Waterways Board and North Thames Gas).

King's Cross Railway Lands Group

In response to the proposals, the local community established a group to investigate their impact and ultimately to make their own proposals for the site. The group, known as the King's Cross Railway Lands Group (KXRLG) is unique in making proposals that have been fully costed, with complete regard for the prevailing property market, its aspirations and its requirements for profit. To enable this sophisticated understanding, the KXRLG employed a number of experts (including economists from University College London, Bartlett School) to assist in the preparation of alternative schemes. Their first method of approach was to employ the bottom-up process of planning-for-real, where local people are given an opportunity to state their own aspirations in an accessible way. The method was devised by Dr Tony Gibson in the late 1960s and was first used in Birkenhead. People are invited to view a large-scale model of the area, upon which they place their proposals for demolition, rehabilitation, change of use or new building. A town planner collates the numerous comments and ideas and produces a community plan. This is an example of a more imaginative form of public participation than is usually undertaken as part of the statutory planning process, and no doubt increased the public's understanding of, and interest in, the site's future. At King's Cross, a large number of planning-for-real events have been held over the years since the submission of the LRC proposals in 1988. The principles embodied in the resulting land use plan were location of some offices at the southern end of the site, using much of the rest for housing, community facilities, workspace and open space. The *People's Brief* (Parkes 1990) complemented the borough brief produced by Camden (1988).

People or profit?

The King's Cross Railway Lands Group carefully examined its proposals for their financial implications (KXRLG 1989). It posed the question, Who would really benefit from the developers' proposals? The developers alleged that the number of offices was necessary to fund the purchase of the land, infrastructure and building and interest charges, but the KXRLG needed to discover if this was necessarily true. The Economic Assessment Working Party of the Railway Lands Group estimated the gross profits of the LRC scheme to be £2.2 billion (based on 1989 figures and before the recession had deepened). They based their own calculations on the mixture of uses revealed in the aforementioned surveys, that is, 39.5% to housing, 14% to industry and 8.5% to offices. It was discovered that even with land divided on this basis, there could still be gross profits of £400 million. The KXRLG wondered how much profit the developers should be allowed to make and what should be the price, social or otherwise, borne by the community. Its 1989 paper had argued that whatever was built on the railway lands, the profit should be shared out between the landowners, the developers and the community. The options for the community should be

(1) Freely provided land to be used for social facilities
(2) The building of the social facilities and housing, which would be handed over to the community to run
(3) A financial share – lump sum paid into a community trust
(4) A lump sum to Camden Council as direct planning gain

The KXRLG concluded that, given the potential for profit, alternatives to the LRC scheme were possible. Schemes more advantageous to the community could still show millions of pounds of profit.' Crucially it concluded that the value of the development and of the land depended on the planning permission. The scheme could be influenced by Camden Council, which did not need to grant planning permission. The huge values (and therefore profits) would only accrue if planning permission were given for the predominantly office scheme. In this situation it would doubtless be argued by Camden that a refusal of planning permission would merely force an appeal to the secretary of state and a potential award of costs against the council for unreasonable refusal of planning permission. It was surprising in the case of the King's Cross proposals that the secretary of state did not call in the application. This was expected, based on the national importance of the Channel Tunnel terminal.

The People's Plan

In the event, Camden Borough Council did not reach a decision on the LRC scheme until 1993, when it was 'minded to permit'; no decision notice has ever been issued. In the meantime, the KXRLG produced the *People's Plan*, and based upon its findings, submitted a planning application on behalf of the community. In 1991, the KXRLG evaluated four schemes for the railway lands. One of them was the commercial scheme by LRC, the subject of the planning application. Another scheme, proposed by KXT, had many of the aims of the LRC scheme, including just over 4 million square feet of offices, a low-level terminal and the establishment of a community development trust. Two schemes were proposed by KXRLG itself.

KXRLG1 was a mixed development including over two hundred housing units, 1.8 million square feet of offices and a high-level terminal at St. Pancras.

KXRLG2 contained some 300,000 square feet of offices and no Channel Tunnel terminal of any kind, but considerable amounts of affordable housing and workspace.

KXRLG1 was based on conventional cross-subsidy of elements, for example, affordable housing from returns on office and other commercial floor space, while still giving the landowners and developers an acceptable rate of return. Implementation was envisaged via a series of interlocking trusts, a quite new 'organisational landscape.' To some extent, the differences in levels of office floor space between the LRC scheme and KXRLG1 reflect the markedly different costs of the low-level terminal as against a high-level terminal at St. Pancras. KXRLG2 refused to accept any significant direct relationship between public works, social services and returns on commercial development. It was based upon a supposedly well-funded housing corporation, a local authority and access to European and other regeneration grants. Parkes and Mouawad (1991) evaluates the financial implications of all the schemes. The first three schemes rely on private profits to cross-subsidise non-profitable elements (i.e. planning gain). KXRLG2 does not rely solely on private profits but depends upon public funding to be implemented. Of the four schemes, only the first three have the potential to be commercially viable, assuming no recession in the property market.

Community planning brief

The revised brief, prepared by Camden (1993), for the King's Cross railway lands acknowledges the massive impact that the community has had upon the planning and proposals for the area since 1988. The new brief outlines the opportunities for inner city regeneration through cooperation and partnership between the local community, developers, landowners, the local authority and other public agencies. The 1993 brief acknowledges a shift away from, or less reliance upon, the private sector alone for inner city urban regeneration. In London, unitary development plans have been published advocating a greener, more sustainable approach to development, recognising that the office market has collapsed, and office growth might not feature strongly in subsequent economic recovery. The main aim of Camden's strategy is to achieve a balanced mix of uses that

> should remain attainable throughout the development of the Railway Lands by means of planning agreements and implementation, through, for example, a development trust on which all participants are represented.

> (Camden 1993)

The objectives reflect some of the planning agreements on planning gain that might be sought. These include employment measures (on-site training,

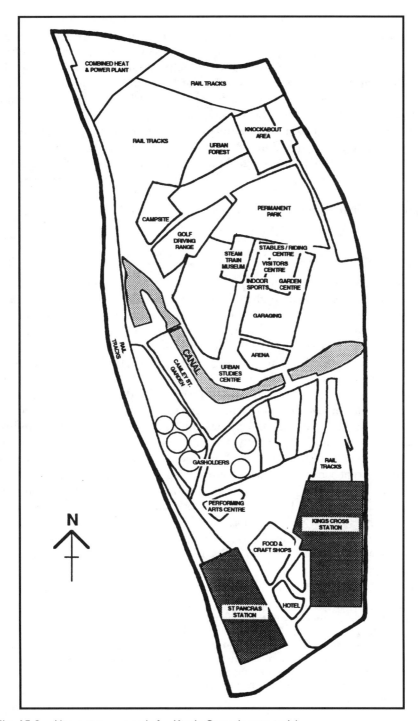

Fig. 15.2 Alternative proposals for King's Cross (not to scale)

retraining local employment during construction phase); affordable housing; leisure, social and welfare facilities, including community centre, sports, day and child care provision. To this end, the council welcomes the setting up of a community development trust to help design, fund and manage the variety of land uses and activities on the site. Since then the office market has collapsed. Uncertainty over the location of the Channel Tunnel terminal continued until 1994, when St. Pancras was announced to be the site for it. This has meant increased uncertainty over the use of the King's Cross railway lands, and following revision of the community planning brief, Camden Borough Council has asked the LRC to withdraw its application. The Channel Tunnel rail link is still dependent upon a joint public/private sector project. It is possible that the earliest the link could be built is 2002, but the completion date could be as late as 2015 (Parkes 1993).

Interim uses initiative

The KXRLG plans were commended by the Royal Town Planning Institute (RTPI) for being 'convincingly drawn up' with an analysis that was comprehensive. This wealth of information and knowledge derived over the past five years has been put to use in the preparation of a plan for interim uses published in 1993. The KXRLG had long been aware of the collapse in office rental values and the growing over supply of office floor space in London. In January 1994 it published the Interim Uses Initiative for King's Cross. This coincided with the announcement by the government that St. Pancras would be the London terminal for the Channel Tunnel link, which rendered much of the earlier schemes (and particularly the LRC planning application) unviable. After six years and many millions of pounds in fees (said to be £30 million), the schemes produced by the developers are unlikely to reach fruition. Interim uses are gaining momentum and reference was made to the concept in the draft advice of the London Planning Advisory Committee, which stated the possibilities of ten years' temporary uses at King's Cross. Some refer to this as the 'now, soon, later' approach, which advocates time-scales for the short-, medium- and long-term development of an area. The Interim Uses Initiative outlines its vision for the future.

> The traveller arriving on the TGV from Paris or Milan in 2003 should thus expect to emerge from St. Pancras into a many faceted, thriving district, combining a wide variety of both temporary and permanent activities. Such offices as there may be are likely to be spin-offs from the University, the British Library, Contemporary Dance or the dozens of charities and trade unions in the area – rather than corporate headquarters. The resident population may have increased, making a contribution to reverse commuting and to begin pedestrian and cycle trips, helping to support all-day and year-round activity and sustaining a strong multi-ethnic culture.

The objectives of the initiative include

- Immediate action to improve the area
- Improving security of existing residents and enterprises rather than displacing them
- Uses which can 'ebb and flow'
- New functions for existing land, buildings and people
- Building a harmonious set of interim activities, lasting from two to twenty years, without preventing a shift to long-term investments if and when funds become available from private, government or European sources.

A very comprehensive survey of all land and buildings on the site revealed those which were capable of renovation, those at risk, land which was contaminated or could be reclaimed, conservation areas and listed buildings. It was discovered that there were three elements common to all proposed long-term schemes for the railway lands, namely, a permanent park and the retention of the goods yard complex of buildings. Suggestions for interim uses were invited via a steering group and canvassed through a series of planning-for-real exercises. Uses put forward included a garden festival; city farm, training; sports facilities, including horse-riding, athletics, roller-skating and other sports which could be accommodated in a former goods shed (tenpin bowling, weight training, etc); exhibition centre, many different types of housing, including self-build, short-life housing, some schemes incorporating construction training; parkland (Fig. 15.2). The vision includes a plan for the area, and in common with the rigour of earlier reports, each use is carefully costed, using a variety of funds. The initiative centres upon

Image: this is considered crucial if investment is to be attracted to the area, now, soon and later, and in getting the blight lifted from the area. It is argued that money spent now on environmental improvements to upgrade the image of King's Cross will be more than repaid through increased investment in the future.

Temporary and permanent uses: this includes a reorganisation of car parking, involving the resiting of certain parking areas and their usage for markets and food stalls, and the release of land currently used for parking for other uses. Parking land could be used more economically. A short-term arts/performance centre is proposed within a former warehouse, as well as short-term prefabricated housing with construction training. Temporary gardens and allotments, along with a festival garden, are proposed. These proposals are made to fit in with the permanent park, and the permanent use of the two aforementioned buildings, the Fish and Coal Offices and the Western Transit Shed.

Linkages: pedestrian and cycle links across the site are crucial in the short-term and might survive to become permanent.

The initiative describes this vision as a change from the 'comprehensive master planning' approach of the 1980s, inimical to the 'now, soon, later' approach of the post-modernist 1990s. The plan includes pilot projects, which are important to illustrate the potential success of the interim uses scheme. The implementation of the entire initiative depends upon striking a balance between community aspirations towards economic and social improvements and sound business capitalism. The report explores existing sources of finance, which include various urban regeneration mechanisms such as development trusts, urban partnerships, private development, regeneration agencies and community cooperatives.

Most are based upon the concept of partnership between the private and public sectors, but a bottom-up approach is their hallmark, rather than the top-down approach advocated by government-led initiatives such as City Challenge. Additional sources of funds are likely to include the European Social Fund, the Sports Council, English Partnerships, English Heritage and the Training and Enterprise Councils. The National Lottery and the Millennium Fund may be available after 1995 for certain projects, and may be particularly relevant to the proposals for interim uses at King's Cross.

Approaches to the implementation of development

Different approaches on the two sites

Various conclusions can be drawn from King's Cross and Canon's Marsh by considering the means of implementing development on large inner city sites. The case studies illustrate a number of approaches to implementation, some unsuccessful, others with the potential for success. It is possible to conclude from these case studies that there are five different approaches: comprehensive or master plan; ad hoc; flexible development framework; parcelisation; and interim uses. This section first draws conclusions from the analysis of the use of planning gain as a way forward in the 1980s, then poses a way forward for the 1990s.

Comprehensive or master planning approach

This involves the drawing up of a scheme for the whole site, which aspires to be implemented at one time, but which could be phased over a given period. It depends upon cleared sites, a clean slate, upon which grandiose plans can be drawn. It works best when there is only one landowner or a consortium, and one developer prepared to implement the entire scheme. It can only occur during an upturn in the economic cycle, depending, of course upon a thriving economy. It does allow for the negotiation of planning gain because a successfully implemented comprehensive scheme could yield massive gain, possibly in the form of public works. Comprehensive schemes tend towards a single-use scenario, sometimes associated with high risk, high cost and high gain. They require a flow in organisation and long-standing commitment to good management and maintenance.

The comprehensive or master planning approach has lost favour with town planners in recent years, although it is still referred to in local authority documents. It is too inflexible to respond to changing market or economic conditions. Negotiations over the scheme and any planning gain element are likely to be protracted, delaying development. The long development profile suffers from unsynchronised planning and property cycles, i.e. the development is probably catering for a market one or two property cycles hence. Conflict with the local authority is likely. Failure of the approach is most likely to arise out of the economic difficulties of financing a single development, especially on a large site. In practice, it is unlikely that a site would be in single ownership, or that any single developer would be able to fund a single scheme. It militates against a mixture of uses. The upturn in the market might not be sustained long enough for large-scale development to occur. It depends, too, upon the provision of infrastructure. Putting huge amounts of development down all at once can inbuild vast social and infrastructural problems. Postwar housing estates built on the urban fringe illustrate the kind of problems likely to occur. There are likely to be problems in ensuring that the less profitable elements are delivered in the later phases and on the marginal sites (e.g. on contaminated land).

Early briefs for Canon's Marsh realised the shortcomings of the comprehensive approach, and for a time, Bristol City Council has abhorred the approach. It seems unusual that the deposit version of the Bristol Local Plan seems to return to the idea of a comprehensive approach. Now, both the community group and the local planning authority in Camden advocate abandonment of a comprehensive approach at King's Cross, partly due to the downturn in the economy and partly due to uncertainty about the funding of the major railworks. But the Fosters scheme for King's Cross is a comprehensive scheme and it does allow for cross-subsidisation; the high value uses were intended to subsidise the building of the hugely expensive low-level Channel Tunnel rail terminal. The recession and uncertainty over strategic decisions relating to the Channel Tunnel have already shown how the approach has failed, leading to massive amounts of money being wasted on schemes which will never be implemented.

Ad hoc approach

The ad hoc approach arises from there being no particular plan or framework for the site, but a commitment by the local planning authority to allow development there and to permit any development proposal that is made. There can be a number of developers; each makes its own arrangements for land purchase and determines the use, density and design of the development. Such an approach usually happens by default, rather than in any planned way. This usually results in the best sites being used first and for the most intensive and profitable purposes; those with problems are left undeveloped. It leaves the local planning authority with even less control than they might have in the presence of a plan. It opens the way for an entirely market-led, property-led regeneration of the site in question, which might not consider the needs of the local community. The lack of guidance could result in unacceptable urban design and a feeling that the buildings on the site do not relate to each other. Crucially, cross-subsidisation cannot occur, although individual developers may negotiate their own planning gain.

Development would occur only as and when the market conditions were right. This has happened at Canon's Marsh with the allowance of the Lloyds office on the best site, without any regard for the rest of the site, and with no commitment to enabling cross-subsidisation.

Flexible development framework

Flexible development depends upon the local planning authority taking a strong lead in guiding and promoting development. In the absence of a statutory local plan, planning or development briefs may provide this framework, which will be the better for having been compiled with public consultation. Objectives are drawn up, which will include a preference for certain uses, and should be based upon a financial knowledge of what is viable and possible. Financial arrangements are likely to include a partnership between public and private sector interests. The framework is not rigid in its approach, allowing for changes in market conditions and in public demands, a factor considered crucial in any property-led urban regeneration, and because of the cyclical nature of the property market. American examples show the need for development to be set within a conceptual framework, which is possible even when funding is not secure and development is unlikely to occur at the same time. It does not mean an ad hoc approach. The disadvantages centre around the strength of the framework, which depends upon a strong local authority or pivotal organisation to take the lead. It also depends upon a balanced framework, firm enough to offer guidance but flexible enough to allow for changing conditions. It also raises questions of infrastructure provision and timing.

Should it be provided first, perhaps to promote investment? Or later, when development has occurred? Flexible development can be construed by developers as the opportunity to continue negotiations with planning officers, because they perceive there to be an open agenda, with no firm desires by the local authority. Neither King's Cross nor Canon's Marsh illustrates an example of this kind of approach. It is almost certainly what was being attempted in Bristol, but the local authority failed to take the necessary lead from an early stage; the permission granted to Lloyds Bank exemplifies this failure, opening the way for an ad hoc approach. The planning briefs produced for Canon's Marsh were inadequate and uninspired, and did not come to terms with the main issues. The employment of consultants, each of whom produced new plans, and ignored the previous briefs, took the strength out of the local authority's position.

Parcelisation

Parcelisation goes further than the flexible development framework because it divides the land into parcels for development. Each parcel of land contains proposals for a mixture of uses, which can cross-subsidise. It works well when there is more than one owner and when there are problems with some parts of the land. It allows for phasing and for time to resolve problems. Different developers can be involved. Its potential success may depend upon the size of the parcel, which is small enough to be developed, yet large enough to allow for the mixture of uses. It depends upon a thriving economy because it utilises mainly private sector finance. Landowners must be prepared to cooperate with the approach and accept that cross-subsidisation will only occur within the parcel, rather than across the wider site. Criticisms of the approach may suggest that it is inflexible, which it can be, as it is more difficult to make it responsive to changing economic conditions.

There is also the possibility that the best-placed parcels will be developed first, leaving problem land undeveloped. Such an approach was proposed at Canon's Marsh (see Fig. 14.3, p. 188), as a way of promoting development, but only after the Lloyds office had been proposed. The merits of the concept were recognised by the city council and other commentators, but the latest plans for the area do not employ the concept.

Partnership approach

A partnership approach involves a joint approach to the planning and funding of a development between the public and private sectors. Planning and development are closely linked, and evolve together in cooperation. The landowners, developers, the local community and the local planning authority evolve a common language and build up enough common ground to give confidence to a potential scheme. One way forward may be to transfer publicly and privately owned land into the control of a community development trust. In this way, the development accounts are open to the public; those involved will appreciate the risks involved, and who is likely to pay for what, when, where and how. A wide variety of funding sources can be tapped in a coordinated fashion. The main problems of the approach are likely to arise out of reluctance by developers and landowners to cooperate on one project or to see their land transferred into single ownership under control of a trust. It has long been recognised at Canon's Marsh that the landowners should have cooperated, but there was a reluctance because of the unequal nature of the land, i.e. some contaminated, some more attractive to developers and some easier to develop. The approach probably depends upon a proactive local planning authority, prepared to take the lead in bringing together the necessary parties to form a trust. An intransigent local authority with rigid views about how a site should be developed is unlikely to make the partnership work. Secrecy, so often present in the negotiations between local authorities and potential developers, will undermine the partnership approach, as at Canon's Marsh.

Interim uses

The interim uses approach depends upon building up development on a site from what is already there, from available resources and uses, based upon the needs of existing residential and business communities and the short- and medium-term interests of the landowners and managers. At the same time, it allows for outside interests to invest in an area slowly as confidence builds up. There needs to be a flexible development framework, which facilitates a 'now, soon, later' approach, and which incorporates uses that can ebb and flow. Temporary uses can be permitted alongside permanent uses to promote interest and investment in the area. This improves its security, image and marketability, so the area can earn the landowners income and help to meet local needs. Interim approaches enable parties who have never previously met each other to work together on small-scale, manageable projects. They work when there is a multitude of owners and uses, and may be when an existing community is threatened with relocation or eviction by other types of plans, perhaps living under blight and the problems it creates. Although they depend upon a mixture of public and private sector capital, funding is on a much reduced scale, so interim schemes can be appropriate in a recession.

The interim uses approach is unlikely to find favour with large-scale developers or landowners. There is no interest in developing during a recession, and when the economy allows for development, a developer may not want to devise plans around existing uses. Profit margins are likely to be lower. This is the approach currently being proposed for the way forward at King's Cross. The King's Cross Railway Lands Group has devised a 'now, soon, later' approach which can accommodate the current needs of the local community and draw upon its enthusiasm. The plan allows for investment in the area, which will in turn attract further investment, perhaps on a small scale. It also allows for permanent commercial development to occur, when the time is right. It does not rely upon planning gain to provide facilities for the community, because to do so would be to wait until the end of the recession and to rely upon protracted negotiation over a large scheme, which might never be implemented. American examples emphasise the importance of staging major events on a site. This has also occurred at King's Cross and Canon's

Marsh, with various festivals and events being held there. But Bristol City Council has resisted attempts to use various buildings on the site for temporary uses.

During the early 1970s, just after the closure of Covent Garden Market, sites began to be developed in an incremental way in a well-documented community-led scheme. Interim uses began to creep in, but in an unplanned way. Undeveloped sites were used as gardens; one famous example is the Japanese Garden in Neal Street, now redeveloped for housing. Interim uses can currently be seen to be working at Spitalfields, for example. Adjacent to the Broadgate scheme, the former market has been put to use for food stalls, sports, shops and cafes, and is alleged to be commercially viable. A swimming-pool is planned on the basis of commencing with a cheap structure, which might become permanent as and when finance is available for improvement. There are sites around Bristol's docks (notably Redcliffe Wharf) for which interim uses have been devised and are believed to be viable. A rejection of earlier interim use schemes in the early 1980s recession has left that particular site undeveloped ever since, awaiting a permanent proposal. Another example is the garden festivals, held in various British cities during the 1980s. They provided a temporary greening, but more importantly, they enabled large areas of derelict and often contaminated land to be treated and prepared for future development. While the festival garden is open to the public, there is a commercial return and the provision of some local facilities. In the long term, the site is ready to receive more permanent development whenever economic conditions allow.

The interim uses approach can be summarised as follows:

- A conceptual framework for development is necessary.
- The framework must be flexible.
- The residential and business community should be involved in the planning of the area, and their specific needs incorporated into the plans.
- Plans are drawn up for the short, medium, and long term – for 'now, soon, later'.
- The finances for implementation must be creatively costed and the sources researched.
- A planning and development partnership could involve the setting up of a community development trust, which has control of development.
- The finance will depend upon a wide range of small-scale sources – not from one major development, but including a private/public partnership.
- The plan should aim to encourage immediate investment (however small-scale) to environmentally improve the area to attract further investment.
- Uses should be capable of ebb and flow.
- Development does not need to await the end of the recession.
- Planning gain is not relied upon as a means of financing community and public facilities.

Conclusion

One of the main lessons to emerge from the case studies is that town planners must come to terms with the finances of development, and that plans must be flexible enough to be accommodated within the economic cycle. When lead-in times for development can be as long as five years, experience of the 1980s and 1990s illustrates that the property market can rise and fall more than once in a period of fourteen years. The early 1980s were characterised by recession in the property market, followed by a property boom, which peaked in 1987. Since then, a further recession has deepened, with no indications yet that the situation will change in the near future. Some argue that economic conditions will never reach the peaks of 1987. If that is true, how is land ever to be developed? Is there to be eternal blight? This chapter has shown how the concept of planning gain has taken root – in plans, in government advice and in court decisions. Planning gain has come to be accepted as a means of providing infrastructure and facilities in association with major development. This kind of property-led regeneration of urban sites, which relies excessively upon private sector finance, only has the potential to be successful during an economic boom. Blight ensues during a recession, and although communities are less threatened by rising land and rental values, some of their needs may go unmet. Derelict land in the inner city is undesirable – for investment, for the environment, for business and for the people who live and work in a city. Waiting for an economic upturn, and relying upon the rather dubious and uncertain methods of planning gain, does not have to be the only way to proceed with development.

In both case studies, there is evidence of some new thinking; in particular, there will have to be some public funding of certain facilities. There is a realisation of the need for partnership between public, private and community interests. In the case of Canon's Marsh, Bristol City Council has failed to apply this to the implementation of a realistic scheme, and at King's Cross, it is the community that is leading the way, alongside the local authority. There are undoubtedly lessons to be learnt from the interim uses scheme for King's Cross. When the property industry begins to emerge from recession, there is likely to be gradual redevelopment and refurbishment of large inner city sites; the interim uses plan will allow this to happen. Right now this approach could be applied to development at many sites, including Canon's Marsh.

Chapter 16

EQUALITY AND PLANNING: RACE

Linda Davies

| Policy development in the United Kingdom |

During the 1970s and 1980s the larger and more radical local authorities in Britain developed political strategies which incorporated many elements of equal opportunity thinking. They were led by the Greater London Council, and individual London boroughs such as Lambeth; provincial cities such as Leicester and Sheffield also played a major part. Such strategies reflected, and built on, national legislation, in particular the Equal Pay Act of 1970, the Sex Discrimination Act of 1975, the Race Relations Act of 1976 and the Disabled Persons Acts of 1944, 1958 and 1981. The 1981 act places a duty on local authorities to draw developers' attention to the requirements of the 1970 Chronically Sick and Disabled Persons Act in providing access to buildings and facilities for the disabled as an integral part of the development process. Local authorities as employers also have to comply with European regulations, just like any provider of goods or services. The range of EU requirements and directives includes Article 119 of the original Treaty of Rome and the Equal Treatment Directive 76/207 (CEC 1991).

Because of the high political profile adopted by the local authorities and the desire of the government to gain greater control over local authority expenditure, conflicts arose between the Conservative government and the local authorities (generally Labour controlled) which were promoting equal opportunities policies. The conflict came to a head in the mid 1980s when the government disbanded the Greater London Council (GLC) led by 'Red Ken' Livingstone. The government's position was subsequently confirmed by the introduction of the Local Government Act of 1988, which used financial and organisational controls to restrict authorities' ability to require compliance with equal opportunities policies in contracts let to the private sector. Herman Ouseley, formerly chief executive of Lambeth Borough Council and now chief executive of the Equal Opportunity Commission, recently expressed his view on the situation. At last, he believes, it has begun to stabilise, with the current Conservative government now starting to accept as the 'norm' equal opportunities for all. But the situation varies from one authority to another.

Policies on race and other aspects of equality fell from popularity for a time because of the overzeal of some of the authorities in the introduction of such policies and programmes. More recently, as local authorities have been pressurised through the growing demands of competition and contracting out of services, equal opportunities policies have been seen as a luxury which cannot easily be afforded. Many race equality officers, for example, have lost their jobs or been redeployed into more mainstream activities. However, the continuing influence of the European Union and the duties of existing United Kingdom legislation have left the Government with little alternative but to accept equal opportunities for all. Such changes in national thinking are ultimately reflected, to a greater or lesser extent, in town planning policies and, in particular, in the development plan system.

Professor Patsy Healey, head of planning at the University of Newcastle upon Tyne, has shown that, although such social and economic policies could, indeed should, be the subject of policy statements in plans, DoE guidance has changed over the years. Policy guidance prior to Circular 22/84 *Memorandum on Structure Plans and Local Plans* (replaced by PPG 12) was concerned only with land use and development issues. Any other factors, such as social considerations in the form of equal opportunity issues, were considered to be outside the remit of the planning acts and were therefore *ultra vires*. Central government guidance at that time was such that, although policy plans could take social considerations into account, planning control should concern itself only with the use applied for, not with the user of the land. Land use considerations were to be the sole consideration in planning decision making throughout the 1970s. However, the situation was to change to allow the inclusion of social issues in the 1980s. Nowadays, the DoE situation on these matters is still somewhat indeterminate and variable.

The GLC's radical strategies during the 1980s were not only reflected in the implementation of its own planning policies, but were taken up by other forward-looking planning authorities throughout the United Kingdom (although the GLC itself was abolished in 1986). Thus, by the end of the 1980s, many planning authorities had equal opportunities policies built into their development plans, for example, provision of special needs housing and access for the disabled. What had seemed radical planning in the 1980s became good practice in the 1990s as there developed in society a general awareness of the need to enable women, ethnic minorities and the disabled, with the opportunities to achieve their full potential.

Government planning guidance of the early 1990s reflected this awareness (as in PPG 12). It arguably increased local authorities' chances of having social policies accepted as approved policy and thus raised the likelihood of their implementation. Nevertheless, many of the emerging policies in the latest development plans can be justified, not only in terms of increasing the opportunity of the individual, but in terms of the economic benefits conferred by increased employment take-up. The equal opportunities policies which have survived the stages of the draft plans and the scrutiny of the DoE at the public local inquiry, must be implemented to be of any effect. As indicated elsewhere in Volume II, especially by Janet Askew, in spite of the above policy guidance, it is by no means a foregone conclusion that such policies will be accepted or acted upon. This chapter now considers the specific background to the development of planning policies for black people and ethnic minorities.

Planning for ethnic minorities

In this section the overall situation will be discussed, looking firstly at the national context and governmental planning guidance. In the following section details of the study undertaken in the South-West will be given (Davies 1993). This is an important area of research as it is often imagined that ethnicity is an urban issue, and that there is likely to be no problem in rural areas. In fact, problems do exist, though they are different problems.

Planning Policy Guidance 12, 'Development Plans and Regional Planning Guidance', 1992, in paragraph 5.48 states that

> the Regulations [on the preparation of development plan documents] also require planning authorities to have regard to social considerations in preparing their general policies and proposals in structure plans and UDP Part I documents [the policy aspect]. . . . But, in preparing detailed plans too, authorities will wish to consider the relationship of planning policies and proposals to social needs and problems, including their likely impact on different groups in the population such as ethnic minorities.

A brief history from the Second World War onwards will illustrate the growth of ethnic minority groups in Britain. By 1961 immigration to the United Kingdom grew to between 30,000 and 50,000 people per year. (In 1962 this was reduced somewhat owing to new legislation, which defined and limited the right of British citizenship.) Some three-fifths of incoming people during this period were non-white. Many of these immigrants at that time were West Indians invited to Britain to supplement the labour shortages in the postwar period. Later there were influxes of more affluent Asian business people (Greed 1993, 225), for example, those who left Uganda because of its oppressive regime.

Black people and ethnic minorities are not a single group; they comprise many different classes, cultures and ethnic groupings. This can be seen from the 1991 census, which records some nine categories of ethnic minority, including black Caribbean, black African, Indian, Pakistani, Bangladeshi, Chinese and Asian. According to the London Research Centre (1993), 5.5% of the population in the United Kingdom is of black or ethnic minority origin. Of the 3 million people who are of black and/or ethnic origin, 1.3 million live within the London area and 1.7 million live elsewhere but are concentrated in urban areas, predominantly in the Midlands. For example, 28.5% of Leicester's population of Asian origin.

Table 16.1 Ethnic minority population

Borough council	% of population of black and ethnic origin
Brent	44.8
Newham	42.3
Tower Hamlets	35.6
Hackney	33.6
Ealing	32.3
Lambeth	30.3

Source: London Research Centre, 1993

Within the London boroughs (Fig. 16.1), Brent Borough Council has the highest level of people of black and ethnic minority origin (44.8%), followed by Newham with 42.3%. Table 16.1 gives figures for the six London boroughs which have the highest percentages of black and ethnic origin. The phrase 'black and ethnic minority' is used because in terms of potential racism and discrimination, matters of 'colour' are as significant as matters of origin and previous nationality. In fact, over half the people in Britain of Afro-Caribbean origin were born in Britain, but they are still seen as 'immigrants' by many, and this may affect attitudes towards them when they apply for jobs, houses or planning permission. But immigration itself has now declined, as a result of growing restrictive trends in immigration legislation in the form of the Commonwealth Immigration Act of 1962, The Race Relations Act of 1965, the Immigration Act of 1971, the Nationality Act of 1981 and further controls in the late 1980s and early 1990s.

Over the period 1980–1993 some thirty new immigration rules were introduced, mostly published in the form of Command Papers, which have increased regulation and restriction of the entry of immigrants to Britain, especially from some 'black' Commonwealth areas. Most 'white' immigration from North America, Australia and Europe is not seen as a problem, although there is concern about immigration from Eastern Europe following the collapse of former socialist states; non-black ethnic minorities also experience discrimination.

Postwar planning policy direction from central government shows a remarkable lack of awareness of ethnic issues. However, some local authorities, especially those which are Labour controlled, have sought to give their planning policies an equal opportunities dimension. It has no doubt occurred to the reader that the earlier case studies gloss over the ethnicity of the residents not as a major consideration in the planning process. But St. Pauls district, in particular, and other parts of Bristol's inner city ring of residential areas have a significant ethnic minority population. As a result of an increasing awareness of the lack of provision of race equality programmes, specifically in the inner cities, in 1983 the Royal Town Planning Institute (RTPI) and the Commission for Racial Equality (CRE) commissioned a report, its recommendations 'explicitly aimed at the bureaucracies concerned with statutory town planning, at central and local government' (RTPI 1983).

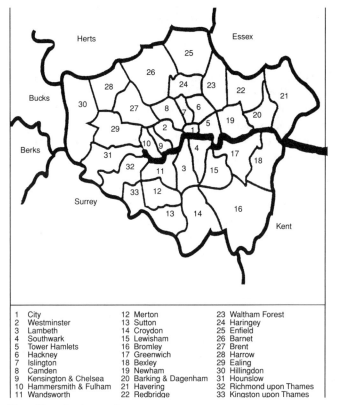

1	City	12	Merton	23	Waltham Forest
2	Westminster	13	Sutton	24	Haringey
3	Lambeth	14	Croydon	25	Enfield
4	Southwark	15	Lewisham	26	Barnet
5	Tower Hamlets	16	Bromley	27	Brent
6	Hackney	17	Greenwich	28	Harrow
7	Islington	18	Bexley	29	Ealing
8	Camden	19	Newham	30	Hillingdon
9	Kensington & Chelsea	20	Barking & Dagenham	31	Hounslow
10	Hammersmith & Fulham	21	Havering	32	Richmond upon Thames
11	Wandsworth	22	Redbridge	33	Kingston upon Thames

Fig. 16.1 Map of London boroughs

The Report further stated

> [This report] says as much about town planning as about race. . . . The delibera-
> tions showed the importance of planning recognising and responding to wider
> patterns of social need than is often the case. Concern for the physical environ-
> ment must not become an obsession, obstructing effective action to assist people in
> need, be they black or white.'
>
> (ibid.)

Also mentioned above, PPG 12 requires planning authorities to have regard
to social considerations in preparing their general policies and proposals in
development plans. For the first time a document specifically lists ethnic
minorities as one of the groups required to be considered in the relationship
between planning policies and proposals for social needs, but significantly
does not list women (see Section 5.48, and see Greed 1994: 6). In 1993, a study
was published by the Royal Town Planning Institute (RTPI 1993b) (written by
V. Krishnarayan and H. Thomas) entitled 'Ethnic Minorities and the Planning
System'. The recommendations of the study suggested change at a national
level in promoting race equality in planning and that the RTPI and the CRE
should produce advice on best professional practice in this area of ethnicity.

219

Ethnicity and planning in the South-West

A large region

In 1993 I produced a report (Davies 1993) which built on previously published research (Davies 1992) and sought to research in greater depth the awareness of the needs of ethnic minorities in the South-West region. The South-West region, as defined by the South West Regional Planning Conference, comprises the seven counties of Avon, Gloucestershire, Somerset, Dorset, Devon, Cornwall and Wiltshire.

The report focused on the role that local authorities can play in improving their approaches to planning for black people and ethnic minorities. There are fifty-eight authorities, including county councils and district councils, in the South-West region. Of these, forty-four responded to the questionnaire, as shown in the appendix accompanying the study (Davies 1993).

Approach to the research

As work of this nature has not previously been carried out in the South-West region it was essential to ascertain the breadth and depth of issues to address. This was achieved by the following means:

(1) Deciding that the study would take the form of a postal survey questionnaire of all local authorities in the South West region.
(2) Running a pilot study in May 1993 in two local authorities where it was already known that there was an awareness of ethnic minority issues in the field of town planning.
(3) Appreciating that there would subsequently be the opportunity to focus in detail on a particular approach taken by an authority or a combination of authorities if examples of good practice were to emerge.

The South-West region is predominantly rural in character with some large urban centres of population and it therefore stands in contrast to predominantly urban areas such as the London boroughs. Nevertheless, the report does provide a profile of equality of opportunities issues tackled by local authorities in a large and not untypical part of the country.

Survey results

Of the seven counties, Avon has the highest percentage of black and ethnic minority population (2.8%) while Somerset and Cornwall have the lowest percentage (0.5% each). Ethnic minority groups in Avon are concentrated mainly in the urban districts of Bristol. Of the districts, the highest percentage of black and ethnic minority population was in Gloucester District

(5.7%), followed by Bristol City (5.1 %), Thamesdown Borough (3.1%) and Bath City (2.6%).

Recruitment and training

The survey showed that only ten staff employed in six local planning authorities in the South-West region were of black or ethnic minority origin. Four of these posts were at a technical grade, three were at administrative grades and three were professionally qualified. In the larger urban areas such as Bristol (376,146 population), Plymouth (243,373) and Swindon (170,850, Thamesdown administrative area), where there was a relatively higher percentage of black and ethnic minority population, one might expect to find a localised higher percentage of black and ethnic minority staff. However, there were only a few staff from black and ethnic minority backgrounds in Bristol and Swindon and none at all in Plymouth.

Bristol City council, for example, included one administrative officer (scales 2–5), one planning officer (unqualified and on scale 6) and a coordinator in urban design matters (no scale given). Swindon (Thamesdown Borough Council) employed two male professionals from black or ethnic minority background, one a planner and the other an architect, on senior officer (SO 2) salary grading (middle grade).

A similar situation emerged in the county councils. Wiltshire County Council employed two black or ethnic minority staff, one female administrator (scale 2) and a male technical senior assistant on transportation matters (grade SO 1/20). Gloucestershire County Council employed one black or ethnic minority female administrative officer, as a word processing operator (scale 2). Dorset County Council employed one male technical assistant surveyor (grade not given). And Avon County Council employed one male administrator in its Regional Waste Division.

Therefore in only a few local authority planning departments were there staff employed from a black and ethnic minority background. The type of work carried out was predominantly administrative or technical (seven out of ten posts), with a top salary scale of SO 2 in the case of the three professionally qualified black and ethnic minority officers. The profile which tended to emerge is one of non-employment of black and ethnic minority staff in 86% of planning departments in the South-West region, with the occasional black or ethnic minority staff member in relatively low grade, non-managerial posts. Many factors could contribute to this situation: few or no black or ethnic minority potential employees presenting themselves for employment; lack of relevant qualifications among black and ethnic minority people. But there is evidence of promotional work being carried out in certain local authorities to redress this position (see later).

A relevant aspect is the way in which planning schools attract black and ethnic minority students to their courses. A recent survey (Mahmood 1993) showed that some 50% of the ethnic minority students whom he interviewed were not aware of a course in town and country planning when choosing from a university prospectus. When asked how much they knew about town and country planning, the popular reply was 'something to do with architecture.' If this is truly the case, the marketing of planning schools to black and ethnic minority students is currently not effective. Urban centres in the South-West with higher black and ethnic minority populations, such as Gloucester, Bristol, Swindon and Bath, should show a commitment to town planning as a vocation. They should encourage positive marketing of the region's educational institutions, especially its one and only recognised planning school at the University of the West of England. Secondary schools and colleges also have a role to play in specifically targeting recruitment of students from black and ethnic minority backgrounds into town and country planning courses. If this is not carried out at source by the planning schools and educational establishments, it is inevitable that town and country planning will remain unattractive to black and ethnic minority people, and the profession will remain unrepresentative.

Internal organisations of local authorities

The local authorities were asked if they monitored the composition of applicants for posts by their ethnic background. Twenty-four of the authorities said that they did, 54.5% of all the responses. They were also asked if they produced any policy documents which acknowledged career progression of black and ethnic minority staff. It was apparent that equal opportunities policies were the most popular policy areas in force. Twenty-eight of the authorities (64% of responses) had in place equal opportunities policy statements either corporately within the council or departmentally. Although at face value this appeared to be a healthy response, the converse position was that 36% of local planning authorities were not so well organised or concerned. Other responses showed that three authorities (7%) produced racial equality policies and only one authority (2.3%) had a harassment policy.

Equal opportunities legislation takes the form of the Sex Discrimination Act of 1975 and the Race Relations Act of 1976 (Section 71); the Race Relations Act imposes a general duty on local authorities to promote equality of opportunity. Given this relatively long-standing legislation and the generic nature of its principles there would appear to be little excuse for local authorities not having an equal opportunities policy. Equal opportunities policies are generally concerned to ensure that no applicant or employee receives less favourable treatment on grounds of gender, disability, age, race, marital status, religion, colour, ethnic or national origin or because they are gay or lesbian. The lack of a code of practice on these issues does not encourage the council formally to take account of these needs when taking decisions and formulating policy.

Approaches to training

Local authorities were asked if training programmes were held for either officers or members on black or ethnic minority issues. Of the respondents, an overwhelming 75% said they did not; only 18% said that they did. (The remaining 7% left the question unanswered. Brief illustrations were given of the local authorities who did hold training programmes. Equal opportunities training courses were organised by Bristol City Council, West Wiltshire District Council, Thamesdown Borough Council, Stroud District Council, Exeter City Council, Wiltshire County Council, Somerset County Council and Gloucestershire County Council. This represents 18% of responding local authorities. Most of the training programmes comprised one-off courses. Wiltshire County Council organised two courses, namely, Recruitment and Selection and Supervisory Management, but numbers attending were not given. Bristol City Council, in addition to its equal opportunities training, runs a course on understanding racism.

Use of the media

Local authorities gave few examples of methods of liaising with black and ethnic minority groups. Radio is used in Gloucestershire County Council (Severn Sound and BBC Radio Gloucester). The Council also uses *The Voice*, a black British newspaper, and other local minority press to reach black and ethnic minority groups. The local Council for Race Equality (CRE) is used by Gloucestershire County Council, Cheltenham Borough Council and Thamesdown Borough Council to communicate with black and ethnic minority community groups. Cheltenham Borough Council holds a quarterly open forum with black and ethnic minority groups; Bristol City Council simply liaises with community groups.

Equal opportunities officers

However, the effectiveness of these policies depends on other related factors, such as the existence or otherwise of an equal opportunity officer in post to carry out these duties and the attendance of that officer at interviews. Only 7% of local authorities have a race relations office in post (Bristol City Council, Avon County Council and Gloucester City Council). The race relations post-holders are located in the chief executive office (Bristol), equal opportunities unit (Avon) and the human resources department (Gloucester). Only Bristol's race relations adviser has been in post any length of time (since 1985) and the posts at Avon County Council and Gloucester City Council have been in existence since 1990 and 1991 respectively. This function in Thamesdown Borough Council forms part of the work of the social policy officer. In Wandsdyke District Council, equal opportunities are

seen as part of personnel practice and advice is given 'as and when necessary.' This poses the questions of how it is decided and what is necessary. In
none of the responding local authorities were the race relations advisers normally present at interview sessions. Even in the few local authorities who
corporately employed a race relations adviser, the presence of that post-
holder was therefore seen as neither essential nor integral to the interview
process – a presence that would have shown a serious commitment in terms
of local authority practice of equal opportunities policies.

Equal opportunities monitoring

Monitoring is arguably one of the more important internal organisational
aspects of equal opportunities for the black and ethnic minority population.
Monitoring is recommended because it is only as a result of awareness of the
facts that local authority officers can have attention drawn to equal opportunity issues when reporting to members on planning applications or policy.
Yet it seems that in the survey questionnaire, not one of the respondents was
monitoring planning applications by the ethnic origin of the applicant. As
one local authority pointed out, ethnic origin is not always apparent by name
and by the information provided; this matter is not addressed within the
standard planning application forms. Asked whether planning officers were
to consider black or ethnic minority implications in drafting policy, only
three authorities (7% of respondents) said that they were, and only two
authorities (5%) were looking at the implications of such issues when reporting on planning applications.

Consultation procedures

In 1983 the report *Planning for a Multi-Racial Britain* by a Royal Town
Planning Institute (RTPI) and Council for Racial Equality (CRE) Working
Party (RTPI 1983), recognised that, while the lack of involvement of black
people and ethnic minorities was not primarily due to poor communication,
an improvement in communication is a necessary prerequisite to greater
understanding and influence in the planning system. In the South-West
region, the survey of local authorities revealed that 91% of respondents had
no consultation arrangements on planning applications and 89% had none
on policy for black ethnic minority groups. Only three local authorities (7%
of respondents) consulted on planning policy matters and only one authority
(2.3%) consulted on development control matters. It was disappointing that
so few local authorities consulted black and ethnic minority groups on planning reports before submitting them to their committees.

Gloucester City Council and Thamesdown Borough Council consulted
black and ethnic minority groups on both planning policy and planning
application matters. While Bristol City Council apparently consulted only on

policy matters, Gloucestershire County Council stated that black and ethnic minority groups were treated no differently from other organisations and in line with other legislation. Thamesdown Borough Council stated that consultation with the local Council for Racial Equality took place on planning issues and it was thought that perhaps this was more prevalent in local authorities than had been made known in the survey questionnaire. Probing further on consultation procedures, only two authorities (5% of respondents) of planning department/divisions undertook research to ascertain the needs of local black and ethnic minority groups.

Examples given include awareness through the population census and employer information in Gloucestershire County Council, and leaflet translation in Bristol City Council and Thamesdown Borough Council. Avon County Council promotes translation services in development plan summaries. Cheltenham Borough Council had access to Gloucester City Council's translation services and West Wiltshire District Council claimed to provide a translation service 'as and when required.' Only Gloucestershire County Council, Gloucester City Council and Thamesdown Borough Council listed the languages in which they provided a translation. Each of the three local authorities provided translations in six languages – including Urdu, Bengali, Hindi, Gujarati, Punjabi and Chinese – except Gloucestershire County Council, which did not provide Gujarati translations. Gloucester City Council's Hindi and Punjabi translations were only given orally and Thamesdown Borough Council also translated into Polish and Italian.

Editor's postscript

The investigation of racial issues or the needs of other minority groups within the planning system often requires one to look for what or who is *not* there, and then to ask why. The fact that there are relatively few ethnic minority communities in a region, or for that matter that there are few senior planning officers, or indeed minority planners at all (see Table 2.1) within the profession does not mean there is no problem. It should not be assumed that 'the numbers are so small as to be statistically insignificant' (Greed 1991: 7), and that therefore it is not an important issue. Minorities may be keeping clear of certain geographical areas or public institutions and professions precisely because there *is* a problem, that of discrimination by the dominant group. Indeed, ethnic minority issues and the people themselves are often presented as problems, even within discourse on social inequality when the teaching claims to be socially aware. They are often portrayed in a negative light, not from a positive perspective as citizens of British cities. In order to carry out effective, appropriate and sensitive planning policy, the needs of minority groups must be fully taken into account throughout the different stages of plan making and the subsequent implementary process. If minority groups are 'missing', the implementary process may not be complete, or the professionals involved 'competent' (CISC 1993), and its objectives may not be representative of the whole community's needs. The 'missing' groups are not adequately drawn into the public partici- pation exercises and are not themselves members of the professional groups who make the decisions in the first place. These issues will be revisited by the editor in the final chapters.

Chapter 17

EQUALITY AND PLANNING: GENDER AND DISABILITY

Linda Davies

| Planning for women |

Women comprise the majority of the population and are not a homogenous group; they are divided on the basis of class, race, age and income among other factors, it is therefore difficult to define exactly what their needs are. Indeed it is argued women qua women do share many common problems in their use of the built environment and in relation to their position in urban society (Greed 1994, Ch. 3). However, inequalities continue to exist and policies should ensure that these are not exacerbated (Calder et al. 1993). As Foulsham (1990) points out. 'awareness of the impact on women of planning as a state service has come relatively late.' The women's movement of the 1960s and 1970s has been influential (indirectly at first) in shaping planning policy through its general work on sex discrimination. For example, the Sex Discrimination Act was introduced in 1975. The 1981 Greater London Council (GLC) election brought with it Valerie Wise, who was a leading light in setting up and chairing the GLC Women's Committee in 1982. The GLC and other progressive Labour London councils had the political and professional will to shape planning policies, and in turn encouraged other local authorities to review their policies and practices and to identify potential discrimination (GLC 1986, 1994).

Throughout Britain, including Scotland (CSLA 1991), a range of regional women-and-planning reports were produced by voluntary groupings of professional women planners. They suggested planning policies which were subsequently included in planning policy documents such as the Greater London Development Plan of 1984. Issues covered ranged from staff training and recruitment to detailed planning policy concerned with women as carers and their special needs in the fields of transport, leisure facilities and safety aspects of urban design. More recently women's policy statements are being incorporated in the new wave of unitary development plans. Research by Calder et al. (1993) in a report *Women and Development Plans* produced by Newcastle University identifies the following issues as the most important 'gender issues' expressed in development plan policy statements:

- *Housing*: access to affordable housing, design sensitive to the needs of women
- *Retailing*: easy access to a wide range of shopping facilities which are both locally based and in town centres
- *Employment*: training and education; removal of barriers which prevent women taking up employment opportunities, including access and child care facilities
- *Transport and personal mobility*: the ease of personal mobility both within and between buildings and access to an adequate and safe public transport system
- *Recreation*: access to conveniently located recreational facilities for use by women and children
- *Community facilities*: the caring responsibilities of women require the provision of facilities which are easily accessible
- *Crime prevention and safety*: overlapping many of the other issues, sensitive design and the development of community spirit can help to alleviate the fear of crime and vandalism

The big question is whether these women-and-planning issues should be the subject of a separate policy section in a development plan policy document, or whether they should be integrated along with other policies under the appropriate topic heading (briefly mentioned in other chapters). It was found in the course of undertaking a review of current literature and governmental guidance that the DoE apparently prefers integration as stated in the *Development Plans: Good Practice Guide* for development plan preparation (DOE, 1992: para 3.79; Greed 1994: 6), as they do not consider separate chapters on any of the so-called minority issues good practice.

Planning policy guidance

Planning Policy Guidance note 12 'Development Plans and Regional Guidance', while not giving guidance on gender issues, specifically, does point out that, in preparing their development plans, local authorities

> will wish to consider the relationship of planning policies and proposals to social needs and problems including their likely impact on different groups in the population
>
> (PPG 12: para 5.48)

Also the DoE's good practice guide within a discussion of social issues and 'particular sections of the population', suggests 'perhaps children, women and homeless people should be added to the list' (Department of the Environment 1992a: para 3.75). Clearly these statements provide some scope for concerned local authorities to include gender-related policies in their development plans. But PPG 12 also insists 'the underlying approach must be to limit the plan content to social considerations that are relevant to land use policies' (para 5.51). PPG 12 does, however, specifically identify provision for single parent families as an area appropriate for development plan policies, but it is notable that, while the government apparently recognises the problem, it appears unwilling to accept that the vast majority of single parent families are headed by women, and to address specific policies accordingly.

Section 106 of the 1990 Town and Country Planning Act allows for planning authorities to enter into planning agreements to 'restrict or regulate the development and use of land.' This is elaborated in Circular 16/91 on planning obligations. As illustrated in earlier chapters, (including those by Janet Askew) planning gain is sometimes used by local authorities to obtain contributions (either financial or in kind) from developers towards the needs of different social groups. But a major limitation of its use is that such contributions have to be directly related to the use of land for which planning permission is applied. Although it may be reasonable to require, for example, a crèche to be provided as part of a new shopping centre, it will not generally be reasonable to ask for funding for a women's study group. In general, when a planning authority proposes to require contributions from developers for social needs, it should include details of these contributions in its development plan, so that developers know what they are expected to provide and can discount the land value accordingly.

Women's needs research

In 1992 my research on women's special needs was undertaken in the sixty-nine unitary authorities in England, to ascertain the extent to which their social needs were being recognised in the preparation of the unitary development plans (Davies 1992). Typical of the key women-centred policies which were then emerging are shopping-related policies (35%), employment (33%), transport and movement (31%), recreation and leisure (28%) and environment (27%). The study looked separately at policies in the six London boroughs of Islington, Kensington and Chelsea, Hammersmith and Fulham, Newham, Bromley and Wandsworth and the six metropolitan districts of Wolverhampton, Oldham, Coventry, Dudley, Manchester City and Tameside. These will be considered under the relevant headings, chosen in a slightly different sequence from the Newcastle study discussed above.

On *retail* policies, five of the six London boroughs, except Kensington and Chelsea, showed some appreciation of the need to provide draft policies for facilities in new large-scale shopping developments (exceeding 2,000 square metres gross floor space). These included child care facilities, crèches, toilets, baby changing and feeding areas. Hammersmith and Fulham even promoted a policy in its consultative draft plan for sheltered lockable spaces for buggies. This draft policy was subsequently removed following the planning inspector's report. A less specific policy along the same lines was promoted by both Islington and Bromley. Many of these policies were subsequently altered (London Women and Planning Forum 1994) as the DoE apparently does not like policies which specify quotas of such-and-such an amount of provision per so many thousand square feet, as is illustrated by the employment policies below.

As to employment-oriented policies in the London Boroughs, there was popular support in five of the six boroughs for the provision of child care in major new employment-generating schemes. In fact, Kensington and Chelsea Borough Council specified that all new employment-generating developments with more than fifty employees were required to provide nursery facilities. This became an integral part of the employment strategy for the borough, and it was argued that it was discriminatory to pretend women could compete 'equally' in the job market when they were hampered by lack of child care provision. This draft policy for a quota requirement was eventually modified by the Department of the Environment at the public local inquiry stage of the unitary development plan, following objection by a large retail concern. The modified version of the unitary plan subsequently deleted the standard of fifty employees and applied the policy only to 'medium and large companies', those occupying a floor space greater than 465 square metres.

In the area of *transport and movement* certain London boroughs (Newham in particular) specifically asked for public transport operators to incorporate measures to maximise personal security, including adequate levels of staffing, lighting and alarm points. Newham Borough Council also intended to investigate the possibility of establishing safe transport for women. In their draft unitary development plans, both Islington and Wandsworth specifically mentioned the need to establish convenient, safe pedestrian routes for women as well as for everybody. Islington specifically mentioned the need to avoid constructing subways and narrow, hidden, poorly lit footways, as such design was detrimental to pedestrian safety. Wandsworth along with Hammersmith and Fulham were encouraging public transport services to improve access, including continuing to support specialised door-to-door services, e.g. Dial-a-Ride, Taxicard and Mobility Bus.

On *environmental* matters, Newham, Wandsworth and Hammersmith and Fulham showed consistent evidence of good practice in design to promote safety and security by, for example, increasing over-looking of public areas, eliminating residential pockets of land with no specific purpose, in a development, increased use of lighting and by encouraging mixed land uses to increase use of public spaces. In March 1994 the Department of the Environment issued Circular 5/94 *Planning Out Crime* to consolidate current thinking on planning and crime prevention and to request the employment of a wide range of anticrime measures within development control, especially in the field of environmental considerations. (The editor notes, that while this policy incorporates some of the concerns of the women-and-planning movement, some women planners in London consider the approach is rather insensitive and likely to create a threatening 'fortress' mentality concerned with protecting property rather than people (see London Women and Planning Forum 1994)).

Recreation and Leisure policies for women were virtually ignored in the selected plans for detailed survey. However, Wolverhampton Metropolitan District did provide a general policy stating that proposals in this policy category would be assessed against access and facilities for people with disabilities and for people with young children. Although not part of the study, it was noted in passing that some unitary authorities did reserve a special chapter within their development plan for women's needs and other 'special' issues (in spite of DoE advice to the contrary). Lambeth initially adopted this approach in the mid 1980s but thereafter preferred to integrate special needs policies for women, and other groups, throughout their development plan, in accordance with Paragraph 3.79 of the DoE's good practice guide. Another advantage of integration is that policies are less likely to be eliminated in a local authority cost-cutting exercise, but this requires to be balanced against policies being lost within the development plan, if not separately prioritised. Indeed, some would argue it is better to try to put them in twice, once on their own and once under the relevant topic heading, in the hope that at least one version will get through the local inquiry stage.

Public funding

The research also looked at the current funding of women's special needs policies. This showed that 20% of women's special needs policies had been publicly funded, 18% through planning agreements and undertakings, 11% by the private sector and 9% by jointly supported funding arrangements. Future funding of women's special needs policies, although not possible to predict in some authorities, showed 24% funding from planning agreements and undertakings, thereby increasing the reliance of future funding on this source of revenue.

In conclusion, it is noticeable that many of the hopes and good policy initiatives conceived in the late 1980s, at the start of the new round of UDP preparation, have since fallen by the wayside or been 'removed' from planning documents. According to Greed (1994: Ch. 11), there is a feeling around that women-and-planning has become somewhat passé although the problems it set out to solve have not been remedied. Now 'everyone' is talking about green issues and sustainability, often, sadly, it appears (to the editor) with little cross-referencing to women's issues or other minority policies. However, it is argued that these present equal opportunities issues have by no means been addressed and that they should be taken on board as an integral part of the implementary agenda within the planning process alongside other uses.

Planning for the disabled

Accessibility

There are over six million people with disabilities in the United Kingdom, many of whom are denied access to jobs, housing and services because of an inaccessible environment (OPCS survey 1988). People with disabilities are not just wheelchair bound. According the Royal Town Planning Institute's Practice Advice Note No. 3 'Access for Disabled People';

> Disability includes a wide range of conditions: it covers more than the obvious such as blindness or confinement to a wheelchair. Breathlessness, pain, the need to walk with a stick, difficulty in gripping because of paralysis or arthritis, lack of physical co-ordination, partial sight, deafness and pregnancy can all affect a person's mobility in the environment. Access for the disabled will also benefit parents with buggies and the elderly.
>
> (RTPI 1985)

PPG 12 emphasises that the planning system now must 'have a regard to social considerations such as the needs of people with disabilities,' but the history of building legislation over the last twenty years shows that the provision of good access to buildings for those with disabilities has been achieved slowly in some cases and not at all in others. The Chronically Sick and Disabled Person's Act of 1970 required the provision of access and facilities for the disabled where reasonable and practicable. This was followed by the Disabled Person's Act of 1981 which inserted Sections 29A and 29B into the 1971 Town and Country Planning Act (now Section 7b of the 1990 Town and Country Planning Act). When they were granting planning permission, it required local authorities to draw the attention of developers to provisions under the Chronically Sick and Disabled Person's Act of 1970 and also to relevant design guidance (BS 5810 *Access for Disabled People* DoE 1992, originally 1979). However, there were no enforceable requirements to this legislation until 1985, when Part M of the Building Regulations came into being. As explained in Chapter 4, and also presented in the References section under 'British Standards', the Building Regulations specify no in-house standards of their own. Instead they validate a range of approved documents, including British Standards and other codes as the basis of the enforceable standards required under Parts A to M of Schedule 1 of the 1984 Building Act, which came into force in 1985. Otherwise, the British Standards Institutes standards remain advisory unless empowered by other legislation. However, as will be seen in later chapters they may still be taken as the minimal baseline for the purposes of controlling local government finance on publicly provided facilities.

Indeed, other statutory bodies which have control over the built environment, alongside the town planners, be they environmental health departments, fire and safety authorities or building regulations inspectors, can by their activities either reinforce or undermine the implementation of satisfactory planning policy. Although planners have considerable control over some aspects of the built environment, again and again one finds their powers are rather weak when it comes to making developers or other statutory bodies provide access into and within buildings. Likewise, planners have little power to specify the internal provision of essential facilities or design modifications which might benefit both the abled and the disabled. Attempts at comprehensive policies, which deal with the external built environment and the internal layout of individual buildings, are riven by this insides/outsides dichotomy. Building authorities control the insides; planners shape the outside of the built environment. This theme is revisited in the final chapters.

Founded in 1984, the Access Committee for England (ACE), which also covers Wales aims to provide a national focus on issues of access for all disabled people. The following year saw the publication of a PAN *Access for Disabled People* (RTPI 1985) and *Access for the Disabled* (Department of the Environment (DCPN 16) 1985). The booklet *Access for Disabled People: Design Guidance Notes* was published by ACE.

A revised edition of PAN *Access for Disabled People* was published by RTPI in 1988. Unfortunately, Part M of the Building Regulations is not itself comprehensive and does not require all buildings to be fully accessible to the disabled. According to PPG 3, 'developers should already be considering whether the internal design of housing, and access to it, can meet the needs of the disabled, whether as a resident or a visitor. The Government looks to the Building Regulations and not the planning system to impose requirements.' In an attempt to resolve the current confusion between the building regulations and planning control, the DoE is now assessing the practicality of extending Part M of the Building Regulations to all new dwellings. This does not solve the problem in respect of old dwellings. According to annual housing and construction statistics (Department of the Environment 1994a), most of the built environment consists of old buildings. And when it comes to providing access for the disabled, they are covered by a confusing variety of controls or no control at all. For instance, DoE Design Note 18 specifies special provision for access for disabled people to educational buildings, but again these only apply to new buildings. (The editor wishes to add that the headquarters of the Royal Town Planning Institute (a quasi-public building) is far from accessible for the disabled; it has front steps, difficult doors, no lift and no disabled toilets. But because it is an existing building, it is unlikely to be subject to such controls unless it undergoes major building works, or the law is changed.)

Disabled access policies, like those for women and ethnic minorities, should be included in development plan policy. After 1986, when the London boroughs commenced their unitary development plans, the group access officers felt it was very important that access policies should be consistent across borough boundaries and produced a twofold strategy which they hoped would be adopted by all London boroughs.

(1) To encourage access throughout the authority for everyone, including wheelchair users and people with disabilities.

(2) To ensure that people with access difficulties were not prevented from playing a full role in the life of the community.

It was against this background that I carried out research on the extent to which unitary development plans were incorporating policies to give access for the disabled (Davies 1992).

Disabled access research

In my research I found that transport and movement was the most popular policy area, as manifested in the percentage of development plan documents which contained policy topic statements related to the disabled. Transport and movement (85%) was followed by housing (80%), leisure, recreation and tourism (78%) then shopping (76%). In the area of *transport and movement*, a wide range of types of policies were drafted by all London boroughs. Concern over safety and design was reflected in policy statements, which covered similar issues to those related to the needs of women. But there was also a wider concern about the need to provide adequate access to and parking facilities for disabled persons. Quota policies requiring the allocation of a percentage of parking spaces for the disabled in off-street car parks with greater than twenty parking spaces were pursued in Newham, Bromley and Wandsworth. Wandsworth sought sensitive local policies highlighting the design of riverside walkways and public areas for the needs of the disabled.

In the area of *housing*, all six of the sampled boroughs had drafted unitary development plans containing policies requiring that all new single storey houses would be built to mobility standard, in accordance with the DoE Housing Directorate Occasional Paper 2/74. Four out of the six had drafted policies to provide access for the disabled into new buildings, conversions or premises to which the public have access. By comparison, the metropolitan districts were keener to draft quoted policies for encouraging disabled person's housing within large-scale residential developments; notably Wolverhampton and Coventry. But this was also true in the London boroughs of Bromley and Kensington and Chelsea.

In the area of *recreation, leisure and movement*, all of the six London boroughs had access for disabled policies. Most popularly they were policies concerned with the need to provide access for the disabled in converted and newly constructed buildings for leisure and recreational use.

Kensington and Chelsea pointed out that shopping centres are public places and it is important that high standards prevail. Policies in this area often overlapped or complemented those found under conservation and development. Occasionally reference was made to Part M of the Building Regulations, particularly if shop-front design policies were being promoted by the council. In four of the six London boroughs, policies required that all shop-fronts should be accessible to wheelchair users. Two of the metropolitan districts, Oldham and Manchester City, requested in their draft plans that toilet facilities for the disabled should be provided in new retail developments of floor space greater than 1,000 square metres. In new shopping centres and some other developments, Wandsworth claimed it was now normal to request a range of facilities for the disabled, including toilet facilities, ramped accesses and reserved parking spaces.

The future

A strategy to tackle inequalities of opportunity requires the participation of many different bodies. Alongside self-help from special needs groups, there is a role for local authorities, for the private sector and for central government. We examine each one in turn, with respect to our three social issues: planning for ethnic minorities, for the special needs of women and for the disabled. Local authorities in the 1990s are facing two major hurdles, the continuation of local authority financial cut-backs and compulsory competitive tendering (CCT), whereby most white-collar services in local authorities will have to be opened to competition from the private sector. How will this affect the implementation of development plan policy?

Recruitment and training budget cut-backs in local authorities have meant that the post of race equality officer is one which can no longer be afforded, and many have been lost or redeployed within authorities. Research shows that many authorities in the South-West did not even achieve such posts within their organisations. The role of the local authority to make equal opportunity policies an integral part of policy formulation, not a bolt-on extra, may well continue as the draft plans emerge from the public local inquiry process. In terms of implementing social issues policy, there is a very real danger that, should drafted policy in development plans survive the public local inquiry system, it may never be implemented due to lack of funds on the part of the local authority. With the introduction of CCT, local authorities are now pared to the bone in terms of what they can achieve, as increasingly their role is one of letting contracts to the private sector and normally to the lowest tenderer. In these circumstances, the local authority has little if any opportunity to insist on the incorporation of social needs policies. The local authorities must have a continuing role in cajoling and persuading business to participate in equal opportunities planning policies, but this role again has been subject to continuous attacks and dilution since the introduction of the 1988 Local Government Act, restructuring authorities' ability to require compliance with equal opportunities policies in contracts let to the private sector.

In terms of central government's role, there is a need for clear guidance and the promotion of good practice so as to encourage a partnership between public and private sectors in working towards implementing equal opportunities policies in development plans. This could be achieved by the introduction of additional annexes in PPG 1 (Annexes B, C and D) to complement the design considerations in Annex A. Such annexes could encourage local authorities and the private sector to adopt social needs policies to give access for the disabled (Annex B), women's special needs (Annex C) and race equality (Annex D). With such central government support there would be the essential encouragement, currently missing, to guide others in their policies.

Performance criteria: Editor's comment

Appendix 3 covers performance criteria for *doing* equal opportunities. Originally prepared by the editor as feedback to the consultation document on the CISC professional competence model, it is written in 'ciscese' and forms an additional element in the CISC 'map' (see Appendix 2 and Fig. 2.3). It is included here as so often practitioners seem vague as to how to implement equal opportunities policy in the construction industry and built environment professions, including town planning practice. It is argued that not only must the types of policies identified in the past two chapters by Linda Davies be taken on board, but also there must be monitoring of the evidence that progress is taking place. The CISC format is particularly apt in first setting performance criteria (objectives), identifying the range of professional activities to which they apply and distinguishing between product evidence and process evidence that demonstrates where or not the policy has been achieved. The definition of evidence dovetails with one of this book's themes: planning implementation as a process with a product as its outcome. The manner of the implementation would take into account the differential levels of power and the traditions of different cultures, particularly with regard to negotiating techniques when dealing with minority clients, and also public participation methods. By paying special attention to minority groups over matters of power and culture, it is possible to increase the competence and efficiency of the implementation process as seen from these minority viewpoints.

PART VI

ALTERNATIVE PERSPECTIVES

IMAGINING THE FUTURE

Having looked at the problems of implementation, firstly in respect of the needs of specific development sites and secondly of particular groups in society, the first chapter in this concluding section takes a broader policy oriented view of planning and the city. A city-wide approach is taken from the perspective of the planning policy maker, in contrast to the developer's viewpoint of concentrating on the details of a specific site, which has been focused upon in some earlier chapters. This exercise is relevant to exploring the basic questions underlying planning policy choice, What do we want? and how do you want to live? (Department of the Environment 1972a). The policies suggested in this section represent the views of the editor and they were produced as part of a brainstorming exercise on future scenarios. Readers (and for that matter some of the other contributors to the book) may have different views on what should be done.

Chapter 19 returns to the theme of implementation to consider the problems of achieving what we want, with reference to just one ostensibly 'little' policy area. It may be worthwhile, as in Chapter 18, to bring some of the vision back into planning and to imagine how our cities might become, but to be realistic we must constantly acknowledge that our power is only relative; it can never be absolute. Planners work alongside representatives of other statutory bodies and government departments, who hold other powers of control over the design of the built environment. The present nature of local government finance, or rather the lack of it, creates additional problems for policy implementation and the wider political context. The planner's role must always be set against the backcloth of power held by the private property sector, whose reason for wanting development might be one of speculative opportunism rather than a concern with society's needs or urban form and structure. Indeed, this whole section reflects the theme running right through the book, namely, that of the complex interrelationship of town planning legislation and policy with other statutory controls and policy areas concerned with managing the built environment.

Chapter 19 places emphasis on shifts from macrolevel policy issues to the nitty-gritty of detailed implementation, to illustrate the problems associated with trying to get just one small change, city-wide. After the more visionary approach of Chapter 18, it seeks to bring the reader down to earth and to balance some of the more conceptual and idealistic policies. To illustrate the problems which the wider legislative context creates for those who seek to implement detailed urban policies, it considers the problem of providing public lavatories – toilets – a key component in the implementation of accessibility policies. This is an issue which so often features in women-and-planning discussions, not only because women are the ones more likely to be responsible for children, but also because it is estimated by researchers in this field that men have approximately two-thirds more provision than women (Jones 1994; and a survey for *Here and Now* broadcast on BBC1 on 20 April 1994 and referred to in *Hansard* for 19 April 1994, p. 742, 3:31 pm speech by Jon Owen Jones). Toilets affect men too, especially elderly men in areas where there is underprovision for everyone. But women are more likely to be the ones who are out more in the daytime, doing the shopping and travelling around in the city on other essential care related trips, without their own central area 'base' in an office or other workplace having its own facilities.

Some readers still might wonder what this has to do with town planning. But that's the problem – compartmentalised thinking. It separates functions and creates artificial demarcations that prevent the comprehensive planning of urban areas. Bristol considers toilet provision a planning issue to be treated in the customary manner – alongside a policy statement, its planning documents contain an implementation section. Bristol apart, Chapter 19 centres on the experience of London boroughs which have already sought to implement such policies in their unitary development plans. However, one could choose a range of other issues or facilities to prioritise and investigate, such as provision for cyclists, designing against crime, access to housing, creating more jobs, leisure and sports centre provision, improving urban design. Indeed, the achievement of the policies would in reality be hampered as much by the nature of the implementation system as by a lack of agreement over their desirability among planners and policy makers, and thus the political support to make them happen. This reflects the considerable debate over the legitimate content of what we call town planning, which topics to let in or to leave out.

Chapter 20 the editor develops certain themes and subtexts running throughout the book – jagged edges or unfinished business requiring a little more discussion. First comes an attempt to define *implementation* and what its objectives should be. It has been accepted throughout that contributors have differences of opinion over definitions. These differences are healthy and are manifested more broadly right across the real world of planning and development. Each contributor instinctively seemed to know what the term meant to them 'in practice', but this aspect still needs some further clarification.

Next comes a re-examination of the public's role in the implementation process. Up to now the public has been portrayed as a key actor, but except for Chapter 15, its role in policy formulation has been rather neglected. Indeed, this might reflect a trend in planning practice, because central government pressures to speed up and streamline planning (including self-certification by planning authorities of their own plans, as described by John Allinson) have no doubt reduced the procedures and time devoted to official public participation. Nowadays, people have to take more responsibility themselves, to create a fuss and to make the running. It is significant that one sees more direct action nowadays taking the form of civil disobedience, particularly in respect of road proposals, possibly because people have become alienated from the official channels or feel they are ineffective, purely window-dressing to diffuse potential conflict. It is intended to resume this discussion in later volumes, because it is undoubtedly pressure from community groups, environmental groups and user organisations, rather than planners themselves, that has created the new planning agenda, focused around green issues, urban conservation, minority group needs and transport issues.

Finally comes the question of power. How much power do planners possess to carry out effective implementation? Town planners do not have total control over the built environment; they share control with other central and local government bodies and professional groupings. Although planners have considerable development control powers, arguably they are negative on the whole, not positive or proactive. Refusal for development may be given, but powers are limited to require a certain type of development to take place. The Building Regulations, British Standards and highways authority policies can either reinforce or undermine the good intentions of the planners. This is particularly manifest in the case of planning adequate access for the disabled and facilities for the disabled (Chapter 17). The planners might specify a step-free, highly accessible *external* layout, but the disabled might still find their path restricted *internally*. Beyond the building's threshold there may not be sufficient power to control internal design. It only takes one badly placed step to bar a person's access to the built environment. It is a curious paradox in town planning that planners have (or at least had) great powers to control the growth and zoning of entire cities, but at the other end of the scale they cannot necessarily specify that a ramp instead of a step be provided in relation to access to a particular building. This problem has become much more noticeable with the growth of the women-and-planning movement, and also because of pressure from disability groups, both groups being concerned with how people *uze* cities. Chapter 20 ends with a list of proposals to improve the chances for the implementation of planning policy.

Remember, it is important not just to read about the issues, but to get out there in the urban laboratory. Have a look at the range of projects suggested in Appendix 1. In particular, an assignment linked to the last section of the book suggests choosing a single policy area of interest then evidence of implementation.

Chapter 18

POLICY: WHAT DO WE WANT?

Clara Greed

How do you want to live: policy

It all depends on what you want

While planning legislation appears quite precise, and the implementation process technical, when it comes down to what policies should be implemented through these measures, there appears to be considerable difference of opinion among the planners and the public. For example, if one believes that cities should be based on unrestricted car usage, then it is likely one would want to plan for low density cities, with the different facilities and centres quite spread out, and possibly well separated by extensive zoning of land uses, with lots of roads and car parking areas. This approach to city planning is manifested in many North American cities, and to a lesser extent in postwar British planning, especially during the 1960s; its influence is still with us. Such a decentralised, dispersed, large-scale approach to planning policy undoubtedly governs the way in which individual planning applications are dealt with, and the overall approach to local site-specific development.

Thus the way a city is conceived at the macro city-wide level inevitably affects the way local areas will be planned. If it is assumed that everyone has a car, it may be considered that there is little need to implement policies which ensure that every residential area has within it a balanced range of shops, local facilities and amenities. If on the other hand there is an emphasis upon urban containment, human-scale planning, discouragement of motor car use and emphasis upon public transport and walking as the main means of getting around the city, then this will create quite different constraints on the way in which local areas are planned. In order for such a city and its inhabitants to function, there will be a need for adequate local provision of basic land uses and facilities, and also perhaps, more mixing rather than zoning of land uses so that, for example, a predominantly residential area will also contain a component of uses providing local employment, retail facilities, leisure provision and adequate public transport, reducing the need for people to make car journeys to meet the basic needs of human existence; work, play, education, shopping, health and child care.

In Bristol the city form is perhaps midway between the two scenarios presented above, with current policy moving towards the latter urban concept, although, like many British cities, Bristol bears the marks of previous attempts to plan on a more grandiose scale as manifested in zoning patterns, emphasis on dispersed development, its road structure and (as shown in Bedminster and Canon's Marsh) inner areas which are still blighted and stunted by previous inappropriate planning proposals. This city-wide or macro level of planning policy cannot be divorced from the more detailed micro level of site development explored in some of the case studies in this book.

Implementation and the levels of planning

In Volume I much was made of city-wide approaches to planning, as exemplified by the ideas of Ebenezer Howard (the low density, garden city school of thought) and Le Corbusier (the high-rise, and generally high density European city approach to planning). The history of these ideas was traced within an account of the development of twentieth century British town planning. The outworkings of the macrolevel conceptualisation of what the planners believe a city should take are translated down into the implementation of local planning at the district and neighbourhood level (as manifested in, say, the Bedminster Local Plan, or the local plans for the central area of Bristol at what might be called a meso level between city and site.) These city wide policies and local area planning principles then determine the planners' attitudes and expectations about development on a particular scheme, the micro level of actual site development.

These three levels of macro (city-wide), meso (local district level), and micro (site development level) are mirrored in the statutory planning framework (as outlined in Chapters 2 and 3). The structure plan (or Part I of the UDP (Unitary Development Plan)) provides the overall city-wide policies and strategic policy guidance at macro level. The local plan level (Part II of the UDP) provides the local district planning level at the meso level. The development control level constitutes the main implementatory level, in which decisions in respect of proposals for a particular site (such as York Gate) at the micro level are guided and informed by policies set at the city-wide and local area levels. It is an important principle of good planning that individual development control decisions are governed by higher policy statements, or looking at it the other way around, that development control is used to carry through and implement overall policy. **The planning process, particularly at the local plan and development control levels provides the opportunity for implementation of planning policy.**

There are so many other factors which come into play that this policy path is not always clearly defined, or the pipeline may get blocked. The individual development control planner may, in the heat of the moment, not necessarily adhere entirely to these higher principles. As operators of the planning system, they possess a considerable level of individual unofficial power to use their own discretion and professional judgement. Indeed, in the real world, structure plan policy makers and development control officers do not always see eye to eye. They may work for separate authorities and work in different buildings, the development plan being a county function, and the local plan and development control being a district function. Each authority may have quite different views on how the area for which they are responsible should be planned.

Perhaps the above representation of policy paths in planning is not entirely realistic because some policies may relate to problems that are found in one place but nowhere else, for example, only the centre of Bristol has the docklands area. Alternatively, there might be detailed aspects of planning at the micro level of site layout which cannot be contained within overall macrolevel policy statements but which are best presented as detailed site layout or urban design principles, possibly in the form of a planning brief for a particular area, a conservation area policy area document or a residential area design guide. However, as seen in the case studies (and this is where the crunch comes), if one does not put such detailed aspects of planning design in macrolevel structure plan and UDP policy statements, in the present pro-developer political climate, it may be argued on appeal that they are not in the policy statement and therefore not approved policy. If on the other hand one does put detailed local plan and urban design principles in high-level policy documents, it might be argued by the planning inspector, as in the case of some of the women-and-planning type London borough UDP policy statements, that a high-level policy document is no place for putting in standards, detailed design principles and quotas.

Although the levels of policy described above work well when dealing with area-based physical land use planning issues, it is more problematic to know in which level of policy document to put some of the more socially oriented policies. Social policy considerations cannot always be tied down to a particular area, and this is particularly the case when dealing with matters like equal opportunities, when dealing with inbuilt discrimination against the disabled within the planning system or when dealing with women-and-planning issues. (They are 'everywhere and nowhere like the sky,' as some famous philosopher once commented.) Social issues affect every dimension of human life and cannot necessarily be provided for by the provision of a piece of land or a building (although some aspects definitely can), but rather may require a change in attitude, perspective and priorities which runs through all aspects of planning practice. Nor can equal opportunities issues be solved in isolation, just by the planning authority; there is a need for liaison with other local authority departments and government bodies. In fact, this is also true of most social policy areas, if not most mainstream planning matters.

Policy suggestions

'Town planning's history is a story of unfulfilled ideas ... of well meant futures and bitter failures' (Sorenson in 'Planning comes of age' *The Planner*, Vol 68: 184, 1982).

In this section the editor is going to present her personal view of ideal policy at the three levels identified above: macro, meso and micro. At the same time, she will try to incorporate an equal opportunities component into the ideas. But, as the dire quotation above indicates, planners seldom see all their ideas fulfilled, and one must accept this. This is another opportunity to give an airing to some of the controversial undercurrents swirling around under the apparently placid surface of policy making. The last chapter of Volume I also provided some such policy ideas, and also Appendix III of Greed (1994) summarises policy directives specifically related to women-and-planning. It is suggested that, as a useful exercise, the reader makes up a personal policy checklist. In the final section the editor will return to the question, how? She will reflect upon the levels of power (or lack of it) held by the planners to carry out such policy. One cannot plan for equal opportunities in isolation, as one must also take on board all the other policy issues, no more than the Bristol football supporters party can just field councillors who can only talk about football at every council meeting. This issue of synergy is reflected upon in the following section. But it might be argued that a concern for equal opportunities (or possibly for some football) informs and affects to some extent all other policy areas discussed.

Reservations

Much is made nowadays of the ideal city form and structure based upon the principles of sustainability and equality. It may be argued that the former includes the latter. According to Blowers (1993) sustainability policy has four elements: to conserve the stock of natural assets, to avoid damaging the regenerative capacity of ecosystems, to achieve greater social equality and to avoid imposing risks and costs on future generations. It has an ecological and environmental agenda. The editor feels some uneasiness with certain manifestations of the current sustainability movement because it has been seen, in some cases, to shift the emphasis away from social and political issues, particularly when hijacked by the right to legitimate elitist conservation policies in the countryside, but that is another story. It is suspected (paradoxically and heretically) that sustainability is a passing craze, which will be replaced by some other all-encompassing new perspective in due course. Possibly the key issues remain valid but the language (or planning jargon) changes according to fashion. Planning has always had a remarkably changeable discourse. There should be no conflict between women-and-planning and sustainable development, provided the conceptualisation of sustainability is informed by an awareness of social inequality. It is significant that the Avon Environmental Strategy and Action Plan (Avon 1993), based on principles of sustainability, was particularly promoted by three women councillors.

Both environmentalists and women planners are keen to increase the provision of public transport and reduce the need to travel by car, perhaps for somewhat different reasons. But many women with household and child care responsibilities do object to green planners making them feel guilty for using cars when there is no other means of transport available to do the shopping. They object because the local planning authority previously gave permission for out-of-town shopping development by a superstore, which subsequently undercut local shops and put them out of business. Indeed the airing of this example demonstrates another problem with planning cities, one is always living in the overlap between putting up with the results of past bad planning decisions and trying to implement better policies for the future. Short of knocking it all down and starting again one cannot make everything perfect all in one go, but the aim of the planner (as stated in Volume I) is to make things at least a little better, and to do less harm than good. But planners cannot work instant miracles. The problem arises when restrictive policies are introduced, perhaps preventing car use or the location of essential facilities but without providing alternative positive solutions.

City-wide: macro level

The editor's ideal city form at the macro level would be based upon urban containment and a higher overall density than exists today; this would facilitate accessibility and movement, chiefly by means of public transport. Having said this, there is no intention to demolish existing development to make it conform to this ideal, but a long-term approach is envisaged of gradually training and pruning the city in this way. Welcome applications might be for utilisation of infill sites and intensification of use; unwelcome applications might be for yet more out-of-town development, especially housing estates. There would be a comprehensive, frequent, cheap, reliable public transport system running throughout the city; every new development or change of use would be subject to a transport levy payment, proportionate to the numbers of new journeys generated by the development, but reduced by the level of non-car accessibility of the location. The editor admits funding is a complex issue and it would need to be taken on board alongside policy making otherwise it is all pie in the sky.

District: meso level

At the meso level of the local district or neighbourhood, there would be an emphasis upon encouraging a balanced mix of land uses and facilities, and generally upon dezoning. However, there would also be very high urban design standards and environmental regulations to ensure that the resulting mixing of work and home, was created sensitively in a manner acceptable to residents. This policy would particularly be encouraged in respect of light manufacturing and office employment; there would still be a case for the more traditional zoning principles to be applied on large-scale and potentially noxious land uses. But colleagues working on sustainable development and related environmental controls would no doubt ensure an overall reduction in such uses. Dezoning, and the provision of local employment opportunities within residential areas, would particularly benefit women workers seeking to combine home and work duties. And it would massively improve the traffic congestion problems, reducing the numbers of commuters heading to and from the central area each day. Indeed, with time, and in the light of new telecommuting trends, central area offices would become redundant, and therefore the task of setting policy guidelines for new uses – redevelopment and perhaps in a few cases conservation – would be allocated to a team within the central area local plan section of the planning office.

Also at the meso district level there would be considerable emphasis upon providing a full range of local businesses, shops and amenities in each area, backed up with new central government grants where necessary. Retail policy would be directly linked to social policy, and a full range of adequate shopping provision must be provided within each local district, with grants and incentives for new ventures being linked to each district's proportions of elderly, children and young people, disabled and carless. New out-of-town centres would not receive planning permission; existing uses would be extinguished and compensation would be paid at the subsequent market value. Alternative uses for existing developments, or demolition and site reclamation (e.g. for urban fringe community forest plantations) would be reflected in county-level planning policy documents. Bristol is a pioneer in urban forest development; see Avon (1993) for the greening of the county, and Policy Statement NE16 and para 3.4.60 of Bristol, November, 1993).

However, policies as to the nature of retail development within residential areas would he flexible, and might run from small shops through to large supermarket developments, with the proviso that close control must be maintained on the likely competition and mix of outlets within sites, through new planning regulations which would control tenure, frequency of distribution, internal layout and occupancy, as well as controlling use in respect of all types of development. Encouragement would be given to large retail outlets willing to relocate in specified residential area infill sites; the local authority would take over their existing out-of-town sites in a direct swap, thus avoiding any unpleasant side-effects of the otherwise harsh compensation regulations. As in the overlap, we do not want the entire retail sector collapsing, as this would be highly impractical.

Motor cars would continue to be accommodated, but people would have more choice not to use them because of the vastly improved public transport system. The dezoning of land uses taking away the need to travel so much for work, because of the decentralisation of central area office uses. It is envisaged that the city centre would be retained providing traditional retail outlets, cultural and educational facilities, and touristic provision, with a strong policy emphasis on quality townscape and urban conservation. It is estimated that approximately 50% less people would actually work in or commute to the centre each day. Office uses would still be allowed in the centre, but it is likely that smaller-scale professional and financial services offices, which are highly dependent on face-to-face contact, may wish to stay because of the ambience of the centre. But many of the administrative, routine, office uses and their staffs would move out, finding cheaper solutions in decentralised locations or telecommuting. People would then be nearer local shops, schools and facilities, enabling them to combine home and work responsibilities and to split caring roles between parents. Possibly dezoning of itself would not lead to decentralisation of office development, but other trends are on our side to reinforce this policy, in particular, teleworking. Teleworking enables people to work away from a centralised office base, which property developers are already taking very seriously as to the implications for office space requirements (*Estates Times*, Teleworking: Computers' remote chance', 14 October 1994, pp. 29–30).

Current car parking standards and quotas in respect of office floor space would be reviewed and possibly made more flexible in view of reduced pressure. New quota regulations would be introduced to enable the female workforce to combine child care and career pressures. One child care space must be provided per 1,000 square feet of net office space. Commercial rates reductions would be allowed for all additional spaces provided, or for space surplus to requirements. In office development over 50,000 square feet this provision must be provided as an integral part of the building. For smaller office premises, funding towards initial construction (or conversion of disused office buildings) would be required and an annual levy would be charged for running costs. In the same way that car parking policy has nowadays been used to encourage or restrict office development, child care spaces would be utilised in a similar manner to ensure that developers and occupiers preferred to locate in decentralised locations within existing inner areas or residential suburbs. In the case of Bristol, the city already manifests a multinucleated land use pattern – lots of little district centres – so these policies could be easily grafted on to existing land use patterns. In other cities, more drastic measures might be required to create district business use cores within areas that were solely residential.

Local estate: micro level

At the micro site development level, a range of measures would be implemented in relation to urban design, street layout, townscape and the general format of the local urban environment. This would be achieved by two means.

In the case of new development, by producing clear design guides which required compliance with the relevant design standards. In the case of existing streets, buildings and local vicinities, grants would be available through a new localised type of town scheme to bring areas up to standard. There is already available a mass of expertise and design principles on planning to create safer and more accessible environments. In order to prioritise these aspects, local planning authorities would be encouraged, by means of the operation of new local government finance regulations, to employ planners, designers and advisers who themselves were disabled and/or belonged to other minority groups, with particular emphasis upon including more women and ethnic minority planners. In conjunction with the Open University and local colleges, scholarships and training programmes would be made available for local residents to study town planning, irrespective of age, class and previous educational record. Indeed, no university town planning course would be validated without showing evidence of involvement in such schemes, and without showing that at least 25% of its student body came from such a local scheme. Positive discrimination quotas would be based on age, gender, class, race and disability; these criteria would be applied both to students and planning lecturers, and ultimately to planning officers themselves.

The sort of microlevel design principles adopted in different residential areas might vary somewhat according to the character, age and architecture of an area. Enforced design uniformity in the name of so-called equal opportunities planning is to be discouraged as it will lead to a mechanical, municipalised system in which all professional judgement and sensitivity is lost. However, certain general principles must be adhered to, such as adequate lighting; steps only to be used as a last resort; all passageways and doorways to be at least wide enough for a double buggy to pass through easily; no unnecessary planting, meandering footpaths or blind corners on pedestrian routes. All buildings would eventually be subject to a much improved update of Approved Document M, including private residential properties. This policy would start with controls on new buildings then gradually move to improvements on existing properties, with grants being made available accordingly. No pedestrian/vehicular segregation of footpaths in housing schemes would be permitted unless the paths were fully lit and received adequate surveillance from overlooking buildings.

As Hayden (1984) suggests in her book *Redesigning the American Dream*, each neighbourhood would be provided with all-purpose community buildings containing good quality child care facilities and other amenities. There would be a range of basic backup services to households, such as a tele-commuting office centre. Other suggestions have been made that such neighbourhood child care and community centres might also be combined with aspects of health, education and leisure facilities to create a new multi-use building in each area. Alternatively they could be combined with local employment centres. These buildings would provide essential facilities, especially for working parents, and some 'care in the community' relief for those looking after the elderly or disabled. In no way should they be compared with present-day community centres. Their name strikes me as somewhat meaningless when so often they seem dominated by evening activities, such as youth clubs, with limited daytime use for toddler groups, and no twenty-four hour provision of facilities and services.

All bus-stops and car parks are to be lit. As long as large car parks remain part of the urban scene (in the overlap period before some of the above policies take full affect), all of them should be staffed. Preferably they should have pay-as-you-leave barriers to reduce car thefts and vandalism. It is considered risky to leave a parking ticket on a windscreen if the ticket shows when the driver is likely to return. In view of the fact that nowadays people may have to travel considerable distances by car or public transport, either into the centre or out to retail parks, public conveniences should be a feature of all main car parks, bus stations, railway stations and other public transport interchanges. These facilities should generally be supervised by an attendant and should be at surface level to avoid steps. They should include baby-changing facilities, feeding facilities and children's toilets, ideally designed or duplicated in such a way that either parent may utilise these facilities without embarrassment to themselves or other users. Adequate provision should also be made for cyclist parking, possibly under cover and in close proximity to toilet provision, for refreshment areas and for other appropriate uses. Indeed, one can envisage a similar type of multi-use set of clustered facilities developing along the principles suggested in the residential neighbourhoods, but with somewhat different components.

The provision of public conveniences should be a comprehensive part of any accessibility policy, for both abled and disabled. Indeed, it is argued that it is often a minimalistic and cost-cutting exercise to divide people into these two categories, as manifested in toilet provision. It is particularly inappropriate in view of the fact that many people at different times in their lives may effectively be disabled, because of illness, injury, pregnancy or old age, but may not qualify for a coveted, orange disabled parking badge or receive any other special considerations. Notwithstanding, such groups are expected to tackle that Krypton factor assault course called the built environment, which can sometimes be a challenge even for the perfectly healthy fully abled citizen.

Extreme care must be given to all the details of any planning policy, with full public participation by users, that is, those who *uze* the built environment, as against those who plan the land uses (see the introduction to Part V). For example, it was recently realised that the maximum distance that pedestrians, as specified in some UDP documents, should be expected to walk from bus-stop or car park to their destination should not be more than 250 metres. This was in fact greater than the distance specified in relation to eligibility for mobility allowance rules (Centre for Independent Transport Research in London, see LWPF 1994). Sharing of footpaths with bicycles should be discouraged; sharing is often adopted to please the cycling lobby, but it makes footpaths unsafe for pedestrians.

The power to implement and control?

This chapter began with a consideration of vital city-wide planning issues and went right down to the very detailed but important 'little' issues which affect how people, especially women and children *uze* the city (p. 197). The discussion has moved from the more traditional realms of land use strategy, to the details of how people *uze* land. Paradoxically, planners still have considerable power over deciding the land use patterns of entire cities, their power spreading over vast tracts of urban land. But their great weakness, their Achilles heel, as highlighted by the demands of the women-and-planning movement, residents and users groups and the disability groups, is their weakness and ineffectiveness in dealing with all those little issues which make up good urban design and usable cities, namely, pavements, ramps, kerbs, steps, crime and safety, lighting, widths of doorways, provision of public conveniences and car park design (see Appendix 4).

However, the situation is patchy in that the planners do possess considerable power over some very detailed matters. For example, they have great powers over controlling kitchen extensions on residential property; over the diameter of satellite dishes, which should not exceed 70 cm (or 90 cm in specified counties); over the heights of walls, which should not normally exceed 2 metres; over where to put advertisements and flag-poles; and over whether a greengrocery can change into a fish and chip shop. Many of these controls are bewildering and irksome to the public, and have given the planners a bad name. Indeed, residential extensions might need to be encouraged in the future to create a more compact, higher density city, which allows for accommodation for extended families and more economical household structures. If one looks into how and why the planning system, in particular, as against say the building regulation system, got lumbered with some of the more curious controls, one finds a tangled, illogical and often contradictory web of Victorian legislation, covering public health, housing and what is now town planning. It has been suggested that the government should undertake to rationalise and harmonise all these regulations, creating a modern system, in which legislation is framed in a manner which is more relevant and responsive to present-day land uses and problems.

There are also much larger issues which planners have little control over, such as public transport, local government finance, housing policy, the activities of the private property sector and the policies and controls established by other governmental and regulatory bodies. Although not the subject of this volume, if one looks into the realms of rural planning and controls over farm buildings, trees, hedgerows and such like, one encounters another set of bewildering and incomplete legislation. For example, there are fines for the destruction of one urban tree under a tree preservation order (TPO), but entire field patterns can be altered without getting planning permission.

Indeed the Ministry of Agriculture, Fisheries and Food has in the past given farmers grants to do so, undermining conservation directives from the Department of the Environment. Likewise, control over the location of refuse disposal sites and waste tips is a county planning function, but the planners can only control these uses in so far as they relate to land use. Incredibly, the fact a site smells or is a danger to health may be irrelevant in planning law, this being an environmental health matter, and not, strictly speaking, the province of planning law, although again it clearly is a matter related to how a site is *uzed*.

In order to increase coordination to achieve effective implementation and to transcend legalistic compartmentalisation, some cities are now creating city centre manager posts for this very reason, giving one person the overview and authority to promote coordination between different departmental functions, including the planners, the police, the environmental health department, the parks department and the local chamber of commerce. This is aimed to ensure, for example, that when tourists and shoppers visit the city of Bath, they find a well-planned, unvandalised, beggarless and crime-free centre with convenient shopping hours that include evenings and with adequate street signs to public conveniences and other facilities which are kept open and hygienic.

Bath has had a major crackdown on what it terms 'aggressive begging'. It is said that no on-street beggars are allowed, unless they are willing to sell copies of *The Big Issue*, produced by the homeless to make money for rehousing. One of its London representatives was brought in specially to publicise the scheme across Bath. In an ideal world, comprehensive housing and employment policies would resolve the situation. Such tactics and terminology might not be seen as politically correct by some. But they are important in the short run, because women, in particular, who may be seen as easy targets for intimidation, increasingly find city centres to be threatening or unsafe places. This clean-up, crimebuster role is a far cry from the traditional land use role of the planner, a trend reflected by Circular 5/94 (Planning out Crime) and in the growing installation of closed circuit television (CCTV, not to be confused with CCT). It is for the reader to consider whether the new trend towards city centre management should be seen as a valid extension of town planning or as something more worrying. However, it does manifest a positive emphasis on day-to-day monitoring and management of the city, rather than the remote, hit-and-run planning of the past, in which the land uses were zoned and then people were left to *uze* the city – with difficulty.

Means of implementation

On discussing these proposals with colleagues, the comment has often been made that it would all cost too much. Not necessarily, as the process of change would not be sudden, but gradual, as indicated by the concept of having an interim period of overlap. It may be a trap to start at the city-wide level of change and become overwhelmed, when in fact local, grassroots change within communities may in fact be more effective as its influence spreads up through the urban system. Indeed, at a recent conference on the city (OECD 1994) I witnessed a discussion of these very issues. The conference was organised by the Organisation for Economic Cooperation and Development (OECD), an international organisation which seeks to provide research and expert advice on a wide range of planning and related issues covering economic development, the environment, the problems of developed and developing countries and urban affairs. Drawing ideas from the example of other European countries is particularly helpful.

A general theme arising from the conference was the importance of the 'city of short journeys' which ties in with the multinucleated city proposed above, and creates a more sustainable, environmentally efficient city form. Its achievement does not necessarily require vast economic expenditure. It involves a change in planning policy to discourage decentralisation and out-of-town development and to encourage infill, reuse and refurbishment of existing structures, with particular attention given to the planning of inner city areas, which in many UK and continental cities still contain surprisingly large underused tracts of derelict land and depressed areas. The present government's attempt towards the single regeneration budget is a welcomed move to prioritise such policies, but its critics point to the funds it takes away from mainstream local government finance.

Dezoning may be gradually achieved in respect of existing development by relaxing controls on change of use, so as to enable shops and small businesses to develop in residential areas, though this would not be a free-for-all but a carefully controlled approach with built-in safeguards to protect the environment. Government subsidies towards small businesses, especially shopping provision in residential areas, is a key factor worthy of consideration. Traditionally there has been a tendency towards putting government expenditure and subsidy into large-scale firms and schemes when a more fine-grained and detailed approach which targets much smaller concerns might in fact be more cost-effective in generating jobs, stimulating the local economy and providing essential small retail outlets in residential areas. Nowadays, small retailers cannot break even in competition with large stores. Policies based on multiple, smaller-scale intervention, in conjunction with local community groups, are generally seen as more effective than the one-off big investment approach, particularly in respect of creating sustainable development. In the final analysis, this is because environmental responsibility is all about how we live our ordinary lives on the day-to-day level. This fact may get obscured in the macrolevel debates about the ozone layer and a general globalisation both of economies and environmental debates.

A fundamental issue which needs tackling is transport, especially public transport, and any realistic planning policy requires government investment in such provision. But improvements can be made to the ways in which existing road space and passenger transport units are used without necessarily incurring vast amounts of expenditure. In some Italian cities, for example, Modena, Milan and parts of Tuscany and Liguria, the urban development plan has been accompanied by a development plan for times (timetables) which has sought to coordinate transport provision, shop opening hours, school days, office hours so that facilities are open when people need them, and existing road space and transport stock is used in the most efficient manner. This is particularly important in historic Italian cities where there is simply not the road space to take higher numbers of cars, or indeed buses (Belloni 1994).

As to achieving social facilities – child care provision and a better quality of environment for *uzers* – planning gain cannot be ruled out. But a more effective and formalised system needs to be developed. The OECD conference cited environmental impact assessment; in some countries this resulted in developers being expected to modify their proposals or pay towards ameliorating measures. In the same way, social impact assessments should be carried out on any large new development or for any change of use of existing properties. The cost of the development to the community, in terms of gains and losses, could provide a basis for calculating the requirement level of planning gain payment, and apparently such an approach has been tried out in some Australian cities. Certain basic standards should be established for the provision of child care facilities, disability provision, public conveniences, etc. according to fixed zoning compliance regulations as are found in some North American cities (Cullingworth 1993). Arguments against such mandatory measures are always made by developers, who argue it would all cost far too much. In fact, if such provision was an integral part of the costing of new development or was carried out gradually for maintenance and modernisation of existing property, it would not be such a major expense within the context of the millions of pounds spent on construction each year.

Do not be overwhelmed by the immensity of implementation and the sheer scale of cities. Start at the human scale, in respect of individual buildings and local areas then implement changes that work their way up through the system. Do not to seek to implement change by means of town planning in isolation to other high-level governmental functions, but to coordinate and reinforce proposed changes in the built environment with policies concerned with employment, economic development, housing and simply the way in which people use cities, as evidenced in the Italian example. It is argued we really know very little about how people use cities, because of the emphasis in the past on impersonal, high-level statistics, and strangely peopleless transport studies. Effective policy implementation puts great emphasis on research and on listening to what people want. It is certainly not the intention in this chapter to present a rigid master plan, for as times change and ordinary people become more involved in the planning process, who knows what will happen? The future possibilities and preferences are as yet impossible to imagine. It is vital to maintain a flexible and interactive approach to policy making, while maintaining a structured macrolevel overview of where the city is going.

Chapter 19

IMPLEMENTATION: CAN WE ACHIEVE IT?

Clara Greed

Planning for access and convenience

CS18 'The City council will seek to improve deficiencies in the provision and quality of public toilets across the city. Where appropriate this may be achieved in new development. New public toilets must be fully accessible to disabled people and include separate children's changing and feeding facilities. They must also be designed to ensure maximum safety and security'.

Implementation: Through the use of planning conditions and planning obligations. Also through close liaison with the Directorate of Health and Environmental Services to identify suitable locations for new toilet provision.

Source: *Deposit Bristol Local Plan* (Bristol, November 1993a)

In seeking to make city centres more accessible both for the abled and disabled it is important that not only should people be able to get there, and that their route should not be impeded by steps, or barriers, but once there they should be able to find available to them basic social amenities and facilities, such as eating-places, toilets, sitting-areas and possibly crèches and play areas for their children. The editor has heard it said by some planners that *accessibility* is about *movement* not *facilities*, and therefore not a land use matter. But this is seen as a blinkered view. It has been found that some people seldom travel precisely because of fear of the lack of availability of such provision, or in anticipation of trying to negotiate a modern city centre by foot being just too tiring for them. As explained in Linda Davies' chapter (and covered briefly in the last chapter of Volume 1, and at more length in the last two chapters of the editor's book on 'women and planning' (Greed 1994), various local authorities have sought to make the provision of both toilets and shoppers crèches an integral component of their planning policy documents, so their provision is a condition of development. These include the London boroughs but also cities such as Southampton (Southampton 1991), Dublin (Barrett and Caffrey 1991) and Birmingham (1991, and in the video *Positive Planning*, Birmingham 1994). But they have found that such provision has often been ruled *ultra vires*. Among shire counties, Cheshire is particularly concerned about toilet policy.

It has long been argued by women planners that such provision *is* a land use matter, because it affects the way people *uze* land. Women, for example, uze city centre retail development differently from men, because 80% of shoppers are women, and they are also likely to be responsible for child care at the same time. 'Well they could always use a pub,' is the usual comment at this point in a tutorial. But the argument is invalid because children are not allowed in pubs. This dates back to the 1933 Children and Young Persons Act which made it illegal for children under fourteen years of age to be in a bar, this restriction subsequently being incorporated in s.168 of the 1964 Licensing Act (see *New Law Journal*, Vol. 91, No. 18: 17–18 'Licensing Update.' by Graham Glover). However, in early 1995 a new system of children's certificates was introduced by the government, enabling a limited number of pubs to allow under age children into bars with their parents. Apparently the reason for this is to create a 'family atmosphere' to deter violence rather than primarily to reflect the needs of women and children. This divisive legislation has ensured that children, and thus effectively women and families, have been kept out of many pubs, and also prevented from benefiting from the original purpose of inns to provide rest and refreshment for travellers. These days few parents would dream of leaving children outside unattended, and so either a parent (usually the mother) has to wait outside with them, or they simply stay at home.

Nevertheless, some planning inspectors have ruled that provision of such facilities as toilets counts as imposing quotas on developers, and this is frowned upon. But there seems to be considerable difference of opinion. Some boroughs consider it perfectly reasonable to provide covered buggy parking space for supermarket shoppers. Other planning inspectors have seen this as most irregular. Yet again it comes back to the old insides/outsides debate – planners should not control what happens within a building; their jurisdiction stops at the threshold. This is rather a ridiculous attitude nowadays when so much shopping space is enclosed, it is under cover in a mall or a superstore, and likely to be in private ownership. But should the public space enclosed within a shopping mall or for that matter a huge railway station concourse, or sports centre really be *inside* space and therefore private rather than public space? Should it be like the inside of someone's home or little shop and therefore beyond the realms of the planners?

In North America, where the enclosed shopping centre originated, the planning position appears to be significantly different; the controls are greater. North American planning is based on meeting certain criteria as to each type of land use, types enforced by zoning regulations. The owner has considerably less control over internal, as well as external, layout than in Britain, and developers are required to provide high quality public conveniences and a wider range of amenity provision overall. This is expected as normal provision; it is not used as a bargaining tool or a form of planning gain to get a better planning permission, as in the rather grubby British system (Cullingworth 1993; Cullingworth and Nadin, 1994: 251 and 272, n. 17).

On-street public provision

The provision of public conveniences can take two forms: on-street provision by the local authority and private off-street provision by the developer or owner of a private building to which the public has access (such as a department store or bus station). This public/private distinction should be borne in mind as, like the insides/outsides and use/uze debates over the jurisdiction of planning law within enclosed shopping centres, it has implications for enforcement. Section 87, subsection 3 of the 1936 Public Health Act gave local authorities the right to build and run on-street public conveniences and to charge such fees as they thought fit 'other than for urinals.' The 1848 Public Health Act was the first act to deal with the topic, giving more general powers. Conditions on charging actually mean it is illegal that men nowadays have to pay to use public or at least quasi-public urinals in some public places. As explained in detail (WDS 1991) a long campaign ensued to get adequate free public conveniences for women as well as men. But a survey back in 1928 of public conveniences in London (WDS 1991, 16) found that men had more than two-thirds the public provision than women, plus they had the benefit of many pub toilets whose entrance was straight off the street. Recent surveys have found the situation has got worse not better (ibid., 499). Needless to say this aspect of the 1936 act contravenes modern anti-sex discrimination legislation, under British and EU law, and therefore should be repealed.

The situation has got worse not better with subsequent legislation. BS6465 (Part I), (see Reference section on British Standards, Building Regulations and Linked Approved document G), which has provided the national guideline standards for toilet provision since the mid 1980s, has provided an extremely imbalanced set of standards 'normally' resulting in men legally being provided with approximately 2 to 3 times more provision per set of toilets than women. In general men have more provision than women because they are likely to have the same number of cubicles and the same floor space area as in the Ladies but with the addition of urinal provision (indeed in the case of some public conveniences only a Gents is provided). This principle is inherited from and reflected in other toilet-related acts such as the 1936 and 1961 Public Health Acts, the various Building Acts, and the 1963 Offices, Shops and Railway Premises Act (the latter is currently being replaced, but not necessarily improved upon by the provisions of the Work Place Directive). The logical answer is to provide a compensatory number of additional cubicles for women. This factor alone explains why there are always queues for women's toilets! In enclosed shopping centre development, even when 80% of shoppers are women, it is quite normal still to provide equal provision for men. In fact the editor was informed by one developer that he did not like providing public conveniences for women beside food courts as they generated queues, but he did not seem able to grasp the obvious remedy to this problem – more, not less, provision. Indeed, private developers, have had no legal obligation to provide for shoppers only shop workers under the current legislation, and local authority provision need only be '-sufficient' (as they think fit) a word which is frequently used but poorly defined in much of the legislation covering the provision of both public and private conveniences (cf s.43 of the 1936 Public Health Act, and Section 28 of the 1984 Building Act and successive legislation).

Discrepancies in provision are also evident in relation to leisure and recreation related provision. BS 6465 (Part I) recommended that toilets in public houses should be provided upon a 75:25 ratio in favour of men. Other authorities suggest calculation for provision at football stadia and sporting facilities should be on a 90:10 basis, in spite of the fact that many such venues are used for mixed audiences for pop festivals, religious gatherings and public events. Currently a new Sports Council consultative document *Toilet Provision in Stadia Planning, Design and Types of Installation* (produced by Simon Inglis consultant, and author of *The Football Grounds of Great Britain*, and numerous other football design publications) improves on this ratio, suggesting 85:15, but also suggesting that clubs should research their own ratio as appropriate to local demand. The lack of awareness of the need for the provision of public toilets to be linked to sport planning, especially in view of the numbers of visitors, tourists and spectators generated, is epitomised by the fact that Manchester closed over two-thirds of its public toilets during the very same period that it was making itself out to be the ideal European city to hold the next Olympic Games. (Presumably cutbacks in toilet provision was one of the many prices to pay for the diversion of vast amounts of public money spent on promoting and reconstructing the city's sports facilities for the Olympics. Australian cities are well provided with public toilets; Sydney was preferred over Manchester.

Not only were there quantitative problems; it must be added that, although men have more provision, there are significantly large areas of cities where there is no provision for men either, and this particularly creates problems for an aging population, male and female. There are also major qualitative problems, not least in terms of hygiene and design. In fact there had always been basic public health standards about provision of washing and drinking water and cleanliness hidden away in the various public health acts but these had often been flouted. Indeed BS 6465 (Part I), which governs toilet design standards emphasises the hygiene aspect among other design factors. The Victorians should be commended, as the builders of palatial public lavatories and proponents of improved urban standards, often driven by a sense of civic pride and a concept of citizenship for both women and men. Nevertheless they would insist on putting them underground, down steps, partly out of a sense of misdirected modesty and also because the legislation of the time allowed the area of the subsoil beneath the public highway to be used for such facilities and for sewer routing. The existence of steps has caused untold problems for large groups of the population, for many generations, not only the disabled, but the elderly, and people with luggage, shopping, pushchairs, and small children.

To add insult to injury, in that they were already recipients of lesser provision, in the past women were likely to find their access to public toilets further blocked by the existence of turnstiles at the entrance and had to pay (because as stated above under the 1936 Public Health Act local authorities had the right to charge for facilities 'other than urinals'). After a heated campaign turnstiles were eventually outlawed under the 1963 Public Lavatories (Turnstiles) Act. However, the rules outlawing turnstiles and other vital details never did apply to *private* conveniences, only *public* ones, and strangely they never applied to British Rail even when it was clearly a nationalised, public sector institution. The question of getting wheelchairs through turnstiles apparently never occurred to councils in those days, and indeed it does not seem to occur to some supermarkets and DIY stores nowadays, who put a type of turnstile across their shop entrances with a little gap to push trolleys under. In fact turnstiles are 'everywhere'.

Section 5 of the 1970 Chronically Sick and Disabled Act required much better provision for the disabled (as previously mentioned by Linda Davies in Chapter 17, with reference to linked Document M of the Building Regulations). In the 1970s following pressure from the women's movement, and legislation requiring the equal provision of goods and services, in many parts of the country public conveniences became free for women and men, and possibly slightly more numerous. This, plus pressure for baby-changing facilities, led to some improvements in some areas, but overall the level of provision remains very poor indeed (Jones 1994). There were no pre-existing governmental requirements on provision of children's toilets or facilities for babies, although design guidelines exist for provision in both the public and private sector in a range of sources. For example *The New Metric Handbook* (Tutt and Adler, 1993, first published 1979, and soon to be updated) provides vastly more equal, realistic and modern, standards than the official minimum standards, and states that the standards were upgraded where it was considered existing legislative standards were inadequate.

However, in the 1980s things took a turn for the worse. Car ownership had increased, cities had spread, tourism had grown, people were away from home for longer periods of time when they went shopping in the new out of town centres, and the population contained a higher proportion of elderly people. Demand for public conveniences therefore increased. Significantly many out of town centres, and regional enclosed shopping centres were originally constructed without any adequate provision (some are still extremely badly provided for). For these reasons, eventually, the provision of public conveniences began to be seen as possibly a matter more of town planning than of public health. Firstly, because of increased vandalism, and cutbacks in local government funding, many public conveniences were closed. Secondly, as traditional city form patterns were restructured, and uses were decentralised, new demands developed. In particular, the old clear cut division between public and private areas was confused, as indicated above by the establishment of enclosed shopping centres.

Just at the time when the 'women and planning' movement seemed to be reaching new heights in the mid 1980s, and it seemed that everyone knew about the importance of creating accessible environments, and everyone knew how wide a pushchair or baby buggy was, and that steps were 'very bad', sinister new reactionary trends were to be found here and there throughout the country. These included the installation of turnstiles on exempted premises, such as railway stations and some shopping malls; existing conveniences being moved downstairs (usually to provide more so-called 'useful' retail floorspace on station concourses); and closure because of vandalism. Such practices effectively undermined good planning practice, by reducing the facilities people needed as part of their access to the built environment. But because of the division of regulatory powers planners could do nothing about them, assuming they even saw it as a serious town planning matter. Indeed, there is no compulsion under the legislation for the local authority to provide on-street public conveniences. There is, surprisingly, no standard of provision based on either floorspace, other spatial criteria, frequency of distribution, or population related numerical factors, just the vague use of the word 'satisfactory' [provision] (to whom?) in the various acts. Likewise there is no requirement to map such facilities on any town planning documents, nor for information purposes for the general public. However, under the Citizen's Charter an account must be given of the number of public conveniences provided by a local authority, but not the ratio of male to female (see *Staying the Course*, Section J: The Local Environment, paras 3 a and b, Audit Commission, 1994)

Private provision

As the situation is not very promising in view of public cutbacks in providing for public on-street toilets, the state of play will now be examined in respect of 'public' toilets in buildings to which the public have access, that is off-street public toilets. Again the situation deteriorated in the 1980s. The Building Regulations on toilets were revised in 1984–5, based on Approved Document G, which was based on impractical, and discriminatory standards dating from many years back (including 1950s standards) as subsequently embodied in BS 6465 (Part I) setting out requirements for different categories of building (see Chapter 4 for the link between Building Regulations and British Standards and enforceable planning requirements). The enforcement of the standards in these documents as introduced in 1985, experts concluded, resulted in reduced standards of provision (CAE 1992). BS 6465 was itself based outdated documents, including Statutory Instrument 966 from 1964 (the legislative background is explained in detail in CAE 1992). It is significant that both the BSI and Building Regulations committees responsible consisted entirely of men, including engineers and architects. Although there was some consultation (mainly with other committees like their own), there was, and still is, no open compulsory public participation to enable people to scrutinize and question the standards proposed. (All this was going on behind closed doors while the women-and-planning movement, and disability groups, innocently imagined they were at last making progress.)

Not only was this a retrograde step but, according to Nigel Ward (a leading authority on these matters from the Environmental Health (Consumer Protection) Department of Waltham Forest), Section 20, subsection 3, of the 1976 Local Government (Miscellaneous Provisions) Act prohibited local authorities enforcing higher standards in privately owned businesses in providing facilities for the use of the public in restaurants, pubs and other places of entertainment, in excess of the standards required under the Building Regulations (CAE 1992). This means they can still set their own standards provided they are not better than current BS 6465 standards. Many London Boroughs and the GLC (under its Public Entertainment Licence Requirements) had previously had much higher and more equitable standards and, prior to the establishment of these new national standards, were free to impose them, because the Building Regulations were silent on such specific standards until the 1976 Act, Section 20, subsection 3, first came in.

Local authorities have only been able to invoke s.20 of the Act (inadequate as it is) and require and control the provision of toilets in private premises used by the public, such as for sport, entertainment (including betting offices), and those serving food and drink, when the building is first being built, or when it is undergoing improvement or alteration. This means that many pre-existing facilities are never upgraded. It should be noted, most significantly, in respect of the debates about shopping developments, that (as stated earlier) no customer toilets are required under s.20 or any other legislation, although facilities must be provided for staff in shops under other health and safety at work legislation, and the new Work Place Directive (Cunningham and Norton 1993:1). Therefore there has been no compulsion for stores such as Marks and Spencers (who do not have restaurants in their stores) to provide customer toilets. Some central area shopping streets, and out-of-town shopping centres, remain toiletless if the private sector chooses not to make provision. However, many department stores do provide facilities especially those seeking to attract family shoppers, as does Mothercare and Children's World. IKEA the Scandinavian furniture store is also renowned for above average facilities including shoppers crèche and toilet provision, being one of the few stores located in mainly out-of-town locations to provide such facilities. (In contrast see *Planning Week*, 5.5.94: page 7, in which it is reported that Tesco have objected to Lewisham's requirement, and especially to the word 'expect' in the UDP which states, 'in major developments which attract large numbers of visitors, such as shopping centres and leisure facilities, the council will expect developers to provide an adequate amount of accessible, good quality sanitary accommodation'. Ian Arnold, the council's environmental services chair has called for 'urgently needed new planning powers in respect of internal facilities in stores' (reflecting the insides/outsides debate highlighted in this book).

Some local authorities have sought to get facilities provided through planning gain, such as the London Borough of Haringey which recommends one male and one female customer toilet per 1000–2000 sq metres of net floor space plus a unisex disabled toilet, and between 2000–4000 square feet of net floorspace another two male and two female toilets and one additional unisex toilet, and thereafter in proportion to the area of the retail store floorspace. But, it has been found in practice, as again in the case of Waltham Forest still struggling to implement its equitable toilet policy, that PPG 1 can be used to prohibit such toilet facility provision by private developers in supermarkets and shopping malls. Therefore the proposed UDP (as of 1992) for that borough has had to be amended to take out the toilet provision policy requirements (from a talk presented by Nigel Ward at a seminar by the Centre for Accessible Environments, CAE 1992). Also, in addition to s.20 subsection 3 of the 1976 Local Government Act discussed above, local authorities may also find their planning gain negotiations limited by the 1989 Local Government and Housing Act which requires 50% of capital receipts (such as inducements from developers not specifically related to the development site) to be set aside to repay current debts (and unfortunately toilets, and especially baby-changing and breast-feeding areas might fall into this category) (Ainsbett 1990). While all natural functions have been banned from public view, and little alternative provision has been made, in contrast, cities are turned upside down to accommodate the needs of the motor car. As stated earlier it is never said that car parking provision is not a land use matter, although also related to the way people 'uze' land, rather than the 'use' itself.

Gains and losses

However, as a result of the campaigning activities of All Mod Cons, and other groups for better provision, and the cooption of a woman on to the BS committee, Susan Cunningham of All Mod Cons, BS 6465 has now been revised and improved with much better (but by no means ideal, and still unequal) standards, which were published in April 1995. BS 6465 should now officially be called BS 6465 Part I, because a Part II is currently under preparation, which will deal in more detail with the quality of facilities, especially space requirements. In due course, the new BS 6465 will have a knock-on effect on Building Regulation standards, but it should be remembered that toilet standards only relate to new premises, and their likely implementation is also dependent on other linked enabling legislation. Also, current legislation only states that local authorities 'may' provide toilet provision, not that they or private developers 'must' do so. But, a totally new set of standards governing, for the first time, toilet provision in retail development has been incorporated as BS 6465 Part I, Table 5.[1]

Customer toilets are now required in shops and shopping malls on the basis of two female toilets, one male toilet, one urinal and one disabled toilet per 1000 to 2000 square metres of net sales area (and so forth) (twice the Haringey standard, but still inadequate in that women constitute at least three-quarters of shoppers). This is a great improvement which will reduce the problems of obtaining such facilities through planning gain by means of Section 106 Agreements. But it should be noted that it requires quite a large retail store to achieve the minimum floor space. For example a traditional high street shop of 660 square feet is only 60 square metres. But from a reasonably sized supermarket, or say a bigger Marks and Spencers of 3000–8000 square feet we can now expect several toilets. A typical old 1960s shopping precinct of say 300 000 sq ft or the huge Metro Centre, at Gateshead, of 1.55 million square feet (c. 144 000 square metres) should yield many toilets. But the management aspects of who pays and who manages the upkeep of toilets in multiple retail unit centres is unclear. Also the requirements are not retrospective as yet, and therefore will only apply to new developments.

Transport

While the problem in relation to retail development is being resolved, there are still major problems in relation to transport facilities which enable people to travel to town centres in the first place. As other buildings or facilities become privatised, and thus move out of the control of legislation covering public buildings to those covering private premises, further controls will be difficult. For example, it has been noted turnstiles are being introduced into a range of newly privatised public facilities, such as in bus stations. This is so in the case of the privatised bus station owned by Badgerline in Bristol where there are now turnstiles, the toilets have been moved downstairs and private security guards patrol the bus station. Badgerline (now known as First Bus) have also acquired bus companies and related stations elsewhere, including *inter alia* Ryder in South Yorkshire, Western National in Plymouth and Cornwall; Eastern National in East Anglia; the local company in Stoke-on-Trent; and Midland Red, the Birmingham 'country' bus company. Mainline railway stations such as Paddington, Euston and King's Cross now have turnstiles at the entrances to female (and some male) toilets, all of which are located downstairs, with a charge of 20p being made. (It is not apparently a lack of money which prevents moving facilities to ground level, or which has caused them to charge 20p, as it is reported £1 000 000 was spent on the refit, *The Sunday Times*, 'Style and Travel Supplement', 24.5.94: page 6.) The entrance thus provided is 15$\frac{1}{2}$ inches across, hardly enough room for pushchairs or luggage, especially when the average pushchair is at least 18 inches across or more. But mothers with pushchairs at railway stations might be told they are not allowed to use the disabled toilet or baby changing facilities (which are typically locked requiring a trek across several platforms to get the key from another office). But these facilities constitute the only passenger accessible toilets with an adequate width entrance now that turnstiles have been installed. Such restrictions, it is argued are town planning matters because they restrict the way in which people 'uze' land, and their access to vital transportation systems, and force people to use cars, or not travel at all, because of the impossibility, for many, of using public transport. Also fire evacuation risk is increased with turnstile installation.

As from 1st April 1994 British Rail left the control of the public sector. Railway stations are now denationalised and so the likelihood of influence is even less than before. (Compare Chapter 15 on the King's Cross situation.) Any realistic integrated land use–transportation planning strategy would incorporate these issues, and also vastly improve the provision for the disabled and babies in railway stations, and on board trains (disabled passengers are often expected to travel in the guards van). Likewise if the government is serious about reducing dependence on the motorcar (PPG 13 *Transport*) the London Underground system would be made more user friendly. More lifts, and wider step escalators, would be installed for people with pushchairs, luggage (which travellers are bound to be carrying), and the disabled. As was commented to the author in the course of research by interested 'uzers', both British Rail and London Underground seem to assume the average passenger will be carrying nothing more than a rolled-up newspaper.

Many groups are in fact rendered 'disabled' (although not officially registered as such) because of the extremely poor design of the built environment. As stated BS 5810 has introduced rules about wheelchair accessible toilets, but again the controls do not necessarily cover older buildings, and many people consider the design standards required are not particularly enlightened. As stated, Part I of BS 6465 on toilets has recently been revised (by a committee which this time had one coopted woman on it, namely Susan Cunningham of All Mod Cons). It is hoped that the new BS 6465 Part II might actually include standards on childcare and baby provision. One must ask why there always has to be 'special' provision for the disabled, women with children, and other so-called minority groups who together make up a sizeable chunk of the population. Perhaps it is indicative of the poor quality of the 'normal' provision, and a symptom of dichotomised thinking which always divides people on the basis of abled/disabled; male/female; normal/abnormal dualisms. (Also a peculiarly Victorian mentality lingers on in the built environment professions, which tends to divide land uses into clean/dirty, polite/unmentionable categories.) The logical solution would be to upgrade all facilities to standards which would break down the false abled/disabled division. This would not reduce, or take away, the benefits to the majority, rather it would make life easier for everyone. It is suspected that those who possess RADAR keys giving access to 'special' disabled toilets, are only a minority of the real numbers who have special needs, particularly in areas where a large proportion of the population is elderly as in the South-West. A survey found that 42% of local authorities have only one public convenience per 5–10000 people, and facilities are closing down every day.

Other 'bright ideas' include APC's (Automatic Public Conveniences), that is the Superloo, originally pioneered by the French who used to be notorious for their public conveniences, with the limited provision there was mainly being aimed at the on-street needs of the male population, in the form of the nineteenth century 'pissoir'. However, the French have a little known law (even to some French patrons it would seem) that all restaurants and cafés must provide toilet provision for customers, although the standard of provision may leave much to be desired. The public generally do not much like APCs, although in their favour, the companies responsible for their provision have pioneered 'loo-franchising' schemes whereby APCs combined with news stands, even small tourist shops are leased out as complete units in areas that otherwise were poorly served. Indeed, in some European capitals APCs are covered on three sides by an array of advertising, news stands and snack bars (possibly a development control nightmare but an ingenious solution to the financial side of provision). Disabled groups, particularly in New York, have campaigned against the dimensions of the standard APC and demanded wheelchair accessible provision. Women's groups have long campaigned that APCs are impractical for mothers with children and pushchairs, having similar problems to the 'turnstile syndrome' associated with restricted individual user access.

There are rumours of the European Union developing a Directive on the Euroloo, in order to harmonise provision across Europe, with the Germans apparently taking a leading role in this initiative. In Britain, it has been recommended that most normal standard cubicles should be a minimum width of 900 mm with a door of 750 mm wide, and a fully accessible cubicle should be 1500 × 2000 with a 1000 mm door (most existing cubicles are much, much smaller). In Appendix 4 the layout of an ideal public convenience to serve the needs of the majority of the population, which provides for the disabled, and for child care, is reproduced with thanks to Sue Cavanagh of the Women's Design Service, as originally drawn by Judi Sissons (Figure A4.3). On the more positive side, it must be stated that there is a range of active pressure groups, and individuals, campaigning on this matter such as Susan Cunningham of All Mod Cons, and that various sympathetic architects and planners are pressing for change within the various relevant committees and organisations to which they belong. For example, David Adler (Tutt and Adler 1993) (author of the *Metric Handbook*) is seeking to incorporate more realistic standards into this famous reference book's next forthcoming revision. It has been noted, however, that some CAD (Computer Aided Design) computer programmes for architects and designers have incorporated a 'toilet block module' which is far too small, and below current standards, and it would seem that no one has challenged this. Also, the provision of toilets was one of the items which eventually got into the revised *Citizen's Charter* which also includes a variety of other urban design type indicators (Audit Commission 1993, 1994). Further improved facilities have been proposed for the disabled (DoE, 1992, c and d).

Conclusion

As can be seen from this one example tremendous problems confront the planners in implementing just one small area of public amenity provision in cities. One could undertake similar studies of other policy areas which are of concern to planners. For example housing is a central issue, but its provision and location is by no means under the control of the planners, but determined to a considerable degree by the activities of the private residential market, and, albeit to a lesser degree nowadays, by local authority housing departments and housing associations, whose agendas and priorities may not be entirely shared by the planners. Employment policy is likewise a key component of many planning documents but in reality the local authority planner has limited influence on creating employment, or indeed on determining its distribution and location in respect of needy groups within the community. While current special area policy initiatives, particularly linked to inner city areas, and urban development corporations, may enable the planners to determine employment policy, if not economic policy, to a small local degree, the continuing separation of economic and physical planning in Britain remains as problematic for those concerned with employment, as does the separation of the social and physical components of planning for those concerned with meeting the needs of minority groups.

---

[1] The BSI (British Standards Institution) standards are now in metric. From 1995 following an EU Directive incumbent on all planning authorities, all measurements shown in planning applications, plans and development schemes must be in metric. Conversion: 1 square foot = 0.09 square metres, and 10.764 square feet = 1 square metre. i.e. divide or multiply by ten approximately.

Chapter 20

THE AGENDA REVISITED

Clara Greed

Plenary: implementation revisited

Definitions

As introduced in Chapter 1, there are a variety of different views of what implementation means. In this concluding section they are gathered together and reconsidered. To the developer, and his (for it is usually his) professional advisers in the private sector, such as the surveyor and property portfolio adviser, implementation simply means getting a scheme up and running, getting it built and let and thus making a profit. This definition seems to be held, in particular, by colleagues who are involved in town planning activities, but are chartered surveyors, either in the general practice division or the planning and development division of the Royal Institution of Chartered Surveyors (RICS). To some members of the construction industry, as exemplified by the CISC map discussion in Chapter 2 the word takes on a much more technical image, associated more with the activities of the civil engineer, construction manager and project manager. Implementation might be viewed as a technological feat. More broadly, the development process may be seen as that all-embracing activity involving each of the different property professions undertaking their respective roles. This comprehensive world-view is also echoed in diagrams, and concepts, developed in the book *The Property Machine* Ambrose and Colenutt (1979). This broad canvas is what suggests a lead body for *all* the construction industry and property professions, in the belief that one can 'map' all their activities, once and for all, as in the CISC exercise for NVQs (CISC 1993). But in reality one may be dealing with many different activities and professional groupings which are significantly different in kind.

As outlined in Chapter 1, implementation entails a whole set of other meanings for the planner; they are many and various as can be seen from the different approaches of the contributors. The planners conceptualisation of implementation seems to be related to a more specific and narrower slice of the development spectrum than is the case in the wide canvas of CISC definition. To town planners, implementations can mean getting development built on a site, with the same meaning as that held by the surveyors (above). This is particularly true of planners working as planning consultants advising private sector clients, including developers, on site potential and the chances of achieving development. But to local authority planners (around 80% of the profession) implementation may not be interchangeable with development, that is, with the end-product; instead it may be seen as a process, the implementary process. Indeed, it has been commented that this book should not be called *Implementing Town Planning* at all, but *The Planning Process in Practice*, and this represents more than a mere semantic shift. One struggles with the precise differences between planning process, implementation process and development process. Each is used variously throughout the book (by each contributor and editor) according to which seemed the most appropriate in the text. (The editor has not sought to tamper with this and standardise usage by different contributors, as each contributor uses words according to the meanings and understandings current in their own professional culture. This is significant in appreciating their conceptualisation and understanding of *implementation*. (Greed 1993: Ch. 1 explores the idea that each different built environment profession has its own culture and way of seeing the world.)

To unpack this further, there appear to be two dimensions or themes to the local government planner's perception of the meaning of implementation and both may be identified in the various chapters, although not necessarily signalled by the writers as being one or the other. Firstly, there is the idea of implementation being parallel to control, or indeed being conflated with the development control process itself, in terms of a development or area being produced in conformity with the various statutory requirements – jumping all the hurdles – and going through all the hoops identified by John Allinson. Secondly, there is the idea that implementation really means opportunities and processes which enable the implementation of higher planning policy objectives; implementation may be seen as a linear activity, a process not a product. The process view reflects the fact that planners are seeking to impose a broader agenda and to achieve wider objectives, by whatever means possible, as and when the opportunity arises. It is likely the influence of this broader agenda may come into play in determining planning applications, much to the annoyance of the developers who are primarily seeking to get the best financial return from the site in question, irrespective of broader, social, economic and environmental considerations. Indeed, the local authority in which such planners are placed may not necessarily support their wider agenda, particularly if it is a relatively non-spending authority, whose own agenda is based on a minimalist view of state intervention and a purely technical view of town planning as an extension of the building control function. The planners, and the planning authority itself, may not be located in a key position in relation to the decision-making hierarchy and thus not in a position to influence corporate municipal policy and the management and governance of the urban area in question.

In this definition the process is one of negotiation, bargaining and mediation in an imperfect world in which planners have limited powers to persuade and haggle with the private sector to implement some of the planner's wider social, economic and environmental policy objectives through planning gain agreements in particular. This view seems to be expressed in Jim Claydon's writings, and within the references to which he refers (such as Barrett and Fudge 1981; Barrett, Stewart and Underwood 1978) much of which emanates from conceptual work undertaken at the School of Advanced Urban Studies in Bristol. In this definition it is by no means a mechanical, preordained process, but one which can be shaped by the planner by means of his/her negotiating skills using professional judgement and expertise. Some of the literature on this subject is highly complex and beyond the ambitions of this textbook, as one is entering into the realms of management theory, decision-making theory and political analysis. However, the reader is recommended to consult the work of Healey, who has recently contributed to an internationally conceived set of papers on policy making, and thus inevitably on policy implementation (Fischer and Forrester 1993). One of the papers (Hoppe 1993) looks at the policy situation *vis-à-vis* planning for ethnic minority groups in Holland; the more advanced student might make interesting comparisons with the British situation as discussed by Linda Davies.

In view of the space constraints of this volume, and the impossibility of the task, the editor will leave the issue of definitions unresolved. Indeed, as in the case of many planning matters, there may be no one right answer, it depends on who you are, what you want, and how you see the world. But whatever one's definition of the implementation process, the planning process or the development process, there usually lurks a latent subtext concerning some concept of success. How does one know one has achieved a satisfactory implementation? This is a fascinating question in a volume which has sought to set practical physical dimensions of development alongside the social policy dimensions. Again there is no one right answer, but much might be learnt about the agenda of the different groups involved by identifying the various interpretations of a successful outcome.

Implementation success

Firstly, to the developer and to his professional advisers, including the surveyor, success might be measured in terms of profit. To construction professionals, success might also be measured in terms of speed and lack of hassle in the course of the development process, and also will include keeping the dreaded cost factor under control by not going excessively over budget. To the architect, civil engineer and other designers, success might variously be measured in the design or technological achievement and in the creative nature of the development. Does it get rave reviews in the *Architects*

Journal and elsewhere in the professional press? What does Prince Charles have to say about it? To community groups, success might be measured in getting at least part of what they want for their area in spite of the activities of the planners, or as preventing their worst fears from being realised, such as their house being demolished.

Looking more broadly, the CISC exercise is fuelled by the need to specify what counts as competence in undertaking professional tasks. Can the somewhat minimalistic NVQ definition of competence be married with any of the definitions of success outlined in relation to the implementation of a particular development? The NVQ exercise grew out of the government department concerned with trade and industry, not the departments responsible for either education or the environment. There has always been more than a passing reference in the mapping exercise to concepts of increasing productivity, efficiency and thus presumably competitiveness and profitability in the whole NVQ exercise. Although this philosophy might be appropriate to manufacturing industries, where there is a range of competing firms, is it appropriate to a process which takes place within a monopolistic situation on one site, under the jurisdiction of one local planning authority in which the end-product is fixed to that site and cannot be exported to Japan or Europe? Indeed, are the definitions of success, as held by town planners ever going to fit into the CISC scenario?

As stated in Chapters 1 and 2, success for planners is sometimes measured in what has *not* been built, in what has been delayed and prevented, rather than in what has been built. If one adds the wider non-commercial objectives of town planning, such as those concerned with social equal opportunities policy and environmental sustainability, the mismatch becomes more stark. However, in passing, one must admit that CISC has shifted ground on this issue, and now appreciates more that competence has many dimensions, and a competent planner might be one who *resists* development and seeks, according to his/her professional brief, to encourage non-profit-making uses on a site because his/her client is society itself.

To the planner, success in the implementation process might mean that he/she was able, through a mixture of negotiation and statutory controls, to get the maximum amount of planning gain from the developer, plus development which exactly tied in with the objectives of the development plan policy document. As was often realised in the CISC exercise, success (and competence) for the planners on a particular site might mean failure (and incompetence) for the surveyors and developers, on the other side, if all their attempts to achieve the most profitable development for the site were thus thwarted. But as implied by Jim Claydon, implementation should not be seen as a confrontational or negative process in which there are winners and losers; one should end up with a reasonably satisfactory result for all parties. Otherwise, as indicated by John Allinson, one is going to have an expensive, time-consuming, litigious planning appeal on one's hands, which local authorities frankly cannot afford to risk in these days of government cut-backs. Indeed, if one looks at the end-product and the tests of success from a wider perspective, one must ask whether a development is acceptable to the people. Janet Askew has argued that, even when massive planning gain is negotiated, the community is always the loser in the long run because the wider costs of development (and the development process itself) will ultimately be paid for by the general public, through taxes to the public sector or through increased prices, interest rates and premiums in the private sector.

The problem with CISC and other individualistic approaches to measuring success or competence is that they do not measure the overall community good for society (cf. Ambrose and Colenutt 1979 in respect of community costs and social capital debates). Mrs. Thatcher is rumoured to have said, 'There is no such thing as Society,' that is, a collective concept of shared interests and identity is politically meaningless, but the editor and most of the contributors believe there is (see the chapter on urban social perspectives in Volume I). The CISC approach and similar methods do not measure the sum total of the corporately undertaken activities of the construction and property professions in producing the built environment, and in particular of the planners in creating the urban reality in which we live. Indeed, much of the professional work undertaken is done in teams, usually on behalf of clients, the whole exercise involving many groups of people, including arguably the people themselves.

Public participation

Planning applications

This brings the editor to a suitable juncture to revisit the question of the role of the people in the planning process. The development process is often presented as a two-cornered fight between the developer and the planner, particularly in respect of planning applications and resultant planning appeals, whereas plan making and the subsequent inquiry procedures seem relatively more open to the general public. People need to have access and opportunity for input to both these processes, namely, planning applications which may affect them and planning policy behind development plan production.

A resident of an area, who has no legal interest in the land in question, has limited legal rights to contest a planning application, as against just comment on it, or make objections within the allocated time period (as explained by John Allinson). Nowadays there has been an extension of neighbour notification and a broadening of the types of applications advertised; the situation is still shifting so consult the most up-to-date legislation. Also one finds windswept site notices tied to lamp-posts informing passers-by of alterations to listed buildings. Few are the lamp-posts without one in the centre of Bristol! People also have the right to consult free of charge, the register of planning applications, held by the local planning office (Section 69 of the 1990 Town and Country Planning Act; and see Chapter 10 of Volume I which deals with development control). But the situation is by no means satisfactory. It is often said that we have the best planning system in the world, but the editor would argue that the British system seems to be very good in some respects and deficient in others. Its actual operation does not always live up to the promise indicated in current legislation, particularly in these days of reduced resources.

Our immediate European neighbours can offer many ideas which might actually benefit the general public. Consider third party interests (alongside the developers and the planners) such as those of local residents, public transport uzers[1] and green pressure groups. In Britain they do not have a guaranteed, automatic, direct legal right to be involved in the development process (although they do have some rights, see Chapter 10); in the Netherlands they do have this right. (Planning in/and Europe will be a topic pursued in the next Volume.) This alone increase the Netherlanders involvement in the planning process and is a far cry from the right to public participation exercised in England and Wales in respect of certain aspects of the planning process.

In Britain there is no official right for the public to be involved in the negotiations on planning gain agreements (and thus planning obligations) although many such agreements are informed by what local community groups have pressed for through community leaders, local councillors and campaigns. Rumour has it that in some countries the public can get more directly involved through coopted community representatives taking part in the negotiation stages over the equivalent of planning gain. It is said that in California they have held auctions in which developers bid for planning permission and for the right to develop. The money thus gained is ploughed back into community facilities and also infrastructure, with local community committees having a say in who gets what. But since the earthquakes of 1994 one is informed the public sector in some areas has temporarily gone over to utilising emergency funds, and the private property market is somewhat in abeyance at present. Indeed, as has been discussed over the years by a wide range of urban academics, The Urban Question, namely, *Who gets what, where and how?* is central to measuring the success of the planning process (as raised in Volume I, Chapter 11, and pursued in Greed 1994).

The question of third party rights in the case of *planning appeals* was discussed by John Allinson in Chapter 10. It would seem that to gain audience one either has to be part of an official consultative body, another governmental body or have an interest in the land. Alternatively, there are some rights for other groups, such as community groups, to make their views known, but this may be dependent on the inspector's discretion, or may be the result of some technicality in the planning system, such as the development being the subject of a development order (s.65 of the 1990 act).

Indeed, unless community groups and similar third parties are proactive, make sure of their involvement and jump through the right legal hoops, no one is necessarily going to go out and seek their views or encourage them to come along as a basic legal right. At present there does seem to be considerable inconsistency in the degrees of access by third parties, in respect of planning application procedures and subsequent planning appeals as well as planning inquiries related to plan approval. However, particularly in respect of development plan preparation, many local authorities undertake good practice at levels over and above the minimum consultation and participation required.

Plan preparation

In contrast to the relatively weak position held by the public in challenging other people's planning applications, the public do have a range of rights for participation and consultation in relation to *plan preparation*. Ironically, some large planning applications by big developers might cover areas greater than those covered by specific local plans. Section 33 of the 1990 Town and Country Planning Act sets out the requirements for publicity and consultation in respect of producing a structure plan, and Section 39 sets out the details for a local plan for those non-metropolitan authorities (mainly the shire counties) operating the two-tier system. Section 12 of the same act sets out the procedures for the preparation of a unitary development plan (UDP). The act is not very specific as to the form public participation should take, but it does require that 'adequate publicity' is undertaken in relation to the policy areas which the local planning authority proposes to include in the plan. Further requirements were introduced under the Planning and Compensation Act of 1991. Section 27 of this act speaks of 'the streamlining of the development plan system' and refers the reader to Schedule 4 (found at the end of the Act). Paragraph 40 of Schedule 4 deals with amendments to public participation procedures. These alterations have been subject to considerable discussion as to whether or not they curtail the public participation process somewhat, as nowadays in the attempt to 'streamline' or 'speed up' the processes and in view of government cut-backs, there is pressure not to 'waste' money on activities which are not seen as absolutely necessary to meeting the minimum statutory requirements of the plan-making process.

Those authorities who have the political will to maintain good practice regardless of pressure to speed up the planning system, still provide imaginative avenues for public participation. For example, Birmingham City Planning Department has worked with Birmingham for People, a voluntary community group within the city as a vehicle for increasing its range and depth of public participation. This group published a planning video in 1993, which expresses the planning aspirations of the local community, especially women. This is an example of a local group taking a very proactive role, not waiting to be asked for its views, but broadcasting them nationally by video, newsletters and generally on the grapevine composed of other like-minded groups (and their ideas were featured in an earlier Channel 4 television programme). Linda Davies' example of King's Cross also exemplifies community groups being well organised and taking a proactive role (almost a case of the tail wagging the dog, that is, the community taking the leading role and the planners following on).

Back in the good old days, before government cut-backs, under the 1971 Town and Country Plan Act, much clearer guidelines were issued as to the format of public participation in respect of structure plan preparation. This was the first time that public participation became mandatory and comprehensive for development plan production, although there certainly had been many earlier attempts pioneered by different local authorities, new town development corporations, and local plan teams. The Skeffington Report People and Planning (1969) provided the guidelines on how to undertake public participation. Admittedly it comes across as somewhat patronising in tone by today's standards but it did set the foundations for a thorough system. As John Allinson has explained, the planning process may be divided into stages: Survey, Analysis and Plan (that is policy making). Public participation should ideally take place at key stages in this process.

It was originally required that at the commencement order stage (when plan making began) initial publicity was given to the public. At the survey stage one component of the survey was required to be a study, possibly a questionnaire, to find out what people wanted. Once the policies had been finalised, taking into account the initial comments of the public, a choice of alternatives was required to be presented for a second round of public participation to reach a final choice. Nowadays, people are lucky if there is one round of public participation, but there are additional requirements for formal consultation with certain named bodies. These tend to be official groups, and insofar as they are representative of the people, they are likely to be more oriented towards middle-class interests and people; many ethnic minority groups, women's groups and working-class communities have virtually no right to formal consultation. The final stage, both then and now, is not participation; it is a formal inquiry in public (examination in public), mentioned by John Allinson, Linda Davies and Janet Askew.

Public participation methods

It is often very difficult to get people interested in participating in structure plan activities. This is because the structure plan is meant to be about long-term, high-level strategic policies. If planners seek to get people's views on the development of the city over the next thirty years, they may find that people do not relate well to such time spans and abstract policy making. They are more likely to relate to planning proposals at a local level, although local plans are where the government has put relatively less emphasis upon public participation. Nevertheless, if planners ask people for their opinions on local plan proposals, they may still receive all sorts of replies or comments that are nothing to do with town planning: The cover's been missing from the drain outside our house for two months. Why is the council closing down all the public lavatories in the area? Why didn't the dustmen come last week? The planners are powerless to control such matters, but such issues are often far more important to people than planning proposals for the area in which they live – unless, of course they find *that road* is going to go through *their garden*! People are often very confused about who does what in local authorities, and anyone 'from the council' who goes out among the general public must be prepared to field questions on all sorts of topics. This situation has probably arisen in the first place because other departments have made little attempt to give attention to public relations, so the planner gets the brunt of it all.

Even people very concerned about town planning issues do not necessarily want to answer their local authority's questions; they ignore the planners' sequence and respond in an order of their own. They might go straight for the issue that is worrying them instead of placing their response within the strategic framework dreamt up by the planners. But the people's input is invaluable. Few may frame their ideas in technical terms and possess professional expertise, but many possess local knowledge, and after all, they are the clients for whom planners are working, at least in theory. People should be treated with respect, not as a nuisance. Likewise, property should not be viewed in an impersonal manner, as just buildings or as obstructions to development objects of compulsory purchase. Buildings may be bricks and mortar but they become part of people's lives and familiar surroundings and they provide their homes, businesses and security. Over the last twenty years a variety of other approaches have tried to get people's interest and thus a reasonable response rate: mounting exhibitions, holding public meetings, leafleting areas and sending out postal questionnaires. Traditional questionnaires based on the yes/no closed question approach often alienate people (or they scribble additional comments all over the feedback form). Top-down interviews in which the planner somewhat awkwardly, even patronisingly, grills the interviewee can be unproductive. This is particularly the case when matters of class, age, gender or ethnicity create a dominance on the part of the interviewer.

It has been found much better, particularly by groups seeking to get feedback from women, school pupils and teenagers, to use a more open-ended discussion setting. To get a meaningful, reasoned response it may first be necessary to run a series of several sessions, gently helping people to learn about the planning system and how to interpret plans and policies. This is instead of plunging in cold and expecting instant replies. If it takes five years to train a planner, it is most unreasonable to expect instant answers from the general public over complex planning policy options. Likewise, informal public meetings often work better for some groups, such as less articulate groups and ethnic minority communities, than a formal meeting with men in suits gazing down from a platform. Such alternative methods may take longer and be more labour intensive but they are probably better at getting at the heart of what people want. All sorts of other methods have been pioneered, including Plan Away Days, when groups of people try to build their own models of what they want an area or site to look like using cardboard or other materials provided by the local authority planners. Plan Away Days help planners to learn a great deal about the details which worry people on housing layouts, and about the practical requirements of daily life in the inner city.

Some might argue that such qualitative methods are not statistically representative, but neither necessarily were the more quantitative traditional methods. In-depth sociological, even ethnographic and anthropological methodologies, are becoming more valued in social policy research, and to a degree this includes town planning (see Hammersley and Atkinson 1983 for an explanation of ethnography). In contrast, methods which go for blanket coverage of large numbers of people are renowned for getting low response rates, so much so that in some cases the final figures are by no means statistically valid. For example, putting a questionnaire into every letter-box, even assuming it is not chewed up by the dog on the way in and that it reaches a member of the household, may only elicit quite low response rates, particularly if people have to post back the replies. Even large-scale surveys are not representative if there is no attempt to structure the composition of the respondent groups. Past questionnaires and other public participation exercises were often addressed to the head of the household; questions about the journey to work were based only on the husband's replies, thus rendering the whole sample inaccurate by leaving out the travel patterns of wives and other working members of the household. It is probably better nowadays to go for an approach which targets a range of people, who together make up a representative spectrum of the population, and to target them in different settings, such as schools, factories, youth clubs, churches, mother and toddler groups, rather than sending individual questionnaires to each household.

There has been particular concern expressed about how to reach ethnic minority groups effectively. Some of the problems have arisen because of language barriers, and Linda Davies has already suggested that information leaflets should be in a range of languages. However, there must always be somebody available (at least at the end of a phone) who can reply to people in their own language. If someone's expectations are raised about the helpfulness of the planning office because they have received a leaflet in Urdu, when they arrive they do not want to find that no one can actually speak to them in Urdu and they are looked upon as visitors from another planet.

There have also been problems contacting English-speaking ethnic minority groups. For example, in inner London it has often been found productive to put information about town planning in Afro-Caribbean hairdressers, barbers and launderettes to get the message across. However, one cannot expect ethnic minorities to respond to planners, answering public participation questions when asked, if for the rest of the year planners fail to respond to ethnic minorities. There is nothing in current legislation on public participation that specifies a certain proportion of each ethnic minority group must be contacted, but it may be seen as discriminatory only to target easily accessible white, articulate, middle-class groups who culturally speak the same language as the planners. Appendix 3 is an equal opportunities element drafted for CISC purposes in respect of measuring competence in professional practice. It suggests that when undertaking survey, analysis, planning and related activities, the needs of ethnic groups and other minorities should be taken into account.

Equal representation?

One could go a step further and suggest that one of the reasons why public participation is necessary in the first place, especially to elicit the views and needs of minority groups, is because women, black people and the disabled are grossly unrepresented within the planning system as planning officers themselves. Some would say that, in order to have a truly representative and competent planning system, the membership of the planning profession and of local government departments should reflect the composition of the population for whom they are planning. It might be argued that the male, white, middle-class planner should be able to plan equally well, in an entirely neutral professional manner, for people unlike himself, but research and human experience has proven otherwise. Admittedly a higher proportion of women are nowadays becoming planners (Table 2.2) but it has been found that less than 5% of the planners in senior positions are women. There are virtually no ethnic minority planners in senior positions and very few in the built environment professions as a whole. It is further argued that it *does* matter that minorities are underrepresented in the higher levels of planning, because it is not until planners reach senior positions that they are in a position to influence policy making and thus shape the built environment through their professional decisions. If these professional decisions are based on limited experience of the lives lived by ordinary people and a lack of understanding of the problems faced by women, the elderly and other minority groups as they *uze* the city – as they seek to travel, shop, go to work and survive in what is often an alienating, impractical and threatening urban environment – then this is likely to result in incompetent plans.

Perhaps traditional mainstream planners feel threatened by change. They are afraid that if all these effective methods of public participation were utilised, and if the planning profession itself became more representative of the population as a whole, then a planner's professional life would become too difficult. Far more decisions would have to be made about how to accommodate the likely plurality (mixture) of opinions that would be put forward on planning policy and implementation priorities. Inevitably, with differences of opinion arising among different minority groups, judgements would have to be made as to priorities. To some planners it might feel as if the whole planning process could get out of control and become too time-consuming or political. The present situation encourages a narrower range of views and there is usually a fall-back position, a compromise which members of the property fraternity hammer out among themselves as to the fate of a particular site or area.

In response to this fear of being overwhelmed by change and variety, it might be stated that it has always been the job of the planners to make decisions as to the best course of action, using their professional expertise and judgement, as well as public feedback, to choose among different options. Many of the policy objectives of minority groups are not particularly earth shattering. In fact some demands are quite simple and straightforward, such as provision for child care, safer environments, non-discriminatory planning permission for ethnic minority food shops and take-aways, fewer steps. But they have been magnified into something enormous because of the disproportionate amount of difficulty encountered by minorities when they have pressed for such changes. Even when the planners themselves have been keen to accommodate such requests, they have encountered a complex legal situation full of contradictory and undermining statutory controls emanating from other regulatory bodies responsible for the built environment.

Political dimensions

Some have commented that this study of the implementation process lacks political dimension and is possibly too concerned with the 'little' issues, as against the matters of grand theory, power and capitalism which ostensibly shape urban form. But what is political? And which aspects and levels of the implementation process are the most politically charged? Which way up should one look at it? It is often said that the personal is political, and this is particularly true when evaluating domestic and so-called individual problems which women encounter in the city of man. This chapter concludes with a few brief reflections. It is true that powerful, but often invisible, political and economic forces are at work in the course of the development process; its relationship to land, private property and potentially vast profits make it a highly political process. But during the course of implementation, one cannot necessarily pinpoint precisely how, when, where and at what level these overarching forces come into play. Local authority councillors as members of the planning committee clearly have considerable political power in the determination of planning permissions, but over and above this there is likely to be a range of levels of power, influence and politicking for or against development. For example, some of the development process in

Bristol is undoubtedly controlled from London, especially in relation to the BDC, whose development corporation is not democratically elected by local people but appointed. Normally, the people have direct political influence on the planning system, through the election of their local authority council-lors. But the people are probably voting according to a range of other factors beyond just planning. Indeed in Bristol, a newly founded football supporters party seems to be doing quite well in fielding its own prospective councillors and attracting considerable support, in spite of all the warnings about one-issue parties never working.

The people may have more direct influence on the planning system through the support of planners who are on 'their side' as in advocacy plan-ning (rather like voluntary legal aid on planning matters) and through the assistance of various planning aid groups, such as Planning Aid for London (PAL) which has strong links with the women-and-planning movement. But much of the academic, analytical material, which has sought to investigate urban power and the political nature of the planners as gatekeepers and urban managers, has focused around traditional structuralist concerns with class conflict and the role of capitalism. Therefore it is of only limited use in trying to understand the mechanics of how gender relations (and patriarchal power), racism and abled/disabled dualistic thinking shapes urban political processes in relation to town planning (Pinch 1985; Dunleavy 1980).

Many minority groups are highly suspicious of the grand theory that belongs to abstract, academic debates, which so often characterise the discus-sion of urban power structures. All their detailed, day-to-day concerns get lost or forgotten. Greed (1994) argues that, collectively, the so-called little things, such as interpersonal interaction, traditional biased assumptions, awkward little bits of unhelpful legislation and silly regulation contain just as much power to block effective policy making and implementation at the day-to-day level of planning practice, especially in respect of equal opportunities. While Neo-Marxists might argue that these factors are all merely predictable mani-festations of the nature of the 'superstructure' (see Volume I), others would argue that they collectively constitute the very building blocks out of which the whole edifice is composed. For further discussion (but *only* for those interested in urban academic theory) from a broadly Neo-Weberian, sym-bolic interactionist perspective see Greed (1991: Ch. 2) and Greed (1994). This debate could go much further but here it has been sufficient to air the underlying issues which shape the implementation process and product.

By concentrating upon the role of town planning and its interaction with the private property development process, only passing reference has been made to economic funding matters, especially the potential role of local and central government finance, in giving town planners the power and the means to be proactive, to create development themselves and to move from a negatively controlling role to a positively initiating role. This issue will be explored at length in the next volume. It will centre around the different manifestations of planning and its varying potential for change. If this book had been written during the twenty-five years following the Second World War, far more attention might, realistically, have been given to this aspect of planning, not least in respect of new town developments and redevelopment schemes. Albeit in different political packaging, elements of this tradition can still be found in partnership schemes, in various inner city initiatives and most recently in the single regeneration budget programme. Perhaps the future political situation will lead to more public investment and a stronger role for local government planners. Readers should check the current situation carefully.

Concluding guidelines

In these final two chapters we have travelled across the spectrum of urban planning issues and purposely confronted two quite different perspectives on town planning. We started with a discussion of high-level, city-wide strategic policy issues and ended with a look at toilet provision. The scope of planning implementation is graphically shown by the book's illustrations. Figure 10.1 shows an entire county; then moving through the local plan and (Figure 15.2) site related levels the last chapter refers to toilet design (Figure A4.3) and ramps which aim at implementing accessibility policy (Appendix IV). Both agendas – strategic land use and detailed *uzer* needs – can be valid within the modern ambit of town planning profession. Quite often when one raises such issues one is told they are not part of 'real' town planning. Indeed, it is a fascinating question when doing qualitative ethnographic research (Hammersley and Atkinson 1983) as to why *culturally* some things are seen as *obviously* part of town planning and some are not. The argument that some women-and-planning matters are far too detailed to be included because they really belong elsewhere is weakened by the fact that very detailed space dimensions and provision standards are involved. It would seem that anything to do with women, children, the disabled, the elderly and the domestic is looked upon with caution. If such matters do not belong in planning, what about putting them in architecture? But architecture seems not to want them either. Designing toilets is seen by many men architects as low status, the equivalent of latrine duty in the army.

The satisfactory implementation of high-level land *use* policy has to take into account the details of how people *uze* the city. Rather than starting with grandiose abstract plans and then translating them into the local area, it is perhaps more realistic to start with the details of daily human need in a particular area or topic and then gradually building up planning policy, stepping from issue to issue, gradually working up to city-wide policy matters. In these post-modernist, post-structuralist, post-grand theory times, few planners still have much enthusiasm for the impossible dreams and delusions of grandeur (Reade 1987) to which planners aspired at the height of the postwar reconstruction period, or for grand schemes of the Surging Sixties in which the whole city was seen as an urban system to be controlled by advanced computerised planning methodologies in splendid isolation from the private property sector and from the people themselves (McLoughlin 1969). Nowadays it is hoped that planners are more tuned into the social needs of the people for whom they are planning and they are more aware of the economic, legal and institutional frameworks in which they work. To make implementation more viable in the light of the problems identified in the various chapters, the following proposals are made:

1 Harmonisation of all current built environment legislation, including British Standards, Building Regulations and the laws governing town and country planning, fire and safety, environmental health, housing, disability and real property. Apparently this is on the government agenda but there is little evidence as yet.

2 Full public consultation and participation over the contents and standards of the new body of law thus produced, with minority representations on policy-making committees being commensurate to their representation in the population.

3 Redefinition of the scope and nature of planning, to include the insides as well as the outsides of buildings, private as well as public spaces, and to include not only land use matters but matters related to how people *uze* land.

4 The promotion and provision of statutory powers for a wider social and economic agenda for town planning alongside and in conjunction with established physical land use planning concerns.

5 Great emphasis on how people *uze* cities in planning education, upon the nitty-gritty of people's daily lives in cities and upon detailed urban design which affects people access to, safety within and satisfaction with the built environment.

6 Reinvestment in local government and greater funding for public works, physical infrastructure and social infrastructure.

7 Greater liaison between the different areas of planning, especially on local government committees and initiatives, so that for example environmental policy bodies, especially those concerned with sustainability and environmental impact, are fully cognisant of equal opportunities agendas. A more central corporate management role for senior planning officers within local government.

8 Introduction of social impact assessment (SIA) for all new schemes and any significant change of use, in a similar manner to environmental impact assessment (EIA).

9 Priority on dezoning and non-decentralisation in order to create the sustainable city of short journey.

10 Relaxation of controls over change of use within residential areas to enable diversification of uses, especially to meet the needs for retail outlets and local employment opportunities, with the proviso of adequate environmental and design control, not a free-for-all by any means.

11 Subsidies to small shops, businesses and social facility providers (such as crèches and their classification as essential uses, in order to enable such enterprises to be viable against market forces, against competition from large stores and businesses and against governmental pressure for economies of scale. In the long run one might envisage a subsidy system being an integral part of development control. Based on evaluation under SIA, small essential land uses might be granted financial support whereas large and socially negative uses might pay a charge.

12 Greater control and monitoring by the DoE on the decisions of its planning inspectors in order to cut down on the variability of decisions on similar issues in different parts of the country and among different London boroughs.

13 Clearer support for development-led planning, and the creation of some more compulsory, less arbitrary form of planning gain, not necessarily as a fixed development tax, but greater ground rules to support and endorse planning officers in their negotiations. Possibly a system based on mandatory zoning compliance should be introduced as in North America, in which the provision of certain social and amenity facilities is an integral part of the zoning.

14 National and improved compulsory standards on such matters as provision of public conveniences, access to all buildings, child care provision, disability and urban safety issues. This is similar to item 1.

15 Vastly improved public transport provision for both bus and car users. Existing routes (including roads, pavements, footpaths and bridleways) to receive clearer national standards as to allocation to pedestrians, bicycles, cars, goods vehicles and public transport.

16 Greater representation of third party and community interests in planning appeals.

17 More effective organisation of the levels of planning authorities, with particular emphasis upon retaining a city-wide (or county-wide) strategic policy level, but possibly more decentralisation of policy functions to district level, where the so-called little issues which so matter to *uzers* of the built environment are centred, and with an intermediate (non-policy-making) development control level in between. In view of the restructuring of current legislation, the remit of planning policy-making and control bodies would substantially alter in agenda and scope to prioritise the issues highlighted in Part VI.

18 Proper research is required on the actual needs of the public, for example, on toilet provision in relation to different locations, land uses, developments and activities. This would provide a basis to support the standards and policies identified. Far more research in general on how people actually use cities related to mobility, accessibility and the daily patterns of movement.

19 Introduction of timetable plans alongside urban development plans (as explained in Chapter 18) to enable the coordination and most efficient

use of road space and transport units with public buildings, shops, schools and places of employment.

20 Greatly improved public transport and a policy-making and management role for the planning authority in such provision, in order to make a reality of planning for a practical relationship between land uses and transportation provisions.

---

[1] To refresh the reader on the use of *uze*, here is a brief explanation. The whole agenda of such user groups centres around detailed considerations of how people *use* streets, buildings and facilities. Traditional planners took a somewhat detached view and looked down on the urban areas, as set out in the maps on their drawing-boards and in their carefully drawn development plans. They were more concerned about land *use* zoning than about how people might *use* (uze) land, that is, the shops, houses and all the other developments one finds in an urban area. They paid very little attention to how one might achieve access to and within these land uses. Indeed, as many women planners have commented, senior male planners might never themselves have tried to use a shopping centre, particularly not while trying to push a baby buggy along at the same time. *Women and Planning*, one of my recent books, introduced the term *uze* and pursued its implications for understanding the different perspectives often held by the planners and the planned – those who *uze* the city and those who provide the land uses. It was decided to spell *use* as *uze* to demonstrate a quite different perspective on policy priorities. The same convention will be adopted in this chapter.

PART VII

APPENDICES

Appendix 1

INDICATIVE PROJECT WORK

| Introduction |

Unlike Volume I, the following projects are not chapter specific, except perhaps those projects related to Parts I and II. In some of the projects, the case studies from Parts III and V might help to suggest possible topics. The projects are based on a range of work at the University of the West of England (UWE) Faculty of the Built Environment. In the past, UWE projects were often confined to individual departments within the Faculty of the Built Environment, and perhaps they were not so ambitious. Nowadays the whole faculty is undertaking interprofessional and cross-school projects, although not as yet at the more advanced levels of courses. However, it is known that other built environment faculties have explored similar avenues or even pioneered extremely ambitious projects. The execution of the following projects very much depends on time, staff resources and student numbers. The intention is to give readers, be they students, lecturers or general readers, some ideas for finding out more about the planning process and implementation, something which cannot be learnt from books alone.

| Project 1: mapping project |

Develop your own 'map' of the functions of the project of the built environment professions with which you are familiar. Firstly identify key areas and functions, then break them down into elements and tasks so that you end up with a matrix (a tree with ever dividing branches). Use the CISC (1993) reference material in Appendix 2 to help you.

| Project 2: legislative controls and development context |

Choose any aspect of site development or building construction with which you are familiar. Write a short report listing the main areas of legislation as well as regulations, orders and directives which have constrained its implementation. Constraints are likely to include the Town and Country Planning Acts, parts of the Building Regulations, Approved documents, British Standards and environmental controls.

Project 3: site development and community needs

Site development and community needs both lead to a variety of projects at different levels. They may be undertaken individually or involve a cast of millions, realistically between ten and fifty students. These tasks are intended to give indicative (directional guidance) examples, as much depends on local circumstances and permission to use a site from developers.

Project 4: individual task

Choose one particular land use as the basis of an individual study such as retail development, residential development or leisure provision. Examine the extent and nature of development in this area, possibly restricting investigations to one section of a town or city. However, to get the overall effect, this could be done as a group project bringing out the competition between out-of-town and in-town locations, for example, and building up an overall picture of development trends, potential and demand for site development.

Find out:

1 What has been developed over the last five years, showing location, market group it is aimed at, land values (and house prices if residential, or office rentals if commercial) and main characteristics. To do this, location maps and site plans may be included as well as some quantitative indication of levels of provision. This information is likely to be available from existing local authority report-of-survey documents or possibly from the local chamber of commerce. Always start with the public reference library and your own investigations. Do not bother the planners or developers, they are usually quite busy, but if needs be then contact them by letter or telephone, not in person. If it is a group project, arrange for one person to go on the group's behalf or ask your lecturer to arrange a visiting speaker who is a local expert on the topic.
2 What is currently being developed? What is proposed? You will need to read the local and national property press. Keep an eye out for advertisements and statutory planning notices on vacant sites.
3 Find out about the current demand, the current land values and the likely rental or sale returns for the type of development you are investigating.
4 Write up all this in a medium-sized student report, with appropriate maps, diagrams, references, sources and acknowledgments. If a presenta-

tion to the whole group is combined in this project (say 40% presentation, 60% written report) then students will readily be able to compare and contrast land values, development demands and planning policies on different types of development within the area studied.

This sort of project might be of use early on in the academic year as a means of getting students out and about, discovering the local urban situation. Over and above the work actually specified, it may generate all sorts of other interesting material. Some students have got holiday jobs on the strength of such projects! Good lecturers might arrange a coach trip around their town or city to identify the main sites and current trends. Good students are likely to find out a lot of this on their own, but those unfamiliar with the property market or the geographical area may require more encouragement. The general reader will also find such an approach useful and instructive.

Project 5: the development process

Choose one particular existing site and investigate it in more depth than in Project 1. Find out who are the actors in the development process and what are their respective aims and objectives for the implementation process. This project might be undertaken by a group of students, any number from four to ten, ideally taken from different specialist course areas. Interprofessional working among students mirrors interprofessional activities in the real world of the development process. For example, the planning students in the group might investigate in depth what the planners, at county and district level, are trying to achieve in respect of the site in question. One can find out the planning history of the site by consulting local plans and reading previous planning application decisions for the site. In particular, aspects of planning gain and other negotiations should be identified. Estate management, valuation and general practice surveying students might concentrate on the financial and market aspects of the site, that is, how the developers are seeking to get the best return from the site and where the money and power behind the development is coming from. Construction and building students might concentrate on what is actually being built, and along with quantity surveying students, might find out how the cost factor and the expediencies of project management affect the overall programme and timescale. Environmental, landscape and geography students might investigate the development's wider environmental impact, its flora and fauna, and its ecological impact. If required, one can extend this project to as many groups as exist in a particular faculty or year group, including subgroups on, for example, transportation policy, legal aspects or infrastructural services. Further, if there is a social, housing and/or political element regarding what local residents and grassroots groups think of the development this element might be tackled by housing students, urban sociology students or better still, any of the other student groups. In fact, this project might be run with students taking the opposite roles from those for which their courses are preparing them. This project would culminate in a group presentation, with maps, diagrams, other visual aids, even videos, of the site development, in order to bring out the different roles and potential conflicts between different interest groups and actors in the development process. The nature of the final agreed plan for the site is likely to be based on compromise, suboptimal choice and negotiation. It is likely the debate will not be limited to that site alone, but will include the viability of alternative sites.

Project 6: conflicts of interest

Building on Project 5, students are asked to choose an existing or proposed development and, in groups of around ten or more, take on the roles themselves of different actors within the development process. All students investigate the development then they present their opinions and findings, taking one of the following roles:

(1) The developer and/or financial backers
(2) The surveyor advising the private sector
(3) The planner representing the city
(4) Local residents
(5) Any interest groups, e.g. green groups and anti-Tesco groups
(6) Local councillors and political pressure groups
(7) Architects and designers
(8) The civil engineers and site development specialists
(9) Perhaps the highways authority
(10) Someone to act as coordinator
(11) Any other roles
(12) Visual aids supervisor

In a class of say fifty students, one would envisage around four groups each choosing a different site. Each group would give a presentation to the rest of the class, with different students taking the roles of the conflicting interests in the development process. The presentation might take the form of a public meeting, and questions would be invited from the floor. At the end, maybe take a vote for or against the development. However, more collaborative, less competitive approaches might be tried too. If there are going to be masses of students swarming over other people's land, it is essential to get the developer's blessing; developers may be willing to give students an official tour of the site and to come and speak at the college. On no account should students be allowed to enter sites still under construction without prior approval and supervision because of insurance and safety considerations. Do not use any confidential documentation or plans without full agreement of the developers or their authorised representatives.

Students have a remarkable ability for obtaining top secret material about site development!

Project 7: site development

An alternative, more practical approach, which may work independently from Projects 1 to 3, or build upon their basis, is a pretend development of a real site. This works best with final-year and more advanced students. Students are given a choice of three real sites for development (with the approval and participation of the real-life agents representing those sites). They are given a development brief, outlining the amount, type and mix of development their client, the developer, wants to achieve in the area. The sites are likely to have a mixture of pros and cons, and with the clock ticking away over the weeks, the students have to decide on which site to go for and how to develop it. The sites are likely to be an out-of-town location, a central area site and a marginal site with potential. They divide into interprofessional groups so that they have planning, valuation, legal, construction, management and other necessary skills among their number.

The lecturers themselves also are arranged into multidisciplinary teams according to their professional qualifications, taking the roles of representatives of the various statutory bodies from which the student developers have to obtain the various permissions to develop (planning, building regs, highways, environmental controls, etc.). Some of the lecturers might take the role of the London financial backers funding the development, who themselves will have a clear agenda as to how far they are willing to go along with local authority requirements as to the form the site development will take. For example, a group of twelve multidisciplinary students would form into a development group, Poly Properties Partnership, and go through all the main initial stages of the development process. Lecturers would act as the planning authority, approving or refusing planning applications, giving (helpful) written reasons for refusal and/or proposed conditions of permission.

The project needs to be structured tightly in terms of time constraints, financial ceilings and client brief. It is likely that a package will be given to students providing some of the information they need to know, but in such a way that they have to go through various decision-making stages to realise the value of this information. Further information can only be gained by approaching the appropriate authorities or representatives of the backers. In practice this means the student developers have to ask role-playing lecturers for information or decisions, by means of letter-box system of written enquiries written in a professional manner, and with only a limited number of actual face-to-face consultations being permitted under strict time constraints. The simulation will probably be designed in such a way that the students discover certain constraints when they make site enquiries (to the appropriate lecturers in their role as local government officials), for example, in relation to archaeological remains on the site, sewerage and drainage problems, restrictive covenants and awkward easements across the site.

At the end of the project the students will have produced a planning report, or rather a development potential report, setting out their recommendations, and also have received (in role play) at least one planning permission, at a detailed level and possibly several abandoned outline applications on the other sites. Obviously the speed of planning application determination has to be remarkably fast, usually less than a week, compared with the real situation. The students will also have done a basic costing and financial projection on the likely returns from the development, again at a fairly basic level within the time allowed. Students are in a position to offer a certain amount of planning gain, according to funds initially identified in their briefing package, on the condition that this is matched and exceeded by enhancement of site value and potential. However, the local planning authority is likely to have some fairly strong policies on social and amenity aspects of site development, which have to be accommodated by the developer.

In terms of time-scale and resources, only a taste of the process can be achieved. But in relating the project to real sites, within real urban economic market scenarios, a degree of valuable learning can be achieved. In theory one could go further than the planning stage, to incorporate construction, architecture and design into the project, but this would extend its length and complexity. However, if students are already undertaking lengthy and detailed project work in these fields, perhaps Project 7 could be dovetailed into this broader interprofessional, site development project.

Projects related to the last section of the book

This section has concentrated on people, plans and 'powers' of implementation.

Public participation

Develop your own public participation exercise using a variety of methods and techniques to get across your proposals. This might be tried on fellow students or possibly some outside cooperating group, such as a school or youth club. Do not do it for real on real people as they may not realise it is only a project and major problems may ensue for the college!

Implementation assignment

Another interesting assignment which might be undertaken individually is to choose a particular social or environmental policy statement from the relevant local plan or unitary development plan. Then go around the area covered by the plan and look for evidence of its implementation, which might be provision for the disabled, child care facilities or provision for cyclists. List the hindrances and hurdles the policy has encountered. Also list the positive aspects which might facilitate development. As a second stage, write a report suggesting ways, means and locations where the elements of the policies might be provided.

Policy assignment

Chapter 18 was very much a brainstorming chapter, containing future policy scenarios. Write your own policy statement for the future development of your town or city (like a mini-UDP policy statement), giving reasons for your views and indicating how the policies might be achieved.

Appendix 2

CISC LIST OF FUNCTIONAL ELEMENTS AND CRITIQUE

KEY PURPOSE: ESTABLISH, MAINTAIN AND MODIFY THE USE OF THE NATURAL AND BUILT ENVIRONMENT, BALANCING THE REQUIREMENTS OF CLIENTS, USERS AND THE COMMUNITY

A   **FORMULATE STRATEGIES AND POLICIES FOR THE DEVELOPMENT, IMPROVEMENT AND USE OF THE ENVIRONMENT**

A1   **Formulate strategies for the environment**

A11   **Monitor and review environmental changes and needs**

A111   **Establish mechanisms for monitoring and reviewing changes and needs in the environment**

A111.1   Establish monitoring and review mechanisms

A111.2   Identify resource constraints on the monitoring and review process

A111.3   Set targets for monitoring and review processes

A112   **Monitor and review changes and needs in the environment**

A112.1   Identify needs and demands for the environment

A112.2   Identify and assess the availability and value of resources

A112.3   Monitor the effects of environmental policies and operations on individuals and communities

A112.4   Monitor the effects of environmental policies and operations on resources

A112.5   Monitor the effects of environmental policies and operations on ecological systems

A113   **Evaluate findings from monitoring and review mechanisms**

A113.1   Assess needs and demands to establish emerging trends and priorities

A113.2   Identify and evaluate alternative resources

A113.3   Assess the ecological and environmental effects of proposed changes

A114   **Recommend policy review options**

A114.1   Evaluate future policy and strategy requirements

A114.2   Evaluate future human and skill resource requirements

A114.3   Evaluate future design, materials, manufacturing and construction requirements

A12   **Formulate strategies for environmental change**

A121   **Review and agree strategic issues and priorities**

A121.1   Evaluate constraints and opportunities which will influence the selection of strategies

A121.2   Develop and present models to explore alternative strategies and options

A121.3   Evaluate alternative strategies and options

A121.4   Set criteria for and evaluate the need for changes in policies and regulations

A122   **Commission and report on policy review surveys and research**

A122.1   Identify, evaluate and prioritise areas for research

A122.2   Plan and commission research and testing programmes

A123	**Prepare and agree a strategic planning framework**
A123.1	Develop alternative planning strategies
A123.2	Present and agree a preferred strategic planning framework
A13	**Implement and evaluate research programmes**
A131	**Establish and agree research projects**
A131.1	Establish, agree and prepare research project objectives and methods
A131.2	Identify and specify project schedules and resources
A132	**Implement and monitor research projects**
A132.1	Implement research data collection
A132.2	Analyse and evaluate research data
A133	**Interpret, evaluate and present research findings**
A133.1	Evaluate the effectiveness of results in meeting research objectives
A133.2	Identify and develop practical applications from research findings
A133.3	Plan, implement and evaluate field tests and pilot projects
A133.4	Communicate research findings and applications to potential users
A2	**Formulate policies and control arrangements**
A21	**Formulate and modify policies for the environment**
A211	**Develop, modify and agree detailed policies and proposals**
A211.1	Identify and evaluate constraints and opportunities
A211.2	Identify options and opportunities for change
A211.3	Consult on and agree policy options
A211.4	Present detailed policies and proposals
A212	**Implement and monitor policies and proposals**
A212.1	Establish operational plans for the implementation of policies and proposals
A212.2	Implement policies and proposals
A212.3	Monitor the implementation of policies and proposals
A22	**Support policy implementation**
A221	**Develop incentives to support policy implementation**
A221.1	Identify needs for incentives to achieve defined objectives
A221.2	Formulate grant, loan an subsidy policies
A222	**Develop controls to support policy implementation**
A222.1	Establish and maintain structures and processes for implementation
A222.2	Identify decision criteria to meet policy guidelines
A222.3	Establish and maintain appeals procedures
A223	**Provide advice and guidance to support policy implementation**
A223.1	Promote and support policy implementation
A223.2	Provide guidance and advice about policy, regulatory requirements and procedures
B	**DEVELOP PROPOSALS FOR THE DEVELOPMENT, IMPROVEMENT AND USE OF THE BUILT ENVIRONMENT**
B1	**Identify requirements and factors which will influence potential developments**
B11	**Formulate and agree a brief which meets client, user and community requirements**
B111	**Investigate, negotiate and agree client, user and community requirements**
B111.1	Identify and agree client requirements and preferences
B111.2	Identify and assess user factors
B111.3	Identify and assess ergonomic factors
B111.4	Identify and assess community factors
B112	**Establish client requirements for professional services, works, goods and materials**
B112.1	Identify key procurement factors
B112.2	Select and agree a procurement procedure with a client
B112.3	Recommend and agree a form of contract

B113 Negotiate and agree a brief
B113.1 Prepare and present a proposal for a brief
B113.2 Revise and agree a brief

B12 Survey the physical characteristics of the natural and built environment

B121 Select, plan and commission surveying methods
B121.1 Identify survey requirements, data standards and outputs
B121.2 Select and plan survey processes and operations

B122 Collect survey data
B122.1 Prepare survey sites and equipment
B122.2 Observe and record measurements

B123 Analyse, process and present survey data
B123.1 Collate and analyse survey data
B123.2 Present survey data

B13 Map the physical characteristics of the natural and built environment

B131 Select, plan and commission mapping methods
B131.1 Identify mapping requirements, data standards and outputs
B131.2 Select and plan mapping processes and operations

B132 Assess and compile mapping data
B132.1 Analyse mapping data
B132.2 Compile mapping data

B133 Process and present mapping data
B133.1 Process mapping data
B133.2 Present mapping data

B14 Investigate the physical characteristics of the natural and built environment

B141 Select, plan and commission test methods
B141.1 Identify test requirements, data standards and outputs
B141.2 Select and plan test processes and operations

B142 Commission and conduct physical tests
B142.1 Prepare sites and equipment for physical testing
B142.2 Investigate and test physical characteristics

B143 Analyse, process and present test data
B143.1 Collate and analyse test data
B143.2 Present test data

B15 Investigate contextual factors relating to the natural and built environment

B151 Investigate historical factors relating to the natural and built environment
B151.1 Prepare and agree an investigation schedule
B151.2 Commission and undertake research into historical factors
B151.3 Identify and evaluate historical factors, likely problems and potential solutions

B152 Investigate social factors relating to the natural and built environment

B152.1 Prepare and agree an investigation schedule
B152.2 Commission and undertake research into social factors
B152.3 Identify and evaluate social factors, likely problems and potential solutions

B153 Investigate visual and spatial factors relating to the natural and built environment
B153.1 Prepare and agree an investigation schedule
B153.2 Commission and undertake research into visual and spatial factors
B153.3 Identify and evaluate visual and spatial factors, likely problems and potential solutions

B154 Investigate ecological and environmental factors relating to the natural and built environment
B154.1 Prepare and agree an investigation schedule
B154.2 Commission and undertake research into ecological and environmental factors
B154.3 Identify and evaluate ecological and environmental factors, likely problems and potential solutions

B16 Investigate and assess the regulatory and legal factors affecting development

B161 Investigate and assess regulatory factors governing site utilisation and development

B161.1 Prepare and agree an investigation schedule

B161.2 Commission and undertake research into regulatory factors

B161.3 Identify and confirm regulatory requirements and constraints

B161.4 Report and advise on potential use options for site development

B162 Investigate and assess legal factors governing site utilisation

B162.1 Prepare and agree an investigation schedule

B162.2 Commission and undertake research into legal factors

B162.3 Identify and evaluate legal factors, likely problems and potential solutions

B17 Assess the financial factors affecting development

B171 Assess and present options for capital funding

B171.1 Identify capital funding requirements

B171.2 Identify and assess capital funding options

B171.3 Advise clients on capital funding decisions

B171.4 Conduct and conclude funding transactions

B172 Estimate, plan and control proposed capital costs

B172.1 Prepare estimates of proposed capital costs

B172.2 Plan proposed capital costs

B172.3 Check proposed capital costs against a cost plan

B173 Assess and present life cycle costings

B173.1 Agree projected project life cycles and methods for cost estimations

B173.2 Identify and estimate cost elements

B173.3 Evaluate cost implications for different design, construction, servicing, financing and use strategies

B18 Assess procurement and resource utilisation factors affecting development

B181 Assess resource procurement factors on the development process

B181.1 Identify and assess resource procurement factors

B181.2 Summarise and present an evaluation of total resource procurement constraints

B182 Assess resource utilisation factors on the development process

B182.1 Identify and assess resource procurement factors

B182.2 Summarise and present an evaluation of total resource utilisation constraints

B2 Prepare and assess design recommendations and solutions

B21 Plan the design process

B211 Develop and present a design development programme

B211.1 Analyse the programme implications of a design brief

B211.2 Prepare a design programme which meets the requirements of the design brief

B211.3 Recommend and agree a structure and timetable for design development

B212 Coordinate the design development process

B212.1 Select and form a design team

B212.2 Induct and brief a design team

B212.3 Establish design team methods and communications

B212.4 Establish research and monitoring systems

B22 Develop and test project design solutions

B221 Identify and assess significant factors affecting project design

B221.1 Synthesize requirements and recommend design parameters

B221.2 Identify structural principles and factors affecting design and construction

B221.3 Identify factors affecting the design of internal and external building environments

B221.4 Identify factors affecting the selection and installation of building services

B221.5	Collate, analyse and evaluate the overall impact of significant factors
B222	**Develop and test the feasibility of alternative design solutions**
B222.1	Identify and test existing design options
B222.2	Originate and test novel design approaches
B222.3	Select test and refine options which best meet the requirements of the brief
B222.4	Evaluate design options against the requirements of the design brief
B23	**Present and agree project design solutions**
B231	**Prepare and present project design proposals**
B231.1	Identify the purpose, methods and techniques for design presentation
B231.2	Prepare and present project design recommendations
B232	**Recommend and advise on the selection of a project design**
B232.1	Advise clients on the selection and modification of a design recommendation
B232.2	Negotiate and agree a detailed design
B233	**Prepare detailed design solutions**
B233.1	Identify the purpose, methods and techniques for preparing detailed designs
B233.2	Identify and select construction processes, techniques and forms
B233.3	Identify, select and assess the performance of building materials
B233.4	Identify the potential effects of building standards on design, construction and control of building work
B233.5	Investigate, calculate and analyse detailed design solutions
B234	**Comply with statutory controls**
B234.1	Identify statutory controls and consent requirements
B234.2	Prepare and submit consent applications
B234.3	Prepare and process appeals and negotiate to secure statutory consent
B3	**Prepare documents for procurement, contract and production**
B31	**Coordinate the production of documents**
B311	**Specify procurement, contract and production documents and their preparation**
B311.1	Specify document requirements
B311.2	Specify programme and assign the production documents
B312	**Assess, integrate and control information for procurement, contract and production purposes**
B312.1	Evaluate design information
B312.2	Collate and integrate design and associated information
B312.3	Integrate and control the design and documentation process
B32	**Prepare procurement, contract and production documents**
B321	**Prepare forms of contract**
B321.1	Draw up contract particulars and preliminaries
B321.2	Prepare and modify standard forms of contract
B321.3	Draft non-standard clauses and forms of contract
B322	**Prepare drawings and schedules**
B322.1	Prepare drawings and associated graphical information
B322.2	Prepare schedules
B323	**Prepare specifications**
B323.1	Prepare prescriptive specifications
B323.2	Prepare performance specifications
B324	**Prepare bills of quantities**
B324.1	Select form of bill for project use
B324.2	Measure quantities from design information
B324.3	Collate and prepare bills of quantities

The CISC mapping exercise and town planning: Critique

The CISC exercise has been evolving during the course of its many workshops and committees over the last four years. Originally it was related only to site-based activities, possibly because of the high level of representation of engineers and construction specialists among the participants. As time went on, greater emphasis was given to all the pre-site activities needed to bring forth development, of which town planning is one key aspect. For CISC purposes, planning is not only seen as a local government activity, although this has been recognised as very important, with separate workshops investigating the specific public sector dimensions of the process. Planning, research and long-term strategy development are also seen as functions which might be undertaken in the private sector, for example, by large building contractors, by property developers and by specialist smaller consultancy firms. From the educational viewpoint, considerable concern has been expressed about an exercise which breaks up the processes into bits; maybe one loses the essential glue that holds the whole thing together. And the richness of built environment higher education is not reflected within the map. The matrix structure and its emphasis upon separate functions has been seen as minimalistic by some, and seems to go against the trend in higher education for interprofessional working, mixed modules and a greater richness of professional expertise overall. Also one can lose the sense of the sequence of events in the map; in the real world, many activities might be going on at once, traversing several parts of the map matrix in the day's work of one professional office. The functions and tasks identified by CISC are more likely to be undertaken in teams, and yet assessment of competence for NVQ purposes is on an individual basis. Professionals might be juggling several balls in the air at once, not doing one little bit at a time; this is particularly true at the higher professional activities, where managerial and professional attributes tend to merge together at senior levels. However, for the purposes of assessment, tasks must be broken down into units, and the later version of the CISC document (CISC 1994) does allow for a broader conceptualisation of the different components which make up the activities, in particular, see the useful concept of range indicators in this document.

One cannot absolutely fit different professional groupings exactly to different parts of the map because the map is function based (and outcomes oriented); it does not seek to reflect or reinforce existing professional divisions. For example, most higher professionals across the construction and property worlds would be likely to undertake at least a few of the strategy and research elements shown under A, and most would be involved in a larger number of the units under F, the management component. In addition to planning being a key element of pre-site activities, it was increasingly accepted by the CISC working group that the financial services, property investment, valuation and funding side of the development process also needed a higher profile on the map. A separate property services group investigated and mapped aspects of pre-site investment, post-site management and valuation functions, subsequently incorporating them into the main document. Members of the Royal Institution of Chartered Surveyors (RICS), especially representatives of its General Practice Division, were particularly concerned that all this non-site-based, apparently invisible work within the world of property development was not marginalised.

It is no secret that there has been considerable debate, if not unease, among the different built environment professions about the scope and nature of the whole process. The problems centre on three areas, all of which impinge upon the nature of town planning. There remains concern about the construction-based image of the exercise, although in fairness, attempts have been made to make the exercise more comprehensive.

The wider aspatial (non-physical, non-site related) aspects of producing the built environment are hard to map and do not fit well into the process, product and project character of the map. Within this aspatial (Foley 1964 gives the original definition) category one might include all the economic, investment and financial dimensions but also all the social and more political policy aspects of decision making. For example, town planning and housing management have a strong tradition of seeking through policy making to deal with social issues, be they inner city problems, poverty, unemployment, homelessness or crime and vandalism. Furthermore, there was initially no equal opportunities element in the map, although mandatory assessment based on the exercise is meant to test professional competence in the full range of management functions. Provisional additions have been made to rectify this situation, but no doubt the original omission was reflective of the very low representation of women, and other so-called minorities in the higher levels of the construction and property professions. There follows a draft equal opportunities element written by the author, aspects of which were subsequently incorporated into Section F of the revised CISC document (CISC 1994).

None of the aforementioned areas are easily mapped as discrete activities with a beginning and end. Indeed, some socio-economic factors essential to good professional practice might be described not as functions one has to do, but more as attitudes of mind; personal attributes such as social awareness; sensitivity in interpersonal professional relationships; or willingness to negotiate instead of taking a confrontational stance. There is also the problem of time-scale and of not having complete control over the activity, circumstances or area one is planning. This problem is particularly evident when one looks at the process of long-term urban plan implementation; a particular problem of the NVQ philosophy (to which CISC is linked) is that the emphasis is upon proving competence, that is, testing an individual's ability to do the job by means of assessing their abilities in their specialist part of the map's functions. How one judges if planning policy making shows competence or indeed that a city itself is competent is quite beyond the realms of human ability. Plans can take many years to come to fruition. Meanwhile, circumstances may change in a way that is quite beyond the control of the planners' competence, for example, planners' policies have in the past been revised in the light of world events such as wars in the Middle East which have raised the price of petrol and thus drastically curtailed plans for motor car based cities. Planners have striven to move from a fixed master plan to a more responsive and flexible system in which the final outcomes may be unknown. A simple competence model might work well in assessing the outcome or product quality of building one fairly uncomplicated little site, but not when dealing with whole cities. Even the smallest, simplest-looking site may be fraught with unimaginable problems encountered in the process of development. Construction colleagues have also commented that the most apparently straightforward building work can be unexpectedly complex and problematic, through no fault of the construction professionals themselves.

Concern has been expressed, particularly from some architects, urban designers and landscape architects, that it is impossible to measure their competence. It is argued that much architectural design is based on such imponderables as intuition, even genius, and these gifts cannot not be quantified for assessment purposes. CISC representatives would argue that genius cannot be measured, but competence is measured in terms of outcomes, so what has been built as result of genius or intuition can be assessed for competence. However, there are still problems. Although one can assess the technical and structural competence of a building, one cannot judge the question of the quality of its style or artistic qualities in the same way. Indeed, who *can* be the judge in this exercise? It was recommended that fellow architects, presumably trained in NVQ assessment, should be the judges. But everyone knows that architecture is notoriously prone to swings in fashion. What was seen as wonderful architecture in the 1960s, namely high-rise development, is seen as a national disaster nowadays. (Granted there are plans to make Centre Point, one of the most infamous of the 1960s London high-rise office developments a listed building worthy of conservation.) The whole debate can become somewhat ridiculous, not only in relation to architecture, but also in respect of large civil engineering projects, especially bridges, where the ultimate test of competence of construction, say of the new Severn Bridge crossing, would be whether it collapsed or not! What time-scale and what weather conditions would one put on such a test?

Most built environment professionals did not seem too bothered about NVQ as long as it stayed down at the manual and trades levels, and did not affect the higher professionals; provided it related to levels 1 and 2, and possibly went to level 3. Now, like rising damp, it is making its way up to levels 4 and 5(5 is the highest level at present). Originally it was imagined that level 4 would be the quasi-professional higher technician level, and level 5 would be the chartered body level. However, because competence must be judged in the workplace on the basis of ability to do the job, it will be necessary for professionals to have proven experience and some seniority to gain level 5. It is not appropriate in a book on the implementation process to enter into a deeper discussion of who is going to pay for it, who will do the assessing, whether you can lose your NVQ once gained and whether this will mean a levy on the construction industry or on professional fees, to name but a few of the uncertainties. Indeed, many of the ideas about NVQing the construction industry came in at the time of the property boom in the mid 1980s; now nobody has the time or money to take them all on board. How can one prove competence as a young professional if one cannot get a job? Well, curiously the answer seems to be do a GNVQ instead! GNVQs in construction also come in a variety of levels starting at advanced, level 3, which is broadly A level or higher technician equivalent. But apparently, in the future, students might be able to do GNVQs at higher level in college, and it is argued that because they will obviously not have had outside professional experience, the GNVQ will test *potential*, whereas the NVQ tests *competence*.

Appendix 3

CISC MAP: DRAFT EQUAL OPPORTUNITIES ELEMENT

Identify and ensure equal opportunities principles are observed in all aspects of professional practice at interpersonal level.
(Element F226.4, to follow Element 226.3 on professional ethics)

Performance criteria

(a) Equal opportunities principles are identified, formulated and agreed for the professional organisation, with reference to existing internal personnel policy statements, and to external, governmental and professional institution requirements.
(b) An equal opportunities statement and a code of practice are produced, publicised and made available to all staff and other relevant persons such as clients and contractors, where appropriate.
(c) Clear objectives are set as to implementation and maintenance of equal opportunities policy; budgets, resources and time-scales, are specified.
(d) An initial equal opportunities audit is undertaken to assess the current situation, then annual monitoring is undertaken to assess progress and ensure compliance.
(e) Equal opportunities criteria are officially referred to, and applied, in relation to job advertisements, staff appraisal, promotion policy, staff relocation and mobility, and allocation of staff to training courses, educational opportunities and other professional opportunities that might be on offer.
(f) Staff training is undertaken at all levels, including senior management and professional partner level to improve knowledge of equal opportunities issues, and to ensure awareness of likely legal, procedural and disciplinary implications of discriminatory practice and harassment.
(g) Equal opportunities policy and procedures are integrated within the business plan, organisational strategy and professional development proposals of the organisation.

(h) The equal opportunities aspects of policy making, and professional decision making should be considered.

(i) Supporting statistical material – sample surveys, questionnaires and survey work – carried out in respect of policy making should fully reflect and represent the composition of the population or client group in question.

(j) A named person or persons is made responsible for dealing with equal opportunities matters and a clear procedure is established for dealing with complaints.

(k) should independent advice or expertise be required, identify external persons, equal opportunities consultants or mentors. In cases of small firms with limited resources, networking links should be established with other small or independent professional practices to ensure a high level of outside equal opportunities advice, on a shared consortium basis, within the context of competence evaluation procedures.

Range indicators

(a) Equal opportunities issues include issues of race, gender, class, age, marital status, disability, child care responsibilities, religion and creed.

(b) Quantitative, statistical and numerical measures to monitor, audit and enforce equal opportunities.

(c) Qualitative, social, cultural and interpersonal matters affecting equal opportunities ethos within organisations should be taken into account.

(d) Equal opportunities affects all levels of employment and staff, ranging from senior partners and chief officers through to middle management, administrative and technical staff.

(e) All forms of communication, all personal and professional dealings are relevant, including committee meetings, teamwork, discussions, written reports, audiovisual material, advertisements, memos, faxes, computer messages, telephone calls and face-to-face encounters.

Performance evidence

Product evidence

(a) Equal opportunities policy statements, codes of practice, budgets, targets and time-scales.

(b) Tangible, physical provision for the disabled, building design, toilet provision, woman-friendly design and child care provision in developments.

(c) Accessible organisations and flexible management structures.

(d) Quantitative representation of members of minority groups at higher management levels.

Process evidence

(a) Training programmes in racial, gender and disability awareness, and in balanced recruitment promotions.
(b) Public participation input and minority representation. A client pool and a range of groups involved in the professional decision-making process.
(c) Qualitative evidence of ethos, management structures, professional habits and employment structures.
(d) Awareness of differential levels of power held by different groups in the negotiating process. Positive discrimination and non-confrontational methods.

At the time of completing this chapter, the proposed new equal opportunities element was still under discussion by the CISC working group. It was also submitted to the RTPI as an appendix to the Draft Equal Opportunities Policy Statement (1994) to indicate how the policy statement might be instrumented and its progress monitored.

Appendix 4

ACCESS ELEMENTS

Typical ramp design

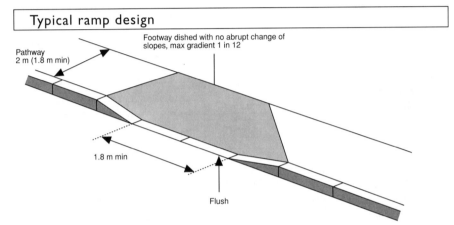

Footway dished with no abrupt change of
slopes, max gradient 1 in 12

Pathway
2 m (1.8 m min)

1.8 m min

Flush

Fig. A4.1 A typical dropped kerb

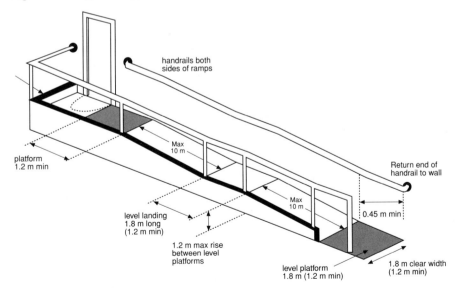

handrails both
sides of ramps

Max
10 m

platform
1.2 m min

Return end of
handrail to wall

level landing
1.8 m long
(1.2 m min)

Max
10 m

0.45 m min

1.2 m max rise
between level
platforms

level platform
1.8 m (1.2 m min)

1.8 m clear width
(1.2 m min)

Fig. A4.2 A typical ramp

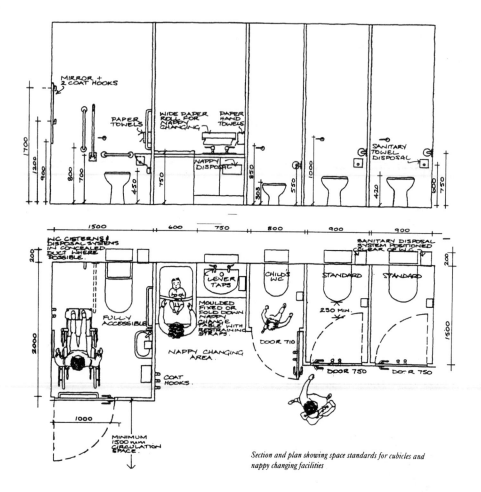

Section and plan showing space standards for cubicles and nappy changing facilities

Fig. A4.3 Public conveniences: section and plan showing space standards for cubicles and nappy changing facilities

PART VIII

SOURCE MATERIAL

SOURCE MATERIAL

Introduction

The references from each chapter are combined in the bibliography. Lists of current acts, circulars and planning policy guidance notes (PPGs) are provided first. References made in individual chapters to the above publications will be found in these lists. If a reference is not found in these lists look under DoE (Department of the Environment) in the bibliography. Also information on the nature of the journals referred to in the bibliography is provided. Since this is a more practically oriented book than Volume I, it contains fewer book references; instead there are more references to legislative requirements and statutes which affect what planners and developers can or cannot do in seeking to achieve development. In fact, in order to find out more about the process of implementation, readers would do well to follow the current professional property press, and to find out what is happening in the world of planning and development in their own area, local authority and development industry. Some suggested project exercises are presented for this purpose in Appendix 1.

List 1

Government publications

Government publications are constantly being changed and updated; updates are shown in brackets on the list. Nevertheless, this list provides a basic picture of the situation. It is *very* important to check the most recent versions for policy chances.

Important planning policy guidance notes (PPGs)

1988

1. *General policy and principles* (revised 1992)
2. *Green belts* (revised 1995)
3. *Land for housing* (revised 1992 as *Housing*)
4. *Industrial and commercial development and small firms* (updated 1992)
5. *Simplified planning zones* (redrafted 1992)
6. *Major retail development* (updated 1993)
7. *Rural enterprise and development* (revised 1992 as *The countryside and rural economy*)
8. *Telecommunications*

1989

9. *Regional guidance for the South East* (RPG)
10. *Strategic guidance for the West Midlands*
11. *Strategic guidance for Merseyside* (and see regional planning guidance notes)
12. *Local plans* (revised 1992 as *Development plans and regional planning guidance*)
13. *Highways considerations in development control* (draft update 1994 *Transport*)

1990

14. *Development on unstable land*
15. *Historic buildings and conservation* (revised 1994)
16. *Archaeology and planning*

1991

17. *Sport and recreation*
18. *Enforcing planning control*

1992

1. *General principles and guidance*
3. *Housing*
4. *Industrial and commercial development in small firms*
7. *The countryside and rural economy*
12. *Development plans and regional planning guidance*
19. *Outdoor advertisement control*
20. *Coastal planning*
21. *Tourism*
22. *Renewable energy*

1993

5. *Major retail development*

1994

2. *Green belts*
9. *Nature conservation*
13. *Transport*
15. *Planning and the historic environment*

Check current DoE lists for updates, current circulars and additional PPGs not referred to in this book (see *The Building, Housing and Planning Catalogue*, HMSO, Annual). Frequently, consultative drafts are produced by the DoE in an ongoing process of updating existing PPGs and creating new ones to reflect current policy issues.

Circulars

This is a selective list based on circulars mentioned in individual chapters plus other key circulars. Nowadays, key policy statements are more likely to appear in PPCs than in circulars or Command Papers (White Papers).

22/80   Development Control: Policy and Practice
38/81   Planning and Enforcement Appeals
22/83   Planning Gain (replaced by 16/91)
14/84   Green Belts
15/84   Land for Housing (cancelled by PPG 3)
16/84   Industrial Development
18/84   Crown Land and Crown Development (see (Department of the Environment 1992b and 1994b exemptions being lifted)

22/84   Memorandum on Structure Plans and Local Plans (see PPG 12)

1/85   The Use of Conditions in Planning Permissions

14/85   Development and Employment

30/85   Transitional Matters (cancelled by PPG 12)

2/86   Development by Small Businesses

8/87   Historic Buildings and Conservation Areas (to be replaced by PPG)

11/87   The Town and Country Planning (Appeals) (Written Representations Procedures) Regulations

12/87   Redundant Hospital Sites in Green Belts

13/87   Changes in the Use of Buildings and Other Land: UCO 1987

16/87   Development involving agricultural land (cancelled by PPG 7)

3/88   Unitary Development Plans (cancelled by PPG 3)

10/88   Inquiries and Appeals Procedure Rules (abbreviated title)

12/89   Green Belts

9/90   Crime Prevention: The Success of the Partnership Approach

7/91   Planning and Affordable Housing (cancelled by PPG 3)

12/91   Redundant Hospital Sites in Green Belts: Planning Guidance

16/91   Planning and Compensation Act 1991: Planning Obligations

17/92   Planning and Compensation Act 1991: Immunity Rules

23/92   Motorway Service Areas

10/93   Local Government Act 1992 (section concerning CCT)

5/94   Planning Out Crime

Command Papers

This list of Command Papers contains only those mentioned in this volume. There are also many more specifically on town planning, although over the last ten years the trend has been to put key policy statements in PPGs rather than DoE Command Papers, but other departments and ministries also produce relevant White Papers.

Ministry of Health (1944) *A National Health Service*, Cmnd No. 6502 (see Leathard 1990).

Ministry of Housing and Local Government (1967) *Town and Country Planning*, Cmnd No. 3333.

Department of Health and Social Security (1989) *Working for Patients: The Health Service: Caring for the 1990s*, Cmnd No. 555.

Department of the Environment (1985) *Lifting the Burden*, Cmnd No. 9517.

Check current policies, such as on inner city renewal and single regeneration budget, which will be discussed in Volume III of this series, *Investigating Town Planning*.

Acts relevant to planning

1848 Public Health Act
1865 Parliamentary Costs Act
1874 Public Health Act
1909 Housing and Town Planning Act
1919 Sex Disqualification (Removal) Act
1919 Housing and Town Planning Act
1925 Law of Property Act
1935 Restriction of Ribbon Development Act
1936 Public Health Act
1945 Distribution of Industry Act
1946 New Towns Act
1947 Town and Country Planning Act
1949 National Parks and Access to the Countryside Act
1952 Town Development Act
1953 Historic Buildings and Ancient Monuments Act
1957 Housing Act
1960 Local Employment Act
1961 Public Health Act
1961 Factories Act
1962 Commonwealth Immigration Act
1963 Offices, Shops and Railway Premises Act
1963 Public Lavatories (Turnstiles) Act
1964 Licensing Act (1995 Childrens Certificates now allow accompanied children into some licensed premises)
1965 Race Relations Act
1967 Civic Amenities Act
1967 Land Commission Act
1968 Countryside Act
1969 Housing Act (General Improvement Areas)
1969 Law of Property Act
1970 Chronically Sick and Disabled Act
1970 Community Land Act
1970 Equal Pay Act
1971 Fire Precautions Act
1971 Town and Country Planning Act
1971 Tribunals and Inquiries Act
1971 Immigration Act
1972 Industry Act
1972 Local Government Act
1974 Town and Country Amenities Act
1974 Housing Act (Housing Action Areas)
1975 Community Land Act

1975   Development Land Tax Act
1975   Sex Discrimination Act
1976   Local Government (Miscellaneous Provisions) Act
1976   Race Relations Act
1980   Highway Act
1980   Local Government Planning and Land Act
1982   Local Government (Miscellaneous Provisions) Act
1981   Disabled Persons Act
1981   Minerals Act
1982   Derelict Land Act
1984   Building Act
1985   Housing Act
1986   Housing and Town Planning Act
1988   Local Government Act
1989   Local Government and Housing Act
1989   Children Act
1990   Town and Country Planning Act
1990   Planning (Listed Buildings and Conservation Areas) Act
1990   Environmental Protection Act
1990   Planning (Hazardous Substances) Act
1990   National Health Service and Community Care Act
1991   New Roads and Street Works Act
1991   Planning and Compensation Act
1992   Local Government Act
1993   Housing and Urban Development Act

Regulations and orders

Department of the Environment (1981, 1986, 1989) *Town and Country Planning (Determination of Appeals by Appointed Persons) (Prescribed Classes) Regulations, 1981, 1986 and 1989.*

Department of the Environment (1985) *The Building Regulations 1985.* London: HMSO, SI No. 1065/1985. Updated as *The Building Regulations 1991*, SI 2768/1991.

Department of the Environment (1987) *Town and Country Planning (Listed Buildings and Buildings in Conservation Areas Regulations.*

Department of the Environment (1987) *Town and Country Planning: Use Classes Order*, SI 764/1987.

Department of the Environment (1987) *Town and Country Planning (Appeal) (Written Representations Procedure) Regulations.*

Department of the Environment (1988) *Town and Country Planning General Development Order.*

Department of the Environment (1992) *Town and Country Planning (Determination by Inspectors) (Inquiries Procedure) Rules.*

Department of the Environment (1992) *Town and Country Planning (Inquiries Procedure) Rules.*

Department of the Environment (1995) *Town and Country Planning (General Development Procedure) Order* 1995.

Department of the Environment (1995) *Town and Country Planning (Permitted Development) Order* 1995.

British Standards

BS 5750   Practice Management Standards
BS 6465   Sanitary Installations (Part I revised 1995 and Part II under revision)
BS 5810   Access for Disabled People (Department of the Environment 1992a)

Disability Design Issues

Disability issues are covered by BS 5810 and by Document M of the Building Regulations (under revision in 1995). Chapter 17 refers to the now out-moded Development Control Policy Note 16 *Access for Disabled People* and the booklet *Access for Disabled People: Design Guidance Notes* ACE (Access Committee for England). Both have been superseded by more recent ACE publications.

Check all publications from the Centre for Accessible Environments, 35, Great Smith Street, London SW1P 3BJ.

Check all Women's Design Service.

The RTPI has previously produced a PAN (advice note) *Access for Disabled People* (RTPI 1985), updated as PAN No. 3. 1988.

Read the various topic sections of the *New Metric Handbook: Planning and Design Data* which include detailed dimensions on requirements (Tutt and Adler 1993). For example, see Diagrams 5.3 and 5.4 of dimensions and reach of wheelchair users

The Relationship between British Standards and the Building Regulations

BS 5810 on disability access is also the basis of Approved Document M of the Building Regulations, and BS 6465 *Sanitary Installations* (which includes design standards and level of provision guidelines) for all toilets, both public convenience and private toilets, is mirrored in Approved Document G

Hygiene under Schedule 1 of the 1984 Building Act which is the basis of the 1985 Building Regulations (updated in 1992). The approved documents run from A to M. In other words, the Building Regulations refer to British Standards and other codes of practice as the basis of their standards, that is, they are linked documents (see Chapter 4).

European Union controls

Article 119 of the Treaty of Rome established the principle of equal opportunities, and the Equal Treatment Directive 76/207 details the scope of its application.

EC Directive 85/337 on Environmental Assessment is applied in Britain under Assessment of Environmental Effects Regulation No. 119 of the 1988 Town and Country Planning Regulations. (All EU legislation, formerly EC legislation, must be embodied in relevant domestic state legislation, and in case of dispute takes precedence.)

List 2

OTHER SOURCES

Other sources and lists

Planning legislation is constantly being updated and amended. Check the *Encyclopaedia of Planning Law* for the most recent versions of use classes orders and general development orders. For the present situation always consult

Grant, M. (ed) *Encyclopedia of Planning Law and Practice.* London: Sweet and Maxwell. Continually updated.

This publication is a loose-leaf, regularly updated set of volumes. Butterworth publishes a planning encyclopaedia that is worth consulting, plus several other legal publications which include planning law. For example, Halsbury's *Statutes of England,* has a separate volume on town and country planning law. Also, readers may need to consult primary law sources such as *The Law Reports* for updates on major planning case law and appeal decisions. Planning decisions are normally determined by the secretary of state for the environment or planning inspectors on the DoE's behalf; only 'big', legally contentious cases go to the higher courts. Several legal reporting systems, and planning information systems, are now on computer disc, electronic networks, or CD-ROM. For example, the Lexis legal system is a computer service giving information on all reported cases, and is available now in many libraries. There are also several planning databases available to which some planning offices subscribe. Also look for various EU databases.

Fuller lists, and more details on specific policy pronouncements, may be obtained by consulting the *Encyclopaedia of Planning Law.* For more information on particular policy pronouncements, consult other textbooks of planning and planning law, including Heap (1994), Cullingworth and Nadin (1994), Grant (1990) and Hall (1992). Slightly different lists of circulars, PPGs and parliamentary acts were provided in Volume I. Volume I also contained a much larger bibliography providing signposts to detailed sources on many aspects of town planning policy and practice. For readers interested in the more social aspects of planning, *Women and Planning* (Greed 1994) gives a breakdown of key texts into different policy and topic areas; it also has an extensive bibliography.

Planning and property journals

Current planning and other built environment professions journals should also be consulted for the current situation.

Planning Week is the weekly journal of the Royal Town Planning Institute. Up to September 1993 it was called *The Planner* and was published fortnightly. Still earlier versions include *Journal of the Town Planning Institute* and *Journal of the Royal Town Planning Institute*. As to references in the bibliography to the RTPI journals, it is often more useful to give the date of an article as the reference, because the frequency and page numbering of the RTPI journal has varied in format over the years.

Planning is a weekly A4 news-sheet from Ambit Publications of Gloucester, quite independent of the RTPI. It is a very useful source of immediate change, and Ambit publishes annual summaries of planning appeals and other planning law issues from a planner's viewpoint rather than a lawyer's. *Planning* has no volume numbers, only issue numbers.

Town and Country Planning is a monthly journal published by the Town and Country Planning Association (TCPA). The TCPA is a voluntary, independent organisation, separate from the RTPI, which grew out of the old Garden Cities Association founded by Ebenezer Howard. Its monthly journal carries fairly substantial articles on a range of planning and environmental issues. It also produces a weekly bulletin.

Chartered Surveyor Weekly is published by the Royal Institution of Chartered Surveyors (RICS). It covers many planning issues, mainly from the viewpoints of the general practice surveyor and the commercial developer. *Estates Gazette* is a similar weekly.

Estates Times is a property press newspaper aimed at a wider audience of property professionals; it has a strong private sector emphasis. Occasional features on different parts of the country are well produced and informative.

There is a range of specialist journals and some of them appear in the bibliography. Planning research journals include *The Journal of Property Research* and *Planning Practice and Research* (Oxford: Carfax Publications). Among the planning law journals is *Journal of Planning and Environment Law*, now increasingly devoted to environmental law and to EU directives which impact upon British town planning. See also European policy documents on environmental issues, prefix EUR in current HMSO publication lists. For specialist issues, readers can consult a dazzling range of other journals in the field of the built environment – a veritable growth area in publications. Also check local authority oriented journals, such as *Local Government Chronicle*, especially for local government finance and current changes.

BIBLIOGRAPHY

Adler, D and P Tutt (1993) *New Metric Handbook: Planning and Design Data*. London: Butterworth Architecture. A revision is forthcoming.

Ainsbett, A (1990) Public/private sector joint ventures: local government and housing act 1989: effects, *Estates Times*, 24 February: 24–9.

Allinson, J (1988) The Community Land Scheme: a study in dichotomy and consensus, *The Planner*, Vol. 74, No. 9:29–32.

Ambrose, P and B Colenutt (1979) *The Property Machine*. Harmondsworth: Penguin.

Architects Journal (1985) *AJ Introduction and Complete Guide to the 1985 Building Regulations*. London: Royal Institution of British Architects. Check updates.

Audit Commission (1991) *NHS Estate Management and Property Maintenance*. London: The Audit Commission for Local Authorities and the Health Service in England and Wales.

—— (1993) *The Citizen's Charter*. London: The Audit Commission for Local Authorities and the Health Service in England and Wales.

—— (1994) *Citizen's Charter Indicators. Consultation on the Audit Commission's Proposals for 1994/5*. The Audit Commission for Local Authorities and the Health Service in England and Wales.

Avon (1980) *County of Avon Structure Plan: Summary*. Bristol: Avon County Council. And subsequent editions.

—— (1993a) *County of Avon Transport Plan: 1993–2013: Consultation Brochure*. Bristol: Avon County Council.

—— (1993b September) *Environmental Strategy and Action Plan*. Bristol: Avon County Council.

Ball, M (1988) *Rebuilding Construction: Economic Change in the British Construction Industry*. London: Routledge.

Barrett, M and G Caffrey (1991) *Women and Planning*. Dublin: Irish Planning Institute.

Barrett, S and C Fudge (eds) (1981) *Policy and Action*. London: Methuen.

Barrett, S and M Hill (1981) *The Theoretical Component of the Research on Implementation*. London: SSRC. Report to SSRC Central/Local Government Relations Panel.

Barrett, S, M Stewart and J Underwood (1979) *The Land Market and Development Process*. Bristol: University of Bristol School of Advanced Urban Studies, Occasional Paper 2.

Bassett, K and J Short (1980) *Housing and Residential Structure: Alternative Approaches*. London: Routledge.

BDC (1990) *A Vision for Bristol*. Bristol: Bristol Development Corporation, Consultation Report.

Bedminster (1980) *Bedminster Local Plan*. Bristol: Bristol City Planning Office. There are earlier versions and later revisions, e.g. June 1988.

Bell, D (1974) *The Coming of Post Industrial Society.* London: Heinemann.

Belloni, C (1994) Policies concerning the organisation of time in Italian cities, in *Proceedings of the Women in the City Conference,* OECD, Paris, and University of Turin.

Benveniste, G (1989) *Mastering the Politics of Planning.* London: Jossey-Boss.

Birmingham (1991) *Caught Short in Brum.* Birmingham: Birmingham for People: Women's Group.

—— (1994) *Positive Planning,* Birmingham: Birmingham for People, video.

Blowers, A (ed) (1993) *Planning for a Sustainable Environment.* London: Earthscan in association with the Town and Country Planning Association.

Bristol (1984) *Canon's Marsh: Planning Brief.* Bristol: Bristol City Council, Planning Department.

—— (1985) *Poverty in Bristol.* Bristol: City Planning Department.

—— (1989) *Conservation Policies.* Bristol: City Planning Department, December. Also see Conservation Area Enhancement Policies, November 1993.

—— (1990) *City Centre Draft Local Plan.* Bristol: Bristol Planning Services, February.

—— (1993a) *Deposit Bristol Local Plan.* Bristol: Planning Services, November.

—— (1993b) *Canon's Marsh Planning Brief.* Bristol: Bristol City Council, Planning and Development Services.

Broady, M (1968) *Planning for People.* London: NCSS/Bedford Square Press.

Burton, I (1992) Agreements on increase though still scarce, *Planning,* No. 965:6–7.

Byrne, S (1989) *Planning Gain: An Overview.* London: Royal Town Planning Institute.

Cadman, D and L Austin-Crowe (1991) *Property Development.* London: Spon.

CAE (1992) *WC Facilities for Women in Public Buildings: Seminar Report.* London: Centre for Accessible Environments.

Calder, N, S Cavanagh, C Eckstein, J Palmer and A Stell (1993) *Women and Development Plans.* Newcastle: Department of Town and Country Planning, Working Paper No. 27.

Camden (1988) *The King's Cross Railway Lands: A Community Planning Brief.* London: London Borough of Camden.

—— (1993) *The King's Cross Railway Lands: A Community Planning Brief.* London: London Borough of Camden.

CEC (1991) *Social Europe: Equal Opportunities for Women and Men.* Brussels: Commission of European Communities.

Cecil, Lord Hugh (1912) *Conservatism.* London: Thornton Butterworth.

CISC (Construction Industry Standing Conference) (1993) *Occupational Standards for Technical, Managerial, and Professional Roles in the Construction Industry.* London: CISC, The Building Centre.

—— (1994) *Occupational Standards for Professional, Managerial, and Technical Occupations in Planning, Construction, Property and Related Engineering Services.* London: CISC, The Building Centre.

Citizen's Charter See Audit Commission

Claydon, J (1991) Negotiations in planning, *The Planner,* 19 October, Vol. 76, No. 41:11–13.

Coupland, A (1989) *King's Cross Development: Real Jobs or False Promises?* London: Crossfire.

Cowan, P (1969) *The Office: A Facet of Urban Growth.* London: Heinemann.

CSLA (1991) *Equal Opportunities and Planning.* Edinburgh: Convention of Scottish Local Authorities. Within this document see extract from *Access for Disabled People,* Glasgow City Planning Department.

Cullingworth, J B (1988) *Town and Country Planning in Britain.* London: Routledge.

—— (1993) *The Political Culture of Planning: American Land Use Planning in Comparative Perspective.* New York: Routledge.

Cullingworth, J B and V Nadin (1994) *Town and Country Planning in Britain*. London: Routledge.

Cunningham, Susan and Christine Norton (1993) *Public Inconveniences: Suggestions for Improvements*. London: All Mod Cons in association with the Continence Foundation.

Daniels, P W (1975) *Office Location: An Urban and Regional Study*. London: Bell.

Davies, L (1992) Aspects of equality, *The Planner*, Vol. 79, No. 3:14–16.

——— (1993) *Black People and Ethnic Minorities in Local Authorities in the South West of England*. Bristol: University of the West of England.

——— (1994) South-west has way to go in planning for ethnic minorities, *Planning*, 25 February, No. 1057:21.

DHSS (1981) *Care in the Community*. London: HMSO.

——— (1989) *Working for Patients: The Health Service, Caring for the 1990s* CMD 555. London: HMSO.

Department of the Environment (1972a) *How do you want to live?* London: HMSO.

——— (1972b) *Development Plan Manual*. London: HMSO.

——— (1985) *Access for the Disabled* (DCPN 16). London: HMSO.

——— (1986) *Planning: Appeals, Call-in and Major Public Inquiries* 1986. London: HMSO.

——— (1991) *Redundant Hospital Sites in Green Belts: Planning Guidelines*. London: HMSO.

——— (1992a) *Development Plans: Good Practice Guidance Note*. London: HMSO.

——— (1992b) *Consultation Paper: The Removal of Crown Exemption from Planning Law*, London: HMSO. See also Circular 18/85, and changes proposed to remove exemptions, 1994.

——— (1992c) *Sanitary Provision for People with Special Needs*. London: HMSO.

——— (1992d) *Access Facilities for Disabled People* (Approved Document M). London: HMSO.

——— (1993) *Planning Inspectorate: Annual Report and Accounts for the Year Ended 31 March 1993*. London: HMSO.

——— (1994a) *Housing and Construction Statistics*. London: HMSO. Updated annually.

——— (1994b) *Removal of Crown Exemption from Planning Controls*. DoE News Release 165, 10 March. London: Department of the Environment.

Dolan, D (1979) *The British Construction Industry: An Introduction*. London: Macmillan.

Dunleavy, P (1980) *Urban Political Analysis*. London: Macmillan.

Edwards, L and J Rowan-Robinson (1980) Whatever happened to the Planning Inquiry Commission? *Journal of Planning and Environment Law*, 307–15.

Edwards, M (1992) A microcosm: redevelopment proposals at King's Cross, in A Thornley (ed) *The Crisis of London*. London: Routledge.

Elson, M and D Payne (1992) *Planning Obligations for Sport & Recreation: A Guide for Negotiation and Action*. London: The Sports Council.

Ennis, C, N Lloyd and R Patterson (1993) *Conceptual Issues Report: The Competences of a Professional*. London: CISC, The Building Centre.

Fischer F and J Forrester (eds) (1993) *The Argumentative Turn in Policy, Analysis and Planning*. London: University College London.

Fisher, R and W Ury (1983) *Getting to Yes*. London: Hutchinson.

Foley, D (1964) An approach to urban metropolitan structure, in M Weber (ed) *Explorations into Urban Structure*. Philadelphia: University of Pennsylvania Press.

Fordham R (1991) Much obliged by better sense of balance, *Planning*, No. 942:7.

——— (1992) Failing to agree on survey, *Planning*, No. 975:7.

——— (1993) Planning gain in ten dimensions, *Journal of Planning and Environmental Law*, August:719–31.

Forester, J (1989) *Planning in the Face of Power*, Los Angeles: University of California.

Fortlage, C (1990) *Environmental Assessment: A Practical Guide.* Aldershot: Gower.

Fothergill, S, S Monk and M Perry (1987) *Property and Industrial Building.* London: Hutchinson.

Foulsham, J (1990) Women's needs and planning: a critical evaluation of recent local authority practice, in J Montgomery and A Thornley (eds) *Radical Planning Initiatives: New Directions in Planning for the 1990s.* Aldershot: Gower.

GLC (1986) *Changing Place: Women and Planning Policies.* London: Greater London Council.

——— (1994) Planning for equality: women in London, in *Draft Greater London Development Plan.* London: Greater London Council, Ch. 4.

Goddard, J B (1975) *Office Location in Urban and Regional Development.* Oxford: Oxford University Press.

Goodchild, R and R Munton (1985) *Development and the Landowner.* London: George Allen and Unwin.

Gore, T and T Nicholson (1991) Models of the land development process: a critical review, *Environment and Planning A,* Vol. 23:705–30.

Grant, M (1990) *Urban Planning Law.* London: Sweet and Maxwell.

——— (ed) (1992) Monthly Bulletin July 1992, in *Encyclopedia of Planning Law and Practice.* London: Sweet and Maxwell, p. 4.

——— (ed) (1993) Update to *Encyclopedia of Planning Law and Practice.* London: Sweet and Maxwell, Vol. 4, pp. 37023–4. This is a frequently updated loose-leaf set of four volumes.

Greed, C (1991) *Surveying Sisters: Women in a Traditional Male Profession.* London: Routledge.

——— (1993) *Introducing Town Planning.* London: Longman.

——— (1994) *Women and Planning: Creating Gendered Realities.* London: Routledge.

Griffiths (1988) *Community Care: An Agenda for Action.* London: HMSO.

Grover, R (1989) *Land and Property: New Directions.* London: Spon.

Hall, P (1992) *Urban and Regional Planning.* London: Routledge.

Hammersley, M and P Atkinson (1983) *Ethnography Principles in Practice.* London: Tavistock.

Harvey, J (1992) Urban Land Economics. London: Macmillan.

Hayden, D (1984) *Redesigning the American Dream.* London: Norton.

Healey, P (1991) Models of the development process: a review, *Journal of Property Research,* 219–38.

——— (1992) An institutional model of the development process, *Journal of Property Research,* 33–44.

——— (1993) Regional variations in the development process: the significance for development activity, urban policy and planning policy. Paper presented at the *Royal Institution of Chartered Surveyors Research Conference,* 2–3 April 1993. London: RICS.

Healey, P and R Nabarro (eds) (1990) *Land and Property Development in a Changing Context.* Aldershot: Gower.

Healey, P, F Ennis and M Purdue (1992) Planning gain and the new local plans, *Town and Country Planning,* February:39–43.

Healey, P, M Purdue and F Ennis (1993) *Gains from Planning: Dealing with the Impacts of Development.* York: Joseph Rowntree Foundation.

Heap, D (1994) *An Outline of Planning Law.* London: Sweet and Maxwell.

Highfield, D (1987) *Rehabilitation and Re-use of Old Buildings.* London: Spon.

Hillier Parker (1983) *Canon's Marsh: Report on Development Potential.* London: Hillier Parker, May and Rowden, Chartered Surveyors.

Hoppe, R (1993) Political judgement and the policy cycle: the case of ethnicity policy arguments in the Netherlands, in F Fischer and J Forrester (eds) *The Argumentative Turn in Policy, Analysis and Planning.* London: University College London.

House of Commons (1968) *Debates* Vol. 757, Column 1372, 31 January. London: Hansard.

—— (1985) *Debates: Chancellor Nigel Lawson's Budget Speech.* London: Hansard.

—— (1986) *Fifth Report from the Environment Committee 1985/86: 'Planning: Appeals, Call-In and Major Public Inquiries' and Government Response Thereto.* London: HMSO.

HSJ (1991) News: slump could wipe £40 million off RHA sales, *Health Service Journal,* 18 April:6.

—— (1993) Media information 1994, *Health Service Journal,* forecast supplement.

Johnson, T (1990) Winning planning appeals, *The Planner,* TCPSS Proceedings Feature, 23 February.

Jones, Jon Owen, MP (1994) *Not at Your Convenience: A Survey of Local Authority Public Convenience Provision.* Cardiff: J. Owen Jones.

Jowell, J (1977) Bargaining in development control, *Journal of Planning and Environmental Law,* 414–33.

Keeble, L (1985) *Fighting Planning Appeals.* London: Construction Press.

Kennedy, J, J Benson and J McMillan (1980) *Managing Negotiations.* London: Business Books.

Kennedy, Henderson and Penrose (1990) *Environmental Assessment: Avon Light Rail Transit Act, 1989.* Bristol: Advanced Transport for Avon.

Keogh, G (1982) *Planning Gain: An Economic Analysis.* University of Reading.

KXRLG (1989) *The King's Cross Development: People or Profit.* London: King's Cross Railway Lands Group.

Lavender, S (1990) *Economics for Builders and Surveyors.* London: Longman.

LDR (1990) *Canon's Marsh Wapping Wharf Concept Report.* London: LDR International Limited. Report to City of Bristol.

Leathard, A (1990) *Health Care Provision: Past, Present and Future.* London: Chapman and Hall.

Little, J (1994) *Gender, Planning and the Policy Process.* London: Elsevier.

Local Government Management Board (1992) *Survey of Planning Staffs in Local Authority Planning Departments.* London: Local Government Management Board.

London Women and Planning Forum (1993) *LWPF Report: UDP Policies.* London: Women's Design Service, Broadsheet No. 7.

London Women and Planning Group (1991) *Shaping our Borough: Women and Unitary Development Plans.* London: Planning Aid for London.

MacCoubrey, H (1988) *Effective Planning Appeals.* London: BSP Professional Books.

MacDonald, G (1993) Planning gain: a must for economic development, *Planning* No. 1005:12–13.

McLoughlin, J (1969) *Urban and Regional Planning: A Systems View.* London: Faber.

Mahmoud, A (1993) *Ethnic Minorities in the Planning Profession, a Study of Recruitment Policies of the Planning School.* BA Dissertation, University of West of England.

Marriott, O (1989) *The Property Boom.* London: Abingdon Press.

Massey, D, P Quintas and D Wield (1992) *High Tech Fantasies: Science Parks in Society, Science and Space.* London: Routledge.

Middleton, J and M Pulford (1993) Street talk, in *Health Service Journal* 9 September: 27.

Millichap, D (1991) The death of planning gain, *Planning,* No. 942:17.

Milne, R (1992) Semblance of new order on planning agreements, *Planning,* No. 955:7.

Ministry of Health (1994) *A National Health Service.* London: HMSO. Ministry of Health, White Paper, Cmnd No. 6502; also see Leathard (1990).

Minton, A (1993) A partnership made in Whitehall, p. 2; New agency announces agenda for partnership, p. 15; *Planning Week,* Vol. 1, No. 11.

Moor, N (1983) *The Planner and the Market.* London: George Godwin.

Morgan, D and S Nott (1988) *Development Control: Policy into Practice.* London: Butterworth.

Mynors, C (1987) *Planning Applications and Appeals: A Guide for Architects and Surveyors.* London: Architectural Press.

—— (1989) *Listed Buildings and Conservation Areas.* London: Longman.

Nadin, V and S Jones (1990) A profile of the profession, in *The Planner,* 26 January, Vol. 76, No. 3:13–24. London: The Royal Town Planning Institute.

OECD (1994) *Women in the City: Houses, Services and the Urban Environment.* Paris: Organisation for Economic Cooperation and Development.

Oldfield King (1989) *York Gate: A New Approach to Bristol.* Bristol: Oldfield King Planning.

—— (1993) *Outlook,* Oldfield King Group Newsletter. Oldfield King, Bristol.

OPCS (Office of Population, Census and Surveys) (1994) *Social Trends.* London: HMSO. Updated annually.

PAG (1980) *Report to Department of the Environment on Planning Gain.* London: HMSO.

—— (1982) *The Development Industry.* London: HMSO.

Parkes, M (1990) *King's Cross Railway Lands: People's Brief.* London: King's Cross Railway Lands Group.

Parkes, M and D C Mouawad (1991) *Towards a Peoples' Plan London.* London: King's Cross Railway Lands Group.

—— (1993) *Interim Uses Initiative.* London: King's Cross Railway Lands Group.

Pickvance, C (1977) *Urban Sociology.* London: Tavistock.

Pinch, S (1985) *Cities and Services: The Geography of Collective Consumption.* London: Routledge.

Planner (no author) (1989a) Framework for the future: Clive Soley's address to the RTPI Council, *The Planner,* 14 July, Vol. 75, No. 12:7–8.

Planner (no author) (1989b) Instant planning appeal decisions: Howard's experiment, *The Planner,* 27 September, Vol. 75, No. 23:5.

Price, D and A Blair (1989) *The Changing Geography of the Service Sector.* London: Belhaven Press.

Punter, J (1990) *Design Control in Bristol 1945–1990.* Bristol: Redcliffe Press.

Ratcliffe, J (1978) *An Introduction to Urban Land Administration.* London: Estates Gazette.

Ravetz, A (1986) *The Government of Space.* London: Faber and Faber.

Reade, E (1987) *British Town and Country Planning.* Milton Keynes: Open University Press.

Rees, C A (1994) Section 54a, planning gain and bargaining power. Paper given at RTPI Conference, 28 January.

Riddall, J G (1993) *Introduction to Land Law.* London: Butterworths.

RTPI (1983) *Planning for a Multi-Racial Britain.* London: Royal Town Planning Institute in conjunction with the Commission for Racial Equality.

—— (1985) *Access for Disabled People.* London: Royal Town Planning Institute. Revised 1988 as practice advice note (PAN) No. 3.

—— (1989) Framework for the future: Clive Soley's address to the RTPI Council. *The Planner,* 14 July, Vol. 75, No. 12:7–8.

—— (1990a) *Careers in Town Planning.* London: Royal Town Planning Institute.

—— (1990b) *Practice Advice Note 8: Development Briefs.* London: Royal Town Planning Institute.

—— (1993a) *Planning for Women.* London: Royal Town Planning Institute, Draft PAN.

—— (1993b) *Ethnic Minorities and the Planning System.* London: Royal Town Planning Institute. Written by V. Krishnarayan and H. Thomas.

—— (1994a) *Code of Professional Conduct.* London: Royal Town Planning Institute.

——— (1994b) *Equal Opportunities Policy Statement.* London: Royal Town Planning Institute, Draft Document.

Rydin, Y (1993) *The British Planning System: An Introduction,* London: Macmillan.

Salt, A (1991) *Planning Applications: the RMJM Guide.* London: BSP Professional Books.

Scarrett, D (1983) *Property Management.* London: Spon.

Sheldon, H and J Claydon (1990) *Local Authority/Developer Negotiations: A Case Study – Development Control.* Bristol: Bristol Polytechnic (now the University of the West of England), Department of Town and Country Planning, Working Paper 15, *The Research Method and Literature.*

——— (1991a) *The Practice of Negotiations in Development Control in Bristol.* Bristol: Department of Town and Country Planning, Working Paper 16.

——— (1991b) *Institutional Influences.* Bristol: Department of Town and Country Planning, Working Paper 17.

Skeffington Report (1969) *People and Planning.* London: HMSO.

Solomos, J (1992) The politics of immigration since 1945, in P Braman (ed) *Racism and Anti-Racism.* London: Sage, pp. 7–29.

Southampton (1991) *Women and the Planned Environment: Design Guide.* Southampton: Directorate of Strategy and Development.

Stapleton, T (1986) *Estate Management Practice.* London: Estates Gazette.

Telling, A E and R Duxbury (1993) *Planning Law and Procedure.* London: Butterworths.

Thomas, H and P Healey (1991) *Dilemmas of Planning Practice.* Aldershot: Avebury Gower.

Thornley, A (1991) *Urban Planning Under Thatcherism: the Challenge of the Market.* London: Routledge.

Tutt, P and D Adler (1993) *New Metric Handbook: Planning and Design Data.* London: Butterworth Architecture. A revision is forthcoming.

Underwood, J (1981) Development control – a case study of discretion in action, in S Barrett and C Fudge (eds) *Policy and Action.* London: Methuen.

WDS (1991) *At Women's Convenience: A Handbook on the Design of Women's Public Toilets.* London: Women's Design Service. Also see its other publications on disabled access, crèches and safety.

Wrenn, D M (1983) *Urban Waterfront Development.* Washington DC: The Urban Land Institute.

INDEX